PEARSON CUSTOM
COMPUTER SCIENCE

CS 1114
Introduction to Software Design
Virginia Tech University

PEARSON

Cover Art: "Blend," courtesy of Getty Images/Jason Reed; "Binary Data Flowing," courtesy of iStockphoto/Andrey Solovyev; "Beech Forest," courtesy of iStockphoto; "Small Plant," courtesy of iStockphoto/Florea Marius Catalin; "Network," courtesy of iStockphoto/Andrey Prokhorov. Additional images courtesy of Photodisc/Getty Images, brandXpictures.

Printed in the United States of America.

V092

Please visit our website at *www.pearsonlearningsolutions.com*.

Attention Bookstores: For permission to return any unsold stock, contact us at *pe-uscustomreturns@pearson.com*.

Pearson Learning Solutions, 501 Boylston Street, Suite 900, Boston, MA 02116
A Pearson Education Company
www.pearsoned.com

PEARSON

ISBN 10: 1-256-59420-2
ISBN 13: 978-1-256-59420-8

Table of Contents

Introduction to the Internet and World Wide Web

Chapter Objectives In this chapter, you will learn how to . . .

- Describe the evolution of the Internet and the Web
- Explain the need for web standards
- Describe universal design
- Identify benefits of accessible web design
- Identify reliable resources of information on the Web
- Identify ethical use of the Web
- Describe the purpose of web browsers and web servers
- Identify networking protocols
- Define URIs and domain names
- Describe HTML, XHTML, and HTML5
- Describe popular trends in the use of the Web

The Internet and the Web are parts of our daily lives. How did they begin? What networking protocols and programming languages work behind the scenes to display a web page? This chapter provides an introduction to some of these topics and is a foundation for the information that web developers need to know. You'll be introduced to Hypertext Markup Language (HTML), the language used to create web pages; eXtensible Hypertext Markup Language (XHTML), the most recent standardized version of HTML; and HTML5—the newest draft version of HTML.

1 The Internet and the Web

The Internet

The **Internet**, the interconnected network of computer networks that spans the globe, seems to be everywhere today. It has become part of our lives. You can't watch television or listen to the radio without being urged to visit a website. Even newspapers and magazines have their place on the Internet.

Birth of the Internet

The Internet began as a network to connect computers at research facilities and universities. Messages in this network would travel to their destination by multiple routes, or paths. This configuration allowed the network to function even if parts of it were broken or destroyed. In such an event, the message would be rerouted through a functioning portion of the network while traveling to its destination. This network was developed by the Advanced Research Projects Agency (ARPA)—and the ARPAnet was born. Four computers (located at UCLA, Stanford Research Institute, University of California Santa Barbara, and the University of Utah) were connected by the end of 1969.

Growth of the Internet

As time went on, other networks, such as the National Science Foundation's NSFnet, were created and connected with the ARPAnet. Use of this interconnected network, or Internet, was originally limited to government, research, and educational purposes. The ban on commercial use of the Internet was lifted in 1991. The growth of the Internet continues: Internet World Stats reported over 2 billion users, about 30% of the world's population, on the Internet in 2011. Figure 1 shows the growth of Internet use by geographic area between 2000 and 2011.

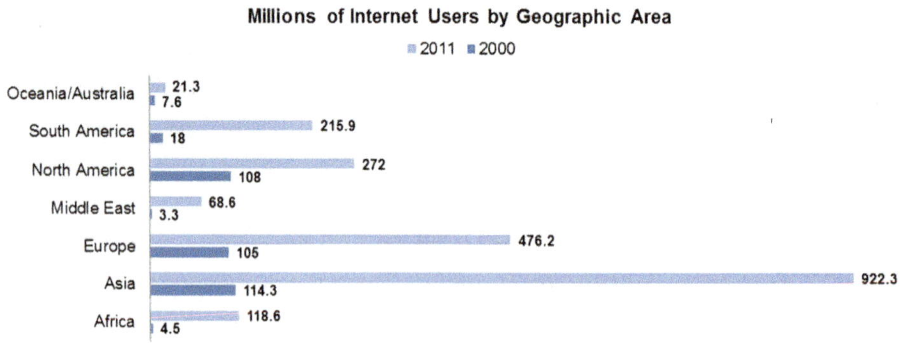

Figure 1 Growth of Internet use
Statistics from http://www.internetworldstats.com. Copyright © 2001–2011, Miniwatts Marketing Group. All rights reserved worldwide.

The lifting of the restriction on commercial use of the Internet set the stage for future electronic commerce: Businesses were now welcome on the Internet. However, the Internet was still text based and not easy to use. The next set of developments solved this issue.

Birth of the Web

While working at CERN, a research facility in Switzerland, **Tim Berners-Lee** envisioned a means of communication for scientists by which they could easily "hyperlink" to another research paper or article and immediately view it. Berners-Lee created the World Wide Web to fulfill this need. In 1991, Berners-Lee posted the code for the Web in a newsgroup and made it freely available. This version of the World Wide Web used **Hypertext Transfer Protocol (HTTP)** to communicate between the client computer and the web server, used **Hypertext Markup Language (HTML)** to format the documents, and was text based.

VideoNote
Evolution of the Web

The First Graphical Browser

In 1993, Mosaic, the first graphical web browser (shown in Figure 2), became available.

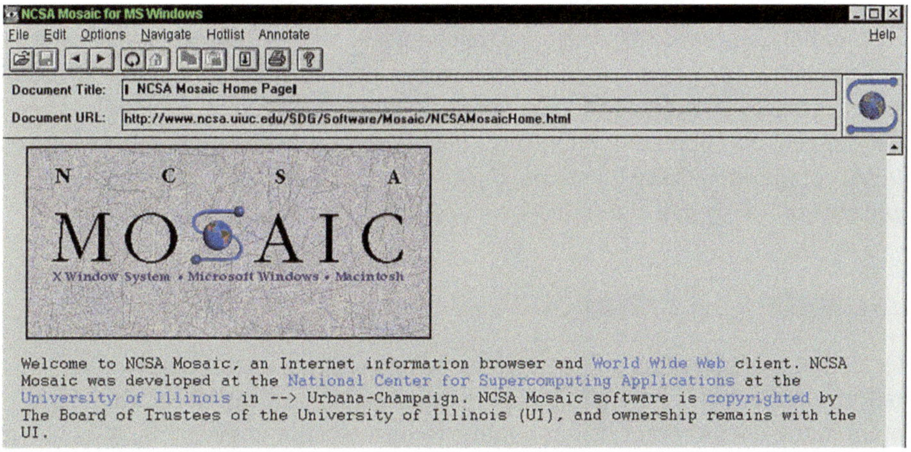

Figure 2 Mosaic: The first graphical browser

Marc Andreessen and graduate students working at the National Center for Supercomputing Applications (NCSA) at the University of Illinois Urbana–Champaign developed Mosaic. Some individuals in this group later created another well-known web browser—Netscape Navigator—which is an ancestor of today's Mozilla Firefox browser.

Convergence of Technologies

By the early 1990s, personal computers with easy-to-use graphical operating systems (such as Microsoft's Windows, IBM's OS/2, and Apple's Macintosh OS) were increasingly available and affordable. Online service providers such as CompuServe, AOL, and Prodigy offered low-cost connections to the Internet. The convergence of available computer hardware, easy-to-use operating systems, low-cost Internet connectivity, the HTTP protocol and HTML language, and a graphical browser made information on the Internet much easier to access. The **World Wide Web**—the graphical user interface to information stored on computers running web servers connected to the Internet—had arrived!

Who Runs the Internet?

You may be surprised that there is no single person "in charge" of the global interconnected network of computer networks known as the Internet. Instead, Internet infrastructure standards are overseen by groups such as the **Internet Engineering Task Force (IETF)** and the **Internet Architecture Board (IAB)**. The IETF is the principal body engaged in the development of new Internet protocol standard specifications. It is an open international community of network designers, operators, vendors, and researchers concerned with the evolution of Internet architecture and the smooth operation of the Internet. The actual technical work of the IETF is completed in its working groups. These working groups are organized into areas by topic, such as security and routing.

The IAB is a committee of the IETF and provides guidance and broad direction to the IETF. As a function of this purpose, the IAB is responsible for the publication of the **Request for Comments (RFC)** document series. An RFC is a formal document from the IETF that is drafted by a committee and subsequently reviewed by interested parties. RFCs are available for online review at http://www.ietf.org/rfc.html. Some RFCs are informational in nature, while others are meant to become Internet standards. In the latter case, the final version of the RFC becomes a new standard. Future changes to the standard must be made through subsequent RFCs.

The **Internet Corporation for Assigned Numbers and Names (ICANN)**, http://www.icann.org, was created in 1998 and is a nonprofit organization. Its main function is to coordinate the assignment of Internet domain names, IP address numbers, protocol parameters, and protocol port numbers. Prior to 1998, the **Internet Assigned Numbers Authority (IANA)** coordinated these functions. IANA still performs certain functions under the guidance of ICANN and maintains a website at http://www.iana.org.

Intranets and Extranets

Recall that the Internet is an interconnected network of computer networks that is globally available. When an organization needs the communication capabilities of the Internet, but doesn't want its information to be available to everyone, either an intranet or extranet is appropriate.

An **intranet** is a private network that is contained within an organization or business. Its purpose is to share organizational information and resources among coworkers. When an intranet connects to the outside Internet, usually a gateway or firewall protects the intranet from unauthorized access.

An **extranet** is a private network that securely shares part of an organization's information or operations with external partners such as suppliers, vendors, and customers. Extranets can be used to exchange data, share information exclusively with business partners, and collaborate with other organizations. Privacy and security are important issues in extranet use. Digital certificates, encryption of messages, and virtual private networks (VPNs) are some technologies used to provide privacy and security for an extranet.

2 Web Standards and Accessibility

Just as with the Internet, no single person or group runs the World Wide Web. However, the **World Wide Web Consortium** (http://www.w3.org), referred to as the W3C, takes a proactive role in developing recommendations and prototype technologies related to the Web. Topics that the W3C addresses include web architecture, standards for web design, and accessibility. In an effort to standardize web technologies, the W3C (logo shown in Figure 3) produces specifications called recommendations.

Figure 3 The W3C logo

W3C Recommendations

The W3C Recommendations are created in working groups with input from many major corporations involved in building web technologies. These recommendations are not rules; they are guidelines. Major software companies that build web browsers, such as Microsoft, do not always follow the W3C Recommendations. This makes life difficult for web developers because not all browsers will display a web page in exactly the same way. The good news is that there is a convergence toward the W3C Recommendations in new versions of major browsers. There are even organized groups, such as The Web Standards Project, http://webstandards.org, whose mission is to promote W3C Recommendations (often called Web standards) not only to the creators of browsers, but also to web developers and designers. You'll follow W3C Recommendations as you code web pages. Following the W3C Recommendations is the first step toward creating a website that is accessible.

Web Standards and Accessibility

Focus on Accessibility

The **Web Accessibility Initiative (WAI)** (http://www.w3.org/WAI), is a major area of work by the W3C. Since the Web has become an integral part of daily life, there is a need for all individuals to be able to access it.

The Web can present barriers to individuals with visual, auditory, physical, and neurological disabilities. An **accessible** website provides accommodations that help individuals overcome these barriers. The WAI has developed recommendations for web content developers, web authoring tool developers, web browser developers, and developers of other user agents to facilitate use of the Web by those with special needs. See the WAI's **Web Content Accessibility Guidelines** (WCAG) at http://www.w3.org/WAI/WCAG20/glance/WCAG2-at-a-Glance.pdf for a quick overview.

Accessibility and the Law

Focus on Accessibility

The **Americans with Disabilities Act** (ADA) of 1990 is a federal civil rights law that prohibits discrimination against people with disabilities. The ADA requires that business, federal, and state services are accessible to individuals with disabilities. A 1996 Department of Justice ruling (http://www.justice.gov/crt/foia/readingroom/frequent_requests/ada_coreletter/cltr204.txt) indicated that ADA accessibility requirements apply to Internet resources.

Section 508 of the Federal Rehabilitation Act was amended in 1998 to require that U.S. government agencies give individuals with disabilities access to information technology that is comparable to the access available to others. This law requires developers creating information technology (including web pages) for use by the federal government to provide for accessibility. The **Federal IT Accessibility Initiative** (http://www.section508.gov) provides accessibility requirement resources for information technology developers.

In recent years, state governments have also begun to encourage and promote web accessibility. The Illinois Information Technology Accessibility Act (IITAA) guidelines are an example of this trend. (See http://www.dhs.state.il.us/IITAA/IITAAWebImplementationGuidelines.html.)

Universal Design for the Web

The Center for Universal Design defines **universal design** as "the design of products and environments to be usable by all people, to the greatest extent possible, without the need for adaptation or specialized design" (http://www.ncsu.edu/project/design-projects/udi/center-for-universal-design/the-principles-of-universal-design/). Examples of universal design are all around us. The cutouts on curbs that make it possible for people in wheelchairs to access the street also benefit a person pushing a stroller or doing a little rollerblading (Figure 4). Doors that open automatically for people with mobility challenges also benefit people carrying packages. A ramp is useful for a person in a wheelchair, a person dragging a rolling backpack or carry-on bag, and so on.

Figure 4 Inline skaters benefit from universal design

Awareness of universal design by web developers has been steadily increasing. Forward-thinking web developers design with accessibility in mind because it is the right thing to do. Providing access for visitors with visual, auditory, and other challenges should be an integral part of web design rather than an afterthought.

A person with visual difficulties may not be able to use graphical navigation buttons and may use a screen reader device to provide an audible description of the web page. By making a few simple changes, such as providing text descriptions for the images and perhaps providing a text navigation area at the bottom of the page, web developers can make the page accessible. Often, providing for accessibility increases the usability of the website for all visitors.

Focus on Accessibility

Accessible websites, with alternative text for images, headings used in an organized manner, and captions or transcriptions for multimedia features, are more easily used not only by visitors with disabilities, but also by visitors using a browser on a mobile device such as a phone or tablet. Finally, accessible websites may be more thoroughly indexed by search engines, which can be helpful in bringing new visitors to a site. As this text introduces web development and design techniques, corresponding web accessibility and usability issues are discussed.

3 Information on the Web

These days anyone can publish just about anything on the Web. In this section we'll explore how you can tell if the information you've found is reliable and how you can use that information.

Reliability and Information on the Web

There are many websites—but which ones are reliable sources of information? When visiting websites to find information, it is important not to take everything at face value (Figure 5).

Questions to ask about web resources are listed as follows;

- **Is the organization credible?**

  Anyone can post anything on the Web! Choose your information sources wisely. First, evaluate the credibility of the website itself. Does it have its own domain name, such as http://mywebsite.com, or is it a free website consisting of just a folder of files hosted on a free web server? The URL of a site hosted on a free web server usually includes part of the free web server's name and might begin with something such as http://mysite.tripod.com or http://www.angelfire.com/foldername/mysite. Information obtained from a website that has its own domain name will usually (but not always) be more reliable than information obtained from a free website.

Figure 5 Who really updated that web page you are viewing?

  Evaluate the type of domain name: Is it for a nonprofit organization (.org), a business (.com or .biz), or an educational institution (.edu)? Businesses may provide information in a biased manner, so be careful. Nonprofit organizations and schools will sometimes treat a subject more objectively.

- **How recent is the information?**

  Another item to look at is the date the web page was created or last updated. Although some information is timeless, very often a web page that has not been updated for several years is outdated and may not be the best source of information.

- **Are there links to additional resources?**

  Hyperlinks indicate websites with supporting or additional information that can be helpful to you in your research as you explore a topic. Look for these types of hyperlinks to aid your studies.

- **Is it Wikipedia?**

  Wikipedia is a good place to begin research, but don't accept what you read there for fact, and avoid using Wikipedia as a resource for academic assignments. Why? Well, except for a few protected topics, anyone can update Wikipedia with anything! Usually it all gets sorted out eventually—but be aware that the information you read may not be valid.

  Feel free to use Wikipedia to begin exploring a topic, but then scroll down to the bottom of the Wikipedia web page and look for "References"—and then explore those websites and others that you may find. As you gather information on these sites, also consider the other criteria: credibility, domain name, timeliness, and links to additional resources.

Ethical Use of Information on the Web

Focus on Ethics

This wonderful technology called the World Wide Web provides us with information, graphics, and music—all virtually free (after you pay your Internet service provider, of course). Let's consider the following issues relating to the ethical use of this information:

- Is it acceptable to copy someone's graphic to use on your own website?
- Is it acceptable to copy someone's website design to use on your own site or on a client's site?
- Is it acceptable to copy an essay that appears on a web page and use it, or parts of it, as your own writing?
- Is it acceptable to insult someone on your website or link to that person's site in a derogatory manner?

The answer to all these questions is no. Using someone's graphic without permission is the same as stealing it. In fact, if you link to it, you are actually using up some of the site's bandwidth and may be costing the owner money. Instead, ask the owner of the website for permission to use the graphic. If permission is granted, store the graphic on your own website and be sure to indicate the source of the graphic when you display it on your web page. The key is to request permission before using someone else's resources. Copying the website design of another person or company is also a form of stealing. Any text or graphic on a website is automatically copyrighted in the United States, regardless of whether a copyright symbol appears on the site or not. Insulting a person or company on your website or linking to the person's or company's website in a derogatory manner could be considered a form of defamation.

Issues like these, related to intellectual property, copyright, and freedom of speech, are regularly discussed and decided in courts of law. Good Web etiquette requires that you ask permission before using others' work, give credit for what you use ("fair use" in the U.S. copyright law), and exercise your freedom of speech in a manner that is not harmful to others. The **World Intellectual Property Organization (WIPO)**, http://wipo.int, is dedicated to protecting intellectual property rights internationally.

What if you'd like to retain ownership, but make it easy for others to use or adapt your work? **Creative Commons**, http://creativecommons.org, is a nonprofit organization that provides free services that allow authors and artists to register a type of a copyright license called a Creative Commons license. There are several licenses to choose from, depending on the rights you wish to grant. The Creative Commons license informs others as to exactly what they can and cannot do with your creative work. See http://meyerweb.com/eric/tools/color-blend to view a web page licensed under a Creative Commons Attribution-ShareAlike 1.0 License with "Some Rights Reserved."

Checkpoint 1

1. Describe the difference between the Internet and the Web.
2. Explain three events that contributed to the commercialization and exponential growth of the Internet.
3. Is the concept of universal design important to web developers? Explain your answer.

4 Network Overview

A **network** consists of two or more computers connected for the purpose of communicating and sharing resources. Common components of a network are shown in Figure 6 and include the following:

- Server computer(s)
- Client workstation computer(s)
- Shared devices such as printers
- Networking devices (router and switch) and the media that connect them

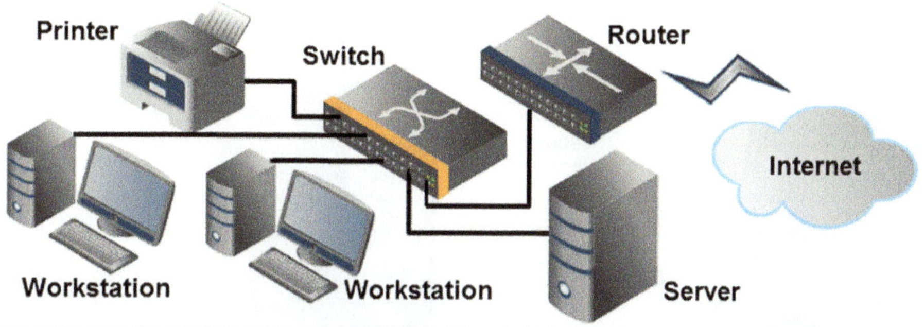

Figure 6 Common components of a network

The **clients** are the computer workstations used by individuals, such as a personal computer (PC) on a desk. The **server** receives requests from client computers for resources such as files. Computers used as servers are usually kept in a protected, secure area and are accessed only by network administrators. Networking devices such as hubs and switches provide network connections for computers, and routers direct information from one network to another. The **media** connecting the clients, servers, peripherals, and networking devices may consist of copper cables, fiber optic cables, or wireless technologies.

Networks vary in scale. A **local area network (LAN)** is usually confined to a single building or group of connected buildings. Your school computer lab may use a LAN. If you work in an office, you probably use a computer connected to a LAN. A **wide area network (WAN)** is geographically dispersed and usually uses some form of public or commercial communications network. For example, an organization with offices on both the East and West Coasts of the United States probably uses a WAN to provide a link between the LANs at each of the offices.

A **backbone** is a high-capacity communication link that carries data gathered from smaller links that interconnect with it. On the Internet, a backbone is a set of paths that local or regional networks connect to for long-distance interconnection. The Internet is a group of interconnected networks with very high-speed connectivity provided by the Internet backbones.

5 The Client/Server Model

The term **client/server** dates from the last millennium (the 1980s) and refers to personal computers joined by a network. "Client/server" can also describe a relationship between two computer programs—the client and the server. The client requests some type of service (such as a file or database access) from the server. The server fulfills the request and transmits the results to the client over a network. While both the client and the server programs can reside on the same computer, typically they run on different computers (Figure 7). It is common for a server to handle requests from multiple clients.

The Internet is a great example of client/server architecture at work. Consider the following scenario: An individual is at a computer using a web browser client to access the Internet. The individual uses the web browser to visit a website, let's say http://www.yahoo.com. The server is the web server program running on the computer with an IP address that corresponds to yahoo.com. It is contacted, locates the web page and related resources that were requested, and responds by sending them to the individual.

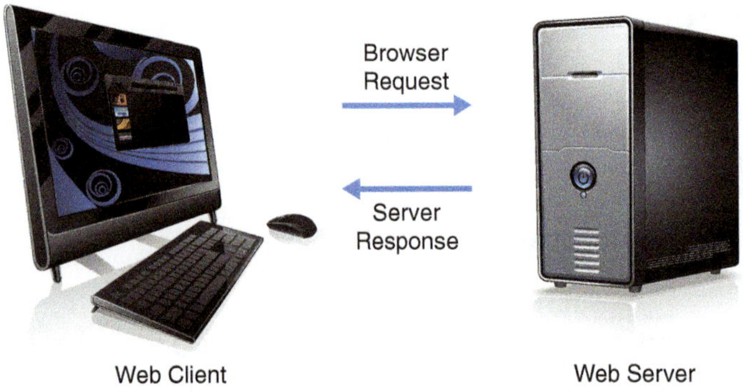

Figure 7 Web client and web server

Here's how to distinguish between web clients and web servers:

Web Client

- Connected to the Internet when needed
- Usually runs web browser (client) software such as Internet Explorer or Firefox
- Uses HTTP
- Requests web pages from a server
- Receives web pages and files from a server

Web Server

- Continually connected to the Internet
- Runs web server software (such as Apache or Internet Information Server)
- Uses HTTP
- Receives a request for the web page
- Responds to the request and transmits the status code, web page, and associated files

When clients and servers exchange files, they often need to indicate the type of file that is being transferred; this is done through the use of a MIME type. **Multipurpose Internet Mail Extensions (MIME)** are rules that allow multimedia documents to be exchanged among many different computer systems. MIME was initially intended to extend the original Internet e-mail protocol, but it is also used by HTTP. MIME provides for the exchange of seven different media types on the Internet: audio, video, image, application, message, multipart, and text. MIME also uses subtypes to further describe the data. The MIME type of a web page is text/html. MIME types of GIF and JPEG images are image/gif and image/jpeg, respectively.

A web server determines the MIME type of a file before the file is transmitted to the web browser. The MIME type is sent along with the document. The web browser uses the MIME type to determine how to display the document.

How does information get transferred from the web server to the web browser? Clients (such as web browsers) and servers (such as a web server) exchange information through the use of communication protocols such as HTTP, TCP, and IP, which are introduced in the next section.

6 Internet Protocols

Protocols are rules that describe how clients and servers communicate with each other over a network. There is no single protocol that makes the Internet and Web work; a number of protocols with specific functions are needed.

File Transfer Protocol (FTP)

File Transfer Protocol (FTP) is a set of rules that allow files to be exchanged between computers on the Internet. Unlike HTTP, which is used by web browsers to request web pages and their associated files in order to display a web page, FTP is used simply to move files from one computer to another. Web developers commonly use FTP to transfer web page files from their computers to web servers. FTP is also commonly used to download programs and files from other servers to individual computers.

E-mail Protocols

Most of us take e-mail for granted, but there are two servers involved in its smooth functioning: an incoming mail server and an outgoing mail server. When you send e-mail to others, **Simple Mail Transfer Protocol (SMTP)** is used. When you receive e-mail, **Post Office Protocol** (POP; currently **POP3**) and **Internet Message Access Protocol (IMAP)** can be used.

Hypertext Transfer Protocol (HTTP)

HTTP is a set of rules for exchanging files such as text, images, audio, video, and other multimedia on the Web. Web browsers and web servers usually use this protocol. When the user of a web browser requests a file by typing a website address or clicking on a hyperlink, the browser builds an HTTP request and sends it to the server. The web server in the destination machine receives the request, does any necessary processing, and responds with the requested file and any associated media files.

Transmission Control Protocol/Internet Protocol (TCP/IP)

Transmission Control Protocol/Internet Protocol (TCP/IP) has been adopted as the official communication protocol of the Internet. TCP and IP have different functions that work together to ensure reliable communication over the Internet.

TCP

The purpose of TCP is to ensure the integrity of network communication. TCP starts by breaking files and messages into individual units called **packets.** These packets (see Figure 8) contain information such as the destination, source, sequence number, and checksum values used to verify the integrity of the data.

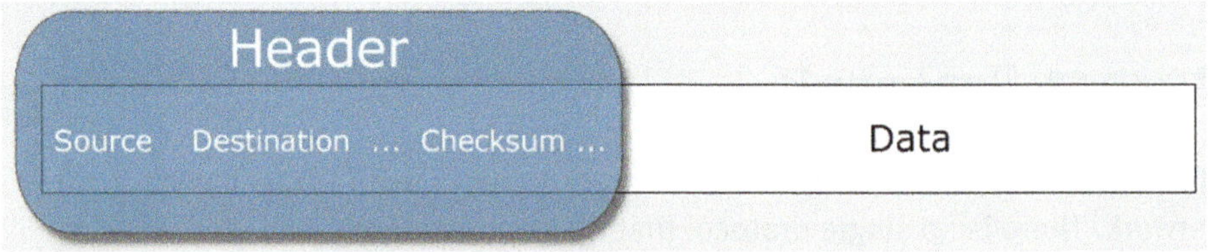

Figure 8 TCP packet

TCP is used together with IP to transmit files efficiently over the Internet. IP takes over after TCP creates the packets, using IP addressing to send each packet over the Internet via the best path at the particular time. When the destination address is reached, TCP verifies the integrity of each packet by using the checksum, requests a resend if a packet is damaged, and reassembles the file or message from the multiple packets.

IP

Working in harmony with TCP, IP is a set of rules that controls how data is sent between computers on the Internet. IP routes a packet to the correct destination address. Once sent, the packet gets successively forwarded to the next closest router (a hardware device designed to move network traffic) until it reaches its destination.

Each device connected to the Internet has a unique numeric **IP address**. These addresses consist of a set of four groups of numbers, called octets. The current version of IP, **Internet Protocol Version 4 (IPv4)**, uses 32-bit (binary digit) addressing. This results in a decimal number in the format of xxx.xxx.xxx.xxx, where each xxx is a value from 0 to 255. Theoretically, this system allows for at most 4 billion possible IP addresses (although many potential addresses are reserved for special uses). However, even this many addresses will not be enough to meet the needs of all of the devices expected to be connected to the Internet in upcoming years.

IP Version 6 (IPv6) will be the next standard IP protocol and will provide a huge increase in the number of possible addresses and many technological advances. IPv6 was designed as an evolutionary set of improvements to the current IPv4 and is backwardly compatible with it. Service providers and Internet users can update to IPv6 independently without having to coordinate with each other. IPv6 provides for more Internet addresses because the IP address is lengthened from 32 bits to 128 bits. This means that there are potentially 2^{128} unique IP addresses possible, or 340,282,366,920,938, 463,463,347,607,431,768,211,456 addresses. (Now there will be enough IP addresses for everyone's PC, notebook, cell phone, tablet, toaster, and so on!)

The IP address of a device may correspond to a domain name. The **Domain Name System (DNS)** associates these IP addresses with the text-based URLs and domain names you type into a web browser address box. For example, at the time this text was written, one of Google's IP addresses was 74.125.73.106. You can enter this number in the address text box in a web browser (as shown in Figure 9), press Enter, and the Google home page will display. Of course, it's much easier to type "google.com," which is why domain names such as google.com were created in the first place! Since long strings of numbers are difficult for humans to remember, the Domain Name System was introduced as a way to associate text-based names with numeric IP addresses.

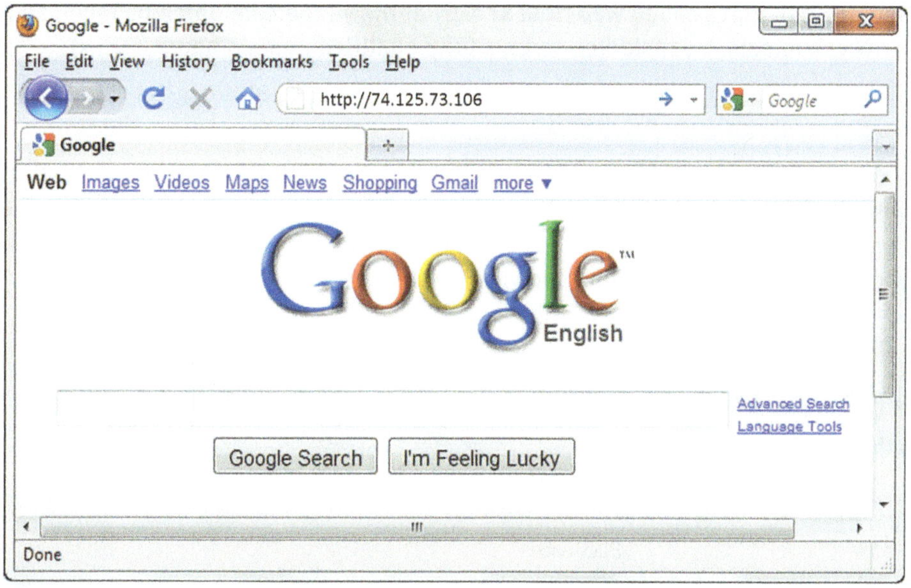

Figure 9 Entering an IP address in a web browser

7 Uniform Resource Identifiers and Domain Names

URIs and URLs

A **Uniform Resource Identifier (URI)** identifies a resource on the Internet. A **Uniform Resource Locator (URL)** is a type of URI which represents the network location of a resource such as a web page, a graphic file, or an MP3 file. The URL consists of the protocol, the domain name, and the hierarchical location of the file on the web server.

The URL http://www.webdevfoundations.net, shown in Figure 10, denotes the use of HTTP protocol and the web server named www at the domain name of webdevfoundations.net. In this case, the root file (usually index.html or index.htm) of the chapter1 directory will be displayed.

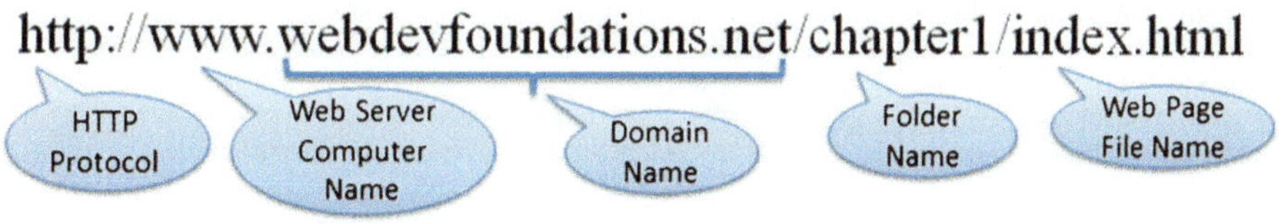

Figure 10 URL Describing a file within a folder

Domain Names

A **domain name** locates an organization or other entity on the Internet. The purpose of the Domain Name System (DNS) is to divide the Internet into logical groups and understandable names by identifying the exact address and type of the organization. The DNS associates the text-based domain names with the unique numeric IP address assigned to a device.

Let's consider the domain name www.yahoo.com. The ".com" is the top-level domain name. The portion "yahoo.com" is the domain name that is registered to Yahoo! and "yahoo" is considered a second-level domain name. The "www" is the name of the web server (sometimes called **web host server**) at the yahoo.com domain. Taken all together, www.yahoo.com is considered to be a **fully qualified domain name (FQDN)**.

Top-Level Domain Names

A **top-level domain (TLD)** identifies the rightmost part of the domain name, starting with the final period. A TLD is either a generic top-level domain, such as .com for commercial, or a country-code top-level domain, such as .fr for France. ICANN administers the generic top-level domains shown in Table 1.

Table 1 Top-level domains

Generic TLD	Used By
.aero	Air-transport industry
.asia	Pan-Asia and Asia Pacific community
.biz	Businesses
.cat	Catalan linguistic and cultural community
.com	Commercial entities
.coop	Cooperative
.edu	Restricted to accredited degree-granting institutions of higher education
.gov	Restricted to government use
.info	Unrestricted use
.int	International organization (rarely used)
.jobs	Human resources management community
.mil	Restricted to military use
.mobi	Corresponds to a .com website—the .mobi site is designed for easy access by mobile devices
.museum	Museums
.name	Individuals
.net	Entities associated with network support of the Internet, usually Internet service providers or telecommunication companies
.org	Nonprofit entities
.post	Universal Postal Union, an agency of the United Nations
.pro	Professionals such as accountants, physicians, and lawyers
.tel	Contact information for individuals and businesses
.travel	Travel industry
.xxx	Adult entertainment

The .com, .org, and .net TLD designations are currently used on the honor system, which means that, for example an individual who owns a shoe store (not related to networking) can register shoes.net.

Country-Code Top-Level Domain Names

Two-character country codes have also been assigned as TLD names. These codes were originally intended to be meaningful by designating the geographical location of the individual or organization that registered the name. In practice, however, it is fairly easy to obtain a domain name with a country-code TLD that is not local to the registrant. See http://register.com and many other domain name registration companies for examples. Table 2 lists some popular country codes used on the Web.

Table 2 Country codes

Country Code TLD	Country
.au	Australia
.de	Germany
.in	India
.jp	Japan
.nl	The Netherlands
.us	United States
.eu	European Union (a group of countries rather than a single country)

The IANA website at http://www.iana.org/cctld/cctld-whois.htm has a complete list of country-code TLDs. Domain names with country codes are often used for municipalities, schools, and community colleges in the United States. For example, the domain name www.harper.cc.il.us denotes, from right to left, the United States, Illinois, community college, Harper, and the web server named "www" as the site for Harper College in Illinois.

The DNS associates domain names with IP addresses. The following happens each time a new URL is typed into a web browser:

1. The DNS is accessed.
2. The corresponding IP address is obtained and returned to the web browser.
3. The web browser sends an HTTP request to the destination computer with the corresponding IP address.
4. The HTTP request is received by the web server.
5. The necessary files are located and sent by HTTP responses to the web browser.
6. The web browser renders and displays the web page and associated files.

The next time you wonder why it is taking so long to display a web page, think about all of the processing that goes on behind the scenes.

FAQ **Will there be any new TLDs soon?**

ICANN has approved the expansion of generic TLDs and announced that it will accept applications for new, customized TLDs. Think of the marketing possibilities—your organization's name, product, or service as a TLD! Sound too good to be true? Well, there's a catch. With a $185,000 application fee and an annual $25,000 fee, deep pockets are needed. Visit http://icann.org for more information.

8 Markup Languages

Markup languages consist of sets of directions that tell the browser software (and other user agents such as mobile phones) how to display and manage a web document. These directions are usually called tags and perform functions such as displaying graphics, formatting text, and referencing hyperlinks.

Standard Generalized Markup Language (SGML)

SGML is a standard for specifying a markup language or tag set. SGML in itself is not a document language, but a description of how to specify one and create a document type definition (DTD). When Tim Berners-Lee created HTML, he used SGML to create the specification.

Hypertext Markup Language (HTML)

HTML is the set of markup symbols or codes placed in a file intended for display on a web browser. The web browser renders the code in the HTML file and displays the web page document and associated files. The W3C (http://www.w3.org) sets the standards for HTML.

Extensible Markup Language (XML)

XML was developed by the W3C as a flexible method to create common information formats and share the format and the information on the Web. It is a text-based syntax designed to describe, deliver, and exchange structured information. It is not intended to replace HTML, but to extend the power of HTML by separating data from presentation. Using XML, developers can create whatever tags they need to describe their information.

Extensible Hypertext Markup Language (XHTML)

XHTML was developed by the W3C to reformulate HTML 4.01 as an application of XML. It combines the formatting strengths of HTML 4.01 *and* the data structure and extensibility strengths of XML. The primary advantages of XHTML include the ability to extend the language by creating new tags and the promise of increased platform interoperability as mobile devices are used more frequently to access the Web.

HTML5—the Newest Version of HTML

As this was being written, the W3C's HTML Working Group (HTML WG) was busy creating a draft recommendation for **HTML5**, which is intended to be the successor to HTML4 and will replace XHTML. HTML5 incorporates features of both HTML and XHTML, adds new elements, provides new features such as form edits and native video, and is intended to be backward compatible. Although this version still in draft form, much of the proposal is stable and supported by modern browsers.

Checkpoint 2

1. Describe the components of the client/server model as applied to the Internet.
2. Identify two protocols used on the Internet to convey information that use the Internet, but do not use the Web.
3. Explain the similarities and differences between a URL and a domain name.

9 Popular Uses of the Web

E-Commerce

Continued growth is expected for **e-commerce**, which is the buying and selling of goods and services on the Internet. Forrester Research projects that by 2014, over $248 billion will be spent on online retail sales (http://techcrunch.com/2010/03/08/forrester-forecast-online-retail-sales-will-grow-to-250-billion-by-2014/). With over 2 billion people online worldwide, as reported by Internet World Stats (http://www.internetworldstats.com/emarketing.htm), that's quite a few potential shoppers! As mobile web access becomes more commonplace, e-commerce will be regularly done not only from stationary computers, but also from portable devices—tablets, netbooks, smartphones, and technology we haven't even imagined yet.

Mobile Access

Accessing the Web with devices other than the standard desktop, notebook, and netbook computers is a growing trend. Gartner predicts that by 2013, mobile phones (including smartphones and browser-equipped phones) will "overtake PCs as the most common Web access device worldwide" (http://www.gartner.com/it/page.jsp?id=1278413). SearchBlog reported a Google 2011 projection that "between 15% and 30% of site traffic will come from mobile devices within eighteen months" (http://www.mediapost.com/publications/?fa=Articles.showArticle&art_aid=147794). Bloomberg Businessweek reported that electronics manufacturers expect a huge demand for **tablet** computers (such as the Apple iPad, Motorola Xoom, and Blackberry Playbook) and anticipate $49 billion in sales by 2015 (http://buswk.co/fK2Q9e). Web designers must consider how their pages will display and function not only on personal computers, but also on smartphones, tablets, and other mobile devices.

Blogs

The trend of keeping a web log, or blog, has been driven by individuals as a forum for personal expression. A **blog** is a journal that is available on the Web; it is a frequently updated page with a chronological list of ideas and links. Blog topics range from politics to technical information to personal diaries. Blogs can focus on one subject or range across a diverse group of topics—it's up to the person, called a blogger, who has created and maintains the blog. Bloggers usually update their blogs daily with easy-to-use software designed to allow people with little or no technical background to update and maintain a blog. Many blogs are hosted at blog communities such as http://www.blogger.com, http://www.wordpress.com, and http://www.tumblr.com. Others are hosted at individual websites, such as the blog kept by the web designer Eric Meyer at http://meyerweb.com. Businesses have noted the value of blogs as communication and customer relationship tools. Companies such as Adobe (http://feeds.adobe.com) and IBM (https://www.ibm.com/developerworks/mydeveloperworks/blogs) utilize blogs in this manner.

Wikis

A **wiki** is a website that can be updated immediately at any time by visitors, using a simple form on a web page. Some wikis are intended for a small group of people, such as the members of an organization. The most powerful wiki is Wikipedia (http://wikipedia.org), an online encyclopedia, which can be updated by anyone at any time. Wikis are a form of social software in action—visitors sharing their collective knowledge to create a resource freely used by all. While there have been isolated incidents of practical jokes, and inaccurate information has occasionally been posted at Wikipedia, the given information and linked resources are a good starting point when exploring a topic.

Social Networking

Blogs and wikis provide web visitors with new methods for interacting with websites and other people—a use referred to as **social computing,** or **social networking**. A trendy activity these days is participating in a social networking site such as Facebook (http://www.facebook.com) or LinkedIn (http://www.linkedin.com). Research firm eMarketer predicts that by 2014, close to two-thirds of all Internet users will regularly access social networking sites (http://www.emarketer.com/Report.aspx?code=emarketer_2000644). If it seems to you as if most of your friends are on Facebook, that may be the case: As of 2011, Facebook had over 500 million active users (http://www.digitalbuzzblog.com/facebook-statistics-stats-facts-2011/). While LinkedIn was created with professional and business networking in mind, businesses have also found it useful to create Facebook sites to promote their products and services.

Twitter (http://www.twitter.com) is a social networking site for **microblogging**, or frequently communicating with a brief message (140 characters or less) called a **tweet**. Twitter users (called twitterers) tweet to update a network of friends and followers about their daily activities and observations. Twitter is not limited to personal use. The business world has also discovered the marketing reach that Twitter can provide. Information Week (http://www.informationweek.com/news/hardware/desktop/217801030) reported that Dell attributes $3 million in sales to its use of Twitter.

RSS

Really Simple Syndication, or **Rich Site Summary (RSS)** is used to create newsfeeds from blog postings and other websites. The RSS feeds contain a summary of new items posted to the site. The URL to the RSS feed is usually indicated by the letters XML or RSS in white text within an orange rectangle. A **newsreader** is needed to access the information. Some browsers, such as Firefox, Safari, and Internet Explorer (version 7 or later), can display RSS feeds. Commercial and shareware newsreader applications are also available. The newsreader polls the feed URL at intervals and displays the new headlines when requested. RSS provides web developers with a method to push new content to interested parties and (hopefully) generate return visits to the site.

Podcasts

Podcasts are audio files on the web that take the format of an audio blog, radio show, or interview. Podcasts are typically delivered by an RSS feed, but can also be made available by providing the link to a recorded MP3 file on a web page. These files can be saved to your computer or to an MP3 player (such as an iPod) for later listening.

Web 2.0

Flickr (http://www.flickr.com/) and del.icio.us (http://del.icio.us/) are two social software sites that provide information-sharing opportunities. Flickr, a photo-sharing site, calls itself the "best way to store, search, sort, and share your photos." Once owned by Yahoo!, but sold to AVOS Systems in April 2011, del.icio.us is a collection of users' favorite sites, or bookmarks. Registered users post lists of favorites, share their favorites with others, and discover new sites by looking at others' favorites. Websites such as Wikipedia, Flickr, Twitter, and del.icio.us are examples of what is called **Web 2.0**. While a consensus on the definition of Web 2.0 has yet to be reached, think of it as the next step in the transition of the Web from isolated static websites to a platform that utilizes technology to provide rich interfaces and social networking opportunities. Visit http://www.go2web20.net and use the search engine to find Web 2.0 sites. You may also read Tim O'Reilly's informative Web 2.0 essay at http://oreillynet.com/pub/a/oreilly/tim/news/2005/09/30/what-is-web-20.html for more information on this developing topic.

The single trend that you can expect to remain the same for the foreseeable future is the trend of constant change. Internet and web-related technologies are in a constant state of development and improvement. If constant change and the opportunity to learn something new excite you, web development is a fascinating field. The skills and knowledge you gain in this text should provide a solid foundation for your future learning.

FAQ **What is the next big thing on the Web?**

The Web is changing by the minute. Check the text's companion website at http://www.webdevfoundations.net for a blog that will help you stay current about web trends.

Chapter Summary

This chapter has provided a brief overview of Internet, Web, and introductory networking concepts. Much of this information may already be familiar to you. Visit the text's website at http://www.webdevfoundations.net for links to the URLs listed in this chapter and to view updated information.

Key Terms

accessibility
backbone
blog
client/server
clients
domain name
Domain Name System (DNS)
extranet
File Transfer Protocol (FTP)
fully qualified domain name (FQDN)
HTML5
Hypertext Markup Language (HTML)
Hypertext Transfer Protocol (HTTP)
Internet
Internet Architecture Board (IAB)
Internet Assigned Numbers Authority (IANA)
Internet Corporation for Assigned Numbers and Names (ICANN)
Internet Engineering Task Force (IETF)
Internet Message Access Protocol (IMAP)
intranet
IP
IP address
IP Version 4 (IPv4)
IP Version 6 (IPv6)
Local Area Network (LAN)
markup languages
media
microblogging
Multipurpose Internet Mail Extensions (MIME)
network
newsreader
packets
podcasts
Post Office Protocol (POP3)
protocols
Really Simple Syndication or Rich Site Summary (RSS)
Request for Comments (RFC)
server
Simple Mail Transfer Protocol (SMTP)
social computing
social networking
Standard Generalized Markup Language (SGML)
tablet
TCP
top-level domain (TLD)
Transmission Control Protocol/ Internet Protocol (TCP/IP)
tweet
Uniform Resource Indicator (URI)
Uniform Resource Locator (URL)
Web 2.0
Web Accessibility Initiative (WAI)
Web Content Accessibility Guidelines (WCAG)
web host server
Wide Area Network (WAN)
wiki
World Intellectual Property Organization (WIPO)
World Wide Web
World Wide Web Consortium (W3C)
XHTML
XML

Review Questions

Multiple Choice

1. Which of the following is a network that covers a small area, such as a group of buildings or campus?
   a. LAN
   b. WAN
   c. Internet
   d. WWW

2. Which of the following markup languages is intended to extend the power of HTML by separating data from presentation?
   a. XML
   b. XHTML
   c. HTML5
   d. SGML

3. Of the following organizations, which one coordinates applications for new TLDs?
   a. Internet Assigned Numbers Authority (IANA)
   b. Internet Engineering Task Force (IETF)
   c. Internet Corporation for Assigned Numbers and Names (ICANN)
   d. World Wide Web Consortium (W3C)
4. What is a unique text-based Internet address corresponding to a computer's unique numeric IP address called?
   a. IP address
   b. domain name
   c. URL
   d. user name
5. Which of the following organizations takes a proactive role in developing recommendations and prototype technologies related to the Web?
   a. World Wide Web Consortium (W3C)
   b. Web Professional Standards Organization (WPO)
   c. Internet Engineering Task Force (IETF)
   d. Internet Corporation for Assigned Numbers and Names (ICANN)

True or False

6. ____ A URL is one type of URI.
7. ____ Markup languages contain sets of directions that tell the browser software how to display and manage a web document.
8. ____ The World Wide Web was developed to allow companies to conduct e-commerce over the Internet.
9. ____ A domain name that ends in .net indicates that the website is for a networking company.

Fill in the Blank

10. A standard language used for specifying a markup language or tag set is ____________.
11. ____________ combines the formatting strengths of HTML 4.0 and the data structure and extensibility strengths of XML.
12. ____________ is the set of markup symbols or codes placed in a file intended for display on a web browser.
13. The newest version of HTML is called ____________.
14. Frequently communicating by posting brief messages at a social networking site is called ____________.
15. The purpose of ____________ is to ensure the integrity of network communication.

Hands-On Exercise

1. Create a blog to document your learning experiences as you study web development. Visit one of the many sites that offer free blogs, such as http://www.blogger.com, http://www.wordpress.com, or http://www.xanga.com. Follow the site's instructions to establish your own blog. Your blog could be a place to note websites that you find useful or interesting. You might report on sites that contain useful web design resources. You might describe sites that have interesting features, such as compelling graphics or easy-to-use navigation. Write a few sentences about each site that you find intriguing. After you begin to develop your own sites, you could include the URLs and reasons for your design decisions. Share this blog with your fellow students and friends. Display your page in a browser, and print the page. Hand in the printout to your instructor.

Web Research

1. The World Wide Web Consortium creates standards for the Web. Visit its site at http://www.w3c.org and then answer the following questions:
   a. How did the W3C get started?
   b. Who can join the W3C? What does it cost to join?
   c. The W3C home page lists a number of technologies. Choose one that interests you, click on its link, and read the associated pages. List three facts or issues you discover.
2. The Internet Society takes an active leadership role in issues related to the Internet. Visit its site at http://www.isoc.org and then answer the following questions:
   a. Why was the Internet Society created?
   b. Determine which local chapter is closest to you. Visit its website. List the website's URL and an activity or service that the chapter provides.
   c. How can you join the Internet Society? What does it cost to join? Would you recommend that a beginning Web developer join the Internet Society? Why or why not?
3. The World Organization of Webmasters (WOW) is a professional association dedicated to the support of individuals and organizations that create and manage websites. Visit its site at http://www.webprofessionals.org and then answer the following questions:
   a. How can you join WOW? What does it cost to join?
   b. List one of the events in which WOW participates. Would you like to attend this event? Why or why not?
   c. List three ways that WOW can help you in your future career as a web developer.

Focus on Web Design

1. Visit a website that interests you. Print the home page or one other pertinent page from the site. Write a one-page summary of the site that addresses the following topics:
   a. What is the URL of the site?
   b. What is the purpose of the site?
   c. Who is the intended audience?
   d. Do you think that the site reaches its intended audience? Why or why not?
   e. Is the site useful to you? Why or why not?
   f. Does this site appeal to you? Why or why not? Consider the use of color, images, multimedia, organization, and ease of navigation.
   g. Would you encourage others to visit this site? Why or why not?
   h. How could this site be improved?

Answers

Checkpoint 1

1. The Internet is a public, globally connected network of computer networks. The Web is a graphical user interface to information stored on computers running web servers connected to the Internet. The Web is a subset of the Internet.
2. The commercialization and exponential growth of the Internet that began in the early 1990s was due largely to a convergence of technologies, including the development of personal computers with graphical operating systems, widespread availability of Internet connection services, the removal of the restriction of commercial use on NSFnet, the development of the World Wide Web by Tim Berners-Lee at CERN, and the development of a graphical browser (called Mosaic) at the NCSA. These events combined to provide the commercial incentive and an easy way to share and access information in a manner that had never been experienced.
3. Universal design is a very important concept for web developers because the websites that they create should be usable by all people. Not only is this the right thing to do, but in developing websites for the government or for educational institutions, access to technology (including websites) is mandated by law.

Checkpoint 2

1. An example of a web client is a computer running a browser software application such as Internet Explorer. Typically, the computer is connected to the Internet only when needed. The web browser software uses HTTP to request web pages and related resources from a web server. A web server is a computer that is continually connected to the Internet and that runs some type of web server software application. It uses the HTTP protocol to receive requests for web pages and related resources. It responds to these requests and sends the resources.
2. In this chapter, several protocols are discussed that use the Internet but not the Web. E-mail messages are transmitted via the Internet. SMTP (Simple Mail Transfer Protocol) is used to send e-mail messages. POP (Post Office Protocol) and IMAP (Internet Message Access Protocol) can be used to receive e-mail messages. FTP (File Transfer Protocol) can be used to exchange (send and receive) files with a computer connected to the Internet.
3. A URL (Uniform Resource Locator) represents the address of a resource that is available on the Internet. A URL consists of a protocol, a domain name, and the hierarchical location of the file or resource. An example of a URL is http://www.webdevfoundations.net/chapter1/index.htm. A domain name locates an organization or other entity on the Internet and is associated with a unique numeric IP address. A domain name is part of a URL.

Review Questions

1. a
2. a
3. c
4. b
5. a
6. True
7. True
8. False
9. False
10. SGML
11. XHTML
12. HTML
13. HTML5
14. microblogging
15. TCP

Credits

All photographs except those noted below © Terry Ann Morris

"Checkpoint" icon (green check mark), "FAQ" icon (orange caption bubble), "Focus on Accessibility" icon (orange key) © Fotolia LLC

"Focus on Ethics" icon (black scales) © so47/Fotolia LLC

Figure 1 © 2001–2011, Miniwatts Marketing Group. All rights reserved worldwide.

Figure 2 © National Center for Supercomputing Applications

Figure 3 © W3C (World Wide Web Consortium)

Figure 4 © Maridav/Shutterstock Images LLC

Figure 6 © Gliffy, Inc. All Rights Reserved (http://www.gliffy.com)

Figure 7 (computer tower) © Viktor Gmyria/Shutterstock Images LLC

Figure 7 (flat-screen monitor, keyboard, mouse) © Lightvision, LLC/Shutterstock Images LLC

HTML Basics

Chapter Objectives

In this chapter, you will learn how to . . .

- Describe HTML, XHTML, and HTML5
- Identify the markup language in a web page document
- Use the html, head, body, title, and meta elements to code a template for a web page
- Configure the body of a web page with headings, paragraphs, line breaks, divs, lists, and blockquotes
- Configure text with phrase elements
- Configure special characters
- Use the anchor element to link from page to page
- Create absolute, relative, and e-mail hyperlinks
- Code, save, and display a web page document
- Test a web page document for valid syntax

This chapter gets you started on your very first web page. You'll be introduced to Hypertext Markup Language (HTML), the language used to create web pages; eXtensible Hypertext Markup Language (XHTML), the most recent standardized version of HTML; and HTML5, the newest draft version of HTML. The chapter begins with an introduction to the syntax of XHTML and HTML5; continues with sample web pages; and introduces HTML structural, phrase, and hyperlink elements as more example web pages are created. You will learn more if you work along with the sample pages in the text. Coding HTML is a skill, and every skill improves with practice.

1 HTML Overview

Markup languages consist of sets of directions that tell the browser software (and other user agents such as mobile phones) how to display and manage a web document. These directions are usually called tags and perform functions such as displaying graphics, formatting text, and referencing hyperlinks.

The World Wide Web is composed of files containing Hypertext Markup Language (HTML) and other markup languages that describe web pages. Tim Berners-Lee developed HTML using Standard Generalized Markup Language (SGML). SGML prescribes a standard format for embedding descriptive markup within a document and for describing the structure of a document. SGML is not in itself a document language, but rather a description of how to specify one and create a document type definition (DTD). The W3C (http://www.w3c.org) sets the standards for HTML and its related languages. Like the Web itself, HTML is in a constant state of change.

HTML

HTML is the set of markup symbols or codes placed in a file that is intended for display on a web page. These markup symbols and codes identify structural elements such as paragraphs, headings, and lists. HTML can also be used to place media (such as graphics, video, and audio) on a web page and describe fill-in forms. The browser interprets the markup code and renders the page. HTML permits the platform-independent display of information across a network. No matter what type of computer a web page was created on, any browser running on any operating system can display the page.

Each individual markup code is referred to as an **element**, or **tag**. Each tag has a purpose. Tags are enclosed in angle brackets, the < and > symbols. Most tags come in pairs: an opening tag and a closing tag. These tags act as containers and are sometimes referred to as container tags. For example, the text that is between the `<title>` and `</title>` tags on a web page would display in the title bar on the browser window. Some tags are used alone and are not part of a pair. For example, a `<br>` tag that configures a line break on a web page is a stand-alone, or self-contained, tag and does not have a closing tag. Most tags can be modified with **attributes** that further describe their purpose.

XHTML

The most recent standardized version of HTML used today is **eXtensible HyperText Markup Language (XHTML)**. XHTML uses the tags and attributes of HTML4 along with the syntax of XML. HTML was originally developed to provide access to electronic documents via a web browser. Web browsers that evolved along with HTML were written to forgive coding errors, ignore syntax errors, and allow "sloppy" HTML code. Web browsers contain many program instructions that are designed to ignore mistakes such as missing ending tags and to guess how the developer meant the page to display. These extra instructions are not a problem for a personal computer, which has relatively large processing power. However, it could be an issue for electronic devices with fewer resources, such as an Internet tablet or mobile phone.

The purpose of XHTML was to provide a foundation for device-independent web access. XHTML was developed by the W3C to be the reformulation of HTML as an application of XML. XHTML combines the formatting strengths of HTML and the data structure and extensibility strengths of XML. Since XHTML was designed using XML, let's take a quick look at XML.

XML (eXtensible Markup Language) is the W3C standard method for creating new markup languages that will support the display of nontraditional content such as mathematical notation, as well as support a variety of display devices. XML can fulfill these diverse needs because it is an extensible language—that is, it is designed to allow the definition of new tags or markup. The syntax of XML is very exacting so that devices do not have to waste processing power guessing how the document should display, but can instead display information efficiently. An XML document must be well formed. A **well-formed document** is a document that adheres to the syntax rules of the language.

HTML5

As this text was being written, the W3C's HTML Working Group (HTML WG) was busy creating a draft recommendation for HTML5, which is intended to be the successor to HTML4 and will replace XHTML. HTML5 incorporates features of both HTML and XHTML, adds new elements of its own, provides new features such as form edits and native video, and is intended to be backward compatible.

It is possible to begin using HTML5 right away! The newest versions of popular browsers, such as Internet Explorer 9, Firefox 4, Safari 5, Google Chrome, and Opera 10, already support some of the new features of HTML5. When new versions of each browser are released, you can expect increased support of HTML5. As you learn to design web pages, you need not only to know what works today in current browsers, but also to get ready to use new HTML5 coding techniques. To meet this challenging goal, this text introduces both XHTML syntax and HTML5 syntax, presents instruction for coding web pages in HTML5 with backward-compatible elements that work in current browsers, and provides practice with the new features of HTML5 that will work only in the latest versions of browsers. Since HTML5 is in draft status and may change after this text is printed, consult http://www.w3.org/TR/html-markup for the most current list of HTML5 elements.

FAQ What software do I need?

No special software is needed to create a web page document; all you need is a text editor. The Notepad text editor is included with Microsoft Windows. TextEdit is distributed with the Mac OS X operating system. (See http://support.apple.com/kb/TA20406 for configuration information.) An alternative to the operating system's basic text editor is one of the many free or shareware editors that are available, such as Notepad++ for Windows (http://notepad-plus-plus.org/download) and TextWrangler for Macs (http://www.barebones.com/products/textwrangler/download.html). Another commonly used alternative is a commercial web-authoring tool, such as Microsoft Expression Web or Adobe Dreamweaver. Regardless of the software or program you use, having a solid foundation in HTML will be useful.

You will need to test your web pages in the most popular browsers, which are listed as follows, along with the URLs where you can download them for free:

- Internet Explorer (http://microsoft.com/ie9)
- Mozilla Firefox (http://www.mozilla.com/en-US/products/download.html)
- Apple Safari (http://www.apple.com/safari/download/)
- Google Chrome (http://www.google.com/chrome)

You will also find the Web Developer Extension for Firefox (https://addons.mozilla.org/en-us/firefox/addon/web-developer) to be useful.

2 Document Type Definition

Because multiple versions and types of HTML and XHTML exist, the W3C recommends identifying the type of markup language used in a web page document with a **Document Type Definition (DTD)**. The DTD identifies the version of HTML contained in your document. Browsers and HTML code validators can use the information in the DTD when processing the web page. The DTD statement, commonly called a **doctype** statement, is placed at the top of a web page document. XHTML is the current standard version of HTML and is supported by popular browsers. HTML5 is the newest version and is currently in draft status. Most of the examples in this text use HTML5 syntax. Except where specifically noted, the HTML5 syntax will display on commonly used browsers.

3 Example XHTML Web Page

In this example, we will use the XHTML 1.0 Transitional DTD, which is the least strict version of XHTML 1.0. The DTD for XHTML 1.0 Transitional is as follows:

```
<!DOCTYPE html PUBLIC "-//W3C//DTD XHTML 1.0 Transitional//EN"
"http://www.w3.org/TR/xhtml1/DTD/xhtml1-transitional.dtd">
```

The rest of your web page document will consist of HTML elements and text. After the DTD, each web page begins with an opening `<html>` tag and ends with a closing `</html>` tag. These tags indicate that the text between them is HTML formatted for display in a browser. Every single XHTML web page you create will include the DTD statement, followed by the html, head, title, meta, and body elements. A basic XHTML web page template (found in the student files at chapter2/templatex.html)[1] is as follows:

```
<!DOCTYPE html PUBLIC "-//W3C//DTD XHTML 1.0 Transitional//EN"
"http://www.w3.org/TR/xhtml1/DTD/xhtml1-transitional.dtd">
<html xmlns="http://www.w3.org/1999/xhtml" lang="en" xml:lang="en">
<head>
<title>Page Title Goes Here</title>
<meta http-equiv="Content-Type" content="text/html; charset=utf-8" />
</head>
<body>
... body text and more XHTML tags go here ...
</body>
</html>
```

[1]Website Case Study starter files are available for download from Pearson's CS Support website at http://cssupport.pearsoncmg.com.

The XHTML tags are lowercase in the code sample. This format conforms to XML syntax. Notice also that the DTD statement does not follow this syntax. The DTD statement indicates the markup language being used and has mixed-case formatting. With the exception of the specific page title, the first eight lines will usually be the same on every XHTML web page that you create.

When using XHTML, the `<html>` tag also needs to describe the XML namespace (xmlns), which is the location of the documentation for the elements being used. This additional information is added to the `<html>` tag in the form of an **attribute**, which modifies or further describes the function of an element. The xmlns attribute points to the URL of the XHTML namespace used in the document, the standard http://www.w3.org/1999/xhtml. The optional **lang** and **xml:lang** attributes specify the spoken language of the document. For example, `lang="en" xml:lang="en"` indicate the English language. Search engines and screen readers may access these attributes.

Don't worry if the concept of specifying a DTD and the xmlns URL seem a bit overwhelming at first—these lines are reused over and over again in every web page. Once you create your web page template, you'll have these statements ready and waiting for all of your future pages.

4 Example HTML5 Web Page

Now that you've seen an example of a web page using XHTML, let's focus on HTML5. The syntax is streamlined and easier to use. We will follow the coding style to use lowercase letters and place quotation marks around attribute values. The HTML5 doctype statement is as follows:

```
<!DOCTYPE html>
```

Just as with XHTML, the doctype statement is the first line in the document. Next, the web page begins with an opening `<html>` tag and ends with a closing `</html>` tag. These tags indicate that the text between them is HTML formatted for display in a browser. Every HTML5 web page contains the doctype statement, followed by the html, head, title, meta, and body elements. A basic HTML5 web page template (found in the student files at chapter2/template.html) is as follows:

```
<!DOCTYPE html>
<html lang="en">
<head>
<title>Page Title Goes Here</title>
<meta charset="utf-8">
</head>
<body>
... body text and more HTML5 tags go here ...
</body>
</html>
```

The next section discusses the purpose of the head, title, meta, and body elements.

5 Head, Title, Meta, and Body Elements

There are two sections on a web page: the head and the body. The **head section**, sometimes called the header section, contains information that describes the web page document. The **body section** contains the actual tags, text, images, and other objects that are displayed by the browser as a web page.

The Head Section

Elements that are located in the head section include the title of the web page, meta tags that describe the document (such as the character encoding used and information that may be accessed by search engines), and references to scripts and styles. Many of these features do not show directly on the web page. The **head element** contains the head section, which begins with the `<head>` tag and ends with the `</head>` tag. You will always code at least two other elements in the head section: a title element and a meta element.

The first element in the head section, the **title element**, configures the text that will appear in the title bar of the browser window. The text between the `<title>` and `</title>` tags is called the title of the web page and is accessed when web pages are bookmarked and printed. The title should be descriptive. If the web page is for a business or organization, the title should include the name of the organization or business.

The **meta element** describes a characteristic of a web page, such as the character encoding. **Character encoding** is the internal representation of letters, numbers, and symbols in a file such as a web page or other file that is stored on a computer and may be transmitted over the Internet. There are many different character-encoding sets. However, it is common practice to use a character-encoding set that is widely supported, such as utf-8, which is a form of Unicode. The meta tag is not used as a pair of opening and closing tags. It is considered to be a stand-alone, or **self-contained**, tag (referred to as a **void element** in HTML5). The meta tag is coded differently in XHTML and HTML5. The XHTML meta tag has more detailed attributes and is coded with an ending />. The HTML5 meta tag is streamlined and includes only the charset attribute to indicate the character encoding.

XHTML Meta Tag

```
<meta http-equiv="Content-Type" content="text/html; charset=utf-8" />
```

HTML5 Meta Tag

```
<meta charset="utf-8">
```

The Body Section

The body section contains text and elements that display directly on the web page in the browser viewport. The purpose of the body section is to configure the contents of the web page. The **body element** contains the body section, which begins with the `<body>` tag and ends with the `</body>` tag. You will spend most of your time writing code in the body of a web page. If you type text into the body section, it will appear directly on the web page.

6 Your First Web Page

Hands-On Practice 1

VideoNote
Your First Web Page

Now that you're familiar with basic elements used on every web page, it's your turn to create your first web page.

Create a Folder

You'll find it helpful to create folders to organize your files as you develop web pages and create your own websites. Use your operating system to create a new folder named mychapter2 on your hard drive or a portable flash drive.

To create a new folder on a Mac:

1. Launch Finder, and select the location where you would like to create the new folder.
2. Choose File > New Folder to create an untitled folder.
3. To rename the folder, select the folder and click on the current name. Type a name for the folder, and press the Return key.

To create a new folder with Windows:

1. Launch Windows Explorer (either press the Windows key or select Start > All Programs > Accessories > Windows Explorer), and navigate to the location where you would like to create the new folder, such as My Documents or your C: drive.
2. Select Organize > New Folder.
3. To rename the New Folder, right-click on it, select Rename from the context-sensitive menu, type in the new name, and press the Enter key.

Your First Web Page

Now you are ready to create your first HTML5 web page. Launch Notepad or another text editor. Type in the following code:

```
<!DOCTYPE html>
<html lang="en">
<head>
<title>My First HTML5 Web Page</title>
<meta charset="utf-8">
</head>
<body>
Hello World
</body>
</html>
```

Notice that the first lines in the file contain the doctype. The HTML code begins with an opening `<html>` tag and ends with a closing `</html>` tag. The purpose of these tags is to indicate that the content between the tags makes up a web page. The head section is delimited by `<head>` and `</head>` tags and contains a pair of title tags with the words "My First HTML5 Web Page" in between, along with a `<meta>` tag to indicate the character encoding. The body section is delimited by `<body>` and `</body>` tags.

The words "Hello World" are typed on a line between the body tags. See Figure 1 for a screen-shot of the code as it would appear in Notepad. You have just created the source code for a web page document.

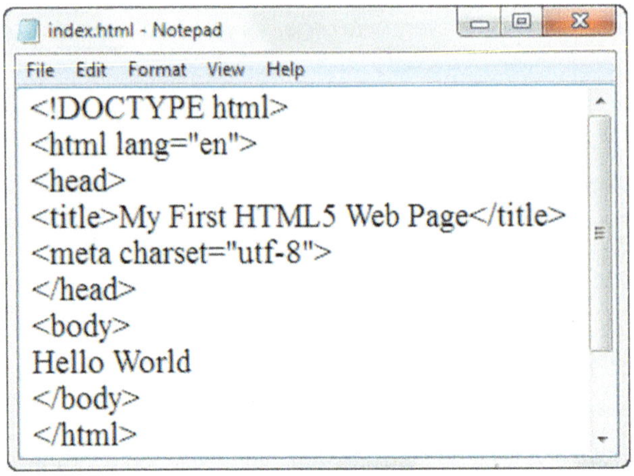

Figure 1 Your web page source code displayed in Notepad

FAQ Do I have to start each tag on its own line?

No, you are not required to start each tag on a separate line. A browser can display a page even if all the tags follow each other on one line with no spaces. Humans, however, find it easier to write and read web page code if line breaks and indentation are used.

Save Your File

You will save your file with the name of index.html. A common file name for the home page of a website is index.html or index.htm. Web pages use either a .htm or a .html file extension. The web pages in this text use the .html file extension. Display your file in Notepad or another text editor. Select File from the menu bar, and then select Save As. The Save As dialog box will appear. Navigate to your mychapter2 folder. Using Figure 2 as an example, type the file name. Click the Save button after you type the file name. Sample solutions for the exercises are available in the student files. If you like, you can compare your work with the solution in the student files at chapter2/index.html before you test your page.

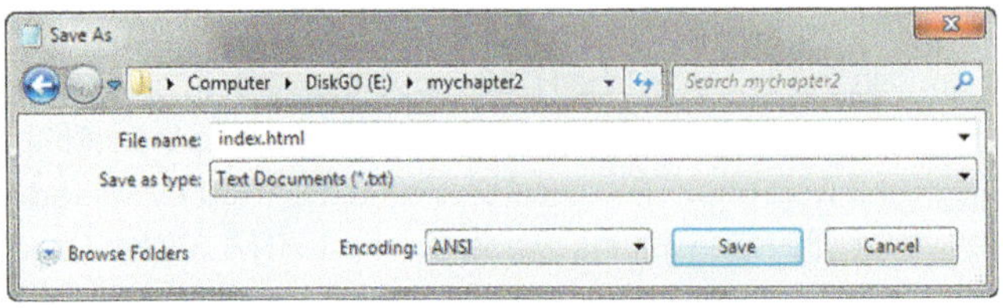

Figure 2 The Save As dialog box

FAQ **Why does my file have a .txt file extension?**

In some older versions of Windows, Notepad will automatically append a .txt file extension. If this happens, type the name of the file within quotation marks ("index.html"), and save your file again.

Test Your Page

There are two ways to test your page:

1. Launch Windows Explorer (Windows) or Finder (Mac). Navigate to your index.html file. Double-click index.html. The default browser will launch and will display your index.html page. Your page should look similar to the one shown in Figure 3.

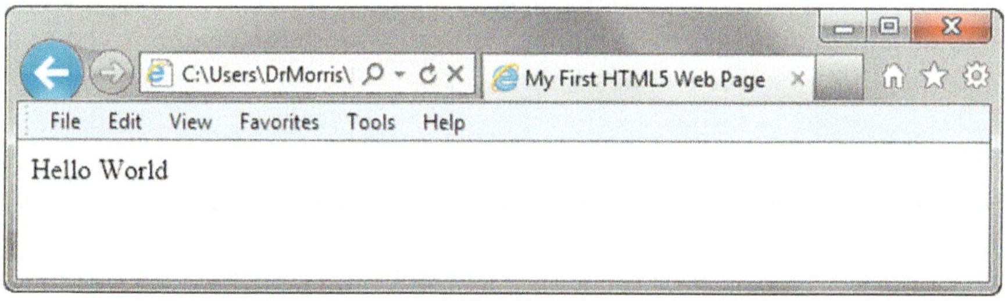

Figure 3 Web page displayed by Internet Explorer

2. Launch a browser. (If you are using Internet Explorer 9, right-click in the area at the top of the browser window and select the Menu bar.) Select File > Open > Browse. Navigate to your index.html file. Double-click index.html, and click OK. If you used Internet Explorer, your page should look similar to the one shown in Figure 3. A display of the page using Firefox 4 is shown in Figure 4.

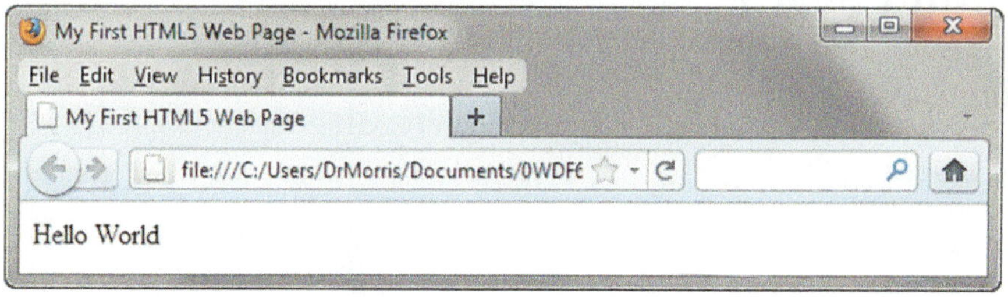

Figure 4 Web page displayed by Firefox

Examine your page. Look carefully at the browser window. Notice how the browser title bar or browser tab displays the title text, "My First HTML5 Web Page." Some search engines use the text enclosed within the `<title>` and `</title>` tags to help determine the relevancy of keyword searches, so make certain that your pages contain descriptive titles. The title element is also used when viewers bookmark your page or add it to their Favorites. An engaging and descriptive page title may entice a visitor to revisit your page. If your web page is for a company or an organization, it's a best practice to include the name of the company or organization in the title.

Checkpoint 1

1. Describe the origin, purpose, and features of HTML.
2. Describe the software needed to create and test web pages.
3. Describe the purpose of the head and body sections of a web page.

7 Heading Element

Heading elements are organized into six levels: h1 through h6. The text contained within a heading element is rendered as a "block" of text by the browser (referred to as block display) and displays with empty space (sometimes called "white space") above and below. The size of the text is largest for **<h1>** (called the heading 1 tag) and smallest for **<h6>** (called the heading 6 tag). Depending on the font being used, the text contained within **<h4>**, **<h5>**, and **<h6>** tags may be displayed smaller than the default text size. All text contained within heading tags is displayed with bold font weight. Figure 5 shows a web page document with six levels of headings.

FAQ Why doesn't the heading tag go in the head section?

It's common for students to try to code the heading tags in the head section of the document, but someone doing this won't be happy with the way the browser displays the web page. Even though "heading tag" and "head section" sound similar, always code heading tags in the body section of the web page document.

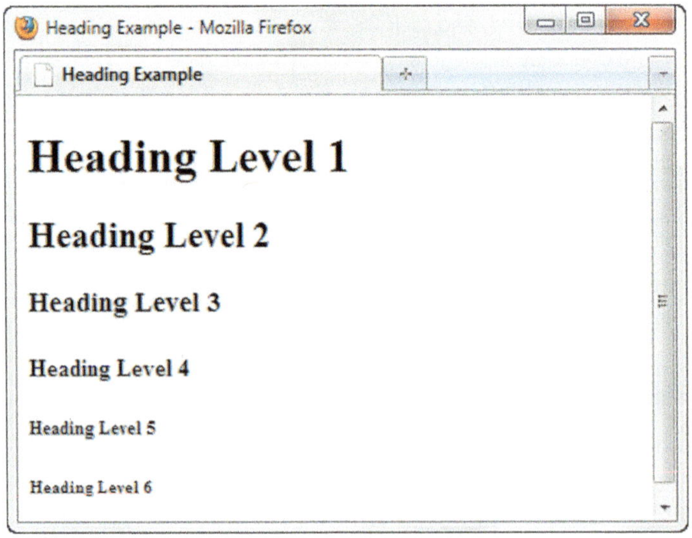

Figure 5 Sample headings

Hands-On Practice 2

To create the web page shown in Figure 5, launch Notepad or another text editor. Select File > Open to edit the HTML5 template file located at chapter2/template.html in the student files. Modify the title element and add heading tags to the body section as indicated by the following highlighted code:

```
<!DOCTYPE html>
<html lang="en">
<head>
<title>Heading Example</title>
<meta charset="utf-8">
</head>
<body>
<h1>Heading Level 1</h1>
<h2>Heading Level 2</h2>
<h3>Heading Level 3</h3>
<h4>Heading Level 4</h4>
<h5>Heading Level 5</h5>
<h6>Heading Level 6</h6>
</body>
</html>
```

Save the document as heading2.html on your hard drive or flash drive. Launch a browser such as Internet Explorer or Firefox to test your page. It should look similar to the page shown in Figure 5. You can compare your work with the HTML5 solution found in the student files (chapter2/heading.html) and the XHTML solution (chapter2/headingxhtml.html). Notice that in this example, the code for both solutions is the same except for the Document Type Declaration, html, and meta tags. This is true for most of the examples in this chapter. The HTML5 solutions for each hands-on practice activity are provided in the student files. The XHTML solution is also provided when deemed useful for comparison.

Accessibility and Headings

Focus on Accessibility

Heading tags can help to make your pages more accessible and usable. You create an outline of the page content when you code heading tags numerically as appropriate (h1, h2, h3, and so on) and configure page content in block display elements such as paragraphs and lists. Visually challenged visitors who are using a screen reader can direct the software to display a list of the headings used on a page to focus on the topics that interest them. Your well-organized page will be more usable for every visitor to your site, including those who are visually challenged.

More Heading Options in HTML5

You may have heard about the new HTML5 header hgroup elements. They offer additional options for configuring headings, but they are supported only in newer browsers.

8 Paragraph Element

Paragraph elements are used to group sentences and sections of text together. Text that is contained by **<p>** and **</p>** tags display as a "block" (referred to as block display) and will appear with empty space above and below it. Figure 6 shows a web page document with a paragraph after the first heading.

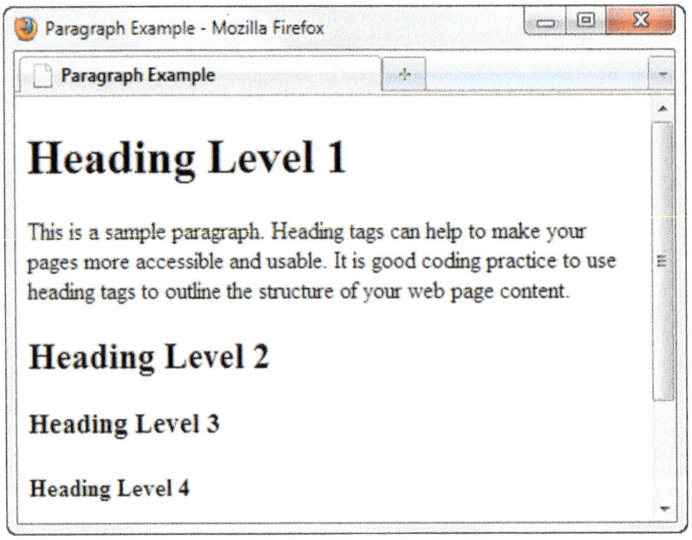

Figure 6 Web page using headings and a paragraph

Hands-On Practice 3

To create the web page shown in Figure 6, launch a text editor. Select File > Open to edit the file located at chapter2/heading.html in the student files. Modify the page title, and add a paragraph of text to your page below the line with the <h1> tags and above the line with the <h2> tags. Use the following code as an example:

```
<!DOCTYPE html>
<html lang="en">
<head>
<title>Paragraph Example</title>
<meta charset="utf-8">
</head>
<body>
<h1>Heading Level 1</h1>
<p>This is a sample paragraph. Heading tags can help to make your
pages more accessible and usable. It is good coding practice to use
heading tags to outline the structure of your web page content.
</p>
<h2>Heading Level 2</h2>
<h3>Heading Level 3</h3>
<h4>Heading Level 4</h4>
<h5>Heading Level 5</h5>
<h6>Heading Level 6</h6>
</body>
</html>
```

Save the document as paragraph2.html on your hard drive or flash drive. Launch a browser to test your page. It should look similar to the page shown in Figure 6. You can compare your work with the solution found in the student files (chapter2/paragraph.html). Notice how the text in the paragraph wraps automatically as you resize your browser window.

Alignment

As you tested your web pages, you may have noticed that the headings and text begin near the left margin. This placement is called **left alignment** and is the default alignment for web pages. There are times, however, when you want a paragraph or heading to be centered or right aligned. The align attribute can be used for this purpose. The purpose of an **attribute** is to modify the properties of an HTML element. In this case, the **align** attribute modifies the element's horizontal alignment (left, center, or right) on a web page. To center an element on a web page, use the attribute `align="center"`. To right-align the text within an element, use the `align="right"` attribute. In XHTML syntax, the align attribute can be used with a number of block display elements, including the paragraph (`<p>`) and heading (`<h1>` through `<h6>`) tags. The align attribute is **obsolete** in HTML5, which means that while it may be used in XHTML, the attribute has been removed from the W3C HTML5 draft specification.

9 Line Break Element

The **line break element** causes the browser to advance to the next line before displaying the next element or portion of text on a web page. The line break tag is not coded as a pair of opening and closing tags. It is considered to be a **stand-alone,** or **void**, element. In HTML5 syntax, the line break tag is coded as **`<br>`**. In XHTML (which follows XML syntax), the line break tag is coded as `<br />`. (The ending /> indicates a self-contained tag.) Figure 7 shows a web page document with a line break after the first sentence in the paragraph.

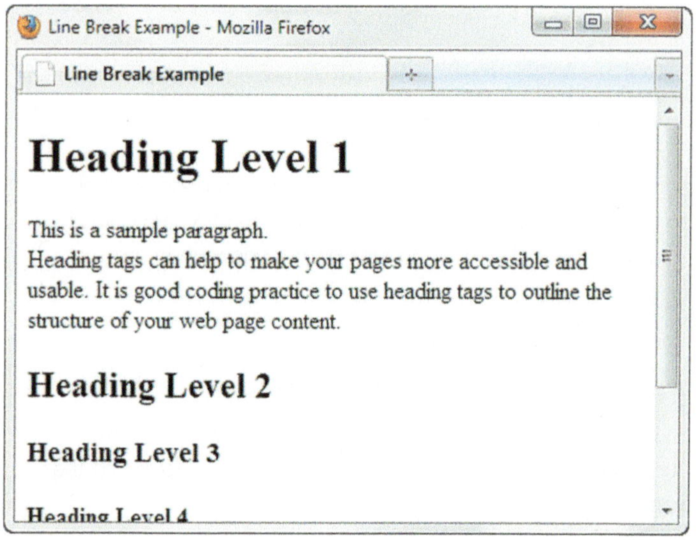

Figure 7 Notice the line break after the first sentence

Hands-On Practice 4

To create the web page shown in Figure 7, launch a text editor. Select File > Open to edit the file located at chapter2/paragraph.html in the student files. Modify the text contained between the title tags to be "Line Break Example". Place your cursor after the first sentence in the paragraph (after "This is a sample paragraph."). Press the Enter key. Save your file. Test your page in a browser, and notice that even though your source code showed the "This is a sample paragraph." sentence on its own line, the browser did not render it that way. A line break tag is needed to configure the browser to display the second sentence on a new line. Edit the file in a text editor, and add a `<br>` tag (the file uses HTML5 syntax) after the first sentence in the paragraph, as shown in the following code snippet:

```
<body>
<h1>Heading Level 1</h1>
<p>This is a sample paragraph. <br> Heading tags can help to make
your pages more accessible and usable. It is good coding practice to
use heading tags to outline the structure of your web page content.
</p>
<h2>Heading Level 2</h2>
<h3>Heading Level 3</h3>
<h4>Heading Level 4</h4>
<h5>Heading Level 5</h5>
<h6>Heading Level 6</h6>
</body>
```

Save your file as linebreak2.html. Launch a browser to test your page. It should look similar to the page shown in Figure 7. You can compare your work with the solution found in the student files (chapter2/linebreak.html). An XHTML solution can also be found in the student files (chapter2/linebreakxhtml.html).

FAQ **Why does my web page still look the same?**

Often, students make changes to a web page document, but get frustrated because their browser shows an older version of the page. The following troubleshooting tips are helpful when you know you modified your web page, but the changes do not show up in the browser:

1. Make sure you save your page after you make the changes.
2. Verify the location that you are saving your page to—a specific folder on the hard drive or removable storage.
3. Verify the location that your browser is requesting the page from—a specific folder on the hard drive or removable storage.
4. Be sure to click the Refresh or Reload button in your browser.

10 Blockquote Element

In addition to organizing text in paragraphs and headings, sometimes you need to add a quotation to a web page. **The blockquote element** is used to display a block of quoted text in a special way—indented from both the left and right margins. A block of indented text begins with a **<blockquote>** tag and ends with a **</blockquote>** tag. Figure 8 shows a web page document with a heading, a paragraph, and a blockquote.

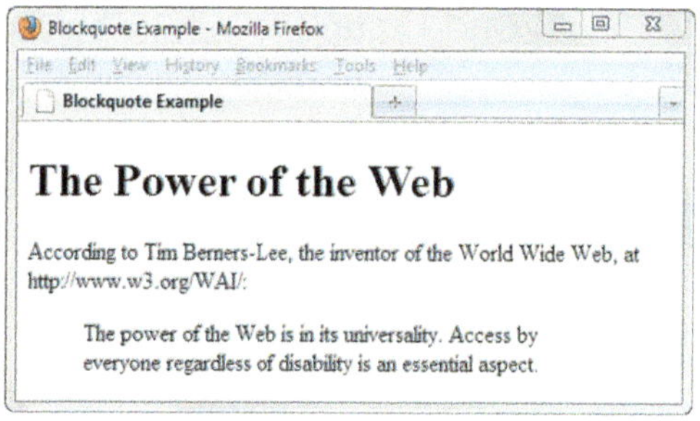

Figure 8 The text within the blockquote element is indented

Hands-On Practice 5

To create the web page shown in Figure 8, launch a text editor. Select File > Open to edit the template file located at chapter2/template.html in the student files. Modify the title element. Add a heading tag, a paragraph tag, and a blockquote tag to the body section as indicated by the following highlighted code:

```
<!DOCTYPE html>
<html lang="en">
<head>
<title>Blockquote Example</title>
<meta charset="utf-8">
</head>
<body>
<h1>The Power of the Web</h1>
<p>According to Tim Berners-Lee, the inventor of the World Wide Web,
at http://www.w3.org/WAI/:</p>
<blockquote>
The power of the Web is in its universality. Access by everyone
regardless of disability is an essential aspect.
</blockquote>
</body>
</html>
```

Save the document as blockquote2.html on your hard drive or flash drive. Launch a browser to test your page. It should look similar to the page shown in Figure 8. You can compare your work with the solution found in the student files (chapter2/blockquote.html).

You have probably noticed how convenient the <blockquote> tag could be if you need to indent an area of text on a web page. You may have wondered whether it would be OK to use the blockquote element anytime you would like to indent text or whether the blockquote element is reserved only for long quotations. The semantically correct use of the blockquote element is only for displaying large blocks of quoted text within a web page. Why should you be concerned about semantics? Consider the future of the Semantic Web, described in *Scientific American* (http://www.scientificamerican.com/article.cfm?id=the-semantic-web) as "[a] new form of Web content that is meaningful to computers [that] will unleash a revolution of new possibilities." Using HTML in a semantic, structural manner is one step toward the Semantic Web. So, avoid using a blockquote element just to indent text.

11 Phrase Elements

Phrase elements, sometimes referred to as **logical style elements,** indicate the context and meaning of the text between the container tags. It is up to each browser to interpret that style. Phrase elements are displayed right in line with the text (referred to as inline display) and can apply to a section of text or even just a single character of text. For example, the **<strong>** element indicates that the text associated with it has strong importance and should be displayed in a "strong" manner in relation to normal text on the page. Table 1 lists common phrase elements and examples of their use. Notice that some tags, such as <cite> and <dfn>, result in the same type of display (italics) as the <em> tag in today's browsers. These tags semantically describe the text as a citation or definition, but the physical display is usually italics in both cases.

Table 1 Phrase elements

Element	Example	Usage
<abbr>	WIPO	Identifies text as an abbreviation; configure the title attribute with the full name
<b>	**bold** text	Text that has no extra importance, but is styled in bold font by usage and convention
<cite>	*cite* text	Identifies a citation or reference; usually displayed in italics
<code>	`code` text	Identifies program code samples; usually a fixed-space font
<dfn>	*dfn* text	Identifies a definition of a word or term; usually displayed in italics
<em>	*emphasized* text	Causes text to be emphasized in relation to other text; usually displayed in italics
<i>	*italicized* text	Text that has no extra importance, but is styled in italics by usage and convention
<kbd>	`kbd` text	Identifies user text to be typed; usually a fixed-space font
<mark>	mark text	Text that is highlighted in order to be easily referenced (HTML5 only)
<samp>	`samp` text	Shows program sample output; usually a fixed-space font
<small>	small text	Legal disclaimers and notices ("fine print") displayed in small font size
<strong>	**strong** text	Strong importance; causes text to stand out from surrounding text; usually displayed in bold
<sub>	$_{\text{sub}}$ text	Displays a subscript as small text below the baseline
<sup>	^{sup} text	Displays a superscript as small text above the baseline
<var>	*var* text	Identifies and displays a variable or program output; usually displayed in italics

Each phrase element is a container element, so an opening and a closing tag must be used. As shown in Table 1, the <strong> element indicates that the text associated with it has "strong" importance. Usually, the browser (or other user agent) will display <strong> text in bold font type. A screen reader, such as JAWS or Window-Eyes, might interpret <strong> text to indicate that the text should be more strongly spoken. In the following line, the phone number is displayed with strong importance:

Call for a free quote for your web development needs: **888.555.5555**

The corresponding code is

```
<p>Call for a free quote for your web development needs:
<strong>888.555.5555</strong></p>
```

Notice that the opening <strong> and closing </strong> tags are contained within the paragraph tags (<p> and </p>). This code is properly nested and is considered to be **well formed**. When improperly nested, the <p> and <strong> tag pairs overlap each other instead of being nested within each other. Improperly nested code will not pass validation testing (see Section 18, "HTML Validation") and may cause display issues.

Figure 9 shows a web page document (also found in the student files at chapter2/em.html) that uses the <em> tag to display the emphasized phrase "Access by everyone" in italics.

The code snippet is

```
<blockquote>
The power of the Web is in its universality.
<em>Access by everyone</em>
regardless of disability is an essential aspect.
</blockquote>
```

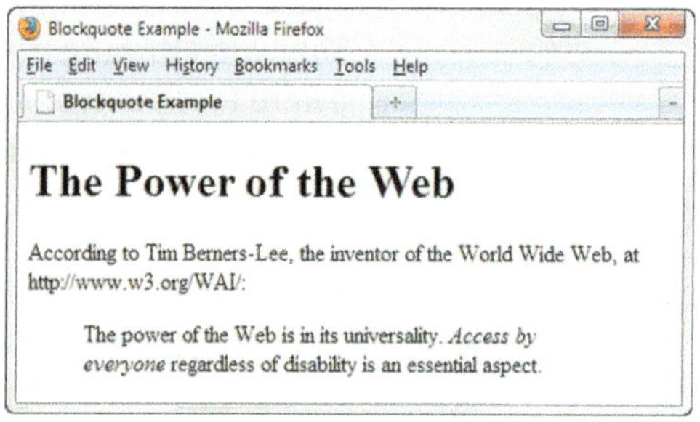

Figure 9 The <em> tag in action

12 Unordered List

Lists are used on web pages to organize information. When writing for the Web, headings, short paragraphs, and lists make your pages clear and easy to read. HTML can be used to create three types of lists: **description lists, ordered lists,** and **unordered lists**. This section focuses on the unordered list, often referred to as a bulleted list when using word processing applications.

An **unordered list** displays a bullet, or list marker, before each entry in the list. This bullet can be one of several types: disc (the default), square, and circle. See Figure 10 for a sample unordered list.

Figure 10 Sample unordered list

Unordered lists begin with a **<ul>** tag and end with a **</ul>** tag. Each list item begins with an **<li>** tag and ends with an **</li>** tag. The code to configure the heading and unordered list shown in Figure 10 is

```
<h1>Popular Web Servers</h1>
<ul>
      <li>Apache Web Server</li>
      <li>Microsoft IIS</li>
      <li>Oracle iPlanet Web Server</li>
</ul>
```

The Type Attribute

The type attribute can be used to change the type of list marker, or bullet. For example, to create an unordered list organized with square list markers, use `<ul type="square">`. Table 2 documents the type attribute and its values for unordered lists.

Table 2 The type attribute for unordered lists

Value	Example
disc (the default)	•
square	■
circle	○

HTML5 and Unordered Lists

The type attribute is widely used in unordered lists and is valid in XHTML. However, be aware that the type attribute on the `<ul>` tag is considered obsolete in HTML5 because it is decorative and does not convey meaning.

Hands-On Practice 6

In this Hands-On Practice, you will use a heading and an unordered list on the same page. To create the web page shown in Figure 11, launch a text editor. Select File > Open to edit the template file located at chapter2/template.html in the student files. Modify the title element and add h1, ul, and li tags to the body section as indicated by the following highlighted code:

Figure 11 An unordered list

```
<!DOCTYPE html>
<html lang="en">
<head>
<title>Heading and List</title>
<meta charset="utf-8">
</head>
<body>
<h1>Popular Web Servers</h1>
<ul>
     <li>Apache Web Server</li>
     <li>Microsoft IIS</li>
     <li>Oracle iPlanet Web Server</li>
</ul>
</body>
</html>
```

Save your file as ul2.html. Launch a browser and test your page. It should look similar to the page shown in Figure 11. You can compare your work with the solution in the student files (chapter2/ul.html). Take a few minutes to experiment with the type attribute. Configure the unordered list to use square bullets. Save your file as ul3.html. Test your page in a browser. You can compare your work with the solution in the student files (chapter2/ulsquare.html).

FAQ **Can I use images as the "bullets" in unordered lists?**

Yes, you can. Cascading Style Sheets (CSS) are used to configure the list markers ("bullets") in an unordered list to display graphic files as list markers.

13 Ordered List

An ordered list displays a numbering or lettering system to itemize the information contained in the list. Ordered lists can be organized by the use of numerals (the default), uppercase letters, lowercase letters, uppercase Roman numerals, and lowercase Roman numerals. See Figure 12 for a sample ordered list.

Figure 12 Sample ordered list

Ordered lists begin with an **<ol>** tag and end with an **</ol>** tag. Each list item begins with an **<li>** tag and ends with an **</li>** tag. The code to configure the heading and ordered list shown in Figure 12 follows:

```
<h1>Popular Web Servers</h1>
<ol>
     <li>Apache Web Server</li>
     <li>Microsoft IIS</li>
     <li>Oracle iPlanet Web Server</li>
</ol>
```

The Type Attribute

The type attribute configures the symbol used for ordering the list. For example, to create an ordered list organized by uppercase letters, use `<ol type="A">`. Table 3 documents the type attribute and its values for ordered lists.

Table 3 The type attribute for ordered lists

Value	Symbol
1	Numerals (the default)
A	Uppercase letters
a	Lowercase letters
I	Roman numerals
i	Lowercase Roman numerals

HTML5 and Ordered Lists

Even though unordered lists and ordered lists are similar, HTML5 treats their type attribute differently. In HTML5, the type attribute is obsolete for use with unordered lists. However, the type attribute is valid when used with ordered lists because the sequencing provides information. The **start attribute** is useful when you need a list to begin with an integer value other than 1 (for example, `start="10"`). Use the new HTML5 **reversed attribute** (set `reversed="reversed"`) to configure the list markers to display in descending order.

Hands-On Practice 7

In this Hands-On Practice, you will use a heading and an ordered list on the same page. To create the web page shown in Figure 13, launch a text editor. Select File > Open to edit the template file located at chapter2/template.html in the student files. Modify the title element and add h1, ol, and li elements to the body section as indicated by the following highlighted code:

```
<!DOCTYPE html>
<html lang="en">
<head>
<title>Heading and List</title>
<meta charset="utf-8">
</head>
<body>
<h1>Popular Web Servers</h1>
<ol>
     <li>Apache Web Server</li>
     <li>Microsoft IIS</li>
     <li>Oracle iPlanet Web Server</li>
</ol>
</body>
</html>
```

Save your file as ol2.html. Launch a browser and test your page. It should look similar to the page shown in Figure 13. You can compare your work with the solution in the student files (chapter2/ol.html).

Figure 13 An ordered list

Take a few minutes to experiment with the type attribute. Configure the ordered list to use uppercase letters instead of numerals. Save your file as ol3.html. Test your page in a browser. You can compare your work with the solution in the student files (chapter2/ola.html).

14 Description List

HTML5 introduces a new element name, **description list**, to replace the definition list element (used in XHTML and earlier versions of HTML). A description list is useful for organizing terms and their descriptions. The terms stand out, and their descriptions can be as long as needed to convey your message. Each term begins on its own line at the margin. Each description begins on its own line and is indented. Description lists are also handy for organizing Frequently Asked Questions (FAQs) and their answers. The questions and answers are offset with indentation. Any type of information that consists of a number of corresponding terms and longer descriptions is well suited to being organized in a description list. See Figure 14 for an example of a web page that uses a description list.

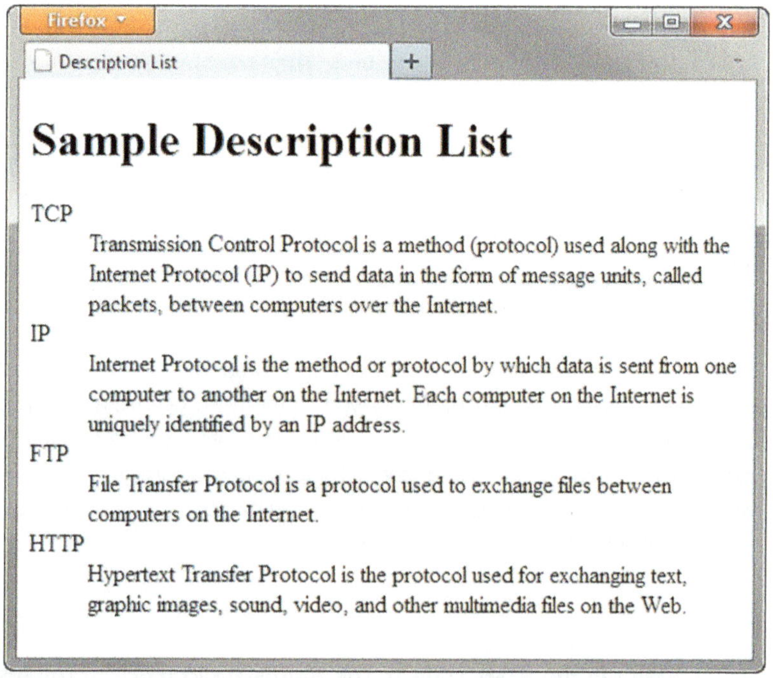

Figure 14 A description list

Description lists begin with the **<dl>** tag and end with the **</dl>** tag. Each term or name in the list begins with the **<dt>** tag and ends with the **</dt>** tag. Each description begins with the **<dd>** tag and ends with the **</dd>** tag.

Hands-On Practice 8

In this Hands-On Practice, you will use a heading and a description list on the same page. To create the web page shown in Figure 14, launch a text editor. Select File > Open to edit the template file located at chapter2/template.html in the student files. Modify the title element and add h1, dl, dd, and dt tags to the body section as indicated by the following highlighted code:

```
<!DOCTYPE html>
<html lang="en">
<head>
<title>Description List</title>
<meta charset="utf-8">
```

```
</head>
<body>
<h1>Sample Description List</h1>
<dl>
    <dt>TCP</dt>
        <dd>Transmission Control Protocol is a method (protocol) used
along with the Internet Protocol (IP) to send data in the form of
message units, called packets, between computers over the Internet.</dd>
    <dt>IP</dt>
        <dd>Internet Protocol is the method or protocol by which data
is sent from one computer to another on the Internet. Each computer
on the Internet is uniquely identified by an IP address.</dd>
    <dt>FTP</dt>
        <dd>File Transfer Protocol is a protocol used to exchange
files between computers on the Internet.</dd>
    <dt>HTTP</dt>
        <dd>Hypertext Transfer Protocol is the protocol used for
exchanging text, graphic images, sound, video, and other multimedia
files on the Web.</dd>
</dl>
</body>
</html>
```

Save your file as description2.html. Launch a browser and test your page. It should look similar to the page shown in Figure 14. Don't worry if the word wrap is a little different; the important formatting is that each `<dt>` term should be on its own line and the corresponding `<dd>` description should be indented under it. Try resizing your browser window, and notice how the word wrap on the description text changes. You can compare your work with the solution in the student files (chapter2/description.html).

FAQ Why is the HTML code in the Hands-On Practice examples indented?

Actually, it doesn't matter to the browser if web page code is indented, but humans find it easier to read and maintain code when it is logically indented. Review the description list created in Hands-On Practice 7. Notice how the `<dt>` and `<dd>` tags were indented. This makes it easier for you or another web developer to understand the source code in the future. There is no rule as to how many spaces to indent, although your instructor or the organization you work for may have a standard. Consistent indentation helps to create more easily maintainable web pages.

Checkpoint 2

1. Describe the features of a heading element and how it configures the text.
2. Describe the difference between ordered lists and unordered lists.
3. Describe the purpose of the blockquote element.

15 Special Characters

In order to use special symbols such as quotation marks, the greater-than sign (>), the less-than sign (<), and the copyright symbol (©) in your web page document, you need to use **special characters**, sometimes called **entity characters**. For example, if you wanted to include a copyright line on your page as follows:

```
© Copyright 2013 My Company. All rights reserved.
```

Use the special character **©** to display the copyright symbol, as shown in the following code:

```
&copy; Copyright 2013 My Company. All rights reserved.
```

Another useful special character is ** **, which stands for nonbreaking space. You may have noticed that web browsers treat multiple spaces as a single space. If you need a small number of spaces in your text, you may use ` ` multiple times to indicate multiple blank spaces. This practice is acceptable if you simply need to tweak the position of an element a little. However, if you find that your web pages contain many ` ` special characters in a row, you should use a different method, such as configuring the padding or margin with Cascading Style Sheets. Table 4 and the appendix, "Special Entity Characters," provide descriptions of special characters and their corresponding code.

Table 4 Common special characters

Character	Entity Name	Code
"	Quotation mark	"
'	Right single quotation mark	’
©	Copyright symbol	©
&	Ampersand	&
Empty space	Nonbreaking space	
—	Long dash	—
|	Vertical Bar		

Hands-On Practice 9

Figure 15 shows the web page you will create in this Hands-On Practice. Launch a text editor. Select File > Open to edit the template file located at chapter2/template.html in the student files. Modify the title of the web page by changing the text between the `<title>` and `</title>` tags to "Web Design Steps."

The sample page shown in Figure 15 contains a heading, an unordered list, and copyright information. Configure the heading "Web Design Steps" as a level 1 heading (`<h1>`) as follows:

```
<h1>Web Design Steps</h1>
```

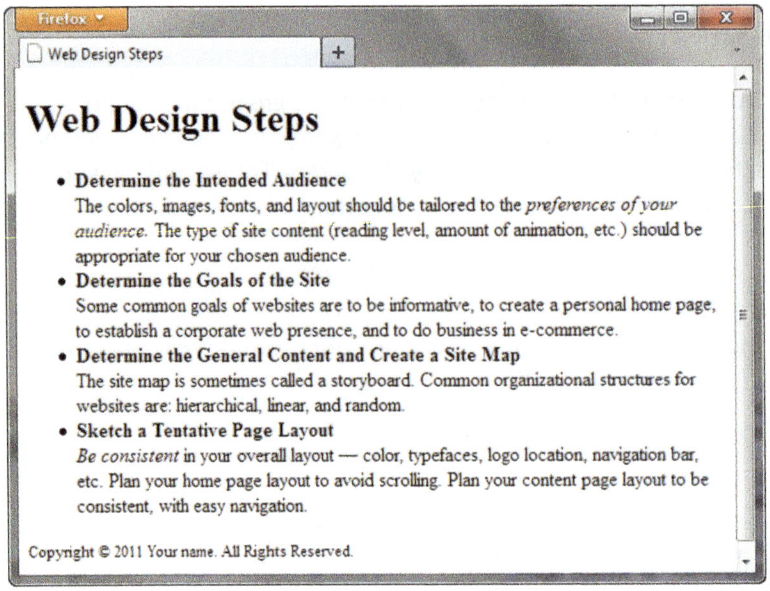

Figure 15 The design.html web page

Now create the unordered list. The first line of each bulleted item is the title of the web design step, which should be strong or stand out from the rest of the text. The code for the beginning of the unordered list is as follows:

```
<ul>
  <li><strong>Determine the Intended Audience</strong><br>
The colors, images, fonts, and layout should be tailored to the
<em>preferences of your audience.</em> The type of site content
(reading level, amount of animation, etc.) should be appropriate for
your chosen audience.</li>
```

Now code the entire ordered list in your design.html file. Remember to code the closing `</ul>` tag at the end of the list. Don't worry if your text wraps a little differently; your screen resolution or browser window size may be different from what is displayed in Figure 15.

Finally, configure the copyright information with the small element. Use the special character `©` for the copyright symbol. The code for the copyright line is as follows:

```
<p><small>Copyright &copy; 2011 Your name. All Rights Reserved.
</small></p>
```

How did you do? Compare your work to the sample in the student files (chapter2/design.html).

16 Div Element

The **div** element configures a structural block area, or "division," on a web page, with empty space above and below. A div element begins with a **`<div>`** tag and ends with a **`</div>`** tag. Use a div element when you need to format an area of a web page, such as a logo, navigation, or footer area. The div element is also useful for configuring a section that contains other block display elements, such as `<p>`, `<ul>`, `<blockquote>`, and even other <div> elements. Cascading Style Sheets (CSS) can be used to style and configure the color, text typeface, and layout of div and other structural elements such as headings, paragraphs, and lists.

Hands-On Practice 10

In this Hands-On Practice, you will practice using the div element as you edit the Trillium Media Design home page, shown in Figure 16. Launch a text editor, and open the starter.html file from the chapter2 folder in the student files. Save your page as div2.html.

Figure 16 This page uses the div element

The code from the body section is as follows:

```
<body>
<h1>Trillium Media Design</h1>
<p>Home  Services  Contact</p>
<h2>New Media and Web Design</h2>
<p>Trillium Media Design will bring your company&rsquo;s Web presence
to the next level. We offer a comprehensive range of services.</p>
<h2>Meeting Your Business Needs</h2>
<p>Our expert designers are creative and eager to work with you.
Take advantage of the power of Web 2.0!</p>
<p><small>Copyright &copy; 2012 Your Name Here</small></p>
</body>
```

Review the code, and notice that the navigation information and the copyright information are configured in paragraph tags, even though they are not really paragraphs (or even sentences). Both a paragraph element and a div element configure text in a block with empty space above and below. However, when the text is not a true paragraph in meaning, a div element is the better choice. Modify the code to replace the paragraph tags that contain the navigation and copyright information with div tags as follows:

```
<body>
<h1>Trillium Media Design</h1>
<div>Home  Services  Contact</div>
<h2>New Media and Web Design</h2>
<p>Trillium Media Design will bring your company&rsquo;s Web presence
to the next level. We offer a comprehensive range of services.</p>
<h2>Meeting Your Business Needs</h2>
<p>Our expert designers are creative and eager to work with you.
Take advantage of the power of Web 2.0!</p>
<div><small>Copyright &copy; 2012 Your Name Here</small></div>
</body>
```

Save your file and display it in a browser. It should look about the same. However, it is now improved "under the hood"—the div elements are a better semantic choice than paragraph elements to configure content areas that are not actually paragraphs, such as the navigation and copyright areas. The student files contain a sample solution at chapter2/div.html. As you continue to develop web pages, you will find that div elements are very handy for configuring areas on web pages.

FAQ **Are there new structural elements in HTML5 that configure areas on web pages?**

Yes, one of the characteristics of HTML5 is an emphasis on semantics. While the div element is useful, it is also quite generic. HTML5 offers a variety of special-purpose structural elements, including section, article, heading, nav, aside, and footer.

17 Anchor Element

Use the **anchor element** to specify a **hyperlink**, often referred to as a *link*, to another web page or file that you want to display. Each anchor element begins with an **<a>** tag and ends with a **</a>** tag. The opening and closing anchor tags surround the text to click to perform the hyperlink. Use the **href** attribute to configure the hyperlink reference, which identifies the name and location of the file to access. Figure 17 shows a web page document with an anchor tag that configures a hyperlink to the text's website, http://webdevfoundations.net.

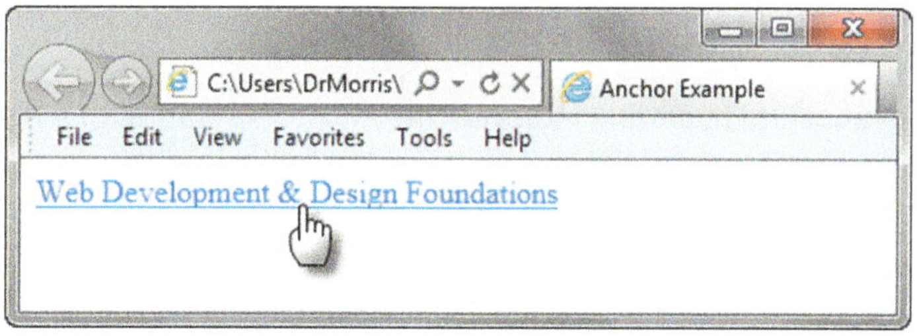

Figure 17
Sample hyperlink

The code for the anchor tag in Figure 17 is as follows:

```
<a href="http://webdevfoundations.net">Web Development &amp; Design
Foundations</a>
```

Notice that the href value is the URL for the website. The text that is typed between the two anchor tags displays on the web page as a hyperlink and is underlined by most browsers. When you move the mouse cursor over a hyperlink, the cursor changes to a pointing hand, as shown in Figure 17.

Hands-On Practice 11

To create the web page shown in Figure 17, launch a text editor. Select File > Open to edit the template file located at chapter2/template.html in the student files. Modify the title element and add anchor tags to the body section as indicated by the following highlighted code:

```
<!DOCTYPE html>
<html lang="en">
<head>
<title>Anchor Example</title>
<meta charset="utf-8">
</head>
<body>
<a href="http://webdevfoundations.net">Web Development &amp; Design
Foundations</a>
</body>
</html>
```

Save the document as anchor2.html on your hard drive or flash drive. Launch a browser to test your page. It should look similar to the page shown in Figure 17. You can compare your work with the solution found in the student files (chapter2/anchor.html).

FAQ **Can images be hyperlinks?**

Yes. Although we'll concentrate on text hyperlinks in this chapter, it's also possible to configure an image as a hyperlink.

Absolute Hyperlinks

An **absolute hyperlink** indicates the absolute location of a resource on the Web. Use absolute hyperlinks when you need to link to resources on other websites. The href value for an absolute hyperlink to the home page of a website includes the `http://` protocol and the domain name. The following hyperlink is an absolute hyperlink to the home page of this text's website:

```
<a href="http://webdevfoundations.net">Web Development &amp; Design
Foundations</a>
```

Note that if we want to access a web page other than the home page on the text's website, we could also include a specific folder name and file name. For example, the following anchor tag configures an absolute hyperlink for a file named chapter1.html located in a folder named 6e on this text's website:

```
<a href="http://webdevfoundations.net/6e/chapter1.html">Web Development
&amp; Design Foundations Chapter 1</a>
```

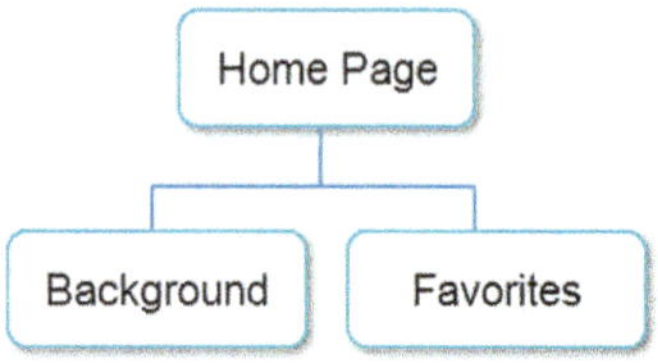

Figure 18 Site map

Relative Hyperlinks

When you need to link to web pages within your site, use a relative hyperlink. The href value for a relative hyperlink does not begin with the http:// and does not include a domain name. For a relative hyperlink, the href value will contain only the file name or file name and folder of the web page you want to display. The hyperlink location is relative to the page currently being displayed. For example, if you were coding a home page (index.html) for the website whose site map is illustrated in Figure 18 and wanted to link to a page named contact.html located in the same folder as index.html, you would use the following code sample:

```
<a href="contact.html">Contact Us</a>
```

Hands-On Practice 12

The best way to learn how to code web pages is by actually doing it! Let's practice and create three pages in a sample website.

1. Create a new folder. Name your folder "mypractice". The site we will create here is an example of a personal website. It will contain a home page called index.html and two content pages called background.html and favorites.html. A sample site map (see Figure 18) shows

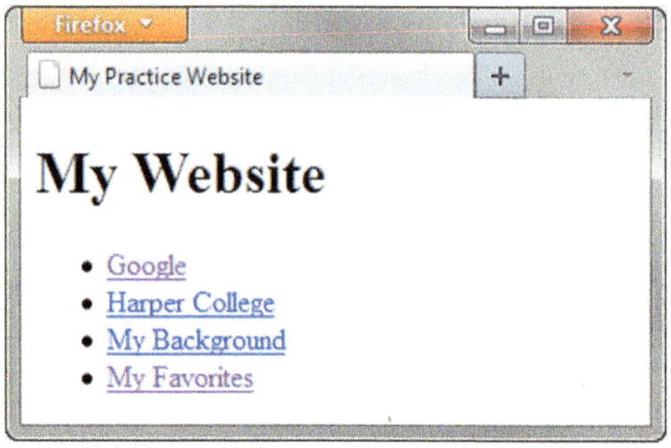

Figure 19 Sample index.html displayed in the Firefox browser

the organization of the site: a home page (index.html) with navigation hyperlinks to two other pages (background.html and favorites.html).

2. Now create the home page for your mypractice website, as shown in Figure 19. Launch a text editor. Select File > Open to edit the template file located at chapter2/template.html in the student files. Modify the title element and configure the following:
   - A "My Website" heading—use `<h1>` tags
   - An unordered list with the following:
     - An absolute link to your favorite search engine
     - An absolute link to the website of your school
     - A relative link to background.html
     - A relative link to favorites.html

   The body section of your web page will be similar to the following code sample:

```
<body>
<h1>My Website</h1>
<ul>
     <li><a href="http://google.com">Google</a></li>
     <li><a href="http://harpercollege.edu">Harper College</a></li>
     <li><a href="background.html">My Background</a></li>
     <li><a href="favorites.html">My Favorites</a></li>
</ul>
</body>
```

   Save your page as index.html in the mypractice folder. Display your page in a browser. It should look similar to the page shown in Figure 19. Compare your work to the sample (chapter2/practice/index.html) in the student files. Test your page by clicking each link. When you click the absolute links to your favorite search engine and your school, you should see those pages displayed if you are connected to the Internet. The relative links should not work yet; let's create the background.html page in Step 3.

3. Create the background.html page, as shown in Figure 20.

Figure 20 Sample background.html page

Let's work efficiently by building on the previous page. Launch a text editor and open the index.html file. Select File > Save As to save the file with the name background.html in the mypractice folder. In order to create a consistent logo for the site, do not change the h1 heading area. Replace the rest of the web page content with the following:

- A subheading of "My Background"—use <h2> tags
- A paragraph that contains one or two sentences about your background
- A navigation bar configured within a div that contains relative hyperlinks to the home page (index.html), the "My Background" page (background.html), and the "My Favorites" page (favorites.html). As shown in Figure 20, you will need to add a blank space between each anchor element. The body section of your web page will be similar to the following code sample:

```
<body>
  <h1>My Website</h1>
  <h2>My Background</h2>
      <p>As a college student majoring in Web Design, I'm interested
    in developing my skills in design principles, HTML, and CSS.</p>
  <div><a href="index.html">Home</a>
      <a href="background.html">Background</a>
      <a href="favorites.html">Favorites</a></div>
</body>
```

Save your file. Now test your index.html page again. This time, when you click the "My Background" hyperlink, your browser should display your new page. Click the "Home" hyperlink on your background.html page to redisplay your home page. Don't worry if these hyperlinks do not work perfectly the first time. If you have problems, carefully examine the source code of the pages, and verify the existence and location of the files by using Windows Explorer or the Mac Finder.

4. Using Step 3 as a guide, create the "My Favorites" page (favorites.html), and configure an unordered list of your favorite topics. See an example in the student files (chapter2/practice/favorites.html).

FAQ What if my relative hyperlink doesn't work?

Check the following:

- Did you save files in the specified folder?
- Did you save the files with the names as requested? Use Windows Explorer, My Computer, or Finder (Mac users) to verify the actual names of the files you saved.
- Did you type the file names correctly in the anchor tag's href property? Check for typographical errors.
- When you place your mouse cursor over a link, the file name of a relative link will display in the status bar in the lower edge of the browser window. Verify that the correct file name appears.

On many operating systems, such as UNIX or Linux, the use of uppercase and lowercase in file names matters, so make sure that the file name and the reference to it are in the same case. It's a good practice to use only lowercase letters for file names used on the Web.

E-Mail Hyperlinks

The anchor tag can also be used to create e-mail hyperlinks. An **e-mail link** will automatically launch the default mail program configured for the browser. The href value of an e-mail link begins with "mailto:", followed by a valid e-mail address. For example, to create an e-mail link to the e-mail address help@terrymorris.net, code the following:

```
<a href="mailto:help@terrymorris.net">help@terrymorris.net</a>
```

It's a good practice to configure the e-mail address as the hyperlink text. Not everyone has an e-mail program configured with his or her browser. You increase usability for all your visitors by displaying the e-mail address as text on the web page.

Hands-On Practice 13

In this Hands-On Practice, you will modify the home page of the website you created in Hands-On Practice 12 by adding an e-mail link to the page's footer area. Launch a text editor, and open the index.html file from your mypractice folder. This example uses the index.html file found in the student files in the chapter2/practice folder.

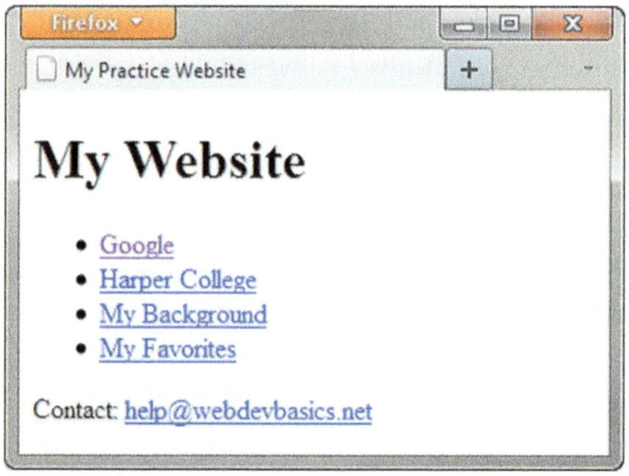

Figure 21 E-mail link added to index.html

Configure a div that contains the text "Contact:" and an e-mail hyperlink at the bottom of the page as shown in Figure 21. Use your e-mail address as the href value. Save the page, and test it in a browser. The browser display should look similar to the page shown in Figure 21. Compare your work with the sample in the student files (chapter2/practice2/index.html). Modify the favorites.html and background.html files in a similar manner. Sample solutions are located in the student files (chapter2/practice2 folder).

FAQ Won't displaying my actual e-mail address on a web page increase spam?

Yes and no. While it's possible that some unethical spammers may harvest web pages for e-mail addresses, chances are that your e-mail application's built-in spam filter will prevent your inbox from being flooded with messages. When you configure an easily readable e-mail hyperlink, you increase the usability of your website for your visitors in the following situations:

- The visitor may be at a public computer with no e-mail application configured. In such a case, clicking the e-mail hyperlink usually causes an error message to display. The visitor will have difficulty contacting you in this manner.
- The visitor may be at a private computer, but prefer not to use the e-mail application (or address) that is configured by default to work with the browser. Perhaps he or she shares the computer with others, or perhaps he or she wishes to preserve the privacy of the default e-mail address.

If you prominently displayed your actual e-mail address, then a visitor in either of these situations can still access your e-mail address and use it to contact you (in either their e-mail application or via a web-based e-mail system such as Google's Gmail). The result is a more usable website for your visitors.

Accessibility and Hyperlinks

Focus on Accessibility

Visually challenged visitors who are using a screen reader can configure the software to display a list of the hyperlinks in the document. However, a list of links is useful only if the text describing each link is actually helpful and descriptive. For example, on your college website, a "Search the course schedule" link would be more useful than a link that simply says, "More information."

Block Anchor

It's typical to use anchor tags to configure phrases, or even just a single word, as a hyperlink. HTML5 provides a new function for the anchor tag: the block anchor. A block anchor can configure one or more elements (even those which display as a block, such as a div, h1, or paragraph) as a hyperlink. See an example in the student files at chapter2/block.html.

FAQ **What are some tips for using hyperlinks?**

- Make your link names descriptive and brief to minimize possible confusion.
- Avoid using the phrase "Click here" in your hyperlinks. In the early days of the Web, this phrase was needed because clicking links was a new experience for web users. Now that the Web is a daily part of our lives, this phrase is slightly redundant, and even archaic.
- Try not to bury hyperlinks within large blocks of text; use lists of hyperlinks instead. Be aware that it is more difficult to read web pages than printed pages.
- Be careful when linking to external websites. The Web is dynamic, and it's possible that the external site may change the name of the page, or even delete the page. If this happens, your link will be broken.

Checkpoint 3

1. Describe the purpose of special characters.
2. Describe when to use an absolute link. Is the http protocol used in the href value?
3. Describe when to use a relative link. Is the http protocol used in the href value?

18 HTML Validation

The W3C's free Markup Validation Service, available at http://validator.w3.org, will validate your HTML code and check it for syntax errors. **HTML validation** provides students with quick self-assessment—you can prove that your code uses correct syntax. In the working world, HTML validation serves as a quality assurance tool. Invalid code may cause browsers to render the pages slower than otherwise.

Hands-On Practice 14

VideoNote
HTML Validation

In this Hands-On Practice, you will use the W3C Markup Validation Service to validate a web page file. This example uses the page completed in Hands-On Practice 8 (located in the student files at chapter2/design.html). Open design.html in a text editor. Add an error to the design.html page by deleting the first closing `</strong>` tag. This modification should generate several error messages.

Next, attempt to validate the design.html file. To do so, launch a browser, and visit the W3C Markup Validation Service file upload page at http://validator.w3.org/#validate_by_upload. Click the Browse button, and select the chapter2/design.html file from your computer. Click the Check button to upload the file to the W3C site (Figure 22).

An error page will display. Notice the "Errors found while checking this document" message. You can view the errors by scrolling down the page, as shown in Figure 23.

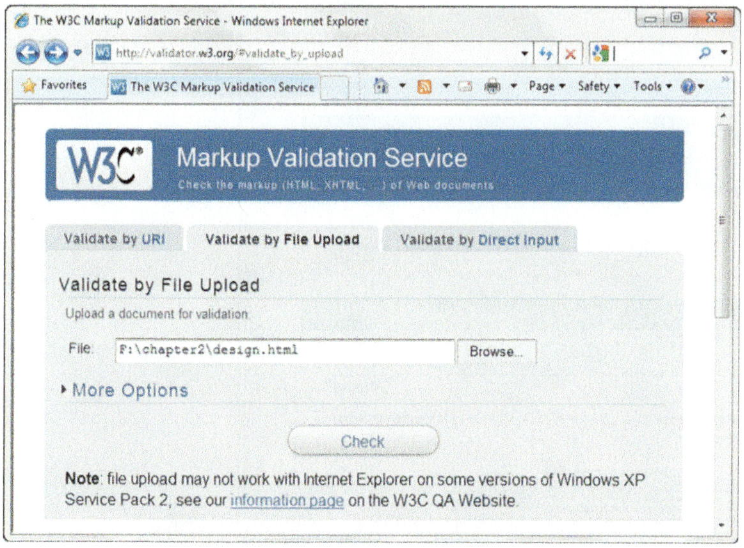

Figure 22 Validating a page with the W3C Markup Validation Service

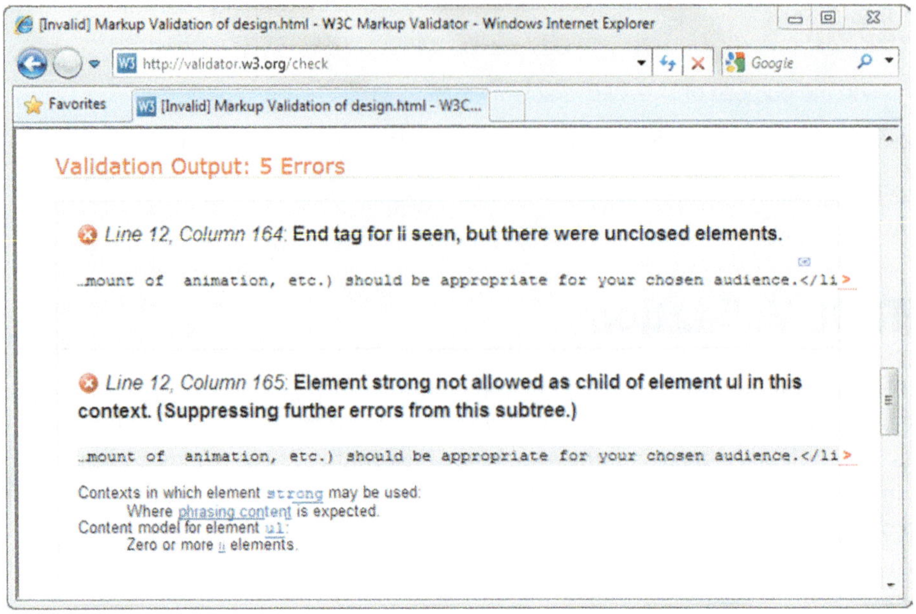

Figure 23 The service indicates that the error is on line 12

Notice that the message indicates line 12, which is the first line after the missing closing `</strong>` tag. HTML error messages often point to a line that follows the error. The text of the message, "End tag for li seen, but there were unclosed elements," lets you know that something is wrong. It is up to you to figure out what it is. A good place to start is to check your container tags and make sure they are in pairs. In this case, that is the problem. You can scroll down to view the other errors. However, since multiple error messages are often displayed after a single error occurs, it is a good idea to fix one item at a time and then revalidate.

Edit the design.html file in a text editor, and add the missing `</strong>` tag. Save the file. Launch a browser, and visit http://validator.w3.org/#validate_by_upload. Select your file, select More Options, and verify that the Show Source and Verbose Output check boxes are checked. Click the Revalidate button to begin the validation.

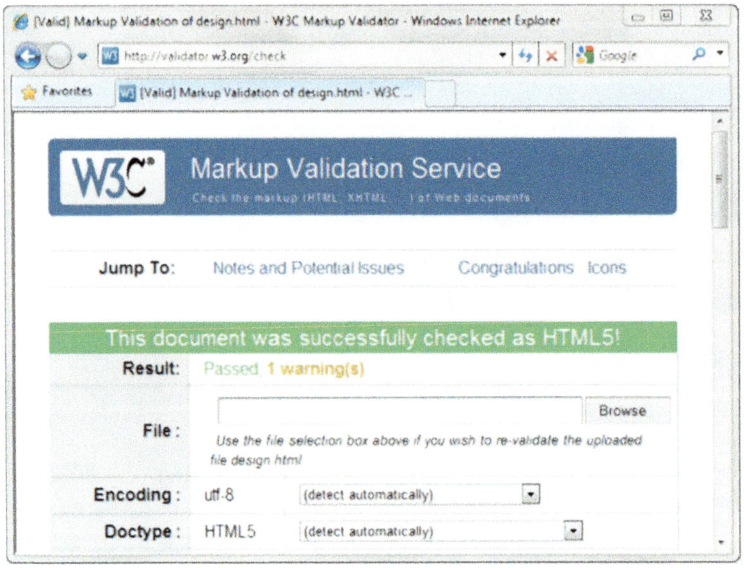

Figure 24 The page has passed the validation test

Your display should be similar to that shown in Figure 24. Notice the "This document was successfully checked as HTML5!" message. This means that your page passed the validation test. Congratulations, your design.html page is valid! You may also notice a warning message, which you can overlook, indicating that the HTML5 conformance checker is in experimental status.

It is good practice to validate your web pages. However, when validating code, use common sense. Since web browsers still do not completely follow W3C recommendations, there will be situations, such as when adding multimedia to a web page, in which HTML code configured to work reliably across a variety of browsers and platforms will not pass validation.

FAQ Are there other ways to validate my HTML?

In addition to the W3C validation service, there are other tools that you can use to check the syntax of your code. Explore the HTML5 validator at http://html5.validator.nu and the HTML5 "lint" tool at http://lint.brihten.com/html.

Chapter Summary

This chapter has provided an introduction to HTML, XHTML, and HTML5. The basic elements that are part of every web page were demonstrated. Structural HTML elements including div, paragraph, and blockquote were presented. Additional topics included configuring lists and using special characters, phrase elements, and hyperlinks. You have practiced testing your HTML5 code for valid syntax. If you worked along with the samples in the chapter, you should be ready to create some web pages on your own. The Hands-On Exercises and Web Case Studies that follow will provide some additional practice.

Visit this text's website at http://www.webdevfoundations.net for links to the URLs listed in this chapter and to view updated information.

Key Terms

©

<a>
<abbr>
<b>
<blockquote>
<body>

<cite>
<code>
<dd>
<dfn>
<div>
<dl>
<dt>
<em>
<font>
<h1>
<h6>
<head>
<html>
<i>
<kbd>
<li>
<mark>
<meta>
<ol>
<p>
<samp>
<small>
<strong>
<sub>
<sup>
<title>
<ul>
<var>
absolute link
anchor element
attribute
block display
body element
body section
character encoding
description list
div element
DOCTYPE
document type definition (DTD)
element
e-mail link
eXtensible HyperText Markup Language (XHTML)
head element
head section
header
heading element
href attribute
HTML5
hyperlink
Hypertext Markup Language (HTML)
inline display
left alignment
obsolete
ordered list
paragraph element
phrase element
relative link
special character
tag
unordered list
validation
well-formed document
XHTML 1.0 Transitional
XML (eXtensible Markup Language)
XML namespace (xmlns)

Review Questions

Multiple Choice

1. Which tag pair is used to create the largest heading?
   a. <h1> </h1>
   b. <h9> </h9>
   c. <h type="largest"> </h>
   d. <h6> </h6>

2. Which tag configures the next element or portion of text to display on a new line?
   a. <line>
   b. <nl>
   c.
   d. <new>

3. Which tag pair configures a structural area on a web page?
   a. <area> </area>
   b. <div> </div>
   c. <cite> </cite>
   d. <strong> </strong>
4. Which tag is used to link web pages to each other?
   a. <link> tag
   b. <hyperlink> tag
   c. <a> tag
   d. <body> tag
5. What is the default alignment for elements on a web page?
   a. center
   b. left
   c. right
   d. wherever you type them in the source code
6. Which type of HTML list will automatically number the items for you?
   a. numbered list
   b. ordered list
   c. unordered list
   d. definition list
7. Which of the following is a reason that the text contained by the title tag should be descriptive and include the name of the business or organization?
   a. The title is saved by default when a visitor bookmarks a web page.
   b. The title may be printed when a visitor prints a web page.
   c. The title may be listed in search engine results.
   d. All of the above are reasons that the text contained by the title tag should be descriptive and include the name of the business or organization.
8. When do you need to use a fully qualified URL in a hyperlink?
   a. always
   b. when linking to a web page file on the same site
   c. when linking to a web page file on an external site
   d. never
9. Which tag pair contains the items in an ordered or unordered list?
   a. <item> </item>
   b. <li> </li>
   c. <dd> </dd>
   d. all of the above
10. What does an e-mail link do?
    a. automatically sends you an e-mail message with the visitor's e-mail address as the reply-to field
    b. launches the default e-mail application for the visitor's browser, with your e-mail address as the recipient
    c. displays your e-mail address so that the visitor can send you a message later
    d. links to your mail server

Fill in the Blank

11. The <meta> tag can be used to ____________.
12. ____________ can be used to display characters such as the copyright symbol.
13. Use the ____________ element to configure text to have strong importance and display in a bold font weight.
14. The ____________ is used to place a nonbreaking space on a web page.
15. Use the ____________ element to configure text to be emphasized and displayed in an italic font style.

Short Answer

16. Explain why it is good practice to place the e-mail address on the web page and within the anchor tag when creating an e-mail link.

Apply Your Knowledge

1. **Predict the Result.** Sketch out and briefly describe the web page that will be created with the following HTML code:

```
<!DOCTYPE html>
<html lang="en">
<head>
    <title>Predict the Result</title>
    <meta charset="utf-8">
</head>
<body>
    <h1><i>Favorite Sites</i></h1>
    <ol>
      <li><a href="http://myspace.com">My Space</a></li>
      <li><a href="http://google.com">Google</a></li>
    </ol>
    <div><small>Copyright &copy; 2013 Your name here</small></div>
</body>
</html>
```

2. **Fill in the Missing Code.** The web page defined by the given code should display a heading and a description list, but some HTML tags, indicated by <_>, are missing. Fill in the missing code.

```
<!DOCTYPE html>
<html lang="en">
<head>
    <title>Door County Wildflowers</title>
    <meta charset="utf-8">
</head>
<body>
    <_>Door County Wild Flowers<_>
    <dl>
      <dt>Trillium<_>
        <_>This white flower blooms from April through June in
        wooded areas.<_>
      <_>Lady Slipper<_>
        <_>This yellow orchid blooms in June in wooded areas.</dd>
    <_>
</body>
</html>
```

3. **Find the Error.** All the text on the web page defined by the given code displays in large and bold font typeface. Explain why this is happening.

```
<!DOCTYPE html>
<html lang="en">
<head>
    <title>Find the Error</title>
    <meta charset="utf-8">
</head>
<body>
    <h1>My Web Page<h1>
    <p>This is a sentence on my web page.</p>
</body>
</html>
```

Hands-On Exercises

1. Write the HTML to display your name with the largest heading element.
2. Write the HTML to create an absolute link to a website whose domain name is google.com.
3. Write the HTML for an unordered list to display the days of the week.
4. Write the HTML for an ordered list that uses uppercase letters to order the items. This ordered list should display the following terms: HTML, XML, and XHTML.
5. Think of a favorite quotation by someone you admire. Write the HTML code to display the person's name in a heading and the quotation in a blockquote element.
6. Modify the following code snippet to indicate that the terms "site map" and "storyboard" should have strong importance:

```
<p>A diagram of the organization of a website is called a site
map, or storyboard. Creating the site map is one of the initial
steps in developing a website.</p>
```

7. Modify the blockquote.html web page you created in Hands-On Practice 5. Configure the URL http://www.w3.org/WAI/ as a hyperlink. Save the file as blockquote2.html.
8. Create a web page that uses a description list to display three network protocols and their descriptions. Include a hyperlink to a website that provides information about the protocols. Add an appropriate heading to the page. Save the page as network.html.
9. Create a web page about your favorite musical group. Include the name of the group, the individuals in the group, a hyperlink to the group's website, your favorite three (or fewer if the group is new) CD releases, and a brief review of each CD.
   - Use an unordered list to organize the names of the individuals.
   - Use a description list for the names of the CDs and your reviews.

   Save the page as band.html.
10. Create a web page about your favorite recipe. Use an unordered list for the ingredients and an ordered list to describe the steps needed to prepare the food. Include a hyperlink to a website that offers free recipes. Save the page as recipe.html.

Web Research

There are many HTML5 tutorials on the Web. Use your favorite search engine to discover them. Choose two that are helpful. For each, print out the home page or other pertinent page and create a web page that contains the answers to the following questions:

a. What is the URL of the website?

b. Is the tutorial geared toward the beginner level, intermediate level, or both levels?

c. Would you recommend this site to others? Why or why not?

d. List one or two concepts that you learned from this tutorial.

Focus on Web Design

You are learning the syntax of HTML5. However, coding alone does not make a web page; design is also very important. Surf the Web and find two web pages, one that is appealing to you and one that is unappealing to you. Print each page. Create a web page that answers the following questions for each of your examples:

a. What is the URL of the website?

b. Is the page appealing or unappealing? List three reasons for your answer.

c. If the page is unappealing, what would you do to improve it?

WWW WEBSITE CASE STUDY

This section introduces four website scenarios, presents the site maps, and directs you to create two pages for each site.

JavaJam Coffee House

Julio Perez is the owner of the JavaJam Coffee House, a gourmet coffee shop that serves snacks, coffee, tea, and soft drinks. Local folk music performances and poetry readings are held a few nights during the week. The customers of JavaJam are mainly college students and young professionals. Julio would like a web presence for his shop that will display his services and provide a calendar for the performances. He would like a home page, menu page, music performance schedule page, and job opportunities page.

A site map for the JavaJam Coffee House website is shown in Figure 25. The site map describes the architecture of the website, which consists of a "Home" page with three main content pages: "Menu," "Music," and "Jobs."

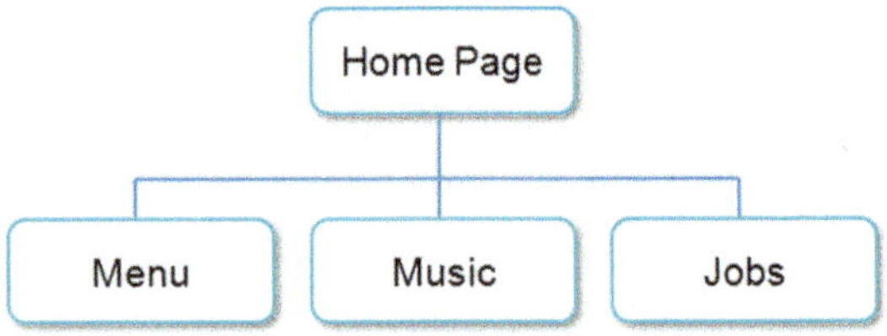

Figure 25 JavaJam site map

Figure 26 displays a wireframe sketch of the page layout for the website. It contains a site logo, a navigation area, a content area, and a footer area for copyright information.

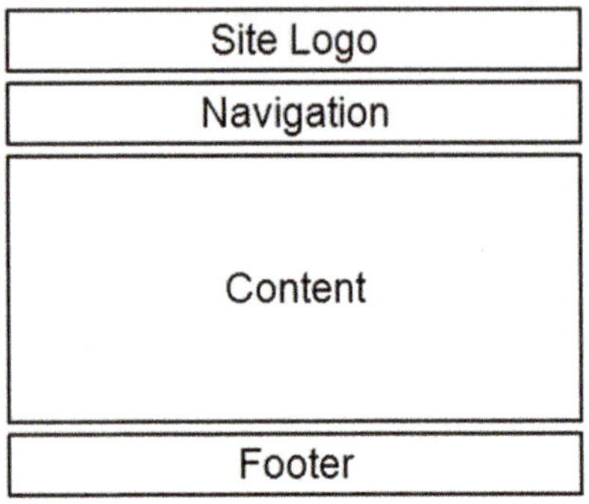

Figure 26 JavaJam wireframe

You have three tasks in this case study:

1. Create a folder for the JavaJam website.
2. Create the Home page: index.html.
3. Create the Menu page: menu.html.

Hands-On Practice Case Study

Task 1: Create a folder on your hard drive or portable storage device (thumb drive or SD card) called "javajam" to contain your JavaJam website files.

Task 2: The Home Page. You will use a text editor to create the Home page for the JavaJam Coffee House website. The Home page is shown in Figure 27.

Figure 27 JavaJam index.html

Launch a text editor, and create a web page with the following specifications:

1. **Web Page Title.** Use a descriptive page title. The company name is a good choice for a business website.
2. **Wireframe Logo.** Use <h1> for the JavaJam Coffee House logo.
3. **Wireframe Navigation.** Place the following text within a div element:

   Home Menu Music Jobs

   Code anchor tags so that "Home" links to index.html, "Menu" links to menu.html, "Music" links to music.html, and "Jobs" links to jobs.html. Add extra blank spaces between the hyperlinks with the   special character as needed.
4. **Wireframe Content.**
   a. Configure the following content in an unordered list:

      Specialty Coffee and Tea

      Bagels, Muffins, and Organic Snacks

      Music and Poetry Readings

      Open Mic Night

b. Code the following address and phone number contact information within a div element. Use line break tags to help you configure this area and add extra space between the phone number and the footer area.

12312 Main Street

Mountain Home, CA 93923

1-888-555-5555

5. **Wireframe Footer.** Configure the following copyright and e-mail link information within a div element. Format it with small text size (use the `<small>` tag) and italics font style (use the `<i>` tag).

   JavaJam Copyright © 2013 Coffee House

   Place your name in an e-mail link on the line under the copyright.

The page in Figure 27 may seem a little sparse, but don't worry; as you gain experience and learn to use more advanced techniques, your pages will look more professional. White space (blank space) on the page can be added with `<br>` tags where needed. Your page does not need to look exactly the same as the sample. Your goal at this point should be to practice and get comfortable using HTML.

Save your page in the javajam folder, and name it index.html.

Task 3: The Menu Page. Create the Menu page shown in Figure 28. A technique that improves productivity is to create new pages based on existing pages so that you can benefit from your previous work. Your new Menu page will use the index.html page as a starting point.

Figure 28 JavaJam menu.html

Open the index.html page for the JavaJam website in a text editor. Select File › Save As, and save the file with the new name of menu.html in the javajam folder. Now you are ready to edit the page.

1. **Web Page Title.** Modify the page title. Change the text contained between the `<title>` and `</title>` tags to the following:

   JavaJam Coffee House Menu

2. Wireframe Content.

a. Delete the Home page content unordered list and contact information.

b. Use a description list to add the menu content to the page. Use the `<dt>` tag to contain each menu item name. Configure the menu item name to have strong importance and display in bold font weight with the `<strong>` tag. Use the `<dd>` tag to contain the menu item description. The menu item names and descriptions are as follows:

Just Java

Regular house blend, decaffeinated coffee, or flavor of the day.

Endless Cup $2.00

Cafe au Lait

House blended coffee infused into a smooth, steamed milk.

Single $2.00 Double $3.00

Iced Cappuccino

Sweetened espresso blended with icy-cold milk and served in a chilled glass.

Single $4.75 Double $5.75

Save your page, and test it in a browser. Test the hyperlink from the menu.html page to index.html. Test the hyperlink from the index.html page to menu.html. If your links do not work, review your work, paying close attention to these details:

- Verify that you have saved the pages with the correct names in the correct folder.
- Verify your spelling of the page names in the anchor tags.

Test again after you make changes.

Fish Creek Animal Hospital

Magda Patel is a veterinarian and owner of the Fish Creek Animal Hospital. Her customers are local pet owners who range from children to senior citizens. Magda would like a website to provide information to her current and potential customers. She has requested a home page, a services page, a page for advice from a veterinarian, and a contact page.

A site map for the Fish Creek Animal Hospital website is shown in Figure 29. The site map describes the architecture of the website, which consists of a "Home" page with three main content pages: "Services," "Ask the Vet," and "Contact."

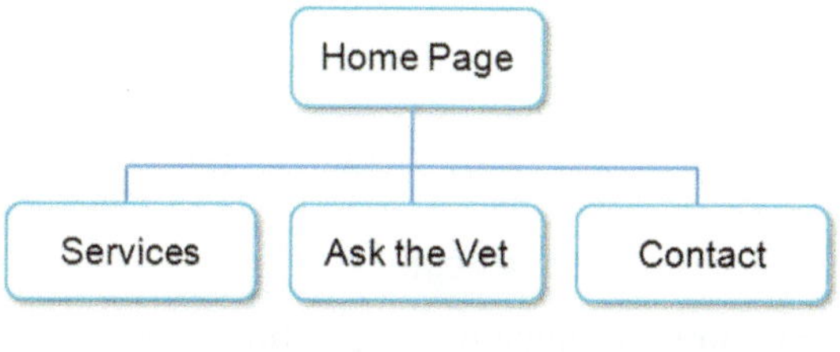

Figure 29 Fish Creek site map

Figure 30 displays a wireframe sketch of the page layout for the website. It contains a site logo, a navigation area, a content area, and a footer area for copyright information.

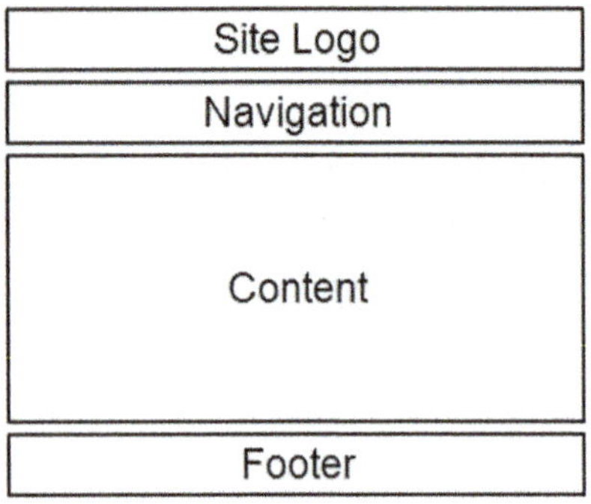

Figure 30 Fish Creek wireframe

You have three tasks in this case study:

1. Create a folder for the Fish Creek website.
2. Create the Home page: index.html.
3. Create the Services page: services.html.

Hands-On Practice Case Study

Task 1: Create a folder on your hard drive or portable storage device (thumb drive or SD card) called "fishcreek" to contain your Fish Creek website files.

Task 2: The Home Page. You will use a text editor application to create the Home page for the Fish Creek Animal Hospital website. The Home page is shown in Figure 31.

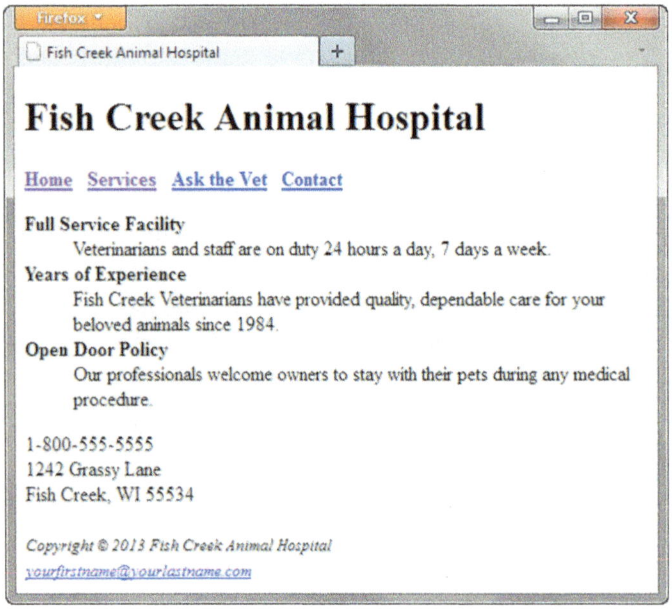

Figure 31 Fish Creek index.html

Launch a text editor, and create a web page with the following specifications:

1. **Web Page Title.** Use a descriptive page title. The company name is a good choice for a business website.
2. **Wireframe Logo.** Use <h1> for the Fish Creek Animal Hospital logo.

3. **Wireframe Navigation.** Configure the following text using the <b> phrase element within a div element:

   Home Services Ask the Vet Contact

   Code anchor tags so that "Home" links to index.html, "Services" links to services.html, "Ask the Vet" links to askvet.html, and "Contact" links to contact.html. Add extra blank spaces between the hyperlinks with the   special character as needed.

4. **Wireframe Content.**

   a. Code the following content in a description list. Configure the text in each dt element to have strong importance and display in bold font weight:

      Full Service Facility

      Veterinarians and staff are on duty 24 hours a day, 7 days a week.

      Years of Experience

      Fish Creek Veterinarians have provided quality, dependable care for your beloved animals since 1984.

      Open Door Policy

      Our professionals welcome owners to stay with their pets during any medical procedure.

   b. Configure the following address and phone number contact information within a div element below the description list. Use line break tags to help you format this area.

      1-800-555-5555

      1242 Grassy Lane

      Fish Creek, WI 55534

5. **Wireframe Footer.** Code the following copyright and e-mail link information within a div element. Format it with small text size (use the <small> tag) and italics font style (use the <i> tag).

   Copyright © 2013 Fish Creek Animal Hospital

   Place your name in an e-mail link on the line under the copyright.

The page in Figure 31 may seem a little sparse, but don't worry; as you gain experience and learn to use more advanced techniques, your pages will look more professional. White space (blank space) on the page can be added with <br> tags where needed. Your page does not need to look exactly the same as the sample. Your goal at this point should be to practice and get comfortable using HTML.

Save your page in the fishcreek folder, and name it index.html.

Task 3: The Services Page. Create the Services page shown in Figure 32. A technique that improves productivity is to create new pages based on existing pages so that you can benefit from your previous work. Your new Services page will use the index.html page as a starting point.

Open the index.html page for the Fish Creek website in a text editor. Select File › Save As, and save the file with the new name of services.html in the fishcreek folder. Now you are ready to edit the page.

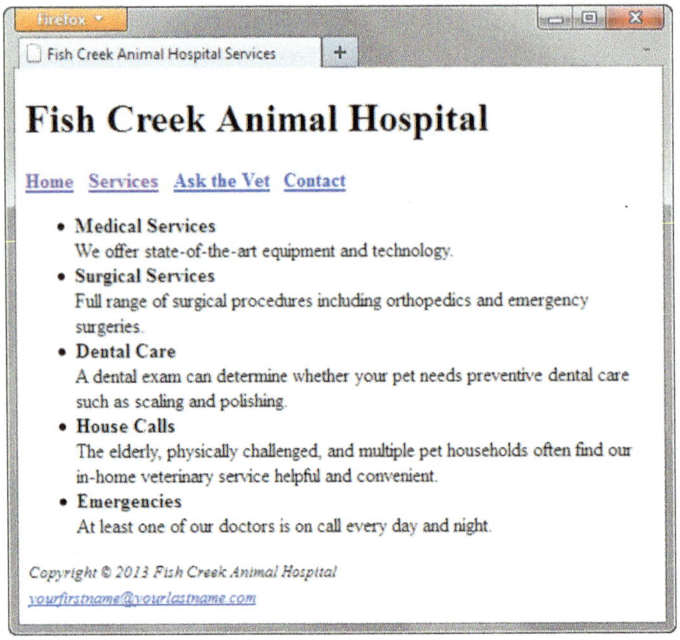

Figure 32 Fish Creek services.html

1. **Web Page Title.** Modify the page title. Change the text contained between the `<title>` and `</title>` tags to the following:

   Fish Creek Animal Hospital Services

2. **Wireframe Content.**

   a. Delete the Home page content description list and contact information.

   b. Use an unordered list to add the services content to the page. Configure the name of each services category to use bold font weight and have strong emphasis. (Use the `<strong>` tag.) Use line break tags to help you configure this area. The service categories and descriptions are as follows:

   Medical Services

   We offer state-of-the-art equipment and technology.

   Surgical Services

   Full range of surgical procedures including orthopedics and emergency surgeries.

   Dental Care

   A dental exam can determine whether your pet needs preventive dental care such as scaling and polishing.

   House Calls

   The elderly, physically challenged, and multiple pet households often find our in-home veterinary service helpful and convenient.

   Emergencies

   At least one of our doctors is on call every day and night.

Save your page, and test it in a browser. Test the hyperlink from the services.html page to index.html. Test the hyperlink from the index.html page to services.html. If your links do not work, review your work, paying close attention to these details:

- Verify that you have saved the pages with the correct names in the correct folder.
- Verify your spelling of the page names in the anchor tags.

Test again after you make changes.

Pacific Trails Resort

Melanie Bowie is the owner of Pacific Trails Resort, located on the California North Coast. The resort offers a quiet getaway, with luxury camping in yurts along with an upscale lodge for dining and visiting with fellow guests. The target audience for Pacific Trails Resort is couples who enjoy nature and hiking. Melanie would like a website that emphasizes the uniqueness of the location and accommodations. She would like the website to include a home page, a page about the special yurt accommodations, a reservations page with a contact form, and a page to describe the activities available at the resort.

A site map for the Pacific Trails Resort website is shown in Figure 33. The site map describes the architecture of the website, which consists of a "Home" page with three main content pages: "Yurts," "Activities," and "Reservations."

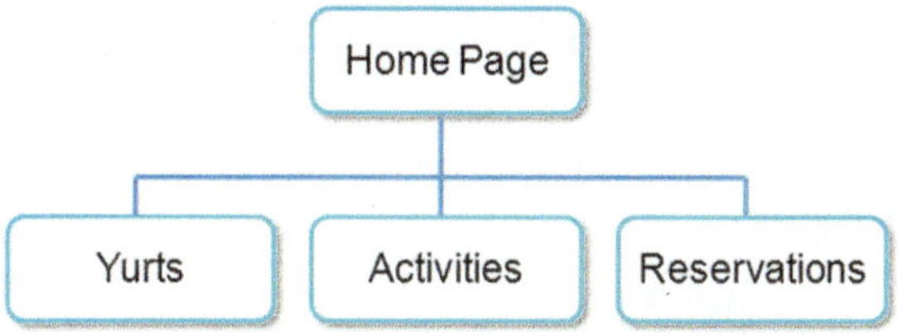

Figure 33 Pacific Trails Resort site map

Figure 34 displays a wireframe sketch of the page layout for the website. It contains a site logo, a navigation area, a content area, and a footer area for copyright information.

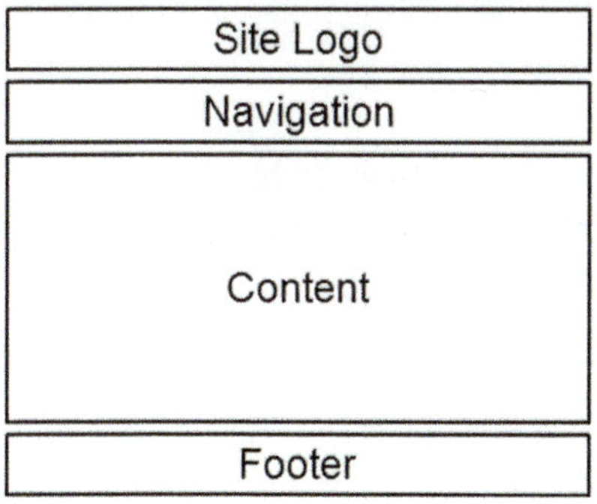

Figure 34 Pacific Trails Resort wireframe

You have three tasks in this case study:

1. Create a folder for the Pacific Trails website.
2. Create the Home page: index.html.
3. Create the Yurts page: yurts.html.

Figure 35 Pacific Trails Resort index.html

Hands-On Practice Case Study

Task 1: Create a folder on your hard drive or portable storage device (thumb drive or SD card) called "pacific" to contain your Pacific Trails Resort website files.

Task 2: The Home Page. You will use a text editor to create the Home page for the Pacific Trails Resort website. The Home page is shown in Figure 35.

Launch a text editor, and create a web page with the following specifications:

1. **Web Page Title.** Use a descriptive page title. The company name is a good choice for a business website.
2. **Wireframe Logo.** Use <h1> for the Pacific Trails Resort logo.
3. **Wireframe Navigation.** Configure the following text using the <b> phrase element within a div element:

   Home Yurts Activities Reservations

   Code anchor tags so that "Home" links to index.html, "Yurts" links to yurts.html, "Activities" links to activities.html, and "Reservations" links to reservations.html.
4. **Wireframe Content.**
   a. Code the following text within an h2 element:

      Enjoy Nature in Luxury

   b. Configure the following sentences in a paragraph:

      Pacific Trails Resort offers a special lodging experience on the California North Coast. Relax in serenity with panoramic views of the Pacific Ocean.

   c. Code the following content in an unordered list:

      Private yurts with decks overlooking the ocean

      Activities lodge with fireplace and gift shop

Nightly fine dining at the Overlook Cafe

Heated outdoor pool and whirlpool

Guided hiking tours of the redwoods

d. Configure the following address and phone number contact information within a div element below the unordered list. Use line break tags to help you format this area.

Pacific Trails Resort

12010 Pacific Trails Road

Zephyr, CA 95555

888-555-5555

5. **Wireframe Footer.** Configure the following copyright and e-mail link information within a div element. Format it with small text size (use the `<small>` tag) and italics font style (use the `<i>` tag).

Copyright © 2013 Pacific Trails Resort

Place your name in an e-mail link on the line under the copyright.

The page in Figure 35 may seem a little sparse, but don't worry; as you gain experience and learn to use more advanced techniques, your pages will look more professional. White space (blank space) on the page can be added with <br> tags where needed. Your page does not need to look exactly the same as the sample. Your goal at this point should be to practice and get comfortable using HTML.

Save your page in the pacific folder, and name it index.html.

Task 3:The Yurts Page. Create the Yurts page shown in Figure 36. A technique that improves productivity is to create new pages based on existing pages so that you can benefit from your previous work. Your new Yurts page will use the index.html page as a starting point.

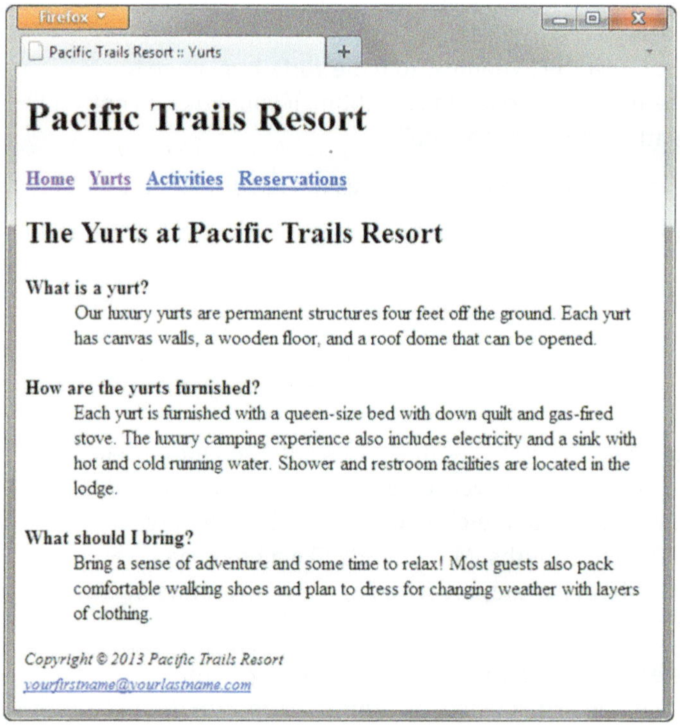

Figure 36 Pacific Trails Resort yurts.html

Open the index.html page for the Pacific Trails Resort website in a text editor. Select File › Save As, and save the file with the new name of yurts.html in the pacific folder. Now you are ready to edit the page.

1. **Web Page Title.** Modify the page title. Change the text contained between the `<title>` and `</title>` tags to the following:

   Pacific Trails Resort :: Yurts

2. **Wireframe Content.**

   a. Replace the text in the h2 element with the following:

      The Yurts at Pacific Trails Resort

   b. Delete the Home page content paragraph, unordered list, and contact information.

   c. Add the yurts content to the page as a FAQs (frequently asked questions) list by using a description list. Configure each question to have strong importance and bold font weight (use the `<strong>` phrase element) within a dt element. Configure each answer within a dd element. The text is shown as follows:

      What is a yurt?

      Our luxury yurts are permanent structures four feet off the ground. Each yurt has canvas walls, a wooden floor, and a roof dome that can be opened.

      How are the yurts furnished?

      Each yurt is furnished with a queen-size bed with down quilt and gas-fired stove. The luxury camping experience also includes electricity and a sink with hot and cold running water. Shower and restroom facilities are located in the lodge.

      What should I bring?

      Bring a sense of adventure and some time to relax! Most guests also pack comfortable walking shoes and plan to dress for changing weather with layers of clothing.

Save your page, and test it in a browser. Test the hyperlink from the yurts.html page to index.html. Test the hyperlink from the index.html page to yurts.html. If your links do not work, review your work, paying close attention to these details:

- Verify that you have saved the pages with the correct names in the correct folder.
- Verify your spelling of the page names in the anchor tags.

Test again after you make the changes.

Prime Properties

Prime Properties is a small real estate company that specializes in residential properties. The owner, Maria Valdez, would like a website to showcase her listings and provide a point of contact for her clients, who are mainly middle-class working adults who are looking for a home in the northwest Chicago suburbs. Maria would like a home page, a listings page that contains information about her properties, a financing page, and a contact page.

A site map for the Prime Properties website is shown in Figure 37. The site map describes the architecture of the website, which consists of "Home" page with three main content pages: "Listings," "Financing," and "Contact."

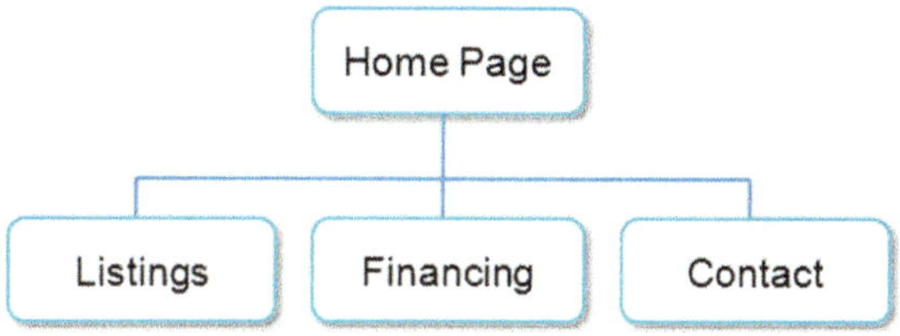

Figure 37 Prime Properties site map

Figure 38 displays a wireframe sketch of the page layout for the website. It contains a site logo, a navigation area, a content area, and a footer area for copyright information.

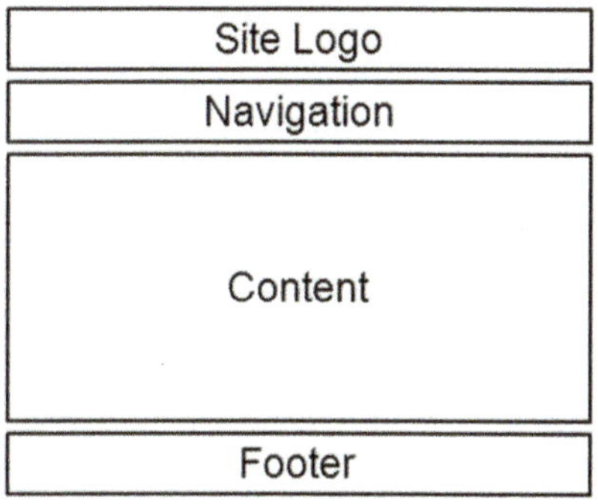

Figure 38 Prime Properties wireframe

You have three tasks in this case study:

1. Create a folder for the Prime Properties website.
2. Create the Home page: index.html.
3. Create the Financing page: financing.html.

Hands-On Practice Case Study

Task 1: Create a folder on your hard drive or portable storage device (thumb drive or SD card) called "prime" to contain your Prime Properties web page files.

Task 2: The Home Page. You will use a text editor to create the Home page for the Prime Properties website. The Home page is shown in Figure 39.

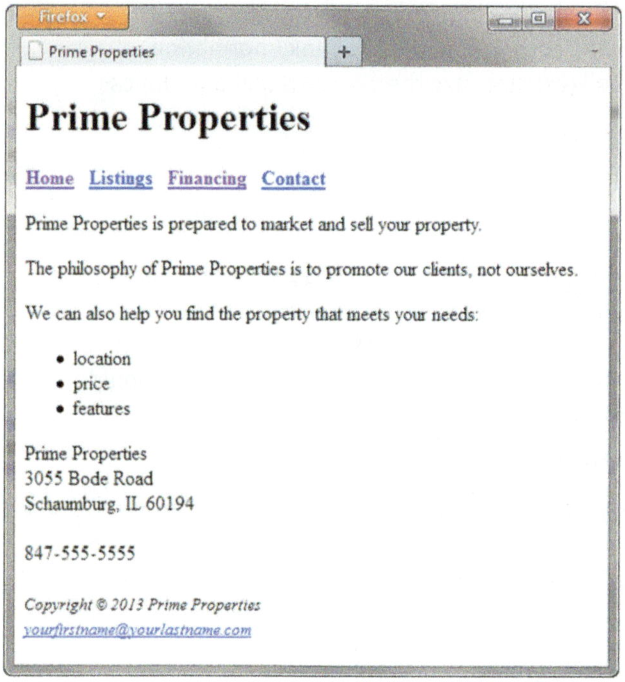

Figure 39 Prime Properties index.html

Launch a text editor, and create a web page with the following specifications:

1. **Web Page Title.** Use a descriptive page title. The company name is a good choice for a business website.
2. **Wireframe Logo.** Use `<h1>` for the Prime Properties logo.
3. **Wireframe Navigation.** Configure the following text using the `<b>` phrase element within a div element:

   Home Listings Financing Contact

Code anchor tags so that "Home" links to index.html, "Listings" links to listings.html, "Financing" links to financing.html, and "Contact" links to contact.html.

4. **Wireframe Content.**
   - **a.** Code each line of the following text in its own paragraph:

     Prime Properties is prepared to market and sell your property.

     The philosophy of Prime Properties is to promote our clients, not ourselves.

     We can also help you find the property that meets your needs:
   - **b.** Configure the following content in an unordered list:

     location

     price

     features
   - **c.** Code the following address and phone number contact information within a div element. Use line break tags to help you configure this area and add extra space between the phone number and the footer area.

     Prime Properties

     3055 Bode Road

     Schaumburg, IL 60194

     847-555-5555
5. **Wireframe Footer.** Configure the following copyright and e-mail link information within a div element. Format it with small text size (use the `<small>` tag) and italics font style (use the `<i>` tag)

   Copyright © 2013 Prime Properties

   Place your name in an e-mail link on the line under the copyright information.

The page in Figure 39 may seem a little sparse, but don't worry; as you gain experience and learn to use more advanced techniques, your pages will look more professional. White space (blank space) on the page can be added with `<br>` tags where needed. Your page does not need to look exactly the same as the sample. Your goal at this point should be to practice and get comfortable using HTML.

Save your page in the prime folder, and name it index.html.

Task 3: The Financing Page. Create the Financing page shown in Figure 40. A technique that improves productivity is to create new pages based on existing pages so that you can benefit from your previous work. Your new Financing page will use the index.html page as a starting point.

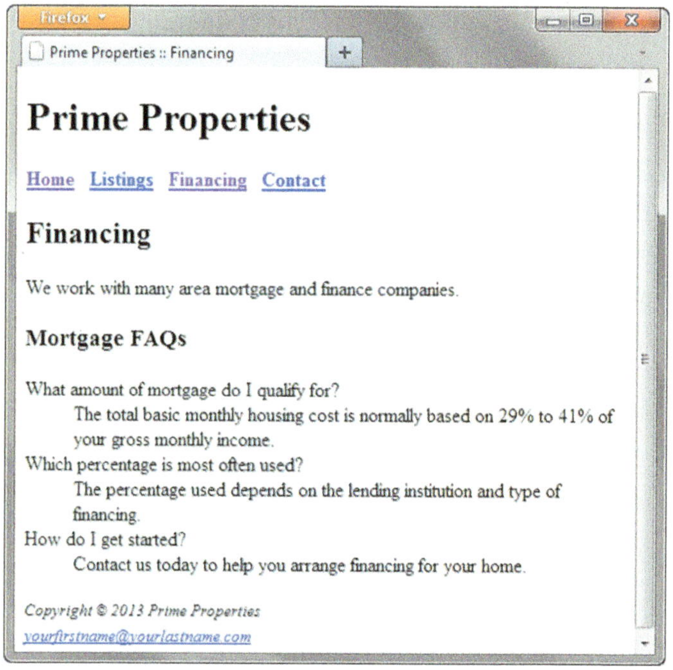

Figure 40 Prime Properties financing.html

Open the index.html page for the Prime Properties website in a text editor. Select File › Save As, and save the file with the new name of financing.html in the prime folder. Now you are ready to edit the page.

1. **Web Page Title.** Modify the page title. Change the text contained between the `<title>` and `</title>` tags to the following:

   Prime Properties :: Financing

2. **Wireframe Content.**

   a. Delete the Home Page content paragraphs, unordered list, and contact information.

   b. Configure the following text in an `<h2>` element:

      Financing

   c. Code the following sentence in a paragraph:

      We work with many area mortgage and finance companies.

   d. Configure the following phrase with an `<h3>` element:

      Mortgage FAQs

   e. Use a description list to configure the FAQs. Configure `<dt>` elements for the questions and `<dd>` elements for the answers. The FAQ questions and answers are as follows:

      What amount of mortgage do I qualify for?

      The total basic monthly housing cost is normally based on 29% to 41% of your gross monthly income.

      Which percentage is most often used?

The percentage used depends on the lending institution and type of financing.

How do I get started?

Contact us today to help you arrange financing for your home.

Save your page, and test it in a browser. Test the hyperlink from the financing.html page to index.html. Test the hyperlink from the index.html page to financing.html. If your links do not work, review your work with close attention to these details:

- Verify that you have saved the pages with the correct names in the correct folder.
- Verify your spelling of the page names in the anchor tags.

Test again after you make the changes.

Answers

Checkpoint 1

1. HTML (Hypertext Markup Language) was developed by Tim Berners-Lee at CERN, using SGML. HTML is the set of markup symbols or codes placed in a file intended for display on a web browser. HTML configures a platform-independent display of information. Each markup code is referred to as an element (or tag).
2. No expensive software is required to create and code web pages. You can use a Windows or Mac text editor application that is part of the operating system. Free text editors and web browsers are also available for download.
3. The head section is located between the `<head>` and `</head>` tags on a web page. This area is used to contain information that describes the web page, such as the title of the page that will display in the menu bar of the browser window. The body section is located between the `<body>` and `</body>` tags. This area is used to code text and tags that show directly in the browser's display of the web page. The purpose of the body section is to describe the contents of the web page.

Checkpoint 2

1. The heading element is used to display headings and subheadings of documents. The size of the heading is configured with the particular heading level used—ranging from 1 to 6. `<h1>` is the largest heading. `<h6>` is the smallest heading. Text contained between heading tags will be displayed in a bold font and will have a line break above and below.
2. Ordered lists and unordered lists can be used to organize information on a web page. Unordered lists display a small symbol or bullet in front of each item. Use the `<ul>` tag to configure an unordered list. By default, ordered lists display a sequence of numbers in front of each item. Use the `<ol>` tag to configure an ordered list. Configure individual items in both ordered and unordered lists using the `<li>` tag.

3. The purpose of the blockquote element is to format a long quotation by indenting a section of text on a web page. Empty space is placed above and below the text contained in the blockquote element. The text is indented from both the left and right margins.

Checkpoint 3

1. Special characters are used to display items such as quotation marks, greater than (>), less than (<), and the copyright symbol © on a web page. These special characters, sometimes called entity characters, are interpreted by the browser when the page is rendered.
2. Use an absolute link to display a web page document from a website other than your own. The http protocol is used in the href value. Example:
```
<a href = "http://www.google.com">Google</a>
```
3. Use a relative link to display a web page document from your website. The http protocol is not used in the href value.
4. Example: <a href = "contact.html">Contact Us</a>

Review Questions

1. a
2. c
3. b
4. c
5. b
6. b
7. d
8. c
9. b
10. b
11. describe a characteristic of a web page, such as the character encoding.
12. special characters
13. strong
14.
15. em
16. It is good practice to place the e-mail address both on the web page and within the anchor tag. Not everyone has an e-mail program configured with his or her browser. By placing the e-mail address in both places, you increase usability for all your visitors.

Credits

All photographs except those noted below © Terry Ann Morris

"Checkpoint" icon (green check mark), "Web Site Case Study" icon (blue "WWW"), "FAQ" icon (orange caption bubble), "Focus on Accessibility" icon (orange key) © Fotolia LLC

"Hands-On Practice" icon (green hand); empty green, yellow, purple, red, and blue icons © Piotr M./Fotolia LLC

Figures 22, 23, 24 © W3C (World Wide Web Consortium)

Configuring Color and Text with CSS

Chapter Objectives In this chapter, you will learn how to . . .

- Describe the evolution of style sheets from print media to the Web
- List advantages of using Cascading Style Sheets
- Configure background and text color on web pages
- Create style sheets that configure common color and text properties
- Apply inline styles
- Use embedded style sheets
- Use external style sheets
- Configure element, class, id, and contextual selectors
- Utilize the "cascade" in CSS
- Validate CSS

Let's explore **Cascading Style Sheets (CSS)**. Web designers use CSS to separate the presentation style of a web page from the information on the web page. CSS is used to configure text, color, and page layout. CSS is not new—it was first proposed as a standard by the W3C in 1996. In 1998, additional properties for positioning web page elements were introduced to the language with CSS level 2 (CSS2), which was used for over a decade before reaching official "recommendation" status in 2011. CSS continues to evolve, with proposals for CSS level 3 (CSS3) properties that support features such as embedding fonts, rounded corners, and transparency. This chapter introduces you to the use of CSS on the Web as you explore how to configure color and text.

1 Overview of Cascading Style Sheets

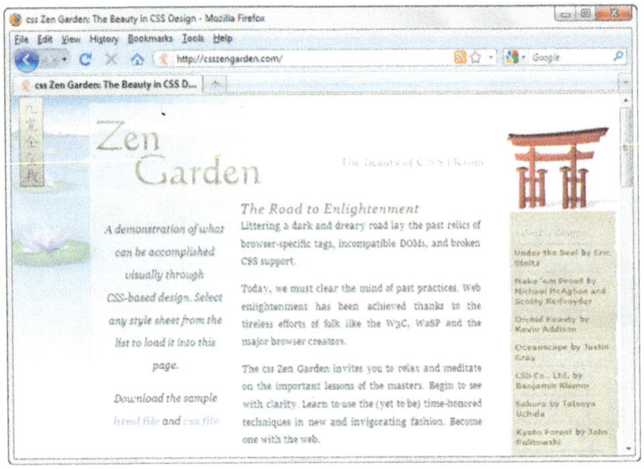

Figure 1 The CSS Zen Garden home page at http://www.csszengarden.com

For years, style sheets have been used in desktop publishing to apply typographical styles and spacing instructions to printed media. CSS provides this functionality (and much more) for web developers. CSS allows web developers to apply typographic styles (typeface, font size, and so on) and page layout instructions to a web page. The CSS Zen Garden, http://www.csszengarden.com, exemplifies the power and flexibility of CSS (Figure 1). Visit this site for an example of CSS in action. Notice how the content looks dramatically different depending on the design (CSS style rules) you select. Although the designs on the CSS Zen Garden are created by CSS masters, at some point these designers were just like you—starting out with CSS basics.

CSS is a flexible, cross-platform, standards-based language developed by the W3C. The W3C's description of CSS can be found at http://www.w3.org/Style. Be aware that even though CSS has been in use for many years, it is still considered an emerging technology, and different browsers do not support it in exactly the same way. We concentrate on aspects of CSS that are well supported by popular browsers.

Advantages of Cascading Style Sheets

There are several advantages to using CSS (see Figure 2):

- **Typography and page layout can be better controlled.** These features include font size, line spacing, letter spacing, indents, margins, and element positioning.
- **Style is separate from structure.** The format of the text and colors used on the page can be configured and stored separately from the body section of the web page document.
- **Styles can be stored.** You can store styles in a separate document and associate them with the web page. When the styles are modified, the HTML remains intact. This means, for example, that if your client decides to change the background color of a set of web pages from red to white, you only need to change one file that contains the styles, instead of modifying each web page document.

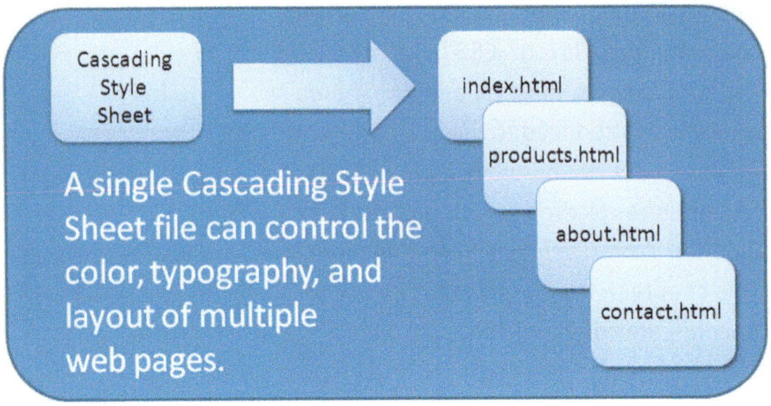

Figure 2 The power of a single CSS file

- Documents are potentially smaller. The formatting is separate from the document; therefore, the actual documents should be smaller.
- Site maintenance is easier. Again, if the styles need to be changed, then it is possible to complete the modifications by changing the style sheet only.

You may be wondering if there are any disadvantages to using CSS. In fact, there is one large disadvantage: CSS technology is not yet uniformly supported by browsers. This disadvantage will be less of an issue in the future as browsers comply with standards. Modern browsers have good support for CSS2 properties. Browser support for new CSS3 features such as rounded corners and color transparency is increasing, although there are differences in syntax, and not all browsers offer the same level of support. See http://caniuse.com/#cats=CSS for a list of CSS3 features supported by various browsers. This text will focus on aspects of CSS that are well supported by modern browsers and note when differences in syntax are needed.

Configuring Cascading Style Sheets

Web developers use four methods to incorporate CSS technology: inline, embedded, external, and imported.

- **Inline styles** are coded in the body of the web page as an attribute of an HTML tag. The style applies only to the specific element that contains it as an attribute.
- **Embedded styles** are defined in the header of a web page. These style instructions apply to the entire web page document.
- **External styles** are coded in a separate text file. This text file is associated with the web page by using a link element in the head section.
- **Imported styles** are similar to external styles in that they can connect styles coded in a separate text file with a web page document. An external style sheet can be imported into embedded styles or into another external style sheet by using the @import directive.

CSS Selectors and Declarations

Style sheets are composed of style rules that describe the styling to be applied. Each **rule** has two parts: a **selector** and a **declaration**:

- CSS Style Rule Selector The selector can be an HTML element name, a class name, or an id name. In this section, we will focus on applying styles to element name selectors. We will work with class selectors and id selectors later in this chapter.
- CSS Style Rule Declaration The declaration indicates the CSS property you are setting (such as color) and the value you are assigning to the property.

For example, the CSS rule shown in Figure 3 would set the color of the text used on a web page to blue. The selector is the body tag, and the declaration sets the color property to the value of blue.

Figure 3 Using CSS to set the text color to blue

The `background-color` Property

The CSS **`background-color` property** configures the background color of an element. The following style rule will configure the background color of a web page to be yellow. Notice how the declaration is enclosed within braces and how the colon symbol (:) separates the declaration property and the declaration value.

```
body { background-color: yellow }
```

The `color` Property

The CSS **`color property`** configures the text (foreground) color of an element. The following CSS style rule will configure the text color of a web page to be blue:

```
body { color: blue }
```

Configure Background and Text Color

Figure 4 displays a web page with a blue text and a yellow background. To configure more than one property for a selector, use a semicolon (;) to separate the declarations as follows:

```
body { color: blue; background-color: yellow; }
```

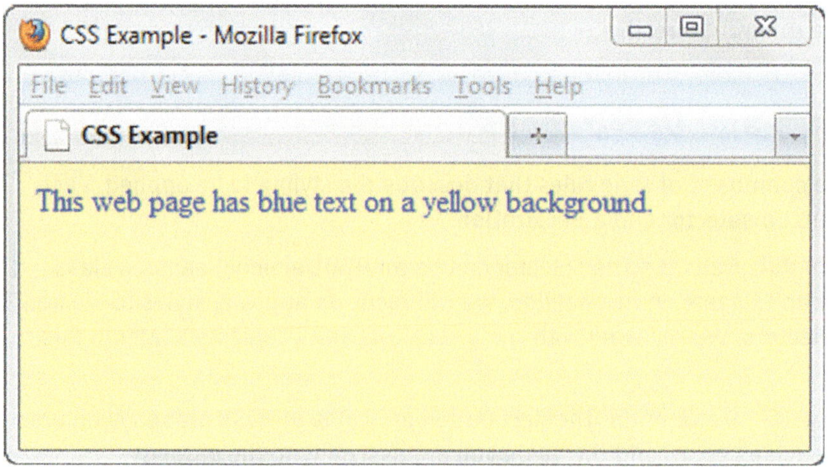

Figure 4 A web page with yellow background color and blue text color

The spaces in these declarations are optional. The ending semicolon (;) is also optional, but useful in case you need to add additional style rules at a later time. The following code samples are also valid:

```
body {color:blue;background-color:yellow}
body { color: blue;
       background-color: yellow; }
body {
      color: blue;
      background-color: yellow;
}
```

You might be asking yourself how you would know what properties and values can be used. See the CSS Property Reference in the appendix for a detailed list of CSS properties. This chapter introduces you to some of the CSS properties commonly used to configure color and text, shown in Table 1. In the next sections, we'll take a look at how color is used on web pages.

Table 1 CSS properties used in this chapter

Property	Description	Values
`background-color`	Background color of an element	Any valid color
`color`	Foreground (text) color of an element	Any valid color
`font-family`	Name of a font or font family	Any valid font or a font family such as serif, sans-serif, fantasy, monospace, or cursive
`font-size`	Size of the font	Varies; a numeric value with pt (standard font point sizes) or px (pixels) units or the unit em (which corresponds to the width of the uppercase M of the current font); a numeric percentage; and the text values xx-small, x-small, small, medium, large, x-large, and xx-large
`font-style`	Style of the font	normal, italic, or oblique
`font-weight`	The "boldness" or weight of the font	Varies; the text values normal, bold, bolder, and lighter and the numeric values 100, 200, 300, 400, 500, 600, 700, 800, and 900
`line-height`	The spacing allowed for the line of text	It is most common to use a percentage for this value; for example, a value of 200% would correspond to double-spacing.
`margin`	Shorthand notation to configure the margin surrounding an element	A numeric value (px or em); for example, body {margin: 10px} will set the page margins in the document to 10 pixels. When eliminating the margin, do not use the px or em unit—for example, body {margin:0}
`margin-left`	Configures the space in the left margin of the element	A numeric value (px or em), auto, or 0
`margin-right`	Configures the space in the right margin of the element	A numeric value (px or em), auto, or 0
`text-align`	The alignment of text	center, justify, left, or right
`text-decoration`	Determines whether text is underlined; this style is most often applied to hyperlinks	The value "none" will cause a hyperlink not to be underlined in a browser that normally processes in this manner
`width`	The width of the content of an element	A numeric value (px or em), numeric percentage, or auto (default)

2 Using Color on Web Pages

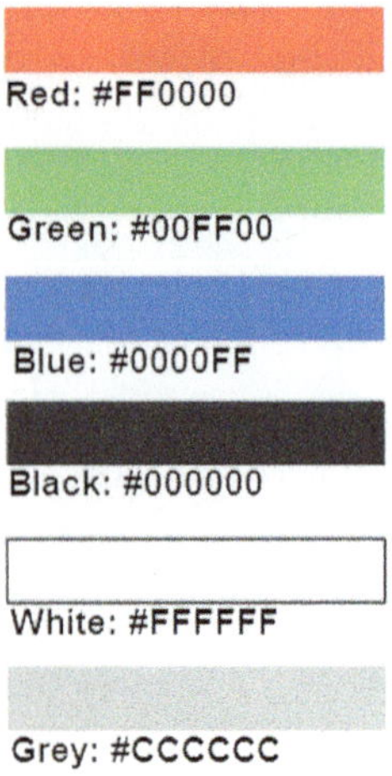

Figure 5 Color swatches and hexadecimal color values

Monitors display color as a combination of different intensities of red, green, and blue, a concept known as **RGB color**. RGB intensity values are numerical from 0 to 255. Each RGB color has three values, one each for red, green, and blue. These values are always listed in the same order (red, green, blue) and specify the numerical value of each color used (see the examples in Figure 5). You will usually use hexadecimal color values to specify RGB color on web pages.

Hexadecimal Color Values

Hexadecimal is the name for the base-16 numbering system, which uses the characters `0, 1, 2, 3, 4, 5, 6, 7, 8, 9, A, B, C, D, E,` and `F` to specify numeric values. **Hexadecimal color** values specify RGB color with numeric value pairs ranging from `00` to `FF` (`0` to `255` in base `10`). Each pair is associated with the amount of red, green, and blue displayed. Using this notation, one would specify the color red as `#FF0000` and the color blue as `#0000FF`. The `#` symbol signifies that the value is hexadecimal. You can use either uppercase or lowercase letters in hexadecimal color values; `#FF0000` and `#ff0000` both configure the color red.

Don't worry—you won't need to do calculations to work with web colors. Just become familiar with the numbering scheme. See Figure 6 for an excerpt from the color chart at http://webdevfoundations.net/color.

Figure 6 Partial color chart

#FFFFFF	#FFFFCC	#FFFF99	#FFFF66	#FFFF33	#FFFF00
#FFCCFF	#FFCCCC	#FFCC99	#FFCC66	#FFCC33	#FFCC00
#FF99FF	#FF99CC	#FF9999	#FF9966	#FF9933	#FF9900
#FF66FF	#FF66CC	#FF6699	#FF6666	#FF6633	#FF6600
#FF33FF	#FF33CC	#FF3399	#FF3366	#FF3333	#FF3300
#FF00FF	#FF00CC	#FF0099	#FF0066	#FF0033	#FF0000

Web-Safe Colors

Back in the day of 8-bit color monitors, web page color could be problematic and it was important to use one of the 216 **web-safe colors**, which display in a similar manner on both the Mac and PC platforms. The hexadecimal color values of web-safe colors use the numerals `00, 33, 66, 99, CC,` and `FF`. The 216 web-safe colors make up the **Web-Safe Color Palette**, shown in the appendix (also at http://webdevfoundations.net/color). Now that most monitors display millions of colors, using web-safe colors is less important. The Web-Safe Color Palette is rather limited, and it is common for today's web designers to choose colors creatively rather than select them only from the palette.

CSS Color Syntax

CSS syntax allows you to configure colors in a number of ways, including hexadecimal color values, color names, and decimal color values. Table 2 shows CSS syntax examples that configure a paragraph with red text.

Table 2 CSS color syntax examples

CSS Syntax	Color Type
`p { color: red; }`	Color name
`p { color: #FF0000; }`	Hexadecimal color value
`p { color: #F00; }`	Shorthand hexadecimal (one character for each hexadecimal pair; used only with web-safe colors)
`p { color: rgb(255,0,0); }`	Decimal color value (RGB triplet)

FAQ **Are there other methods to configure color with CSS?**

Yes, the CSS3 Color Module (currently in proposed recommendation status) provides a way for web developers to configure not only color, but also the transparency of the color, with RGBA (Red, Green, Blue, Alpha).

3 Inline CSS with the Style Attribute

Recall that there are four methods for configuring CSS: inline, embedded, external, and imported. In this section, we focus on inline CSS using the style attribute.

The Style Attribute

Inline styles are coded as an attribute on an HTML tag using the **style attribute**. The value of the style attribute is set to the style rule declaration that you need to configure. Recall that a declaration consists of a property and a value. Each property is separated from its value with a colon (:). The following code will use inline styles to set the text color of an `<h1>` tag to a shade of red:

```
<h1 style="color:#cc0000">This is displayed as a red heading</h1>
```

If there is more than one property, they are separated by a semicolon (;). The following code configures the heading with a red text color and a gray background color:

```
<h1 style="color:#cc0000;background-color:#cccccc">
This is displayed as a red heading on a gray background</h1>
```

Hands-On Practice 1

In this Hands-On Practice, you will configure a web page with inline styles. The inline styles will specify the following:

- Global body tag styles for an off-white background with teal text. These styles will be inherited by other elements by default. For example:

  ```
  <body style="background-color:#F5F5F5;color:#008080;">
  ```

- Styles for an h1 element with a teal background with off-white text. This style will override the global styles configured on the body element. For example:

  ```
  <h1 style="background-color:#008080;color:#F5F5F5;">
  ```

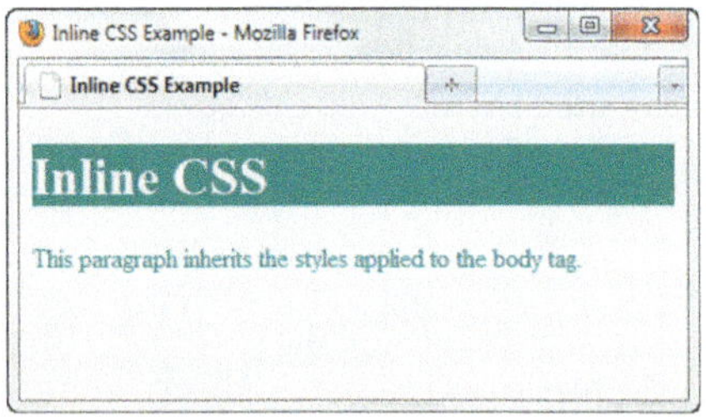

Figure 7 Web page using inline styles

A sample is shown in Figure 7. Launch a text editor. Select File > Open to edit the template file located at chapter2/template.html in the student files. Modify the title element, and add heading tags, paragraph tags, style attributes, and text to the body section as indicated by the following highlighted code:

```
<!DOCTYPE html>
<html lang="en">
<head>
<title>Inline CSS Example</title>
<meta charset="utf-8">
</head>
<body style="background-color:#F5F5F5;color:#008080;">
<h1 style="background-color:#008080;color:#F5F5F5;">Inline CSS</h1>
<p>This paragraph inherits the styles applied to the body tag.</p>
</body>
</html>
```

Save the document as inline2.html on your hard drive or flash drive. Launch a browser to test your page. It should look similar to the page shown in Figure 7. Note that the inline styles applied to the body tag are inherited by other elements on the page (such as the paragraph) unless more-specific styles are specified (such as those coded on the `<h1>` tag). You can compare your work with the solution found in the student files (chapter3/inline.html)[1].

Let's continue and add another paragraph, with the text color configured to be dark gray:

```
<p style="color:#333333">This paragraph overrides the text color
style applied to the body tag.</p>
```

[1]Website Case Study starter files are available for download from Pearson's CS Support website at http://cssupport.pearsoncmg.com.

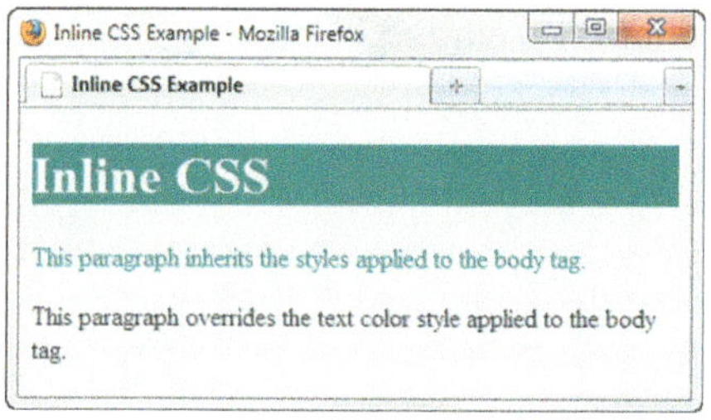

Figure 8 The second paragraph's inline styles override the global styles configured on the body tag

Save the document as inline3.html. It should look similar to the page shown in Figure 8. You can compare your work with the solution found in the student files (chapter3/inlinep.html). Note that the inline styles applied to the second paragraph override the global styles applied to the body of the web page.

FAQ **Are inline styles recommended?**

While inline styles can sometimes be useful, you'll find that you won't use this technique much in practice—it's inefficient, adds extra code to the web page document, and is inconvenient to maintain. However, inline styles can be quite handy in some circumstances, such as when you post an article to a content management system or blog and need to tweak the sitewide styles a bit to help get your point across.

4 Embedded CSS with the Style Element

In the previous Hands-On Practice, you added inline styles for one of the paragraphs. To do so, you coded a style attribute on the paragraph element. But what if you needed to configure the styles for 10 or 20 paragraphs instead of just one? Using inline styles, you might be doing a lot of repetitive coding! While inline styles apply to one HTML element, embedded styles apply to an entire web page.

Style Element

Embedded styles are placed within a **`<style>` element** located in the head section of a web page. The opening `<style>` tag and the closing `</style>` tag contain the list of embedded-style rules. When using XHTML syntax, the `<style>` tag requires a **type attribute** with the value of `"text/css"` to indicate the MIME type. HTML5 syntax does not require the type attribute.

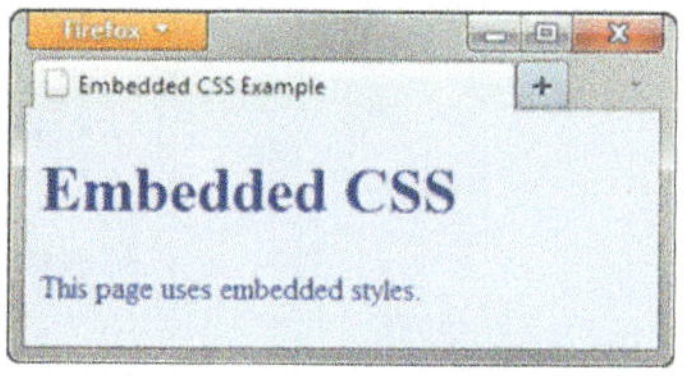

Figure 9 Web page with embedded styles

The web page in Figure 9 uses embedded styles to set the text color and background color of the web page document with the body element selector. See the example in the student files at chapter3/embed.html. The code follows:

```
<!DOCTYPE html>
<html lang="en">
<head>
<title>Embedded Styles</title>
<meta charset="utf-8">
<style>
body { background-color: #CCFFFF;
       color: #000033;
}
</style>
</head>
<body>
<h1>Embedded CSS</h1>
<p>This page uses embedded styles.</p>
</body>
</html>
```

Notice the way the style rules were coded, with each rule on its own line. This formatting is not required for the styles to work, but it makes the styles more readable and easier to maintain than one long row of text. The styles are in effect for the entire web page document because they were applied to the <body> tag using the body element selector.

Hands-On Practice 2

Launch a text editor, and open the starter.html file from the chapter3 folder in the student files. Save your page as embedded.html, and test it in a browser. Your page should look similar to the one shown in Figure 10.

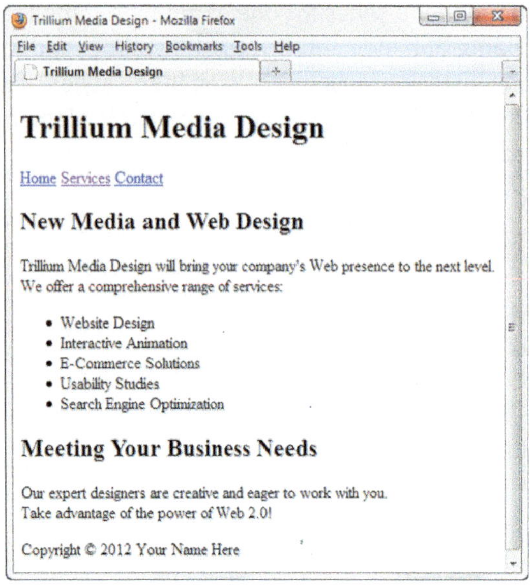

Figure 10 The web page without any styles

Open the file in a text editor, and view the source code. Notice that the web page code uses the `<h1>`, `<h2>`, `<div>`, `<p>`, `<ul>`, and `<li>` elements. In this Hands-On Practice, you will code embedded styles to configure selected background and text colors. You will use the body element selector to configure the default background color (`#e6e6fa`) and default text color (`#191970`) for the entire page. You will also use the h1 and h2 element selectors to configure different background and text colors for the heading areas. Edit the embedded.html file in a text editor, and add the following code below the `<title>` element in the head section of the web page:

```
<style>
body { background-color: #e6e6fa; color: #191970; }
h1 { background-color: #191970; color: #e6e6fa; }
h2 { background-color: #aeaed4; color: #191970; }
</style>
```

Save your file, and test it in a browser. Figure 11 displays the web page along with corresponding color swatches. A monochromatic color scheme was chosen. Notice how the repetition of a limited number of colors unifies the design of the web page. View the source code for your page, and review the CSS and HTML code. An example of this web page is in the student files at chapter3/embedded.html. Note that all the styles were located in a single place on the web page. Since embedded styles are coded in a specific location, they are easier to maintain over time than inline styles. Also, notice that you coded the styles for the h2 element selector only once (in the head section), and *both* of the `<h2>` elements applied the h2 style. This approach is more efficient than coding the same inline style on each `<h2>` element. However, it is uncommon for a website to have only one page. Repeating the CSS in the head section of each web page file is inefficient and difficult to maintain. In the next section, you'll use a more productive approach—configuring an external style sheet.

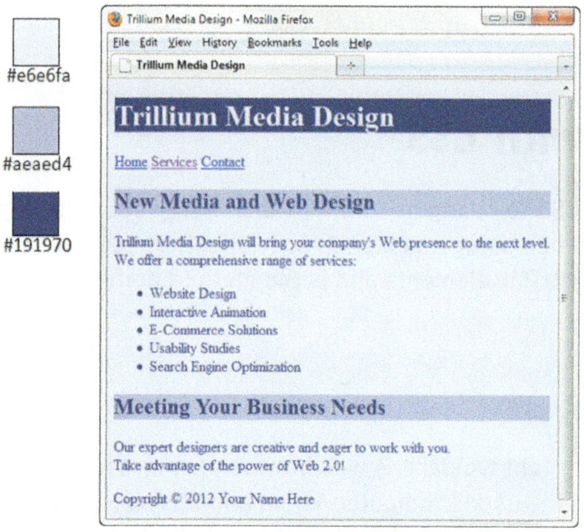

Figure 11 The web page after embedded styles are configured

FAQ My CSS doesn't work; what can I do?

Coding CSS is a detail-oriented process. There are several common errors that can cause the browser not to apply CSS correctly to a web page. With a careful review of your code and the following tips, you should get your CSS working:

- Verify that you are using the colon (:) and semicolon (;) symbols in the right spots—they are easy to confuse. The colon should separate the properties from their values, while the semicolon should be placed between each *property:value* configuration.
- Check that you are not using equal (=) signs instead of colons (:) between each property and its value.
- Verify that curly braces ({ and }) are properly placed around the style rules for each selector.
- Check the syntax of your selectors, the selectors' properties, and the property values for correct usage.
- If part of your CSS works and part doesn't, read through the CSS and determine the first rule that is not applied. Often, the error is in the rule above the rule that is not applied.
- Use a validation application to check your CSS code. The W3C has a free CSS code validator at http://jigsaw.w3.org/css-validator. The W3C's CSS validator can help you find syntax errors. See Section 9 for an overview of how to use this tool to validate your CSS.

Checkpoint 1

1. List three reasons to use CSS on a web page.
2. When designing a page that uses colors other than the default colors for text and background, explain why it is a good reason to configure both the text color and the background color.
3. Describe one advantage to using embedded styles instead of inline styles.

5 Configuring Text with CSS

In this section, you will learn to use CSS to configure font typeface. Using CSS to configure text is more flexible (especially when using an external style sheet, as you will discover later in the chapter) than using HTML elements and is the method preferred by modern web developers.

The `font-family` Property

The **`font-family` property** configures font typeface. A web browser displays text using the fonts that have been installed on the user's computer. When a font is specified that is not installed on your web visitor's computer, the default font is substituted. Times New Roman is the default font displayed by most web browsers. Table 3 shows font family categories.

Table 3 Common fonts

Font Family Category	Font Family Description	Common Font Typeface Names
serif	Serif fonts have small embellishments ("serifs") on the end of letter strokes; often used for headings	Times New Roman, Georgia, Palatino
sans-serif	Sans-serif fonts do not have serifs; often used for web page text	Arial, Tahoma, Helvetica, Verdana
monospace	Fixed-width font; often used for code samples	Courier New, Lucida Console
cursive	Handwritten style; use with caution—may be difficult to read on a web page	Lucida Handwriting, Brush Script, Comic Sans MS
fantasy	Exaggerated style; use with caution—may be difficult to read on a web page	Jokerman, Impact, Papyrus

Not every computer has the same fonts installed. See http://www.ampsoft.net/webdesign-l/WindowsMacFonts.html for a list of web-safe fonts. Create a built-in backup plan by listing multiple fonts and categories for the value of the font-family property. The browser will attempt to use the fonts in the order listed. The following CSS configures the p element selector to display text in Arial (if installed), Helvetica (if installed), or the default installed sans-serif font:

```
p { font-family: Arial, Helvetica, sans-serif; }
```

FAQ I've heard about "embedding" fonts in order to use special fonts on a web page—what's that all about?

Still in draft form and not yet an official standard, CSS3 introduces `@font-face`, which can be used to "embed" fonts within web pages, although what actually happens is that you provide the location of the font and the browser downloads it. For example, if you own the rights to freely distribute the font named MyAwesomeFont and it is stored in a file named myawesomefont.otf in the same folder as your web page, the CSS to make it available to your web page visitors is

```
@font-face { font-family: 'MyAwesomeFont';
             src: url('myawesomefont.otf'); }
```

Current browsers support `@font-face`, but there are file size and copyright issues to consider. You may have purchased a font, but you need to check your license to determine whether you also have the right to freely distribute the font. For more information about `@font-face`, see http://nimbupani.com/font-in-your-face.html and the text's website at http://webdevfoundations.net/6e/chapter3.html. Keep in mind that if you need a nonstandard font just for a logo area or for an image on a web page, there is an easy solution: You are free to use any font that is available to you when you create an image with a graphics application.

More CSS Font Properties

CSS provides you with lots of options for configuring the text on your web pages. In this section, you will explore the `font-size`, `font-weight`, `font-style`, and `line-height` properties.

The `font-size` Property

The **`font-size` property** sets the size of the font. Table 4 lists a wide variety of text and numeric values—there are almost too many choices available. See the notes in Table 4 for recommended use.

Table 4 Configuring font size

Value Category	Values	Notes
Text Value	xx-small, x-small, small, medium (default), large, x-large, xx-large	Scales well when text is resized in browser; limited options for text size
Pixel Unit (px)	Numeric value with unit, such as 10 px	Pixel-perfect display depends on screen resolution; may not scale in every browser when text is resized
Point Unit (pt)	Numeric value with unit, such as 10 pt	Use to configure print version of web page; may not scale in every browser when text is resized
Em Unit (em)	Numeric value with unit, such as .75 em	Recommended by W3C; scales well when text is resized in browser; many options for text size
Percentage Value	Numeric value with percentage, such as 75%	Recommended by W3C; scales well when text is resized in browser; many options for text size

The **em unit** is a relative font unit that has its roots in the print industry, dating back to the day when printers set type manually with blocks of characters. An em unit is the width of a square block of type (typically the uppercase M) for a particular font and type size. On web pages, an em unit corresponds to the width of the font and size used in the parent element (typically the body element). So, the size of an em unit is relative to the font typeface and default size. Percentage values work in a similar manner to em units. For example, `font-size: 100%` and `font-size: 1em` should render the same in a browser. To compare font sizes on your computer, launch a browser and view chapter3/fonts.html in the student files.

The `font-weight` Property

The **`font-weight` property** configures the boldness of the text. Configuring the CSS rule `font-weight: bold;` has a similar effect as the `<strong>` or `<b>` HTML element.

The `font-style` Property

The **`font-style` property** typically is used to configure text displayed in italics. Valid values for `font-style` are normal (the default), italic, and oblique. The CSS `font-style: italic;` has the same visual effect in the browser as an `<i>` or `<em>` HTML element.

The `line-height` Property

The **`line-height` property** modifies the default height of a line of text and is often configured with a percentage value. For example, code `line-height: 200%;` to configure text to appear double spaced.

The `text-align` Property

HTML elements are left-aligned by default; They begin at the left margin. The CSS **`text-align` property** configures the alignment of text and inline elements within block display elements such as headings, paragraphs, and divs. The values for the text-align property are left (default), right, and center. The following CSS code sample configures an h1 element to have centered text:

```
h1 { text-align: center; }
```

While it can be quite effective to center the text displayed in web page headings, be careful about centering text in paragraphs. According to WebAIM (http://www.webaim.org/techniques/textlayout), studies have shown that centered text is more difficult to read than left-aligned text.

The `text-indent` Property

The CSS **`text-indent` property** configures the indentation of the first line of text within an element. The value can be numeric (such as a px, pt, or em unit) or a percentage. The following CSS code sample configures the first line of all paragraphs to be indented:

```
p { text-indent: 5em; }
```

The `text-decoration` Property

The purpose of the CSS **`text-decoration` property** is to modify the display of text. Commonly used values for the `text-decoration` property include `none`, `underline`, `overline`, and `line-through`. Did you ever wonder why some hyperlinks are not underlined? Although hyperlinks are underlined by default, you can remove the underline with the text-decoration property. The following code sample removes the underline on a hyperlink:

```
a { text-decoration: none; }
```

Hands-On Practice 3

Now that you've got a collection of new CSS properties for font and text configuration, let's try them out by modifying the embedded.html page. Launch a text editor, and open embedded.html. You will now code additional CSS style rules to configure the text on the page.

Set Default Font Properties for the Page

As you have already seen, CSS rules applied to the body selector apply to the entire page. Modify the CSS for the body selector to display text using a sans-serif font. The new font typeface style rule shown in the following code will apply to the entire web page unless more specific style rules are applied to a selector (such as h1 or p), a class, or an id (more on classes and ids later):

```
body { background-color: #E6E6FA;
       color: #191970;
       font-family: Arial, Verdana, sans-serif; }
```

Save your page as embedded1.html, and test it in a browser. Your page should look similar to the one shown in Figure 12. Notice that just a single line of CSS changed the font typeface of all the text on the page!

Figure 12 CSS configures the font on the web page

Configure the h1 Selector

Now you will configure the `line-height` and `font-family` CSS properties. Set the `line-height` property to 200%; this will add a bit of empty space above and below the heading text. Next, modify the h1 selector to use a serif font. When a font name contains spaces, type quotes as indicated in the code that follows. While it is generally recognized that blocks of text using sans-serif fonts are easier to read, it is common to use a serif font to configure page or section headings.

```
h1 { background-color: #191970;
     color: #E6E6FA;
     line-height: 200%;
     font-family: Georgia, "Times New Roman", serif; }
```

Save your page, and test it in a browser. If you notice that the "Trillium Media Design" text seems to crowd the left margin, add a ` ` nonbreaking space special character in the body of the web page after the opening `<h1>` tag.

Configure the h2 Selector

Configure the CSS rule to use the same font typeface as the h1 selector and to display centered text.

```
h2 { background-color: #AEAED4;
     color: #191970;
     font-family: Georgia, "Times New Roman", serif;
     text-align: center; }
```

Configure the Paragraphs

Edit the HTML, and remove the line break tag that is after the first sentence of each paragraph; these line breaks look a bit awkward. Next, configure text in paragraphs to display just slightly smaller than the default text size. Use the `font-size` property set to .90em. Configure the first line of each paragraph to be indented. Use the `text-indent` property to configure a 3em indent.

```
p { font-size: .90em;
    text-indent: 3em; }
```

Configure the Unordered List

Configure the text displayed in the unordered list to be bold.

```
ul { font-weight: bold; }
```

Save your page as embedded2.html, and test it in a browser. Your page should look similar to the one shown in Figure 13. The student files contain a sample solution at chapter3/embedded2.html. CSS is quite powerful—just a few lines of code significantly changed the appearance of the web page. You may be wondering if even more customization is possible. For example, what if you did not want all the paragraphs to display in exactly the same way? While you could add inline styles to the web page code, that is usually not the most efficient technique. The next section introduces the CSS class and id selectors, which are widely utilized to configure specific page elements.

Figure 13 CSS configures color and text properties on the web page

FAQ Is there a quick way to apply the same styles to more than one HTML tag or more than one class?

Yes, you can apply the same style rules to multiple selectors (such as HTML elements, classes, or ids) by listing the selectors in front of the style rule. Place a comma between each selector. The following code sample shows the `font-size` of 1em being applied to both the paragraph and list-item elements:

```
p, li { font-size: 1em; }
```

6 CSS Class, id, and Contextual Selectors

The Class Selector

Use a CSS **class selector** when you need to apply a CSS declaration to certain elements on a web page and not necessarily tie the style to a particular HTML element. See Figure 14, and notice that the last two items in the unordered list are displayed in a different color than the others; this is an example of using a class. When setting a style for a class, configure the class name as the selector. Place a dot, or period (.), in front of the class name in the style sheet. The following code configures a class called feature in a style sheet with a foreground (text) color set to red:

```
.feature { color: #FF0000; }
```

The styles set in the new class can be applied to any element you wish. You do this by using the class attribute, such as `class="feature"`. Do not type the dot in front of the class value in the opening tag where the class is being applied. The following code will apply the feature class styles to a `<li>` element:

```
<li class="feature">Usability Studies</li>
```

The id Selector

Use a CSS **id selector** to identify and apply a CSS rule uniquely to a single area on a web page. For example, the copyright information in the page footer in Figure 14 displays in small italic text with a gray color (`#333333`). This style could have been configured with a class. However, because the page will have only one footer area, an id is more appropriate. When setting a style for an id, place a hash mark (#) in front of the id name in the style sheet. The following code will configure an id called footer in a style sheet with gray, small, italic text:

```
#footer { color: #333333;
          font-size: .75em;
          font-style: italic; }
```

The styles set in the footer id can be applied to any element you wish by using the id attribute, `id="footer"`. Do not type the # in front of the id value in the opening tag. The following code will apply the footer id styles to a div tag:

```
<div id="footer">This paragraph will be displayed using styles
configured in the footer id.</div>
```

Using CSS with an id selector is similar to using CSS with a class selector. Use an id selector to configure a single element on a web page. Use a class selector to configure one or more elements on a web page.

Figure 14 Using classes and ids

Hands-On Practice 4

In this Hands-On Practice, you will modify the CSS and the HTML in the Trillium Technologies page to configure the navigation and page footer areas. Launch a text editor, and open embedded2.html.

Configure the Navigation Area

The navigation links would be more prominent if they were displayed in a larger and bolder font. Create a class named nav that sets the font-size and font-weight properties.

```
.nav { font-weight: bold;
       font-size: 1.25em; }
```

Modify the opening div tag of the navigation area. Add a class attribute that associates the div with the nav class as follows:

```
<div class="nav"><a href="index.html">Home</a>
<a href="services.html">Services</a>
<a href="contact.html">Contact</a></div>
```

Configure the Content Area

Trillium Technologies would like to draw attention to its new usability and search optimization services. Create a class named feature that configures the text color to be red (#ff0000).

```
.feature { color: #ff0000; }
```

Modify the last two items in the unordered list. Add a class attribute to each opening li tag that associates the list item with the feature class as follows:

```
<li class="feature">Usability Studies</li>
<li class="feature">Search Engine Optimization</li>
```

Configure the Footer Area

Create an id named footer that sets the text color, font-size, and font-style properties.

```
#footer { color: #333333;
          font-size: .75em;
          font-style: italic; }
```

Modify the opening div tag of the footer area to add an id attribute that associates div with the id class:

```
<div id="footer">Copyright &copy; 2012 Your Name Here</div>
```

Save your file as embedded3.html, and test it in a browser. Your page should look similar to the image shown in Figure 14. The student files contain a sample solution at chapter3/embedded3.html. Notice how the class and id styles are applied.

FAQ How do you choose class and id names?

You can choose almost any name you wish for a CSS class or id. However, CSS class names are more flexible and easier to maintain over time if they are descriptive of the structure rather than of specific formatting. For example, a class name of largeBold would no longer be meaningful if the design were changed to display the area differently; however, a structural class name such as nav, header, footer, content, or subheading is meaningful regardless of how the area is configured. Here are more hints for class names:

- Use short, but descriptive, names.
- Both letters and numbers may be used.
- Avoid spaces in class names.
- Class names are not case sensitive, but consistency will make page maintenance easier.

A final tip about CSS classes is to be wary of "classitis"—that is, creating a brand new class each time you need to configure text a bit differently. Decide ahead of time how you will configure page areas, code your classes, and apply them. The result will be a more cohesive and better organized web page.

The Contextual Selector

Use a CSS **contextual selector** when you want to specify an element within the context of its container (parent) element. Contextual selectors are sometimes referred to as descendent selectors. To configure a contextual selector, list the container selector (which can be an element selector, class, or id) followed by the specific selector you are styling. For example, to specify a green text color only for anchor tags located *within* the footer id declared earlier, code the following style rule:

```
#footer a { color: #00ff00; }
```

The next section introduces a new HTML element that is useful when configuring page areas.

7 Span Element

The div element configures a section or division on a web page with empty space above and below. The div element is useful when you need to format a section that is physically separated from the rest of the web page, referred to as a block display. In contrast, the **span element** defines a section on a web page that is *not* physically separated from other areas; this formatting is referred to as inline display. Use the `<span>` tag if you need to format an area that is contained within another, such as within a `<p>`, `<blockquote>`, `<li>`, or `<div>` tag.

Hands-On Practice 5

You will experiment with the span element in this Hands-On Practice by configuring a new class to format the company name when it is displayed within the text on the page and using the span element to apply this class. Open the embedded3.html file in a text editor. Your web page will look similar to the one shown in Figure 15 after the changes are complete.

Figure 15 This web page uses the span element

Configure the Company Name

View Figure 15, and notice that the company name, Trillium Technologies, is displayed in bold and serif font within the first paragraph. You will code both CSS and HTML to configure this formatting. First, create a new CSS rule that configures a class called companyname in bold, serif font, and 1.25em in size. The code follows:

```
.companyname { font-weight: bold;
               font-family: Georgia, "Times New Roman", serif;
               font-size: 1.25em; }
```

Next, modify the beginning of the first paragraph of HTML to use the span element to apply the class as follows:

```
<p><span class="companyname">Trillium Media Design</span> will bring
```

Save your file, and test it in a browser. Your page should look similar to the one shown in Figure 15. The student files contain a sample solution at chapter3/embedded4.html. View the source code for your page, and review the CSS and HTML code. Note that all the styles were located in a single place on the web page. Since embedded styles are coded in a specific location, they are easier to maintain over time than inline styles. Also notice that you needed to code the styles for the `h2` element selector only once (in the head section), and *both* of the `<h2>` elements applied the `h2` style. This approach is more efficient than coding the same inline style on each `<h2>` element. However, it is uncommon for a website to have only one page. Repeating the CSS in the head section of each web page file is inefficient and difficult to maintain. In the next section, you will use a more efficient approach: configuring an external style sheet.

8 Using External Style Sheets

VideoNote
External Style Sheets

The flexibility and power of CSS are best utilized when the CSS is external to the web page document. An external style sheet is a text file with a .css file extension that contains CSS style rules. The external style sheet file is associated with a web page by using the link element. This approach provides a way for multiple web pages to be associated with the same external style sheet file. The external style sheet file does not contain any HTML tags; it contains only CSS style rules.

The advantage of external CSS is that styles are configured in a single file. This means that when styles need to be modified, only one file needs to be changed, instead of multiple web pages. On large sites, this approach can save a web developer much time and increase productivity. Let's get some practice with this useful technique.

Link Element

The **link element** associates an external style sheet with a web page. It is placed in the head section of the page and is a stand-alone, void tag. In HTML5 syntax, the link element is coded as `<link>`. When using XHTML syntax, the link element is coded as `<link />`. Three attributes are used with the link element: rel, href, and type.

- The value of the **rel** attribute is "`stylesheet`".
- The value of the **href** attribute is the name of the style sheet file.

- The value of the **type** attribute is `"text/css"`, which is the MIME type for CSS. The type attribute is optional in HTML5 and required in XHTML.

Code the following in the head section of a web page to associate the document with the external style sheet named color.css:

```
<link rel="stylesheet" href="color.css">
```

Hands-On Practice 6

Let's practice using external styles. First, you will create an external style sheet. Next, you will configure a web page to be associated with the external style sheet.

Create an External Style Sheet

Launch a text editor, and type in the following style rules to set the background color of a page to blue and the text color to white. Save the file as color.css.

```
body { background-color: #0000FF;
       color: #FFFFFF; }
```

Figure 16 shows the external color.css style sheet displayed in Notepad. Notice that there is no HTML in this file. HTML tags are not coded within an external style sheet. Only CSS rules (selectors, properties, and values) are coded in an external style sheet.

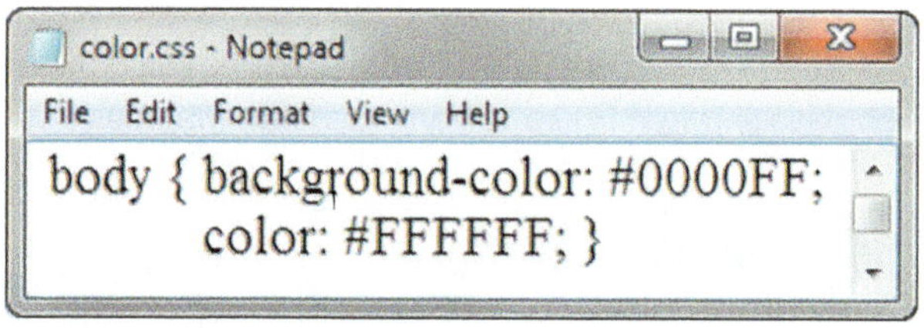

Figure 16 The external style sheet color.css

Configure the Web Page

To create the web page shown in Figure 17, launch a text editor and open the template file located at chapter2/template.html in the student files. Modify the title element, add a link tag to the head section, and add a paragraph to the body section as indicated by the following highlighted code:

```
<!DOCTYPE html>
<html lang="en">
<head>
<title>External Styles</title>
<meta charset="utf-8">
<link rel="stylesheet" href="color.css">
</head>
<body>
<p>This web page uses an external style sheet.</p>
</body>
</html>
```

Save your file as external.html. Launch a browser, and test your page. It should look similar to the page shown in Figure 17. You can compare your work with the solution in the student files (chapter3/external.html). The color.css style sheet can be associated with any number of web pages. If you ever need to change the style of formatting, you need to change only a single file (color.css) instead of multiple files (all of the web pages). As mentioned earlier, this technique can boost productivity on a large site.

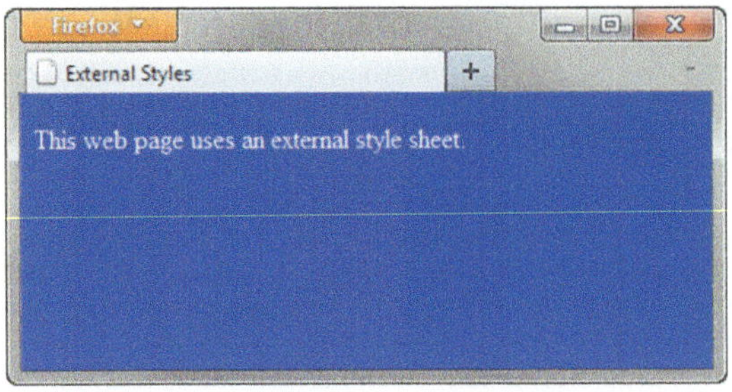

Figure 17 This page is associated with an external style sheet

The advantage of having only a single file to update is significant for both small and large websites. In the next Hands-On Practice, you will modify the Trillium Technologies home page to use an external style sheet.

Hands-On Practice 7

In this Hands-On Practice, you will continue to gain experience using external style sheets as you create the external style sheet file named trillium.css, modify the Trillium Technologies home page to use external styles instead of embedded styles, and associate a second web page with the trillium.css style sheet.

A version of the Trillium home page is in the student files. Open the embedded4.html file in a browser. The display should be the same as the web page shown in Figure 15 from Hands-On Practice 5.

trillium.css - Notepad

```
body { background-color: #E6E6FA;
           color: #191970;
           font-family: Arial, Verdana, sans-serif; }
h1 { background-color: #191970;
        color: #E6E6FA;
        line-height: 200%;
        font-family: Georgia, "Times New Roman", serif; }
h2 { background-color: #AEAED4;
        color: #191970;
        font-family: Georgia, "Times New Roman", serif;
        text-align: center;  }
p { font-size: .90em;
      text-indent: 3em;  }
ul { font-weight: bold; }
.nav { font-weight: bold;
          font-size: 1.25em;  }
.feature { color: #ff0000;  }
#footer { color: #333333;
              font-size: .75em;
              font-style: italic; }
.companyname { font-weight: bold;
                       font-family: Georgia, "Times New Roman", serif;
                       font-size: 1.25em; }
```

Figure 18 The external style sheet named trillium.css

Now that you've seen what you're working with, let's begin. Launch a text editor, and save the file as index.html in a folder called trillium. You are ready to convert the embedded CSS to external CSS. Select the CSS rules (all the lines of code between, but not including, the opening and closing `<style>` tags). Use Edit > Copy, or press the Ctrl + C keys (Cmd + C keys on a Mac), to copy the CSS code to the clipboard. Now you will place the CSS in a new file. Launch a text editor and create a new file. Use Edit > Paste, or press the Ctrl + V keys (Cmd + V keys on a Mac), to paste the CSS style rules. Save the file as trillium.css. See Figure 18 for a screenshot of the new trillium.css file in Notepad. Notice that there are no HTML elements in trillium.css—not even the `<style>` element. The file contains CSS rules only.

Next, edit the index.html file in a text editor. Delete the CSS code you just copied. Delete the closing `</style>` tag. Replace the opening `<style>` tag with a link element to associate the style sheet named trillium.css. The `<link>` tag code is as follows:

```
<link href="trillium.css" rel="stylesheet">
```

Save the file, and test it in a browser. Your web page should look just like the one shown in Figure 15. Although it looks the same, the difference is in the code: The page now uses external, instead of embedded, CSS.

Now, for the fun part—you will associate a second page with the style sheet. The student files contain a services.html page for Trillium at chapter3/services.html. When you display this page in a browser, it should look similar to the one shown in Figure 19. Notice that although the structure of the page is similar to the home page, the styling of the text and colors is absent.

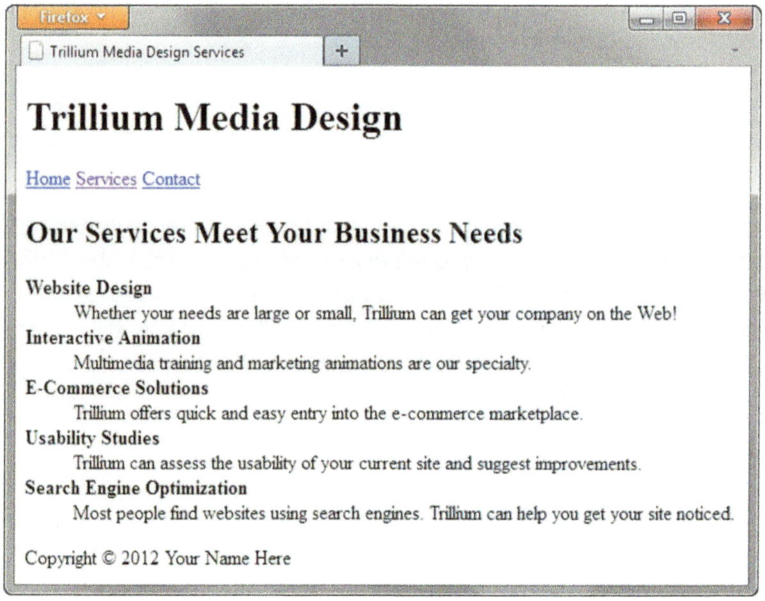

Figure 19 The services.html page is not associated with a style sheet

Launch a text editor to edit the services.html file. As you view the HTML code, you will notice that this page is ready for our trillium.css styles—for example, the nav class and footer id have been coded as attributes in the corresponding navigation and page footer areas. All that is left for you to do is to code an HTML `<link>` tag to associate the services.html web page with the trillium.css external style sheet. Place the following code in the header section above the closing </head> tag:

```
<link href="trillium.css" rel="stylesheet">
```

Save your file, and test it in a browser. Your page should look similar to Figure 20—the CSS rules have been applied!

Figure 20 The services.html page has been associated with trillium.css

If you click the Home and Services hyperlinks, you can move back and forth between the index.html and services.html pages in the browser. The student files contain a sample solution in the chapter3/3.7 folder.

Notice that when using an external style sheet, if the use of color or fonts on the page ever needs to be changed, modifications are made only to the external style sheet. Think about how this approach can improve productivity on a site with many pages. Instead of modifying hundreds of pages to make a color or font change, only a single file—the CSS external style sheet—needs to be updated. Becoming comfortable with CSS will be important as you develop your skills and increase your technical expertise.

Checkpoint 2

1. Describe a reason to use embedded styles. Explain where embedded styles are placed on a web page.
2. Describe a reason to use external styles. Explain where external styles are placed and how web pages indicate that they are using external styles.
3. Write the code to configure a web page to associate with an external style sheet called mystyles.css.

FAQ When designing a new web page or website, how do I begin to work with CSS?

The following guidelines can be helpful when configuring a page using CSS:

- Review the design of the page. Check if common fonts are used. Define global properties (the default for the entire page) for characteristics such as fonts and colors attached to the body element selector.
- Identify typical elements used for organization in the page (such as `<h1>`, `<h2>`, and so on), and declare style rules for these elements if different from the default.
- Identify various page areas such as the logo header, navigation, footer, and so on. List any special configurations needed for these areas. You may decide to configure classes or ids in your CSS to configure these areas.
- Create one prototype page that contains most of the elements you plan to use and test. Revise your CSS as needed.
- Plan and test. These are important activities when designing a website.

9 Center HTML Elements with CSS

You learned how to center text on a web page earlier in this chapter—but what about centering the entire web page itself? A popular page layout design that is easy to accomplish with just a few lines of CSS is to center the entire contents of a web page within a browser viewport. The key is to configure a div element that contains, or "wraps," the entire page content. The HTML follows:

```
<body>
<div id="wrapper">
... page content goes here ...
</div>
</body>
```

Next, configure CSS style rules for this container. The **`margin`** is the empty space surrounding an element. In the case of the body element, the margin is the empty space between the page content and the edges of the browser window. As you might expect, the `margin-left` and `margin-right` properties configure the space in the left and right margins, respectively. The margins can be set to 0, pixel units, em units, percentages, or auto. When margin-left and margin-right are both set to auto, the browser calculates the amount of space available and divides it evenly between the left and right margins. The `width` property configures the width of a block display element. The following CSS code sample sets the width of an id named wrapper to 700 pixels and centers it:

```
#wrapper { width: 700px;
           margin-left: auto;
           margin-right: auto; }
```

You'll practice this technique in the next Hands-On Practice.

Hands-On Practice 8

In this Hands-On Practice, you will code CSS properties to configure a centered page layout, using the files from Hands-On Practice 7 as a starting point. Create a new folder called trillium2. Locate the chapter3/3.7 folder in the student files. Copy the index.html, services.html, and trillium.css files to your trillium2 folder. Open the trillium.css file in a text editor. Create an id named wrapper. Add the margin-left, margin-right, and width style properties to the style rules as follows:

```
#wrapper { margin-left: auto;
           margin-right: auto;
           width: 80%; }
```

Save the file.

Open the index.html file in a text editor. Add the HTML code to configure a div element assigned to the id wrapper that "wraps," or contains, the code within the body section. Save the file. When you test your index.html file in a browser, it should look similar to the page shown in Figure 21. The student files contain a sample solution in the chapter3/3.8 folder.

Figure 21 The page content is centered within the browser viewport

FAQ **Is there an easy way to add a comment for documentation purposes in CSS?**

Yes. An easy way to add a comment to CSS is to type "/*" before your comment and "*/" after your comment, as shown in the following example:

```
/* Configure Footer */
#footer { font-size: .80em; font-style: italic; text-align: center; }
```

10 The "Cascade"

Figure 22 shows the "cascade" (**rules of precedence**) that applies the styles in order from outermost (external styles) to innermost (HTML attributes coded on the page). This set of rules allows the sitewide styles to be configured, but overridden when needed by more granular page-specific styles (such as embedded or inline styles).

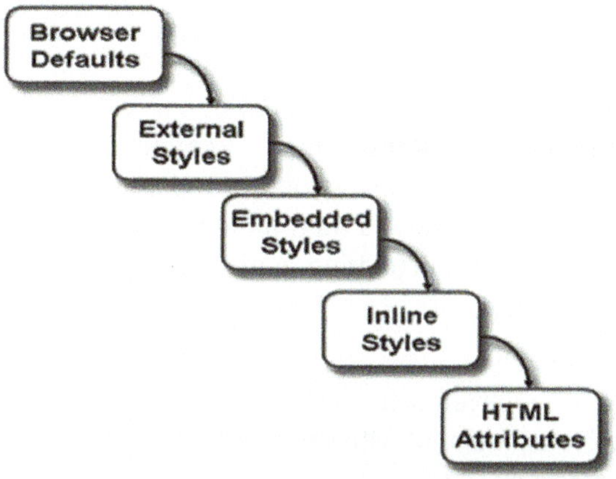

Figure 22 The "cascade" of Cascading Style Sheets

External styles can apply to multiple pages. If a web page contains both a link to an external style sheet and embedded styles, the external styles will be applied first, and then the embedded styles will be applied. This approach allows a web developer to override global external styles on selected pages.

If a web page contains both embedded styles and inline styles, the embedded styles are applied first, and then the inline styles are applied. This approach allows a web developer to override pagewide styles for particular HTML tags or classes.

Any XHTML tag or attribute will override styles. For example, a `<strong>` tag will override corresponding font-related styles configured for an element. If no attribute or style is applied to an element, the browser's default is applied. However, the appearance of the browser's default may vary by browser, and you might be disappointed with the result. Use CSS to specify the properties of your text and web page elements. Avoid depending on the browser's default.

In addition to the general cascade of CSS types described previously, the style rules themselves follow rules of precedence. Style rules applied to more local elements (such as a paragraph) take precedence over those applied to more global elements (such as a `<div>` that contains the paragraph).

Let's look at an example of the cascade. Consider the following CSS code:

```
.content { font-family: Arial, sans-serif; }
p { font-family: "Times New Roman", serif; }
```

The CSS has two style rules: a rule creating a class named `content` that configures text using the Arial (or generic sans-serif) font family, and a rule configuring all paragraphs to use the Times New Roman (or generic serif) font family. The HTML on the page contains a <div> with multiple elements, such as headings and paragraphs, as shown in the following code:

```
<div class="content">
<h1>Main Heading</h1>
<p>This is a paragraph. Notice how the paragraph is contained in
the div.</p>
</div>
```

Here is how the browser would render the code:

1. The text contained in the heading is displayed with Arial font because it is part of the <div> assigned to the `content` class. It inherits the properties from its parent (<div>) class. This is an example of **inheritance**, in which certain CSS properties are passed down to elements nested within a container element, such as a <div> or <body> element. Text-related properties (font-family, color, etc.) are generally inherited, but box-related properties (margin, padding, width, etc.) are not. See http://www.w3.org/TR/CSS21/propidx.html for a detailed list of CSS properties and their inheritance status.
2. The text contained in the paragraph is displayed with Times New Roman font because the browser applies the styles associated with the most local element (the paragraph). Even though the paragraph is contained in (and is considered a child of) the `content` class, the local paragraph style rules takes precedence and are applied by the browser.

Don't worry if CSS and rules of precedence seem a bit overwhelming at this point. CSS definitely becomes easier with practice. You will get a chance to practice with the "cascade" as you complete the next Hands-On Practice.

Hands-On Practice 9

You will experiment with the "cascade" in this Hands-On Practice as you work with a web page that uses external, embedded, and inline styles.

1. Create a new folder named mycascade.
2. Launch a text editor. Open a new file. Save the file as site.css in the mycascade folder. You will create an external style sheet that sets the `background-color` of the web page to a shade of yellow (`#FFFFCC`) and the text color to black (`#000000`). The code follows:

   ```
   body { background-color: #FFFFCC;
          color: #000000; }
   ```

   Save and close the site.css file.
3. Open a new file in the text editor, and save it as mypage1.html in the mycascade folder. The web page will be associated with the external style sheet site.css, use embedded styles to set the global text color to blue, and use inline styles to configure the text color of the

second paragraph. The file mypage1.html will contain two paragraphs of text. The code for mypage1.html follows:

```
<!DOCTYPE html>
<html lang="en">
<head>
<title>The Cascade in Action</title>
<meta charset="utf-8">
<link rel="stylesheet" href="site.css">
<style>
  body { color: #0000FF; }
</style>
</head>
<body>
<p>This paragraph applies the external and embedded styles
&mdash; note how the blue text color that is configured in
the embedded styles takes precedence over the black text color
configured in the external stylesheet.</p>
<p style="color: #FF0000">Inline styles configure this paragraph
to have red text and take precedence over the embedded and
external styles.</p>
</body>
</html>
```

Save mypage1.html, and display it in a browser. Your page should look similar to the sample shown in Figure 23. The student files contain a sample solution at chapter3/cascade/mypage1.html.

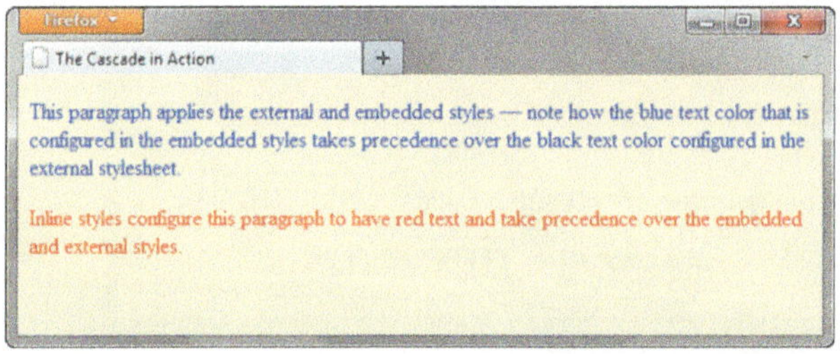

Figure 23 Mixing external, embedded, and inline styles

Take a moment to examine the mypage1.html web page and compare it with its source code. The web page picked up the yellow background from the external style sheet. The embedded style configured the text to be the color blue, which overrides the black text color in the external style sheet. The first paragraph in the web page does not contain any inline styles, so it inherits the style rules in the external and embedded style sheets. The second paragraph contains an inline style of red text color; this setting overrides the corresponding external and embedded styles.

11 CSS Validation

The W3C has a free Markup Validation Service (http://jigsaw.w3.org/css-validator) that will validate your CSS code and check it for syntax errors. **CSS validation** provides students with quick self-assessment—you can prove that your code uses correct syntax. In the working world, CSS validation serves as a quality assurance tool. Invalid code may cause browsers to render the pages more slowly than otherwise.

VideoNote
CSS Validation

Hands-On Practice 10

In this Hands-On Practice, you will use the W3C CSS Validation Service to validate an external CSS style sheet. This example uses the color.css file completed in Hands-On Practice 6 (student files chapter3/color.css). Locate color.css, and open it in a text editor. Now add an error to the color.css file By finding the body element selector style rule and deleting the first "r" in the `background-color` property. Add another error by removing the # from the `color` property value. Save the file.

Next, attempt to validate the color.css file. Visit the W3C CSS Validation Service page at http://jigsaw.w3.org/css-validator and select the "by File Upload" tab. Click the Browse button and select the color.css file from your computer. Click the Check button. Your display should be similar to that shown in Figure 24. Notice that two errors were found. The selector is listed, followed by the reason an error was noted.

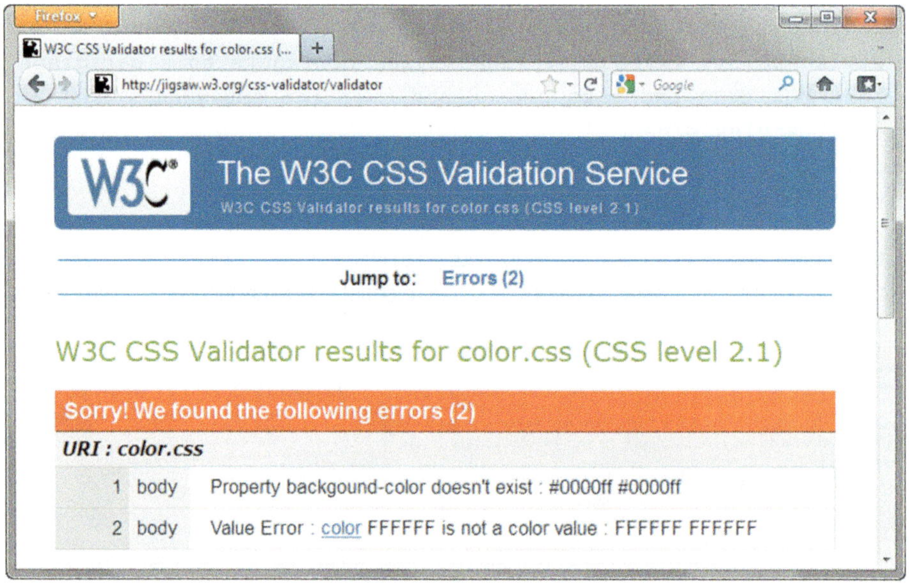

Figure 24 The validation results indicate errors

Notice that the first message in Figure 24 indicates that the "`backgound-color`" property does not exist. This is a clue to check the syntax of the property name. Edit color.css and correct the first error. Test and revalidate your page. Your browser should now look similar to the one shown in Figure 25 and should be reporting only one error.

The error reminds you that `FFFFFF` is not a color value; you are expected to already know that you need to add a `"#"` character to code a valid color value, as in `#FFFFFF`. Notice how any valid CSS rules are displayed below the error messages. Correct the color value, save the file, and test again.

Your results should look similar to those shown in Figure 26. There are no errors listed. The Valid CSS Information contains all the CSS style rules in color.css. This means your file passed

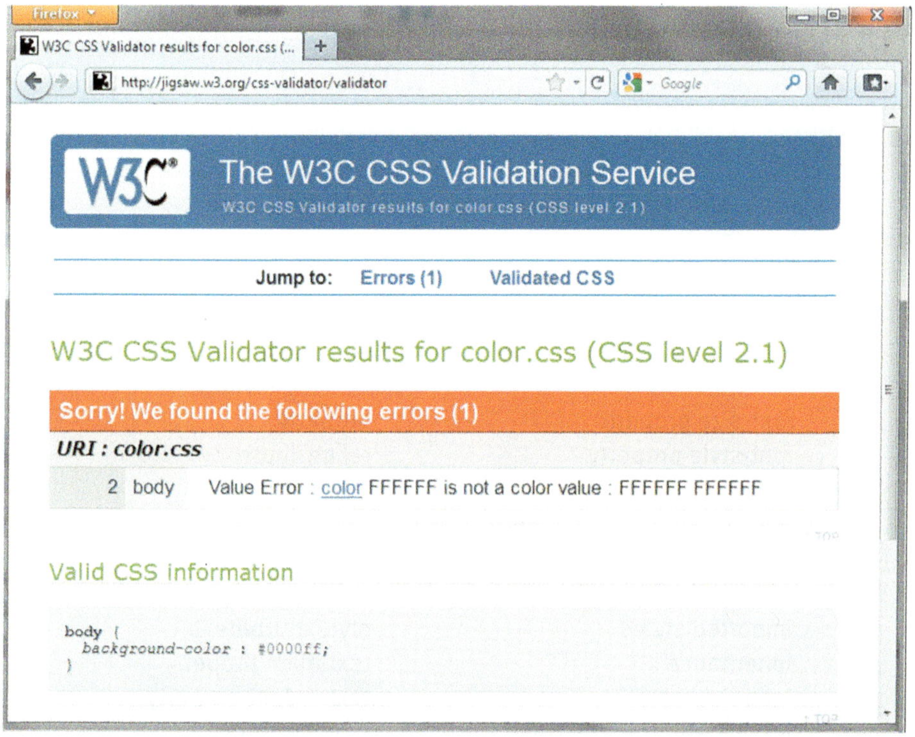

Figure 25 The valid CSS code is displayed below the errors (and warnings, if any)

the CSS validation test. Congratulations, your color.css file is valid CSS syntax! It is good practice to validate your CSS style rules. The CSS validator can help you to quickly identify code that needs to be corrected and indicate which style rules a browser is likely to consider valid. Validating CSS code is one of the many productivity techniques that web developers commonly use.

Figure 26 The CSS is valid!

Chapter Summary

This chapter has introduced Cascading Style Sheet rules associated with color and text on web pages. There is much more that you can do with CSS, including positioning, hiding and showing page areas, formatting margins, and formatting borders. As you continue your study of web development, you will learn about these additional uses. Visit this text's website at http://www.webdevfoundations.net for examples, information on the resources described in this chapter, and to view updated information.

Key Terms

<link>
<span>
<style>
background-color property
Cascading Style Sheets (CSS)
class attribute
class selector
color property
CSS validation
declaration
em unit
embedded styles
external styles
font-family property
font-size property
font-style property
font-weight property
hexadecimal color values
id attribute
id selector
imported styles
inheritance
inline styles
line-height property
margin-left property
margin-right property
pixels
point
property
rel attribute
RGB color
rule
rules of precedence
selector
style attribute
text-align property
text-indent property
type attribute
Web-Safe Color Palette
width property

Review Questions

Multiple Choice

1. Which of the following is the CSS property used to set the background color of a web page?
   a. bgcolor
   b. background-color
   c. color
   d. none of the above

2. Which type of CSS is coded in the body of the web page as an attribute of an HTML tag?
   a. embedded
   b. inline
   c. external
   d. imported

3. Which of the following describe two components of CSS rules?
   a. selectors and declarations
   b. properties and declarations
   c. selectors and attributes
   d. none of the above

4. Which of the following associates a web page with an external style sheet?
   a. `<style rel="external" href="style.css">`
   b. `<style src="style.css">`
   c. `<link rel="stylesheet" href="style.css">`
   d. `<link rel="stylesheet" src="style.css">`

5. Which of the following is the declaration property used to set the font typeface for an area of a web page?
   a. font-face
   b. face
   c. font-family
   d. size

6. Which of the following can be a CSS selector?
   a. an HTML element name
   b. a class name
   c. an id name
   d. all of the above

7. Which of the following do you configure to apply a style to only one area on a web page?
   a. group
   b. class
   c. id
   d. none of the above

8. Where do you place the code to associate a web page with an external style sheet?
   a. in the external style sheet
   b. in the DOCTYPE of the web page document
   c. in the body section of the web page document
   d. in the head section of the web page document

9. Which of the following configures a background color of #FFF8DC for a web page using CSS?
   a. `body { background-color: #FFF8DC; }`
   b. `document { background: #FFF8DC; }`
   c. `body { bgcolor: #FFF8DC;}`
   d. `document { bgcolor: #FFF8DC; }`

10. Which of the following uses CSS to configure a class called news with red text, large font, and Arial or a sans-serif font?

```
a. news { color: red;
          font-size: large;
          font-family: Arial,
          sans-serif; }
b. .news { color: red;
           font-size: large;
           font-family: Arial,
           sans-serif; }
c. .news { text: red;
           font-size: large;
           font-family: Arial,
           sans-serif; }
d. #news { text: red;
           font-size: large;
           font-family: Arial,
           sans-serif;}
```

11. Which of the following is true if a web page contains both a link to an external style sheet and embedded styles?
    a. Embedded styles will be applied first, and then the external styles will be applied.
    b. The inline styles will be used.
    c. External styles will be applied first, and then the embedded styles will be applied.
    d. The web page will not display.

Fill in the Blank

12. The ________________ element is useful for creating areas on a web page that are embedded within paragraphs or other block display elements.

13. The ________________ CSS property can be used to center text within a block display element.

14. The ________________ CSS property can be used to indent the first line of text.

15. CSS was first proposed as a standard by the W3C in ________________.

Apply Your Knowledge

1. **Predict the Result.** Draw and write a brief description of the web page that will be created with the following HTML code:

```
<!DOCTYPE html>
<html lang="en">
<head>
<title>Trillium Media Design</title>
<meta charset="utf-8">
```

```
<style>
  body { background-color: #000066;
         color: #CCCCCC;
         font-family: Arial,sans-serif; }
  h1 { background-color: #FFFFFF;
       color: #000066; }
  .footer { font-size: 80%;
            font-style: italic; }
</style>
</head>
<body>
<h1>Trillium Media Design</h1>
<div>Home <a href="about.html">About</a>
<a href="services.html">Services</a>
</div>
<p>Our professional staff takes pride in its working relationship
with our clients by offering personalized services that listen to
their needs, develop their target areas, and incorporate these
items into a website that works.</p>
<br><br>
<div class="footer">
Copyright &copy; 2012 Trillium Media Design
</div>
</body>
</html>
```

2. **Fill in the Missing Code.** Consider the following code, in which some CSS properties and values, indicated by "_", and some HTML tags, indicated by <_>, are missing:

```
<!DOCTYPE html>
<html lang="en">
<head>
<title>Trillium Media Design</title>
<meta charset="utf-8">
<style>
  body { background-color: #0066CC;
         color: "_"; }
  h1 { "_": "_" }
<_>
<_>
<body>
<h1>Trillium Media Design</h1>
   <p>Our professional staff takes pride in its working
relationship with our clients by offering personalized services
that listen to their needs, develop their target areas, and
incorporate these items into a website that works.</p>
</body>
</html>
```

The web page corresponding to the code should be configured so that the background and text colors have good contrast. The <h1> tag should use Arial. Fill in the missing code.

3. **Find the Error.** Why won't the page corresponding to the following code display properly in a browser?

```
<!DOCTYPE html>
<html lang="en">
<head>
<title>Trillium Media Design</title>
<meta charset="utf-8">
<style>
  body { background-color: #000066;
         color: #CCCCCC;
         font-family: Arial,sans-serif;
         font-size: 1.2em; }
<style>
</head>
<body>
<h1>Trillium Media Design</h1>
   <p>Our professional staff takes pride in its working
relationship with our clients by offering personalized services
that listen to their needs, develop their target areas, and
incorporate these items into a website that works.</p>
</body>
</html>
```

Hands-On Exercises

1. Write the HTML for a paragraph that uses inline styles to configure the background color of red and the text color of white.
2. Write the HTML and CSS code for an embedded style sheet that configures a background color of `#eaeaea` and a text color of `#000033`.
3. Write the CSS code for an external style sheet that configures the text to be brown, 1.2em in size, and in Arial, Verdana, or a sans-serif font.
4. Write the HTML and CSS code for an embedded style sheet that configures a class called new that is bold and italic.
5. Write the HTML and CSS code for an embedded style sheet that configures links without underlines; a background color of white; text color of black; is in Arial, Helvetica, or a sans-serif font; and has a class called new that is bold and italic.
6. Write the CSS code for an external style sheet that configures a page background color of `#FFF8DC`; has a text color of `#000099`; is in Arial, Helvetica, or a sans-serif font; and has an id called new that is bold and italic.

7. **Practice with External Style Sheets.** In this exercise, you will create two external style sheet files and a web page. You will experiment with linking the web page to the external style sheets and note how the display of the page is changed.
   a. Create an external style sheet (call it format1.css) to format as follows: document background color of white, document text color of `#000099`, and document font family of Arial, Helvetica, or sans-serif. Hyperlinks should have a background color of gray (`#cccccc`). Configure the h1 selector to use the Times New Roman font with red text color.
   b. Create an external style sheet (call it format2.css) to format as follows: document background color of yellow and document text color of green. Hyperlinks should have a background color of white. Configure the h1 selector to use the Times New Roman font with white background color and green text color.
   c. Create a web page about your favorite movie that displays the movie name in an `<h1>` tag, a description of the movie in a paragraph, and an unordered (bulleted) list of the main actors and actresses in the movie. The page should also have a hyperlink to a website about the movie. Place an e-mail link to yourself on the web page. This page should be associated with the format1.css file. Save the page as moviecss1.html. Be sure to test your page in more than one browser. Modify the moviecss1.html page to link to the format2.css external style sheet instead of the format1.css file. Save the page as moviecss2.html and test it in a browser. Notice how different the page looks!

8. **Practice with the Cascade.** In this exercise, you will create two web pages that link to the same external style sheet. After modifying the configuration in the external style sheet, you will test your pages again and find that they automatically pick up the new style configuration. Finally, you will add an inline style to one of the pages and find that it takes effect and overrides the external style.
   a. Create a web page that includes an unordered list describing at least three advantages of using CSS. The text "CSS Advantages" should be contained within `<h1>` tags. This page should include a hyperlink to the W3C website. Write the HTML code so that one of the advantages is configured to be a class called news. Place an e-mail link to yourself on the web page. The web page should be associated with the external style sheet called ex8.css. Save the page as advantage.html.
   b. Create an external style sheet (call it ex8.css) to format as follows: document background color of white; document text color of `#000099`; and document font family of Arial, Helvetica, or sans-serif. Hyperlinks should have a background color of gray (`#cccccc`). `<h1>` elements should use the Times New Roman font with black text color. The news class should use red italic text.
   c. Launch a browser, and test your work. Display the advantage.html page. It should use the formatting configured in ex8.css. Modify the web page or the CSS file until your page displays as requested.
   d. Change the configuration of the external style sheet (ex8.css) to use a document background color of black, document text color of white, and `<h1>` text color of gray (`#cccccc`). Save the file. Launch a browser, and test the advantage.html page. Notice how it picks up the new styles from the external style sheet.
   e. Modify the advantage.html file to use an inline style. The inline style should be applied to the `<h1>` tag and configure it to have red text. Save the advantage.

html page, and test in a browser. Notice how the <h1> text color specified in the style sheet is overridden by the inline style.

9. **Practice Validating CSS.** Choose a CSS external style sheet file to validate; perhaps you have created one for your own website. Otherwise, use an external style sheet file that you worked with in this chapter. Use the W3C CSS validator at http://jigsaw.w3.org/css-validator. If your CSS does not immediately pass the validation test, modify it and test again. Repeat this process until the W3C validates your CSS code. Write a one- or two-paragraph summary about the validation process that answers the following questions: Was the CSS validator easy to use? Did anything surprise you? Did you encounter a number of errors or just a few? How easy was it to determine how to correct the CSS file? Would you recommend the validator to other students? Why or why not?

Web Research

1. This chapter has introduced you to using CSS to configure web pages. Use a search engine to find CSS resources. The following resources can help you get started:
   - http://www.w3.org/Style/CSS
   - http://positioniseverything.net
   - http://www.dezwozhere.com/links.html

   Create a web page that provides a list of at least five CSS resources on the Web. For each CSS resource, provide the URL, website name, and a brief description. Configure text and background colors with good contrast. Place your name in the e-mail address at the bottom of the web page.

2. There is still much for you to learn about CSS. A great place to learn about web technology is the Web itself. Use a search engine to search for CSS tutorials. The following resources can help you get started:
   - http://www.echoecho.com/css.htm
   - http://www.w3schools.com/css
   - http://www.davesite.com/webstation/css

   Choose a tutorial that is easy to read. Select a section that discusses a CSS technique that was not covered in this chapter. Create a web page that uses this new technique. The web page should provide the URL of your tutorial, the name of the website, and a description of the new technique you discovered. Place your name in the e-mail address at the bottom of the web page.

Focus on Web Design

In this chapter, you have learned how to configure color and text with CSS. In this activity, you will design a color scheme, code an external CSS file for the color scheme, and code an example web page that applies the styles you configured. Use any of the following sites to help you get started with color and web design ideas:

Psychology of Color

- http://www.infoplease.com/spot/colors1.html
- http://www.sensationalcolor.com/meanings.html
- http://designfestival.com/the-psychology-of-color
- http://www.designzzz.com/infographic-psychology-color-web-designers

Color Theory

- http://www.colormatters.com/colortheory.html
- http://colortheory.liquisoft.com/
- http://www.digital-web.com/articles/color_theory_for_the_colorblind

Color Scheme Generators

- http://meyerweb.com/eric/tools/color-blend
- http://colorschemer.com/schemes
- http://www.colr.org
- http://colorsontheweb.com/colorwizard.asp
- http://kuler.adobe.com
- http://colorschemedesigner.com

Complete the following tasks:

a. Design a color scheme. List three hexadecimal color values in addition to neutral colors such as white (`#FFFFFF`) or black (`#000000`) in your design.

b. Describe the process you went through as you selected the colors. Describe why you chose these colors. What type of website would they be appropriate for? List the URLs of any resources you used.

c. Create an external CSS file named color1.css that configures font properties, text color, and background color selections for the document, h1 element selector, p element selector, and footer class, using the colors you have chosen.

d. Create a web page named color1.html that shows examples of the CSS style rules.

WEBSITE CASE STUDY

Implementing CSS

JavaJam Coffee House

Figure 25 in this chapter shows a site map for the JavaJam website. You will develop a new version of the website that uses an external style sheet to configure text and color. Figure 26 in this chapter depicts the wireframe page layout.

You have the following tasks:

1. Create a new folder for this JavaJam case study.
2. Create an external style sheet named javajam.css that configures the color and text for the JavaJam website.
3. Modify the Home page to utilize an external style sheet to configure colors and fonts. The new Home page and color swatches are shown in Figure 27.
4. Modify the Menu page to be consistent with the new Home page.
5. Configure centered page layout.

Figure 27 New JavaJam index.html

Hands-On Practice Case

Task 1: Create a folder on your hard drive or portable storage device called javajamcss. Copy all the files from your Chapter 2 javajam folder into the javajamcss folder.

Task 2: The External Style Sheet. You will use a text editor to create an external style sheet named javajam.css. Code the CSS to configure the following:

1. Global styles for the document (use the body element selector) with background color `#ffffcc`; text color `#330000`; and Verdana, Arial, or any sans-serif font.
2. Styles for the h1 element selector that configure background color `#ccaa66`, text color `#000000`, `200%` line height, and centered text.
3. Styles for the navigation area (use an id named `nav`) that configure centered text. *Hint*: Use the CSS `text-align` property.
4. Styles for the page footer area (use an id named `footer`) that configure background color `#ccaa66`, text color `#000000`, small font size `(.60em)`, italics, and centered text.

Save the file as javajam.css in the javajamcss folder. Check your syntax with the CSS validator (http://jigsaw.w3.org/css-validator). Correct and retest if necessary.

Task 3: The Home Page. Launch a text editor, and open the index.html file. You will modify this file to apply styles from the javajam.css external style sheet as follows:

1. Add a `<link>` element to associate the web page with the javajam.css external style sheet file. Save and test your index.html page in a browser and you'll notice that the styles configured with the body and h1 element selectors are already applied!
2. Configure the navigation area. Assign the div that contains the navigation to the id named `nav`. *Hint*: `<div id="nav">`.
3. Configure the page footer area. Remove the `<small>` and `<i>` elements, because the `font-size` and `font-style` are configured as part of the footer id. Assign the div that contains the footer information to the id named `footer`.

Save the index.html file, and test it in a browser. Your page should look similar to the one shown in Figure 27 except that your page content will be left-aligned instead of centered. Don't worry—you'll center your page layout in Task 5 of this case study.

Task 4: The Menu Page. Launch a text editor, and open the menu.html file. You will modify this file in a similar manner as you modified the home page: Add the `<link>` element, configure the navigation area, and configure the page footer area. Save and test your new menu.html page. It should look similar to the one shown in Figure 28, except for the alignment.

Task 5: Center Page Layout with CSS. Modify javajam.css, index.html, and menu.html to configure page content that is centered with `80%` width (refer to Hands-On Practice 8 if necessary):

1. Launch a text editor, and open the javajam.css file. Add a style rule for an id named wrapper with `width` set to `80%`, `margin-right` set to auto, and `margin-left` set to auto.
2. Launch a text editor, and open the index.html file. Add the HTML code to configure a div element assigned to the id `wrapper` that "wraps," or contains, the code within the body section. Save and test your index.html page in a browser and you'll notice that the page content is now centered within the browser viewport as shown in Figure 27.
3. Launch a text editor, and open the menu.html file. Add the HTML code to configure a div element assigned to the id `wrapper` that "wraps," or contains, the code within the body section. Save and test your menu.html page in a browser and you'll notice that the page content is now centered within the browser viewport as shown in Figure 28.

Experiment with modifying the javajam.css file. Change the page background color, the font family, and so on. Test your pages in a browser. Isn't it amazing how a change in a single file can affect multiple files when external style sheets are used?

Fish Creek Animal Hospital

Figure 29 in this chapter shows a site map for the Fish Creek website. The Home page and Services page were created in the chapter "HTML Basics". You will develop a new version that uses an external style sheet to configure text and color. Figure 30 in this chapter depicts the wireframe page layout.

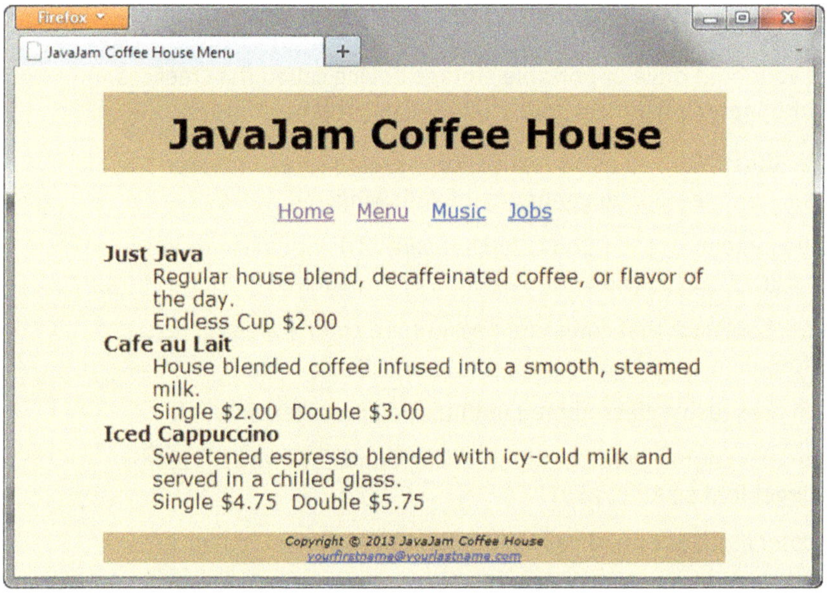

Figure 28
New menu.html page

You have the following tasks:

1. Create a new folder for this Fish Creek case study.
2. Create an external style sheet named fishcreek.css that configures the color and text for the Fish Creek website.
3. Modify the Home page to utilize an external style sheet to configure colors and fonts. The new Home page and color swatches are shown in Figure 29.
4. Modify the Services page to be consistent with the new Home page.
5. Configure centered page layout.

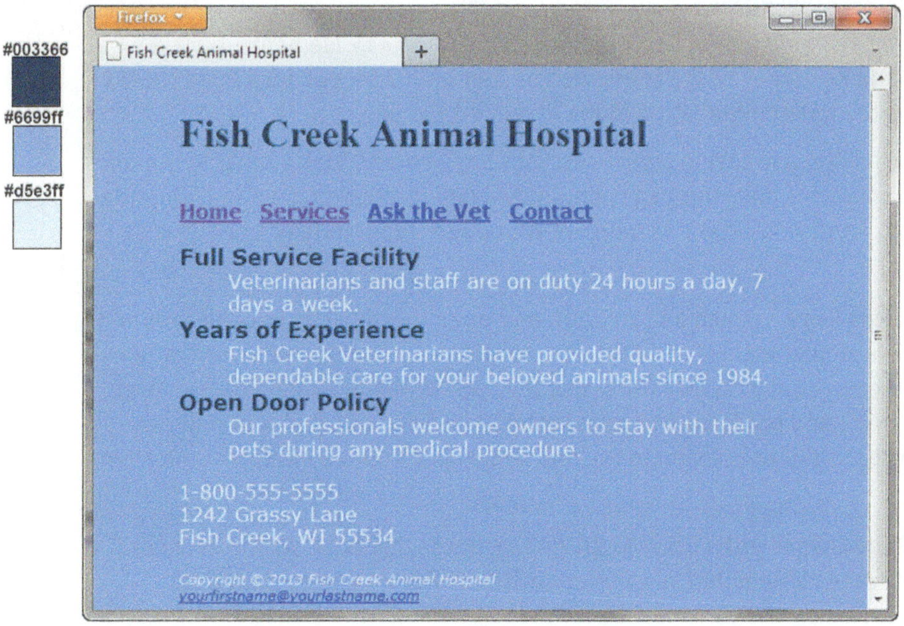

Figure 29
New Fish Creek index.html

Hands-On Practice Case Study

Task 1: Create a folder on your hard drive or portable storage device called fishcreekcss. Copy all the files from your Chapter 2 fishcreek folder into the fishcreekcss folder.

Task 2: The External Style Sheet. You will use a text editor to create an external style sheet named fishcreek.css. Code the CSS to configure the following:

1. Global styles for the document (use the body element selector) with background color `#6699ff`; text color `#d5e3ff`; and Verdana, Arial, or any sans-serif font.
2. Styles for the h1 element selector that configure background color `#6699ff`, text color `#003366`, serif font, and `200%` line height.
3. Styles for a navigation area (use a class named `nav`) that displays text in bold.
4. Styles for a class named `category` with bold font, background color `#6699ff`, text color `#003366`, and larger font size `(1.1em)`.
5. Styles for the page footer area (use an id named `footer`) with a small font size `(.70em)` and italic text.

Save the file as fishcreek.css in the fishcreekcss folder. Check your syntax with the CSS validator (http://jigsaw.w3.org/css-validator). Correct and retest if necessary.

Task 3: The Home Page. Launch a text editor, and open the index.html file. You will modify this file to apply styles from the fishcreek.css external style sheet as follows:

1. Add a `<link>` element to associate the web page with the fishcreek.css external style sheet file. Save and test your index.html page in a browser and you'll notice that the styles configured with the body and h1 element selectors are already applied!
2. Configure the navigation area. Assign the div that contains the navigation to the class named `nav`. *Hint*: `<div class="nav">`. Remove the `<b>` element from the navigation area, because the CSS will configure the bold font style.
3. Configure each `<dt>` element to apply the `category` class. *Hint*: `<dt class="category">`. Remove the `<strong>` elements, because the CSS will configure the bold font style.
4. Configure the page footer area. Remove the `<small>` and `<i>` elements, because the `font-size` and `font-style` are configured as part of the `footer` id. Assign the div that contains the footer information to the id named `footer`.

Save the index.html file, and test in a browser. Your page should look similar to the one shown in Figure 29 except that your page content will be left-aligned instead of indented from the margins. Don't worry—you'll configure your page layout in Task 5 of this case study.

Task 4: The Services Page. Launch a text editor, and open the services.html file. You will modify this file in a similar manner: Add the `<link>` element, configure the navigation area, configure the `category` classes (*Hint*: Use the `<span>` tag to contain the name of each service offered), and configure the page footer area. Save and test your new services.html page. It should look similar to the one shown in Figure 28 except for the alignment.

Task 5: Center Page Layout with CSS. Modify fishcreek.css, index.html, and services.html to configure page content that is centered with `80%` width. Refer to Hands-On Practice 8 if necessary.

1. Launch a text editor, and open the fishcreek.css file. Add a style rule for an id named wrapper with `width` set to `80%`, `margin-right` set to auto, and `margin-left` set to auto.
2. Launch a text editor, and open the index.html file. Add the HTML code to configure a div element assigned to the id `wrapper` that "wraps," or contains, the code within the body section. Save and test your index.html page in a browser and you'll notice that the page content is now centered within the browser viewport as shown in Figure 29.
3. Launch a text editor, and open the services.html file. Add the HTML code to configure a div element assigned to the id `wrapper` that "wraps," or contains, the code within the body section. Save and test your services.html page in a browser and you'll notice that the page content is now centered within the browser viewport as shown in Figure 30.

Experiment with modifying the fishcreek.css file. Change the page background color, the font family, and so on. Test your pages in a browser. Isn't it amazing how a change in a single file can affect multiple files when external style sheets are used?

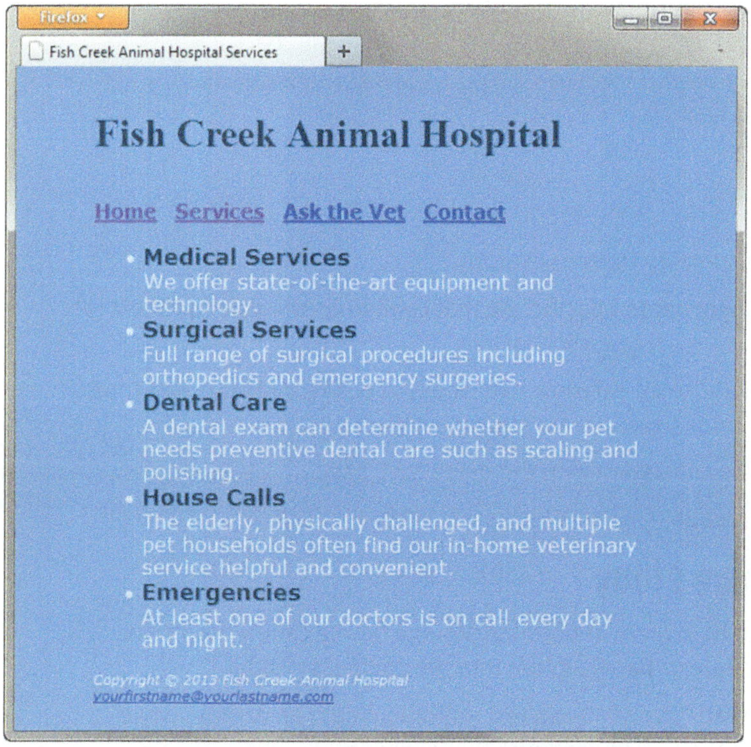

Figure 30 New services.html page

Pacific Trails Resort

Figure 33 in this chapter" shows a site map for the Pacific Trails Resort website. The Home page and Yurts page were created in the chapter "HTML Basics". You will develop a new version of this website that uses an external style sheet to configure text and color. Figure 34 in this chapter depicts the wireframe page layout.

Figure 31 New Pacific Trails index.html

You have the following tasks:

1. Create a new folder for this Pacific Trails case study.
2. Create an external style sheet named pacific.css that configures the color and text for the Pacific Trails website.
3. Modify the Home page to utilize an external style sheet to configure colors and fonts. The new Home page and color swatches are shown in Figure 31.
4. Modify the Yurts page to be consistent with the new Home page.
5. Configure centered page layout.

Hands-On Practice Case Study

Task 1: Create a folder on your hard drive or portable storage device called pacificcss. Copy all the files from your Chapter 2 pacific folder into the pacificcss folder.

Task 2: The External Style Sheet. You will use a text editor to create an external style sheet named pacific.css. Code the CSS to configure the following:

1. Global styles for the document (use the body element selector) with background color `#FFFFFF`; text color `#666666`. and Verdana, Arial, or any sans-serif font.
2. Styles for the h1 element selector that configure background color `#000033`, text color `#FFFFFF`, `200%` line height, and Georgia or any serif font.
3. Styles for a navigation area (use an id named `nav`) that displays text in bold and has a sky-blue background color `(#90C7E3)`.
4. Styles for the h2 element selector that configure medium-blue text color `(#3399CC)` and Georgia or any serif font.

5. Styles for the dt element selector that configure dark-blue text color (`#000033`).
6. Styles for a class named `resort` that configure dark-blue text color (`#000033`) and `1.2em` font size.
7. Styles for the page footer area (use an id named `footer`) with a small font size (`.70em`) and italic, centered text.

Save the file as pacific.css in the pacificcss folder. Check your syntax with the CSS validator (http://jigsaw.w3.org/css-validator). Correct and retest if necessary.

Task 3: The Home Page. Launch a text editor, and open the index.html file. You will modify this file to apply styles from the pacific.css external style sheet as follows:

1. Add a `<link>` element to associate the web page with the pacific.css external style sheet file. Save and test your index.html page in a browser and you'll notice that the styles configured with the body, h1, and h2 element selectors are already applied!
2. Configure the navigation area. Assign the div that contains the navigation to the id named `nav`. *Hint*: `<div id="nav">`. Remove the `<b>` element from the navigation area, because the CSS will configure the bold font weight.
3. Find the company name ("Pacific Trails Resort") in the first paragraph below the h2. Configure a span that contains this text. Assign the span tag to the `resort` class.
4. Configure the page footer area. Remove the `<small>` and `<i>` elements, because the `font-size` and `font-style` are configured as part of the footer id. Assign the div that contains the footer information to the id named `footer`.

Save the index.html file, and test in a browser. Your page should look similar to the one shown in Figure 31 except that your page content will be left-aligned instead of indented from the margins. Don't worry—you'll configure your page layout in Task 5 of this case study.

Task 4: The Yurts Page. Launch a text editor, and open the yurts.html file. You will modify this file in a similar manner: Add the `<link>` element, configure the navigation area, and configure the page footer area. Save and test your new yurts.html page. It should look similar to the one shown in Figure 32 except for the alignment.

Task 5: Center Page Layout with CSS. Modify pacific.css, index.html, and yurts.html to configure page content that is centered with `80%` width. Refer to Hands-On Practice 8 if necessary.

1. Launch a text editor, and open the pacific.css file. Add a style rule for an id named wrapper with `width` set to `80%`, `margin-right` set to auto, and `margin-left` set to auto.
2. Launch a text editor, and open the index.html file. Add the HTML code to configure a div element assigned to the id `wrapper` that "wraps," or contains, the code within the body section. Save and test your index.html page in a browser and you'll notice that the page content is now centered within the browser viewport as shown in Figure 31.
3. Launch a text editor and open the yurts.html file. Add the HTML code to configure a div element assigned to the id `wrapper` that "wraps," or contains, the code within the body section. Save and test your yurts.html page in a browser and you'll notice

that the page content is now centered within the browser viewport as shown in Figure 32.

Experiment with modifying the pacific.css file. Change the page background color, the font family, and so on. Test your pages in a browser. Isn't it amazing how a change in a single file can affect multiple files when external style sheets are used?

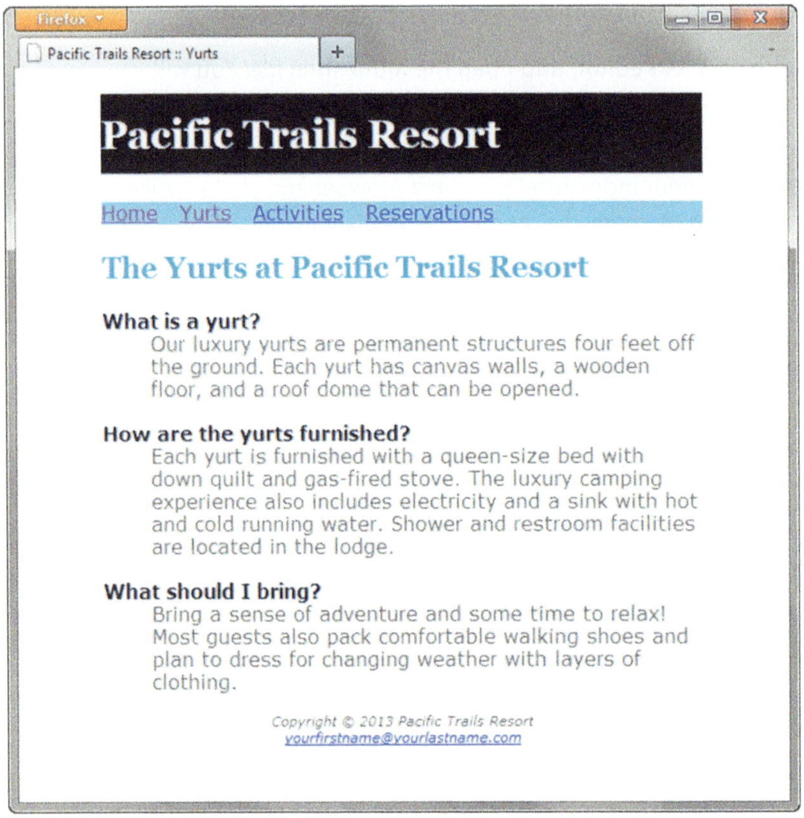

Figure 32 New yurts.html page

Prime Properties

Figure 37 in this chapter shows a site map for the Prime Properties website. The Home page and Financing page were created in the chapter "HTML Basics". You will develop a new version of this website that uses an external style sheet to configure text and color. Figure 38 in this chapter depicts the wireframe page layout.

You have the following tasks:

1. Create a new folder for this Prime Properties case study.
2. Create an external style sheet named prime.css that configures the color and text for the Prime Properties website.
3. Modify the Home page to utilize an external style sheet to configure colors and fonts. The new Home page and color swatches are shown in Figure 33.
4. Modify the Financing page to be consistent with the new Home page.
5. Configure centered page layout.

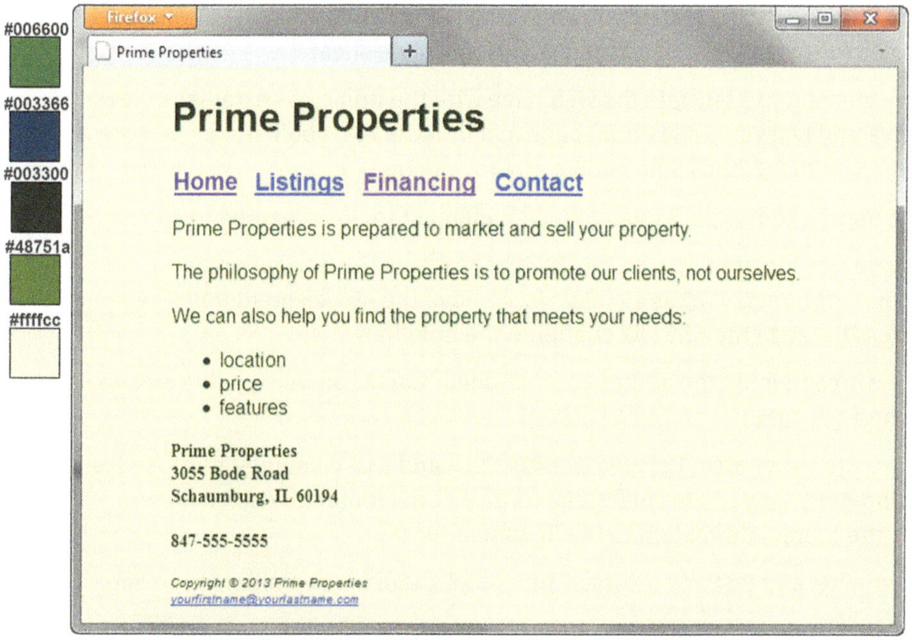

Figure 33 New Prime Properties index.html

Hands-On Practice Case Study

Task 1: Create a folder on your hard drive or portable storage device called primecss. Copy all the files from your Chapter 2 prime folder into the primecss folder.

Task 2: The External Style Sheet. You will use a text editor to create an external style sheet named prime.css. Code the CSS to configure the following:

1. Global styles for the document (use the body element selector) with background color `#ffffcc`; text color `#003300`; and Arial, Helvetica, or any sans-serif font.
2. Styles for the h2 element selector that configure background color `#ffffcc` and text color `#003366`.
3. Styles for the h3 element selector that configure background color `#ffffcc` and text color `#006600`.
4. Styles for the dd element selector that configure italics, font size smaller than the default (`.90em`), and `200%` line height.
5. Styles for an id named `header` that configure background color `#ffffcc` and text color `#48751A`.
6. Styles for a navigation area (use a class named `nav`) that displays text in bold, large (`1.2em`) font.
7. Styles for a class named `contact` that configure boldface, font size smaller than the default (`.90em`), and Times New Roman or any serif font.
8. Styles for the page footer area (use an id named `footer`) with small font size (`.60em`) and italic text.

Save the file as prime.css in the primecss folder. Check your syntax with the CSS validator (http://jigsaw.w3.org/css-validator). Correct and retest if necessary.

Task 3: The Home Page. Launch a text editor, and open the index.html file. You will modify this file to apply styles from the prime.css external style sheet.

1. Add a `<link>` element to associate the web page with the prime.css external style sheet file. Save and test your index.html page in a browser and you'll notice that the styles configured with the body selector are already applied!
2. Configure the logo header area. Assign the `<h1>` element to the id named `header`.
3. Configure the navigation area. Assign the div that contains the navigation to the class named `nav`. *Hint*: `<div class="nav">`. Remove the `<b>` element from the navigation area, because the CSS will configure the bold font style.
4. Configure the div containing the address and phone information. Assign this area to the class named `contact`.
5. Configure the page footer area. Remove the `<small>` and `<i>` elements, because the `font-size` and `font-style` are configured as part of the footer id. Assign the div that contains the footer information to the id named footer.

Save the index.html file, and test in a browser. Your page should look similar to the one shown in Figure 33.

Task 4: The Financing Page. Launch a text editor, and open the financing.html file. You will modify this file in a similar manner: Add the `<link>` element, configure the logo header area, configure the navigation area, and configure the page footer area. Save and test your new financing.html page. It should look similar to the one shown in Figure 34.

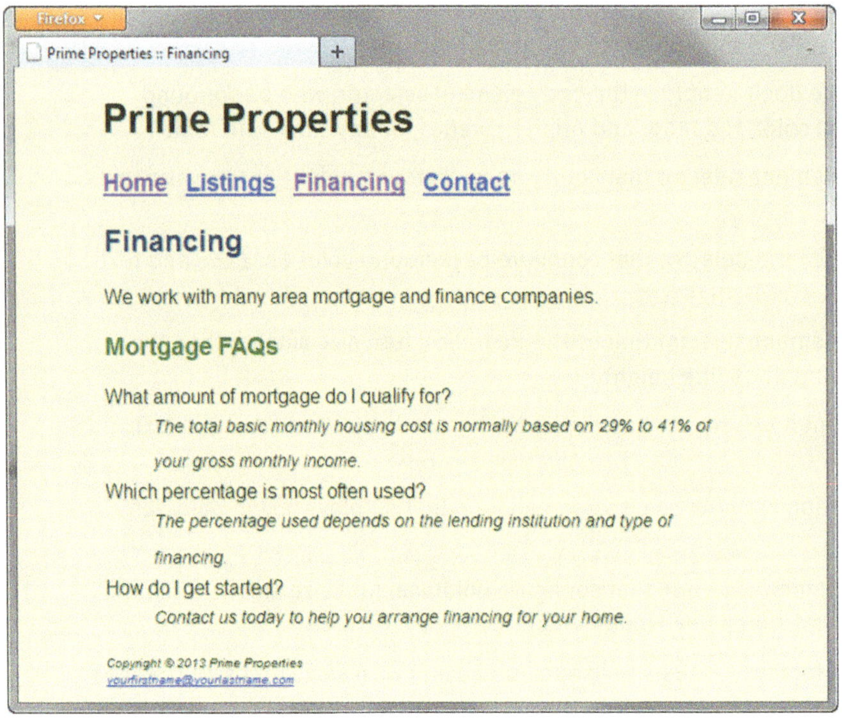

Figure 34 New financing.html page

Task 5: Center Page Layout with CSS. Modify prime.css, index.html, and financing.html to configure page content that is centered with `80%` width. Refer to Hands-On Practice 8 if necessary.

1. Launch a text editor, and open the prime.css file. Add a style rule for an id named `wrapper` with `width` set to `80%`, `margin-right` set to auto, and `margin-left` set to auto.
2. Launch a text editor, and open the index.html file. Add the HTML code to configure a div element assigned to the id `wrapper` that "wraps," or contains, the code within the body section. Save and test your index.html page in a browser and you'll notice that the page content is now centered within the browser viewport as shown in Figure 33.
3. Launch a text editor, and open the financing.html file. Add the HTML code to configure a div element assigned to the id `wrapper` that "wraps," or contains, the code within the body section. Save and test your financing.html page in a browser and you'll notice that the page content is now centered within the browser viewport as shown in Figure 34.

Experiment with modifying the prime.css file. Change the page background color, the font family, and so on. Test your pages in a browser. Notice how a change in a single file can affect multiple files when external style sheets are used.

Answers

Checkpoint 1

1. Reasons to use CSS on a web page include the following: greater control of typography and page layout, separation of style from structure, potentially smaller web page documents, and easier site maintenance.
2. Because visitors may set their browsers to certain colors, it is a good idea when changing a text or background color to configure both the text color and the background color properties to provide good contrast between text and background.
3. Embedded styles are coded once in the header section of the web page and apply to the entire page. This practice is more efficient than using inline styles to code individual styles on HTML elements.

Checkpoint 2

1. Embedded styles can be used to configure the text and color formatting for an entire web page. Embedded styles are placed in the head section of a web page. The `<style>` tag is used to contain the CSS selectors and properties that configure the embedded styles.
2. External styles can be used to configure the text and color formatting for some or all of the pages on a website in one file. This single file can be changed, and all the web pages associated with it will display the new styles the next time they

are rendered in a browser. External styles are placed in a separate text file that uses a .css file extension. Web pages use the `<link>` tag to indicate that they are using an external style sheet.

3. `<link rel="stylesheet" href="mystyles.css">`

Review Questions

1. b
2. b
3. a
4. c
5. c
6. d
7. c
8. d
9. a
10. b
11. c
12. span
13. text-align
14. text-indent
15. 1996

Credits

All photographs except those noted below © Terry Ann Morris

"Checkpoint" icon (green check mark), "Web Site Case Study" icon (blue "WWW"), "FAQ" icon (orange caption bubble)

"Hands-On Practice" icon (green hand); empty green, yellow, purple, red, and blue icons © Piotr M./Fotolia LLC

Figures 24, 25, 26, © W3C (World Wide Web Consortium)

CSS Property Reference

Commonly Used CSS Properties

Property	Description
`background`	Shorthand to configure all the background properties of an element Value: `background-color background-image background-repeat background-position`
`background-attachment`	Configures a background image as fixed in place or scrolling Value: `scroll` (default) or `fixed`
`background-clip`	CSS3; configures the area to display the background Value: `border-box`, `padding-box`, or `content-box`
`background-color`	Configures the background color of an element Value: Valid color value
`background-image`	Configures a background image for an element Value: `url` (*file name or path to the image*), `none` (default) Optional new CSS3 functions: `linear-gradient()` and `radial-gradient()`
`background-origin`	CSS3; configures the background positioning area Value: `padding-box`, `border-box`, or `content-box`
`background-position`	Configures the position of a background image Value: Two percentages, pixel values, or position values (`left`, `top`, `center`, `bottom`, `right`)
`background-repeat`	Configures how the background image will be repeated Value: `repeat` (default), `repeat-y`, `repeat-x`, or `no-repeat`
`background-size`	CSS3; configures the size of the background images Value: Numeric value (px or em), percentage, `contain`, `cover`
`border`	Shorthand to configure the border of an element Value: `border-width border-style border-color`
`border-bottom`	Configures the bottom border of an element Value: `border-width border-style border-color`
`border-collapse`	Configures the display of borders in a table Value: `separate` (default) or `collapse`

(*Continued*)

Property	Description
border-color	Configures the border color of an element Value: Valid color value
border-image	CSS3; configures an image in the border of an element See http://www.w3.org/TR/css3-background#the-border-image
border-left	Configures the left border of an element Value: border-width border-style border-color
border-radius	CSS3; configures rounded corners Value: One to four numeric values (px or em) or percentages that configure the radius of the corners. If a single value is provided, it configures all four corners. The corners are configured in order of top left, top right, bottom right, and bottom left. Related properties: border-top-left-radius, border-top-right-radius, border-bottom-left-radius, and border-bottom-right-radius
border-right	Configures the right border of an element Value: border-width border-style border-color
border-spacing	Configures the space between table cells in a table Value: Numeric value (px or em)
border-style	Configures the style of the borders around an element Value: none (default), inset, outset, double, groove, ridge, solid, dashed, or dotted
border-top	Configures the top border of an element Value: border-width border-style border-color
border-width	Configures the width of an element's border Value: numeric pixel value (such as 1px), thin, medium, or thick
bottom	Configures the offset position from the bottom of a containing element Value: Numeric value (px or em), percentage, or auto (default)
box-shadow	CSS3; configures a drop shadow on an element Values: Three or four numerical values (px or em) to indicate horizontal offset, vertical offset, blur radius, spread distance (optional), and a valid color value. Use the inset keyword to configure an inner shadow.
caption-side	Configures the placement of a table caption Value: top (default) or bottom
clear	Configures the display of an element in relation to floating elements Value: none (default), left, right, or both
color	Configures the color of text within an element Value: Valid color value
display	Configures how and whether an element will display Value: inline, none, block, list-item, table, table-row, or table-cell
float	Configures the horizontal placement (left or right) of an element Value: none (default), left, or right
font-family	Configures the font typeface of text Value: List of valid font names or generic font family names
font-size	Configures the font size of text Value: Numeric value (px, pt, em) percentage value, xx-small, x-small, small, medium (default), large, x-large, xx-large, smaller, or larger
font-stretch	CSS3; configures a normal, condensed, or expanded face from a font family Value: normal (default), wider, narrower, condensed, semi-condensed, expanded, or ultra-expanded
font-style	Configures the font style of text Value: normal (default), italic, or oblique

Property	Description
font-variant	Configures whether text is displayed in small-caps font Value: normal (default) or small-caps
font-weight	Configures the weight (boldness) of text Value: normal (default), bold, bolder, lighter, 100, 200, 300, 400, 500, 600, 700, 800, or 900
height	Configures the height of an element Value: Numeric value (px or em), percentage, or auto (default)
left	Configures the offset position from the left of a containing element Value: Numeric value (px or em), percentage, or auto (default)
letter-spacing	Configures the space between text characters Value: Numeric value (px or em) or normal (default)
line-height	Configures the line height of the text Value: Numeric value (px or em), percentage, multiplier numeric value, or normal (default)
list-style	Shorthand to configure the properties of a list Value: list-style-type list-style-position list-style-image
list-style-image	Configures an image as a list marker Value: url (*file name or path to the image*) or none (default)
list-style-position	Configures the position of the list markers Value: inside or outside (default)
list-style-type	Configures the type of list marker displayed Value: none, circle, disc (default), square, decimal, decimal-leading-zero, Georgian, lower-alpha, lower-roman, upper-alpha, or upper-roman
margin	Shorthand to configure the margin of an element Value: One to four numeric values (px or em) or percentages, auto, or 0
margin-bottom	Configures the bottom margin of an element Value: Numeric value (px or em), percentage, auto, or 0
margin-left	Configures the left margin of an element Value: Numeric value (px or em), percentage, auto, or 0
margin-right	Configures the right margin of an element Value: Numeric value (px or em), percentage, auto, or 0
margin-top	Configures the top margin of an element Value: Numeric value (px or em), percentage, auto, or 0
max-height	Configures the maximum height of an element Value: Numeric value (px or em), percentage, or none (default)
max-width	Configures the maximum width of an element Value: Numeric value (px or em), percentage, or none (default)
min-height	Configures the minimum height of an element Value: Numeric value (px or em), percentage, or none (default)
min-width	Configures the minimum width of an element Value: Numeric value (px or em), percentage, or none (default)
opacity	CSS3; configures the transparency of an element and its child elements Value: Numeric value between 1 (fully opaque) and 0 (completely transparent)
overflow	Configures how content should display if it is too large for the area allocated Value: visible (default), hidden, auto, or scroll
padding	Shorthand to configure the padding of an element Value: One to four numeric values (px or em) or percentages, or 0

(Continued)

Property	Description
`padding-bottom`	Configures the bottom padding of an element Value: Numeric value (px or em), percentage, or 0
`padding-left`	Configures the left padding of an element Value: Numeric value (px or em), percentage, or 0
`padding-right`	Configures the right padding of an element Value: Numeric value (px or em), percentage, or 0
`padding-top`	Configures the top padding of an element Value: Numeric value (px or em), percentage, or 0
`page-break-after`	Configures the page break after an element Value: `auto` (default), `always`, `avoid`, `left`, or `right`
`page-break-before`	Configures the page break before an element Value: `auto` (default), `always`, `avoid`, `left`, or `right`
`page-break-inside`	Configures the page break inside an element Value: `auto` (default) or `avoid`
`position`	Configures the type of positioning used to display an element Value: `static` (default), `absolute`, `fixed`, or `relative`
`right`	Configures the offset position from the right of a containing element Value: Numeric value (px or em), percentage, or `auto` (default)
`text-align`	Configures the horizontal alignment of text within an element Value: `left` (default), `right`, `center`, or `justify`
`text-decoration`	Configures the decoration added to text Value: `none` (default), `underline`, `overline`, `line-through`, or `blink`
`text-indent`	Configures the indentation of the first line of text Value: Numeric value (px or em) or percentage
`text-outline`	CSS3; configures an outline around text displayed within an element Value: One or two numerical values (px or em) to indicate thickness and (optionally) blur radius, and a valid color value
`text-shadow`	CSS3; configures a drop shadow on the text displayed within an element Values: Three or four numerical values (px or em) to indicate horizontal offset, vertical offset, blur radius, or spread distance (optional), and a valid color value
`text-transform`	Configures the capitalization of text Value: `none` (default), `capitalize`, `uppercase`, or `lowercase`
`top`	Configures the offset position from the top of a containing element Value: Numeric value (px or em), percentage, or `auto` (default)
`transform`	CSS3; configures change or transformation in the display of an element Value: A transform function such as `scale()`, `translate()`, `matrix()`, `rotate()`, `skew()`, or `perspective()`
`transition`	CSS3; shorthand property to configure the presentational transition of a CSS property Value: List the value for the `transition-property`, `transition-duration`, `transition-timing-function`, and `transition-delay`, separated by spaces; default values can be omitted, but the first time unit applies to `transition-duration`
`transition-delay`	CSS3; Indicates the beginning of the transition Value: 0 (default) configures no delay; otherwise use a numeric value to specify time (usually in seconds)
`transition-duration`	CSS3; Indicates the length of time to apply the transition Value: 0 (default) configures an immediate transition; otherwise use a numeric value to specify time (usually in seconds)

Property	Description
`transition-property`	CSS3; Indicates the CSS property that the transition applies to Value: A list of applicable properties is available at http://www.w3.org/TR/css3-transitions
`transition-timing-function`	CSS3; Configures changes in the speed of the transition by describing how intermediate property values are calculated Value: `ease` (default), `linear`, `ease-in`, `ease-out`, or `ease-in-out`
`vertical-align`	Configures the vertical alignment of an element Value: Numeric value (px or em), percentage, baseline (default), `sub`, `super`, `top`, `text-top`, `middle`, `bottom`, or `text-bottom`
`visibility`	Configures the visibility of an element Value: `visible` (default), `hidden`, or `collapse`
`white-space`	Configures white space inside an element Value: `normal` (default), `nowrap`, `pre`, `pre-line`, or `pre-wrap`
`width`	Configures the width of an element Value: Numeric value (px or em), percentage, or `auto` (default)
`word-spacing`	Configures the space between words within text Value: Numeric value (px or em) or `auto` (default)
`z-index`	Configures the stacking order of an element Value: Numeric value or `auto` (default)

Web-Safe Color Palette

Web-safe colors look the most similar on various computer platforms and computer monitors. Back in the day of eight-bit color, it was crucial to use web-safe colors. Since most modern video drivers support millions of colors, the use of web-safe colors is now optional. The hexadecimal and decimal RGB values are shown for each web-safe color in the palette above.

Visual Elements and Graphics

Chapter Objectives **In this chapter, you will learn how to . . .**

- Create and format lines and borders on web pages
- Decide when to use graphics and what graphics are appropriate
- Apply the image element to add graphics to web pages
- Optimize an image for web page display
- Configure images as backgrounds on web pages
- Configure images as hyperlinks
- Configure rounded corners, box shadow, text shadow, opacity, and gradients with CSS3
- Configure RGBA color with CSS3
- Use HTML5 elements to caption a figure
- Use the HTML5 meter and progress elements
- Find free and fee-based graphics sources
- Follow recommended web design guidelines when using graphics on web pages

A key component of a compelling website is the use of interesting and appropriate graphics. This chapter introduces you to working with visual elements on web pages.

When you include images on your website, it is important to remember that not all users are able to view them. Some users may have vision problems and need assistive technology such as a screen reader application that reads the web page to them. In addition, search engines send out spiders and robots to walk the web and catalog pages for their indexes and databases; such programs do not access your images. Visitors using a mobile device may have images disabled. As a web developer, strive to create pages that are enhanced by graphical elements, but are usable without them.

1 Configuring Lines and Borders

Web designers often use visual elements such as lines and borders to separate or define areas on web pages. In this section, you'll explore two coding techniques to configure a line on a web page: the HTML horizontal rule element and the CSS border and padding properties.

The Horizontal Rule Element

A **horizontal rule element** visually separates areas of a page and configures a horizontal line across a web page. Since the horizontal rule element does not contain any text, it is coded as a void tag and not in a pair of opening and closing tags. XHTML syntax for the horizontal rule is `<hr />`. HTML5 syntax for the horizontal rule is `<hr>`. The horizontal rule element has a new semantic meaning in HTML5, indicating a thematic break. Horizontal rules are centered within their container element by default.

Hands-On Practice 1

Open the web page found at chapter4/starter1.html[1] in the student files in a text editor. Add an `<hr>` tag above the div element that contains the page footer.

Save your file as hr.html, and test it in a browser. The lower portion of your web page should look similar to the partial screenshot shown in Figure 1. Compare your work with the solution in the student files (chapter4/hr.html). While a horizontal rule can be easily created using HTML, a more modern technique for configuring lines on web pages is to use CSS to configure a border.

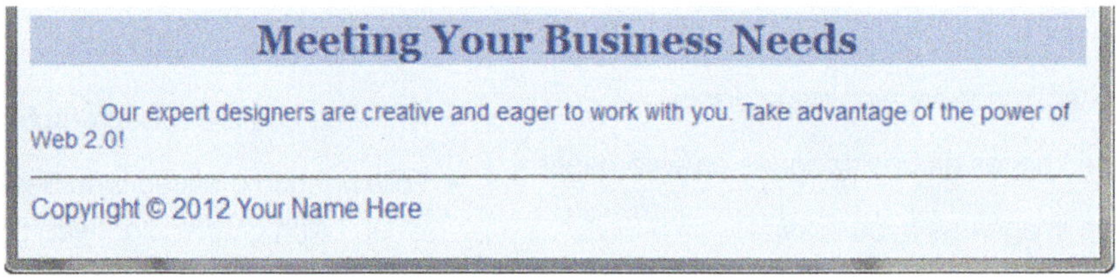

Figure 1 The `<hr>` tag configures a horizontal line

The border and padding Properties

When you configure background colors for heading elements, block display HTML elements form the shape of a rectangular box on a web page. This is an example of the CSS box model. Let's focus on two CSS properties that can be configured for the "box": the border and padding properties.

The border Property

The **`border` property** configures the border, or boundary, around an element. By default, the border has a width set to 0 and does not display. You can set the `border-width`,

[1]Website Case Study starter files are available for download from Pearson's CS Support website at http://cssupport.pearsoncmg.com.

border-color, and border-style with the border property. And there's more—you can even configure individual settings for the top, right, bottom and left borders using the border-top, border-right, border-bottom, and border-left properties.

The border-style Property

The **border-style property** configures the type of line displayed in the border. The formatting options include inset, outset, double, groove, ridge, solid, dashed, and dotted. Be aware that these property values are not all uniformly applied by browsers. Figure 2 shows how Firefox 4 and Internet Explorer 9 render various border-style values.

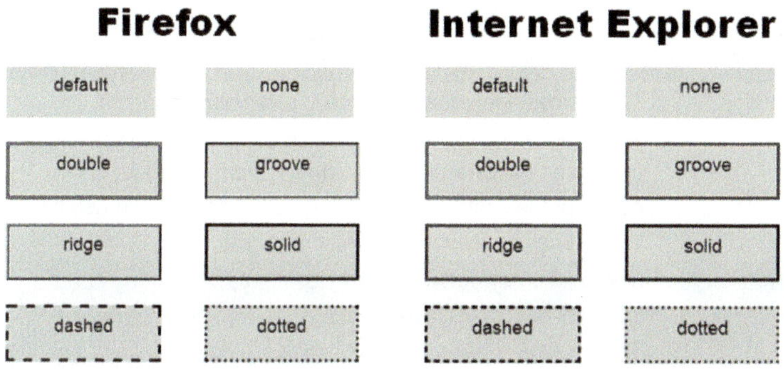

Figure 2 Not all border-style values are rendered the same way by popular browsers

The CSS to configure the borders shown in Figure 2 uses a border-width of 3 pixels, the value indicated for the border-style property, and a border-color of #000000. For example, the style rule to configure the dashed border follows:

```
.dashedborder { border-width: 3px;
                border-style: dashed;
                border-color: #000033; }
```

A shorthand notation allows you to configure all the border properties in one style rule by listing the values of border-width, border-style, and border-color, as in the following example:

```
.dashedborder { border: 3px dashed #000033; }
```

The padding Property

The **padding property** configures empty space between the content of the HTML element (usually text) and the border. By default, the padding is set to 0. If you configure a background color for an element, the color is applied to both the padding and the content areas. You'll apply the padding and border properties in the next Hands-On Practice. You may want to refer to Table 1, which presents a description of the CSS properties introduced in this chapter, as you work through the Hands-On Practice exercises.

Table 1 New CSS properties introduced in this chapter

Property	Description	Values
background-attachment	Configures whether the background image scrolls with the page or is fixed in place	fixed, scroll (default)
background-clip	Configures the background painting area. This CSS3 property is not supported in all browsers.	padding-box, border-box, or content-box
background-image	Background image on an element	To display an image, use url(imagename.gif), url(imagename.jpg), or url(imagename.png). To disable image display, use none (default).
background-origin	Configures the background positioning area. This CSS3 property is not supported in all browsers.	padding-box, border-box, or content-box
background-position	Position of the background image	Two percentage values or numeric pixel values. The first value configures the horizontal position, and the second configures the vertical position starting from the upper left corner of the container's box. Text values can also be used: left, top, center, bottom, and right.
background-repeat	Controls how the background image will repeat	Text values repeat (default), repeat-y, (vertical repeat), repeat-x (horizontal repeat), and no-repeat (no repeat). The new CSS3 values (space, round) are not supported in all browsers.
background-size	Configures the size of the background image. This CSS3 property is not supported in all browsers.	Two percentages, pixel values, auto, contain, or cover. The first value indicates width. The second value indicates height. If only one value is provided, the second value defaults to auto. The value contain causes the background image to be scaled (with aspect ratio intact) to horizontally fill the container. The value cover causes the background image to be scaled (with aspect ratio intact) to vertically fill the container.
border	Shorthand notation to configure the values for border-width, border-style, and border-color of an element	The values for border-width, border-style, and border-color separated by spaces—for example, border: 1px solid #000000;
border-bottom	Shorthand notation to configure the bottom border of an element	The values for border-width, border-style, and border-color separated by spaces—for example, border-bottom: 1px solid #000000;
border-bottom-left-radius	Configures rounded corners on the bottom left corner of a border. This CSS3 property is not supported in all browsers.	One numeric value (px or em) or percentage that configures the radius of the corner.
border-bottom-right-radius	Configures rounded corners on the bottom right corner of a border. This CSS3 property is not supported in all browsers.	One numeric value (px or em) or percentage that configures the radius of the corner.
border-color	The color of the border around an element	Any valid color value
border-left	Shorthand notation to configure the left border of an element	The values for border-width, border-style, and border-color separated by spaces—for example, border-left: 1px solid #000000;

Table 1 *(Continued)*

Property	Description	Values
`border-radius`	Configures rounded corners on a element. This CSS3 property is not supported in all browsers.	One to four numeric values (px or em) or percentages that configure the radius of the corners. If a single value is provided, it configures all four corners. The corners are configured in order of top left, top right, bottom right, and bottom left.
`border-right`	Shorthand notation to configure the right border of an element	The values for **`border-width`**, **`border-style`**, and **`border-color`** separated by spaces—for example, **`border-right: 1px solid #000000;`**
`border-style`	The type of border around an element	Text values **`double`**, **`groove`**, **`inset`**, **`none`** (the default), **`outset`**, **`ridge`**, **`solid`**, **`dashed`**, **`dotted`**, and **`hidden`**
`border-top`	Shorthand notation to configure the top border of an element	The values for **`border-width`**, **`border-style`**, and **`border-color`** separated by spaces—for example, **`border-top: 1px solid #000000;`**
`border-top-left-radius`	Configures a rounded top left corner. This CSS3 property is not supported in all browsers.	One numeric value (px or em) or percentage that configures the radius of the corner.
`border-top-right-radius`	Configures a rounded top right corner. This CSS3 property is not supported in all browsers.	One numeric value (px or em) or percentage that configures the radius of the corner.
`border-width`	The width of a border around an element	A numeric pixel value (such as 1px) or the text values **`thin`**, **`medium`**, and **`thick`**
`box-shadow`	Configures a drop shadow on an element. This CSS3 property is not supported in all browsers.	Two to four numerical values (px or em) to indicate horizontal offset, vertical offset, blur radius (optional), and spread distance (optional), and a valid color value. Use the **`inset`** keyword to configure an inner shadow.
`height`	The height of an element	A numeric pixel value or percentage
`linear-gradient`	Configures a linear blending of shades from one color to another. This CSS3 property is not supported in all browsers.	Numerous syntax options for starting points of the gradient and color values. For example, the following configures a two-color linear gradient: **`linear-gradient(#FFFFFF, #8FA5CE);`**
`min-width`	Configures a minimum width for an element	A numeric pixel value or percentage
`opacity`	Configures the transparency of an element. This CSS3 property is not supported in all browsers.	Numeric values between 1 (fully opaque) and 0 (completely transparent). This property is inherited by all child elements.
`padding`	Shorthand notation to configure the amount of padding—the blank space between the element and its border	1. A single numeric value (px or em) or percentage; configure padding on all sides of the element. 2. Two numeric values (px or em) or percentages; the first value configures the top and bottom padding, and the second value configures the left and right padding—for example, **`padding: 20px 10px;`** 3. Three numeric values (px or em) or percentages; the first value configures the top padding, the second value configures the left and right padding, the third value configures the bottom padding—for example, **`padding: 5px 30px 10px;`**

(Continued)

Table 1 *(Continued)*

Property	Description	Values
		4. Four numeric values (px or em) or percentages; the values configure the padding in the following order: `padding-top`, `padding-right`, `padding-bottom`, `padding-left`.
`padding-bottom`	Blank space between an element and its bottom border	A numeric value (px or em) or percentage
`padding-left`	Blank space between an element and its left border	A numeric value (px or em) or percentage
`padding-right`	Blank space between an element and its right border	A numeric value (px or em) or percentage
`padding-top`	Blank space between an element and its top border	A numeric value (px or em) or percentage
`radial-gradient`	Configures a radial (circular) blending of shades from one color to another. This CSS3 property is not supported in all browsers.	Numerous syntax options for starting points of the gradient and color values. For example, the following configures a two-color radial gradient: `radial-gradient(#FFFFFF, #8FA5CE);`
`text-shadow`	Configures a drop shadow on the text displayed within an element. This CSS3 property is not supported in all browsers.	Two to four numerical values (px or em) to indicate horizontal offset, vertical offset, blur radius (optional), and spread distance (optional), and a valid color value.

Hands-On Practice 2

In this Hands-On Practice you will work with the border and padding properties. Launch a text editor, and open the web page found at chapter4/starter1.html in the student files. You will modify the CSS style rules for the h1 element selector, h2 element selector, and footer id. When you are finished, your page should look similar to the one shown in Figure 3.

Edit the CSS style rules as follows:

1. Modify the style rules for the h1 element selector. Remove the line-height style rule, because you will use padding to configure the empty space. Add a style rule to set the padding to 15 pixels. The code follows:

```
padding: 15px;
```

2. Add a style rule to the h2 element selector to configure a 2-pixel, dashed, bottom border in the color #191970. The code follows:

```
border-bottom: 2px dashed #191970;
```

3. Add a footer id selector to configure a thin, solid, top border in the color #aeaed4 along with 10 pixels of top padding. Also configure the footer to have gray, small, italic text. The code follows:

```
#footer { border-top: thin solid #aeaed4;
          padding-top: 10px;
          color: #333333;
          font-size: .75em;
          font-style: italic; }
```

Edit the HTML, and assign the div that contains the footer information to the id named footer. Save your file as border.html.

Test your page in multiple browsers. Expect your page to look slightly different in various browsers. See Figure 3 for a screenshot of the page using Firefox. Figure 4 shows the page displayed in Internet Explorer. The student files contain a sample solution (chapter4/border.html).

Figure 3 CSS border and padding properties add visual interest to the page

Figure 4 Internet Explorer renders the dashed border differently than Firefox

FAQ **My web page looks different in some browsers. What can I do?**

Do not expect your web pages always to look the same in every browser and every browser version. Web pages that look different in various browsers are a part of life in the world of web developers. The good news is that browser developers are finally beginning to be less inventive and more compliant with the W3C standards. Also, organizations such as The Web Standards Project (http://www.webstandards.org) have lobbied for standards compliance in browsers. Look for improved compliance in the future!

Checkpoint 1

1. Is it reasonable to try to code a web page that looks exactly the same on every browser and every platform? Explain your answer.
2. Describe what is incorrect with the following CSS code, which causes a web page containing it not to display a border when rendered in a browser:

```
h2 { background-color: #ff0000
     border-top: thin solid #000000 }
```

3. True or False: CSS can be used to configure visual elements such as rectangular shapes and lines on web pages.

2 Types of Graphics

Graphics can make web pages compelling and engaging. This section discusses features of graphic files commonly used on the Web: GIF, JPEG, and PNG. A new web graphic format, WepP, is also introduced.

Graphic Interchange Format (GIF) Images

GIF images are best used for line drawings containing mostly solid tones and simple images such as clip art. The maximum number of colors in a GIF file is 256. GIF images have a .gif file extension. Figure 5 shows a logo image created in GIF format.

Figure 5 This logo is a GIF

Transparency

The format GIF89A used by GIF images supports image **transparency**. In a graphics application, such as the open-source GIMP, one color (typically the background color) of the image can be set to be transparent. The background color (or background image) of the web page shows through the transparent area in the image. Figure 6 displays two GIF images on a blue textured background.

Figure 6 Comparison of transparent and nontransparent GIFs

Animation

An **animated GIF** consists of several images or frames, each of which is slightly different. When the frames display on the screen in order, the image appears animated. Animated GIFs can be created in a graphics application such as Adobe Fireworks.

Compression

Lossless compression is used when a GIF is saved. This means that nothing in the original image is lost and that the compressed image, when rendered by a browser, will contain the same pixels as the original.

Optimization

To avoid slow-loading web pages, graphic files should be optimized for the Web. Image **optimization** is the process of creating an image with the lowest file size that still renders a good-quality image—balancing image quality and file size. GIF images are typically optimized by reducing the number of colors in the image by using a graphics application such as Adobe Photoshop, Adobe Fireworks, or GIMP.

Interlacing

Browsers render, or display, web page documents in order, line by line, starting at the top of the document. They display standard images as the files are read in order from top to bottom. The top of a standard image begins to display after 50 percent of the image has been read by a browser. When a GIF graphic file is created, it can be configured as interlaced. An **interlaced** image progressively displays and seems to fade in as it downloads. The image first appears fuzzy but gradually becomes clearer and sharper, which can help to reduce the perceived load time of your web page.

Joint Photographic Experts Group (JPEG) Images

JPEG images are best used for photographs. In contrast to a GIF image, a JPEG image can contain 16.7 million colors. However, JPEG images cannot be made transparent, and they cannot be animated. JPEG images have a .jpg or .jpeg file extension.

Compression

JPEG images are saved using **lossy compression**. This means that some pixels in the original image are lost or removed from the compressed file. When a browser renders the compressed image, the display is similar to, but not exactly the same as, the original image.

Optimization

There are trade-offs between the quality of the image and the amount of compression. An image with less compression will have higher quality and result in a larger file size.

Figure 7 A JPEG saved at 80-percent quality (55KB file size) displays well on a web page

An image with more compression will have lower quality and result in a smaller file size. Most graphics applications allow you to preview the quality–compression trade-off and choose the image that best suits your needs.

When you take a photo with a digital camera, the file size is too large for optimal display on a web page. Figure 7 shows an optimized version of a digital photo with an original file size of 250KB. The image was optimized using a graphics application set to 80-percent quality, is now only 55KB, and displays well on a web page.

Figure 8 was saved with 20 percent quality and is only 19KB, but its quality is unacceptable. The quality of the image degrades as the file size decreases. The square blockiness you see in Figure 8 is called **pixelation** and should be avoided.

Figure 8 JPEG saved at 20-percent quality (19KB file size)

Another technique used with web graphics is to display a small version of the image, called a **thumbnail image**. Often, the thumbnail is configured as an image hyperlink that displays the larger image when clicked. Figure 9 shows a thumbnail image.

Progressive JPEG

When a JPEG file is created, it can be configured as progressive. A **progressive JPEG** is similar to an interlaced GIF in that the image progressively displays and seems to fade in as it downloads.

Figure 9 This small thumbnail image is only 5KB

Portable Network Graphic (PNG) Images

PNG images combine the best of GIF and JPEG images and will be a replacement for GIF images in the future. PNG (pronounced "ping") graphics can support millions of colors, support variable transparency levels, and use lossless compression. PNG images also support interlacing.

Table 2 Overview of common web graphic file types

Image Type	File Extension	Compression	Transparency	Animation	Colors	Progressive Display
GIF	.gif	Lossless	Yes	Yes	256	Interlacing
JPEG	.jpg or .jpeg	Lossy	No	No	Millions	Progressive
PNG	.png	Lossless	Yes	No	Millions	Interlacing

New WebP Image Format

Google's new **WebP image format** offers improved lossy compression for photographic images, but it's not yet ready for use in commercial websites. WebP (pronounced "weppy") graphics are currently supported only by the Google Chrome browser. Visit http://code.google.com/speed/webp for more information on this new image format.

3 Image Element

The **image element** configures graphics on a web page. These graphics can be photographs, banners, company logos, navigation buttons, and so on; you are limited only by your creativity and imagination.

The image element is not coded as a pair of opening and closing tags. It is considered to be a void element. Use `<img />` for XHTML syntax and `<img>` for HTML5 syntax. The following code example configures an image named logo.gif, which is located in the same folder as the web page:

```
<img src="logo.gif" height="200" width="500" alt="My Company Name">
```

The **src attribute** specifies the file name of the image. The **alt attribute** provides a text replacement, typically a text description, of the image. The browser reserves the correct amount of space for your image if you use the height and width attributes with values either equal to or approximately the size of the image. Table 3 lists `<img>` tag attributes and their values. Commonly used attributes are shown in bold.

Table 3 Attributes of the <img> tag

Attribute	Value
`align`	`right`, `left` (default), `top`, `middle`, `bottom`; obsolete—use the CSS float or position property instead
`alt`	Text phrase that describes the image
`border`	Image border size in pixels; `border="0"` prevents the border of an image hyperlink from being displayed; obsolete—use the CSS border property instead
`height`	Height of image in pixels
`hspace`	Amount of space, in pixels, that is blank to the left and right of the image; obsolete—use the CSS padding property instead
`id`	Text name—alphanumeric, beginning with a letter, no spaces; the value must be unique and not used for other id values on the same web page document
`name`	Text name—alphanumeric, beginning with a letter, no spaces; this attribute names the image so that it can be easily accessed by client-side scripting languages such as JavaScript; obsolete—use the id attribute
`src`	The URL or file name of the image
`title`	A text phrase containing advisory information about the image; typically more descriptive than the alt text
`vspace`	Amount of space, in pixels, that is blank above and below the image; obsolete—use the CSS padding property instead
`width`	Width of image in pixels

Notice that several attributes in Table 3 are marked as obsolete. Although obsolete in HTML5, they are still valid in XHTML so you'll see them coded in existing web pages. CSS can be used to re-create the functions of these now-obsolete attributes.

FAQ What if I don't know the height and width of an image?

Most graphics applications can display the height and width of an image. If you have a graphics application such as Adobe Photoshop or Adobe Fireworks handy, launch the application and open the image. These applications include options that will display the properties of the image, such as height and width.

If you don't have a graphics application available, you can determine the dimensions of an image by using a browser. Display the image on a web page. Right-click on the image to display the context-sensitive menu. Select a menu option such as Properties or "View Image Info" to view the dimensions (height and width) of the image. (*Warning*: If the height and width are specified on the web page, those values will be displayed even if the image's actual height and width are different.)

Accessibility and Images

Focus on Accessibility

Use the alt attribute to provide accessibility. Section 508 of the Rehabilitation Act requires the use of accessibility features for new information technology (including websites) associated with the federal government. The alt attribute configures an alternative text description of the image. This alt text is used by the browser in two ways. The browser will show the alt text in the image area before the graphic is downloaded and displayed. Some browsers will also show the alt text as a tool tip whenever a visitor to the web page places the mouse cursor over the image area. Applications such as screen readers will read the text in the alt attribute out loud. A mobile browser may display the alt text instead of the image.

Standard browsers such as Internet Explorer and Safari are not the only type of application or user agent that can access your website. Major search engines run programs called spiders or robots; these programs index and categorize websites. They cannot process text within images, but some process the value of the alt attributes in image tags.

Image Hyperlinks

The code to make an image function as a hyperlink is very easy. To create an **image link,** all you need to do is surround your image element with anchor tags. For example, to place a link around an image called home.gif, use the following HTML code:

```
<a href="index.html"><img src="home.gif" height="19" width="85"
alt="Home"></a>
```

When an image is used as a hyperlink, the default is to show a blue outline (border) around the image. If you would prefer not to display this outline, you could use the `border="0"` attribute in your image tag as follows:

```
<a href="index.html"><img src="home.gif" height="19"
width="85" alt="Home" border="0"></a>
```

A more modern approach is to use CSS to configure the border on the img selector. The next Hands-On Practice will demonstrate this technique as you configure images and add image links to a web page.

Hands-On Practice 3

In this Hands-On Practice you will add a graphical logo banner and image navigation buttons to a web page. Then you'll configure the image buttons as image links. Create a new folder called trilliumch4. The graphics used in this Hands-On Practice are located in the student files chapter4/starters folder. Save the trilliumbanner.jpg, home.gif, services.gif, and contact.gif files in your trilliumch4 folder. A starter version of the Trillium Media Design Home page is ready for you in the student files. Save the chapter4/starter2.html file to your trilliumch4 folder. Launch a browser to display the starter2.html web page; notice that a monochromatic green color scheme has been configured with CSS. When you are finished with this Hands-On Practice, your page will look similar to the one shown in Figure 10.

Figure 10 The new Trillium Home page with a logo banner

Launch a text editor, and open starter2.html in the trilliumch4 folder.

1. Configure the logo banner image:
   - Replace the text contained between the `<h1>` opening and closing tags. Code an `<img>` element to display trilliumbanner.jpg in this area. Remember to include the `src`, `alt`, `height`, and `width` attributes. Sample code follows:

     ```
     <img src="trilliumbanner.jpg" alt="Trillium Media Design"
     width="700" height="86">
     ```

   - Edit the embedded CSS to configure the h1 element selector to have the same height as the image. Add the following style rule:

     ```
     height: 86px;
     ```

2. Configure the image links. Notice that the anchor tags are already coded; you'll just need to convert the text links to image links. However, before you start changing the code, let's take a minute to discuss accessibility. Whenever the main navigation consists of media, such as an image, some individuals may not be able to see the images (or may have images turned off in their browser). To provide navigation that is accessible to all, configure a set of plain-text navigation links in the page footer area as follows:
   - Copy the `<div>` element containing the navigation area to the lower portion of the page, and paste it above the page footer.
   - Modify the style rules in the nav class. Change the font size to .75em.
3. Now, focus on the top navigation area. Replace the text contained between each pair of anchor tags with an image element. Use home.gif for the link to index.html, services.gif for the link to services.html, and contact.gif for the link to contact.html. Sample code follows:

```
<a href="index.html"><img src="home.gif" alt="Home" width="120"
height="40"></a>
```

4. Edit the embedded CSS to create a new style rule that configures no border for the img element selector. The code follows:

```
img { border-style: none; }
```

Save your page as index.html in the trilliumch4 folder. Launch a browser, and test your page. It should look similar to the one shown in Figure 10. *Note*: If an image did not display on your web page, verify that you have saved the trilliumbanner.jpg, home.gif, services.gif, and contact.gif files in the trilliumch4 folder and that you have spelled the file name correctly in the `<img>` element.

As you test your page, resize the browser window, make it smaller, and note how the image links move around. To prevent them from moving, add a new style rule to the body selector that sets a minimum width for the page. This rule will cause the browser to automatically display a horizontal scroll bar if a visitor to the web page resizes the browser window below the size specified. Sample code follows:

```
min-width: 700px;
```

Save and test your page again. The student files contain a sample solution in the chapter4/4.3 folder. Isn't it interesting how just a few images can add visual interest to a web page?

FAQ What if my images don't show?

The following are common reasons for images not displaying on a web page:

- Are your images really in the website folder? Use Windows Explorer or Mac Finder to double-check.
- Did you code the HTML and CSS correctly? Check for common mistakes such as typing scr instead of src and missing quotation marks.
- Do your images have the exact file names that you have used in the background or src attributes in your HTML code? Attention to detail and consistency will be very helpful here.

FAQ How should I name my image files?

Guidelines for naming image files:

- Use all lowercase letters.
- Do not use punctuation symbols and spaces.
- Do not change the file extensions (should be .gif, .jpg, .jpeg, or .png).
- Keep your file names short, but descriptive. Here are some examples:

  i1.gif is probably too short.

  myimagewithmydogonmybirthday.gif is too long.

  dogbday.gif may be just about right.

Optimize an Image for the Web

Photos taken with a digital camera are too large—in both their dimensions and their file size—to display well on a web page. Recall that image optimization requires balancing image quality and file size. It is the process of creating an image with the lowest file size that still renders with good quality. Adobe Photoshop and Adobe Fireworks are often used by web professionals to optimize images for the Web. GIMP (http://gimp.org) is a popular open-source image editor that supports multiple platforms. Pixlr offers a free, easy-to-use, online photo editor at http://pixlr.com/editor.

Hands-On Practice 4

In this Hands-On Practice you will configure an image with a caption on a web page. The photo used in this Hands-On Practice is located in the student files chapter4/starters folder. Save the myisland.jpg file in a folder named mycaption.

Step 1: Launch a text editor. Select File > Open to edit the template file located at chapter2/template.html in the student files. Modify the title element. Add an image tag to the body section to display the myisland.jpg image as follows:

```
<img src="myisland.jpg" alt="Tropical Island" height="480" width="640">
```

Save the file as index.html in the mycaption folder. Launch a browser to test your page. It should look similar to the page shown in Figure 11.

Figure 11 The image is displayed on the web page

Step 2: Configure a figure caption and border for the image. To do so, launch a text editor and open the web page file. Add embedded CSS to the head section that configures an id named figure that is 640 pixels wide, has a border, has padding set to 5px, and has centered text using the Papyrus font typeface (or the default fantasy family font). The code follows:

```
<style>
#figure { width: 640px;
          border: 1px solid #000000;
          padding: 5px;
          text-align: center;
          font-family: Papyrus, fantasy; }
</style>
```

Edit the body section to add a div to contain the image. Add the text "Tropical Island Getaway" below the image but within the div element. Assign the div to the id named figure. Save the file as index.html in the mycaption folder. Launch a browser to test your page. It should look similar to the page shown in Figure 12. The student files contains a sample solution in the chapter4/caption folder.

Figure 12 CSS configures the placement of the border and figure caption

4 HTML5 Visual Elements

In Hands-On Practice 4, you configured an image and a caption on a web page. You used a div element to contain the image and text caption. In this section, you'll explore an approach that implements new HTML5 elements and requires a modern browser that supports HTML5 (such as Safari, Firefox, Chrome, Opera, or Internet Explorer 9). You'll use the new HTML5 figure and figcaption elements.

HTML5 Figure Element

The block display `figure` **element** comprises a unit of content that is self-contained, such as an image, along with one optional `figcaption` element.

HTML5 Figcaption Element

The block display `figcaption` **element** provides a caption for a figure.

Hands-On Practice 5

In this Hands-On Practice you will configure an area on a web page that contains an image with a caption by using the HTML5 figure and figcaption elements. The graphic used in this Hands-On Practice is located in the student files chapter4/starters folder. Save the myisland.jpg file in a folder named mycaption2.

Step 1: Launch a text editor. Select File > Open to edit the template file located at chapter2/template.html in the student files. Modify the title element. Add an image tag to the body section to display the myisland.jpg image as follows:

```
<img src="myisland.jpg" alt="Tropical Island" height="480"
width="640">
```

Save the file as index.html in the mycaption2 folder. Launch a browser to test your page. It should look similar to the page shown in Figure 11.

Step 2: Configure a figure caption and border for the image. Launch a text editor and open the web page file. Add embedded CSS to the head section that configures the figure element selector to be 640 pixels wide, with a border, and with padding set to 5px. Configure the figcaption element selector to have centered text using the Papyrus font typeface (or the default fantasy family font). The code follows:

```
<style>
figure { width: 640px;
        border: 1px solid #000000;
        padding: 5px; }
figcaption { text-align: center;
            font-family: Papyrus, fantasy; }
</style>
```

Edit the body section. Below the image, add a `figcaption` element that contains the following text: "Tropical Island Getaway." Configure a `figure` element that contains both the image and the figcaption. The code follows:

```
<figure>
  <img src="island.jpg" width="640" height="480" alt="Tropical Island">
  <figcaption>
  Tropical Island Getaway
  </figcaption>
</figure>
```

Save the file as index.html in the mycaption2 folder. Launch a browser to test your page. It should look similar to the page shown in Figure 13. The student files contains a sample solution in the chapter4/caption2 folder.

Figure 13 The HTML5 figure and figcaption elements were used in this web page

You might be wondering why these new HTML5 elements were created when the same design can be configured using a div element as a container. The reason is semantics. The div element is useful but very generic in nature. When the figure and figcaption elements are used, the structure of the content is well defined. However, if you are designing pages for commercial websites, hold off on using the new figure and figcaption elements until browser support of HTML5 is more widespread.

HTML5 Meter Element

The **`meter` element** displays a visual gauge of a numeric value within a known range, typically as part of a bar chart. At the time this text was written, this new HTML5 element was supported only in the Chrome and Opera 11 browsers. The meter element is configured with several attributes, including `value` (the value displayed), `min` (the lowest possible value in the range), and `max` (the highest possible value in the range). The following code snippet (from the student files chapter4/meter.html) configures the display of a monthly browser-usage report that shows total visits and the number of visits by users for each browser:

```
<h1>Monthly Browser Report</h1>
<meter value="14417" min="0" max="14417">14417</meter>14,417 Total
Visits<br>
<meter value="7000" min="0" max="14417">7000</meter> 7,000 Firefox<br>
<meter value="3800" min="0" max="14417">3800</meter> 3,800 Internet
Explorer<br>
<meter value="2062" min="0" max="14417">2062</meter> 2,062 Chrome<br>
<meter value="1043" min="0" max="14417">1043</meter> 1,043 Safari<br>
<meter value="312" min="0" max="14417">312</meter>   
312 Opera<br>
<meter value="200" min="0" max="14417">200</meter>   
200 other<br>
```

Figure 14 displays the page in the Opera browser. As time goes on, more browsers will support the new HTML5 meter element. It provides a very handy way to display a bar chart on a web page. Visit http://caniuse.com to get current information on browser support of this element.

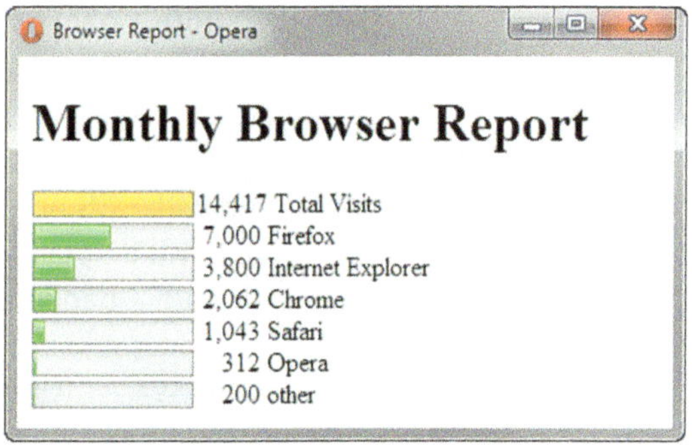

Figure 14 The `meter` element rendered in the Opera browser

HTML5 Progress Element

The **`progress` element** displays a bar that depicts a numeric value within a specified range. At the time this text was written, this new HTML5 element was supported by the Chrome, Firefox 6, and Opera 11 browsers. The progress element is configured with the `value` (the value displayed) and `max` (highest possible value) attributes. The following code snippet (from the student files chapter4/progress.html) shows 50 percent completion of a task:

```
<h1>Progress Report</h1>
<progress value="5000" max="10000">5000 </progress>
Progress Toward Our Goal
```

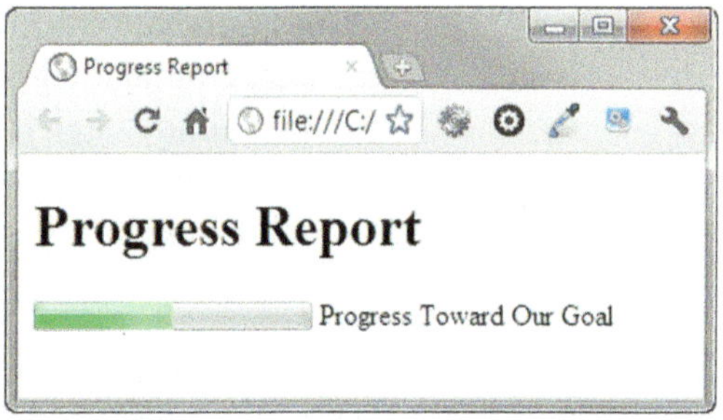

Figure 15 The `progress` element rendered in the Chrome browser

Figure 15 displays the page in the Chrome browser. As time goes on, more browsers will support the new HTML5 elements. Visit http://caniuse.com to get current information on browser support of HTML5.

5 Background Images

VideoNote
CSS Background Images

By now, you should have learned how to configure background color with the CSS `background-color` property. For example, the following CSS code configures the background of a web page to be a soft yellow:

```
body { background-color: #ffff99; }
```

The background-image Property

Use the CSS **`background-image` property** to configure a background image. For example, the following CSS code configures the HTML body selector with a background of the graphic texture1.png located in the same folder as the web page file:

```
body { background-image: url(texture1.png); }
```

Using Both Background Color and a Background Image

You can configure both a background color and a background image. The background color (specified by the `background-color` property) will display first. Next, the image specified as the background will be displayed as it is loaded by the browser.

By coding both a background color and a background image, you provide your visitor with a more pleasing visual experience. If the background image does not load for some reason, the background color will still have the expected contrast with your text color. If the background image is smaller than the web browser window and the web page is configured with CSS not to automatically tile (repeat the image), the background color of the page will display in areas not covered by the background image. The CSS for a page with both a background color and a background image follows:

```
body { background-color: #99cccc;
       background-image: url(background.jpg); }
```

Browser Display of a Background Image

You may think that a graphic created to be the background of a web page would always be about the size of the browser window viewport. However, the dimensions of the background image are often much smaller than the typical viewport. The shape of a background image is often either a thin rectangle or a small rectangular block. Unless otherwise specified in a style rule, browsers repeat, or tile, these images to cover the page's background, as shown in Figures 16 and 17. The images have small file sizes so that they download as quickly as possible.

Figure 16 A long, thin background image tiles down the page

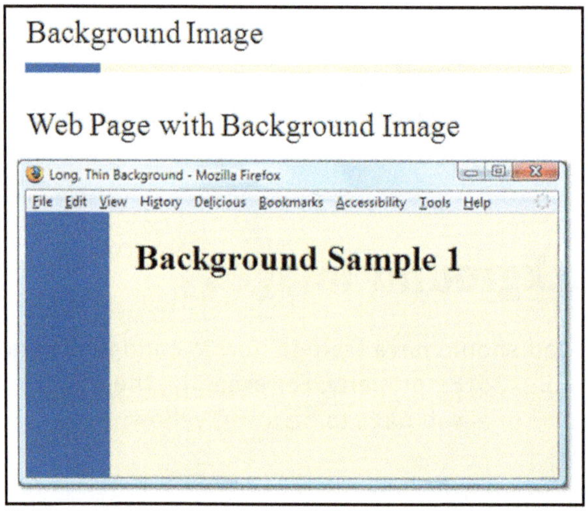

Figure 17 A small rectangular background is repeated to fill the web page window

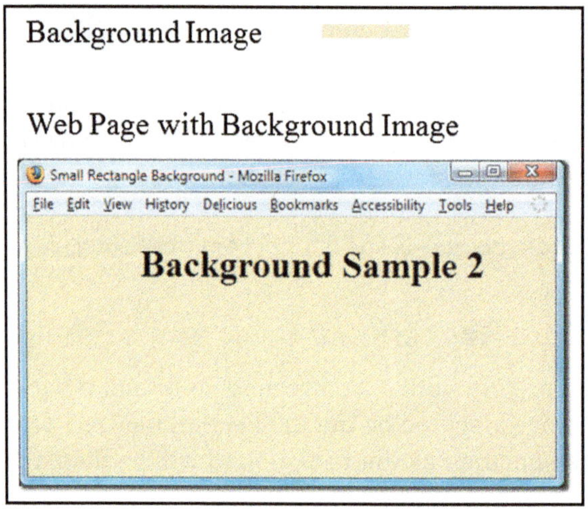

The `background-repeat` Property

As just discussed, the default behavior of a browser is to repeat, or tile, background images to cover the entire element's background. This behavior also applies to other elements, such as backgrounds for headings, paragraphs, and so on. You can change this tiling behavior with the CSS **`background-repeat` property**. The values for the background-repeat property include `repeat` (default), `repeat-y` (vertical repeat), `repeat-x` (horizontal repeat), and `no-repeat` (no repeat). Figure 18 provides examples of the actual background image and the result of applying various background-repeat property values.

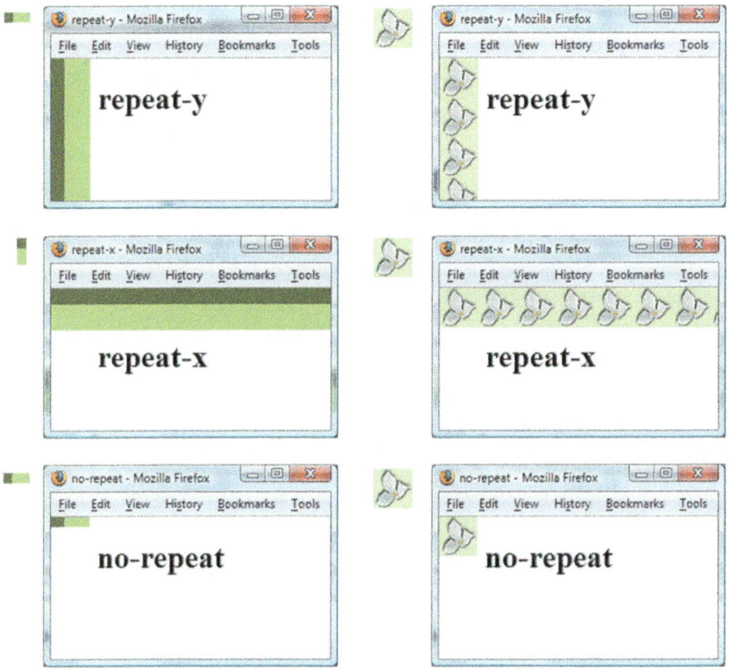

Figure 18 Examples of the CSS `background-repeat` property

CSS3 provides for additional values for the background-repeat property that are not yet well supported by browsers:

- `background-repeat: space;`

  Repeats the image in the background without clipping (or cutting off) parts of the image by adjusting empty space around the repeated images.

- `background-repeat: round;`

  Repeats the image in the background and scales (adjusts) the dimensions of the image to avoid clipping.

The `background-position` Property

You can specify other locations for the background image besides the default top left location by using the **`background-position` property**. Valid values for the background-position property include percentages; pixel values; or `left`, `top`, `center`, `bottom`, and

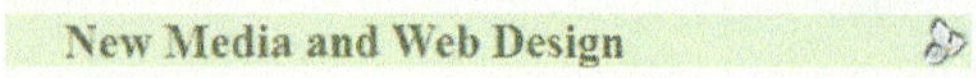

Figure 19 The flower background image was configured to display on the right side with CSS

right. The first value indicates horizontal position. The second value indicates vertical position. If only one value is provided, the second value defaults to center. In Figure 19, the small flower image has been placed in the background on the right side of the element by using the following style rule:

```
h2 { background-image: url(trilliumbg.gif);
     background-position: right;
     background-repeat: no-repeat; }
```

Hands-On Practice 6

Let's practice using a background image. You will update the index.html file from Hands-On Practice 3 (shown in Figure 10). In this Hands-On Practice you will configure the h2 element selector with a background image that does not repeat. Obtain the trilliumbullet.gif image from the student files chapter4/starters folder. Save the image in your trilliumch4 folder. When you have completed this exercise, your page should look similar to the one shown in Figure 20.

Figure 20 The background image in the <h2> areas is configured with background-repeat: no-repeat

Launch a text editor, and open index.html.

1. Modify the style rule for the h2 element selector to configure the background-image and background-repeat properties. Set the background image to be trilliumbullet.gif. Set the background not to repeat. The h2 element selector style rules follow:

```
h2 { background-color: #d5edb3;
     color: #5c743d;
     font-family: Georgia, "Times New Roman", serif;
     background-image: url(trilliumbullet.gif);
     background-repeat: no-repeat; }
```

2. Save your page as index.html. Launch a browser, and test your page. You may notice that the text in the h2 element is displayed over the background image. In this case, the page would look more appealing if there were more space, or padding, before the beginning of the text displayed by the h2 elements. Use the CSS `padding-left` property to add empty space within the left side of the element. Add the following declaration to the h2 element selector to add empty space before the text:

```
padding-left: 30px;
```

3. Save and test your page again. It should look similar to the one shown in Figure 20. The student files contain a sample solution in the chapter4/4.6 folder.

FAQ What if my images are in their own folder?

It's a good idea to organize your website by placing all your images in a folder. Notice that the CircleSoft website whose file structure is shown in Figure 21 contains a folder called images, which contains GIF and JPEG files. To refer to these files in code, you also need to refer to the images folder. The following are some examples:

- The CSS code to configure the background.gif file from the images folder as the page background follows:

```
body { background-image:
       url(images/background.gif); }
```

- The HTML to display the logo.jpg file from the images folder follows:

```
<img src="images/logo.jpg"
alt="CircleSoft" width="588" height="120">
```

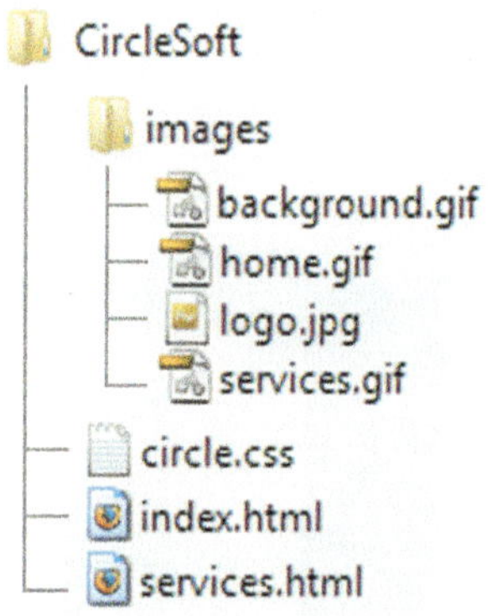

Figure 21 A folder named "images" contains the graphic files

The background-attachment Property

Use the **`background-attachment` property** to configure whether the background image remains fixed in place or scrolls along with the page in the browser viewport. Valid values for the background-attachment property include `fixed` and `scroll` (the default).

Checkpoint 2

1. Describe the CSS to configure a graphic named circle.jpg to display once in the background of all `<h1>` elements. Code the CSS.
2. Describe the CSS that configures a file named bg.gif to repeat vertically down the background of a web page. Code the CSS.
3. Explain how the browser will render the web page if you use CSS to configure both a background image and a background color.

6 More About Images

This section introduces several additional techniques used with images on web pages. Topics discussed include image maps, the favorites icon, image slicing, and CSS Sprites.

Image Maps

An **image map** is an image that can be used as one or more hyperlinks. An image map will typically have multiple clickable or selectable areas that link to another web page or website. The selectable areas are called **hotspots**. You have probably used image maps many times, but never realized it. One common use of image maps is to create interactive maps that website visitors can manipulate to choose a location. Figure 22 shows a page in the http://nerrs.noaa.gov website that displays a map of the Ace Islands. When a visitor selects an island, a new web page displays with detailed information about the island.

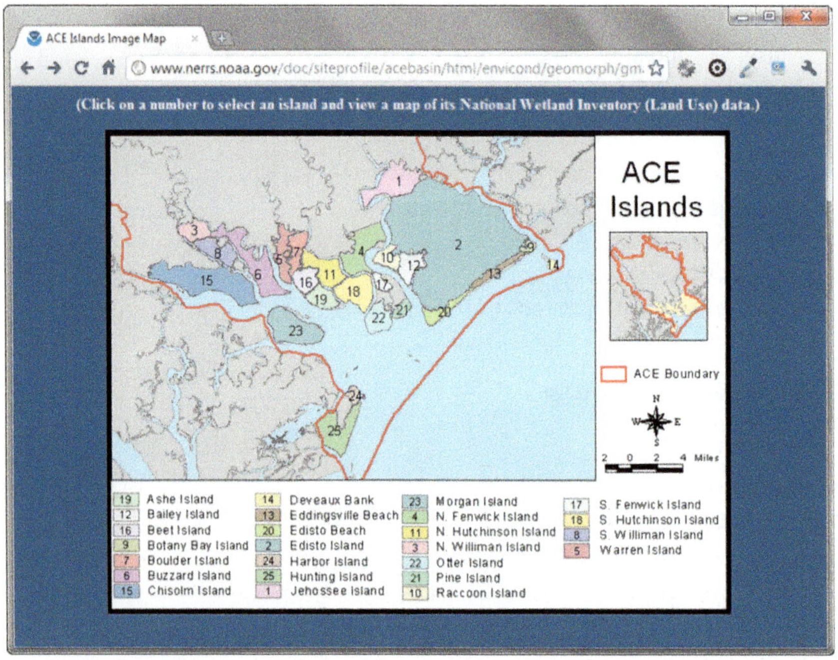

Figure 22 An image map is used to select a location on this website

Most web authoring software, such as Adobe Dreamweaver, provides wizards or other tools to help you create image maps quickly and easily. If you don't have access to a web authoring tool to create an image map, the most difficult part is determining the pixel coordinates of the hyperlink area. The coordinates are in pairs of numbers that signify the number of pixels from the top and the number of pixels from the left edge of the image. If you are working with a graphic artist, he or she may be able to supply you with the coordinates. Another option is to open the image in a graphics application such as Adobe Fireworks, Adobe Photoshop, or GIMP to obtain approximate coordinates. You can modify these coordinate values as you work with the HTML on your web page. Image maps can be used to create clickable areas in three shapes: rectangles, circles, and polygons.

An image map uses two new elements: map and area. The **`map` element** is a container tag and is used to begin and end the image map. The **`name` attribute** is coded to associate the `<map>` tag with its corresponding image. Configure the image tag with the **`usemap` attribute** to indicate which `<map>` to use. For example, `<img src="fishingboat.jpg" usemap="#boat">` will be associated with the image map described by `<map name="boat" id="boat">`. The id attribute uniquely identifies the map area.

The `<area>` tag defines the coordinates or edges of the map area and uses `shape`, `coords`, `alt`, and `href` attributes. XHTML syntax for the horizontal rule is `<area />`. Table 4 describes the type of coordinates (`coords`) needed for each shape value.

Table 4 Shape coordinates

Shape	Coordinates	Meaning
`rect`	"x1,y1, x2,y2"	The coordinates at point (x1,y1) represent the upper-left corner of the rectangle. The coordinates at point (x2,y2) represent the lower-right corner of the rectangle.
`circle`	"x,y,r"	The coordinates at point (x,y) indicate the center of the circle. The value of r is the radius of the circle, in pixels.
`polygon`	"x1,y1, x2,y2, x3,y3", etc.	The values of each (x,y) pair represent the coordinates of a corner point of the polygon.

We'll focus on a rectangular image map. For a rectangular image map, the value of the `shape` attribute is `rect`, and the coordinates indicate the pixel positions as follows: distance of the upper-left corner from the left side of the image, distance of the upper-left corner from the top of the image, distance of the lower-right corner from the left edge of the image, and distance fo the lower-right corner from the top of the image.

Figure 23 shows an image of a fishing boat. The dotted rectangle around the fishing boat indicates the location of the hotspot. The coordinates shown (24, 188) indicate that the top-left corner is 24 pixels from the left edge of the image and 188 pixels from the top of the image. The pair of coordinates in the lower-right corner (339, 283) indicates that this corner is 339 pixels from the left edge of the image and 283 pixels from the top of the image. Visit the text's website at http://webdevfoundations.net/6e/chapter4.html to see an image map in action. The HTML code to create this image map follows:

```
<map name="boat" id="boat">
  <area href="http://www.doorcountyvacations.com" shape="rect"
        coords="24, 188, 339, 283" alt="Door County Fishing">
</map>
<img src="fishingboat.jpg" usemap="#boat" alt="Door County" width="416"
height="350">
```

Most web developers do not hand-code image maps. As mentioned previously, the easiest way to create a client-side image map is to use a web authoring tool, such as Adobe Dreamweaver (http://adobe.com/dreamweaver) or Coffee Cup Software's HTML Editor (http://www.coffeecup.com/html-editor).

Figure 23 Sample image map

The Favorites Icon

Ever wonder about the small icon you sometimes see in the address bar or tab of a browser? That's a **favorites icon**, usually referred to as a **favicon**, which is a square image (either 16×16 pixels or 32×32 pixels) associated with a web page. The favicon, shown in Figure 24, may display in the browser's address bar, tab, or the favorites and bookmarks lists.

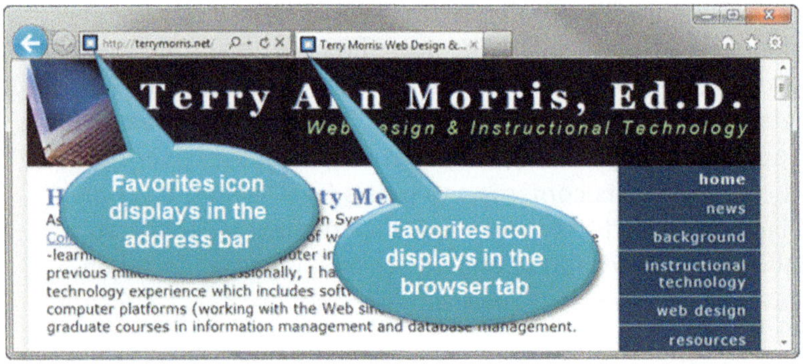

Figure 24 The favorites icon displays in the browser tab and address bar

You can create a favicon in a graphics application, such as Adobe Fireworks, or at a number of websites including http://www.favicongenerator.com, http://www.favicon.cc, and http://www.freefavicon.com. While some versions of Internet Explorer (version 6 and earlier) expected the file to be named favicon.ico and to reside in the root directory of the web server, a more modern approach is to associate the favicon.ico file with a web page by using the link element. The `<link>` tag in the header section of a web page is coded to associate an external style sheet file with a web page file. You can also use the `<link>` tag to associate a favorites icon with a web page.

Three attributes are used to associate a web page with a favorites icon: `rel`, `href`, and `type`. The value of the `rel` attribute is `icon`. The value of the `href` attribute is the name of the image file. The value of the `type` attribute describes the MIME type of the image—which defaults to `image/x-icon` for .ico files. The HTML code to associate a favorites icon named favicon.ico to a web page follows:

```
<link rel="icon" href="favicon.ico" type="image/x-icon">
```

Note that to be compatible with Internet Explorer and follow Microsoft's proprietary syntax, you'll also need to code a second link tag:

```
<link rel="shortcut icon" href="favicon.ico" type="image/x-icon">
```

Be aware that Internet Explorer's support of the favorites icon is somewhat buggy. You may need to publish your files to the Web (see the FTP tutorial in the appendix) in order for the favicon to display even in current versions of Internet Explorer. Other browsers, such as Firefox, Safari, Google Chrome, and Opera, display favicons more reliably and also support GIF and PNG image formats.

Hands-On Practice 7

Let's practice using a favorites icon. Obtain the favicon.ico file from the student files in the chapter4/starters folder. In this exercise, you will use your files in the trilliumch4 folder from Hands-On Practice 6 (also see the student files chapter4/4.6 folder) as a starting point.

1. Launch a text editor, and open index.html. Add the following link tags to the head section of the web page:

```
<link rel="icon" href="favicon.ico" type="image/x-icon">
<link rel="shortcut icon" href="favicon.ico" type="image/x-icon">
```

2. Save your page as index.html. Launch the Firefox browser, and test your page. You should notice the small trillium flower in the Firefox browser tab as shown in Figure 25. The student files contain a sample solution in the chapter4/4.7 folder.

Figure 25 The favorites icon displays in the Firefox browser tab

Image Slicing

Graphic artists and designers can create complex web page images. Sometimes, parts of these images are better optimized as GIFs than as JPEGs, while other parts of the images may be better optimized as JPEGs than as GIFs. By **image slicing** the single, complex images into multiple, smaller images, you can optimize all portions for the most efficient display. In addition, there may be times when you plan special mouse rollover effects for parts of a large, complex image. In this case, parts of the image need to be individually accessible to scripting languages, and so the image needs to be sliced. When an image is sliced, it is broken into multiple graphic files. Most graphics applications, such as Adobe Fireworks and Adobe Photoshop, have features for image slicing that automatically create the HTML for you. Visit the text's website at http://webdevfoundations.net/6e/chapter4.html for more information on image slicing.

CSS Sprites

A modern technique to optimize the use of images on web pages is called CSS Sprites. A **sprite** is an image file that contains multiple small graphics that are configured as background images for various web page elements. The CSS `background-image`, `background-repeat`, and `background-position` properties are used to manipulate the placement of the image. Having just a single image saves download time, because the browser needs to make only one http request for the combined image instead of many requests for the individual smaller images.

7 Sources and Guidelines for Graphics

Sources of Graphics

There are many ways to obtain graphics: You can create them using a graphics application, download them from a website providing them for free, purchase and download them from a graphics website, purchase a graphics collection on a DVD, take digital photographs, scan photographs, scan drawings, or hire a graphic designer to create graphics for you. Popular graphic applications include Adobe Photoshop and Adobe Fireworks. Popular free graphics applications include GIMP (http://gimp.org), Google's Picasa (http://picasa.google.com), and the Pixlr web application (http://pixlr.com/editor). These applications usually include tutorials and sample images to help you get started. Visit the text's website at http://webdevfoundations.net/6e/chapter4.html for tutorials on using Adobe Fireworks and Adobe Photoshop to create a logo banner image.

Focus on Ethics

Sometimes you might be tempted to right-click on an image on a web page and download it for use on your own website. Be aware that materials on a website are copyrighted (even if a copyright symbol or notice does not appear) and are not free to use unless the owner of the site permits it. So, contact the owner of an image and request permission for use rather than just taking it. If you're using Flickr (http://flickr.com) to search for images, select the advanced-search page and check "*Only search within Creative Commons-licensed content.*" Be sure to follow the instructions for attribution when indicated.

There are many web sites that offer free and low-cost graphics. Choose a search engine and search for "free graphics"—you'll get more results than you have time to view. The following are a few sites that you may find helpful when looking for images:

- Microsoft Clip Art: http://office.microsoft.com/clipart/default.aspx
- FamFamFam: http://www.famfamfam.com
- Free Stock Photo Search Engine: http://www.everystockphoto.com
- Free Images: http://www.freeimages.co.uk
- The Stock Solution: http://www.tssphoto.com
- SuperStock: http://www.superstock.com
- iStockphoto: http://www.istockphoto.com

It is also possible to create a banner or button image online. There are a number of sites that offer this feature. Some include advertising with your free image, some offer paid memberships, and others are simply free. Search for "create free online banner" to find sites offering this service. The following are a few useful sites for creating banners and button images:

- Animation Online: http://www.animationonline.com
- Web 2.0 LogoCreator: http://creatr.cc/creatr
- Cooltext.com: http://www.cooltext.com
- Ad Designer.com: http://www.addesigner.com

Guidelines for Using Images

Images enhance your web page by creating an engaging, interesting user experience. Images can also hurt your web page by slowing down its performance to a crawl and discouraging visitors. This section explores some guidelines for using images on web pages.

Reuse Images

Once an image from your site is requested for a web page, it is stored in the cache on your visitor's hard drive. Subsequent requests for the image will use the file from the hard drive instead of another download. This approach results in faster page loads for all pages that use the image. It is recommended that you reuse common graphics such as logos and navigation buttons on multiple pages instead of creating different versions of these common graphics.

Consider the Size vs. Quality Issue

You can choose among varying levels of image quality when using a graphics application to create or optimize an image. There is a correlation between the quality of the image and the size of the image file: The higher the quality, the larger the file size will be. Choose the smallest file that gives you appropriate quality. You may need to experiment until you get the right match.

Consider Image Load Time

Be careful when using images on web pages—it takes time for them to load. Optimize the file size and the dimensions of images for efficient web page display.

Use Appropriate Resolution

Web browsers display images at relatively low **resolution**—72ppi (pixels per inch) or 96ppi. Many digital cameras and scanners can create images with much higher resolution. Of course, higher resolution means larger file size. Even though the browser does not display the depth of resolution, more bandwidth is still used for the large file size. Be careful when taking digital photographs or scanning images. Use a resolution setting appropriate for web pages. A one-inch image saved at 150ppi could appear close to two inches wide on a 72ppi monitor.

Specify Dimensions

Always use accurate height and width attributes on image tags. This will allow the browser to allocate the appropriate space on the web page for the image and load the page faster. Do not try to resize the appearance of an image by modifying the settings of the height and width attributes. While this approach will work, your page will load more slowly, and your image quality may suffer. Instead, use a graphics application to create a smaller or larger version of the graphic when needed.

Be Aware of Brightness and Contrast

Gamma refers to the brightness and contrast of the monitor display. Monitors used with Macintosh and Windows operating systems use a different default gamma setting (Macintosh uses 1.8; Windows uses 2.2). Images that have good contrast on a computer running Windows may look slightly washed out on a Macintosh. Images created on a Macintosh may look darker, with less contrast, when displayed on a computer with a Windows operating system. Be aware that even monitors on the same operating system may have slightly different gamma values than the default for the platform. A web developer cannot control gamma, but should be aware that images will look different on various platforms because of this issue.

Accessibility and Visual Elements

Focus on Accessibility

Even though images help to create a compelling, interesting website, remember that not all your visitors will be able to view your images. The Web Accessibility Initiative's WCAG 2.0 includes a number of guidelines for web developers in the use of color and images:

- Don't rely on color alone. Some visitors may have color perception deficiencies. Use high contrast between background and text color.
- Provide a text equivalent for every nontext element. Use the alt attribute on your image tags.
    - If an image displays text, configure that text as the value of the alt attribute.
    - Use `alt=""` for an image that is purely decorative.
- If your site navigation uses image hyperlinks, provide simple text links at the bottom of the page.

Vinton Cerf, the co-inventor of TCP/IP and the former chairman of the Internet Society, said, "The Internet is for everyone." Follow web accessibility guidelines to ensure that this is true.

Checkpoint 3

1. Search for a site that uses image hyperlinks to provide navigation. List the URL of the page. What colors are used on the image links? If the image links contain text, is there good contrast between the background color and the letters on the image links? Would the page be accessible to a visitor who is sight challenged? How have accessibility issues been addressed? Is the alt attribute used to describe the image link? Is there a row of text links in the footer section of the page? Answer these questions and discuss your findings.
2. When configuring an image map, describe the relationship between the image, map, and area tags.
3. True or False: You should save your images using the smallest file size possible.

8 CSS3 Visual Effects

This section introduces new CSS3 properties that provide visual effects on web pages, including background clipping and scaling, multiple background images, rounded corners, box shadows, text shadows, opacity effects, transparent color with RGBA, and gradients.

The CSS3 `background-clip` Property

The new CSS3 **`background-clip` property** confines the display of the background image with the following values:

- `content-box` (clips the display to the area behind the content)
- `padding-box` (clips the display to the area behind the content and padding)
- `border-box` (default; clips the display to the area behind the content, padding, and border; similar to the padding-box property except that the image will display behind a border configured to be transparent)

The background-clip property is supported by modern browsers, although Safari requires the proprietary `-webkit-background-clip` property instead of the W3C draft `background-clip` property. Be aware that when you code the nonstandard property, your CSS will not pass W3C validation. Figure 26 shows a background image that is configured to clip to the content box. The sample page is located in the student files (chapter4/clip folder).

Figure 26 The CSS3 `background-clip` property

The CSS is shown as follows:

```
.test { background-image: url(myislandback.jpg);
        -webkit-background-clip: content-box;
        background-clip: content-box;
        width: 400px;
        padding: 20px;
        border: 1px solid #000; }
```

The CSS3 background-origin Property

The new CSS3 **background-origin property** positions the background image, using the following values:

- content-box (positions relative to the content area)
- padding-box (default; positions relative to the padding area)
- border-box (positions relative to the border area)

Figure 27 The CSS3 background-origin property

Figure 27 shows a background image that is configured to display in the lower right corner of the content box. The sample page is located in the student files (chapter4/origin folder).

```
The CSS is shown as follows:
.test { background-image: url(trilliumsolo.jpg);
        background-origin: content-box;
        background-repeat: no-repeat;
        background-position: right bottom;
        width: 400px;
        padding: 20px;
        border: 1px solid #000; }
```

You may have noticed that it's common to use several CSS properties when configuring background images. The properties typically work together. However, be aware that the background-origin property has no effect if the background-attachment property is set to the value "fixed".

The CSS3 background-size Property

The new CSS3 **background-size property** can be used to resize or scale the background image. Valid values for the background-size property can be:

- a pair of percentage values (width, height)
- a pair of pixel values (width, height)
- auto, contain, or cover

Figure 28 The CSS3 background-size property

If only one numeric or percentage value is provided, the second value defaults to auto. The value contain causes the background image to be scaled (with aspect ratio intact) to vertically fill the container. The value cover causes the background image to be scaled (with aspect ratio intact) to horizontally fill the container. In Figure 28 (see the student files chapter4/size folder), the background image has been configured to vertically fill the container using the following style rule:

```
div { background-image: url(myislandback.jpg);
      background-size: cover;
      background-repeat: no-repeat;
      width: 200px;
      padding: 20px; }
```

When using new CSS3 properties, be mindful that they are supported only in modern browsers. Be sure to test without the CSS3 properties to verify that the pages are still readable and usable. Visit http://www.quirksmode.org/css/contents.html to get current information about browser support of CSS3 properties.

CSS3 Multiple Background Images

Let's explore applying multiple background images to a web page. Although the CSS3 Backgrounds and Borders module is still in working draft status, current versions of most popular web browsers support the use of multiple background images.

Figure 29 shows a web page with two background images configured on the body selector: a green gradient image that repeats across the entire browser viewport, and a flower image that displays once in the right footer area. Use the CSS3 `background` property to configure multiple background images. Each image declaration is separated by a comma. You can optionally add property values to indicate the image's position and whether the image repeats. The `background` property uses a shorthand notation: Just list the values that are needed for relevant properties such as `background-position` and `background-repeat`.

Figure 29 The Firefox browser displays multiple background images

Progressive Enhancement

Multiple background images are currently supported by recent versions of Firefox, Chrome, Safari, Opera, and Internet Explorer 9. Be aware that multiple background images are not supported by earlier versions of Internet Explorer. You'll use the technique of **progressive enhancement**, which is defined by web developer and HTML5 evangelist Christian Heilmann as "starting with a baseline of usable functionality, then increasing the richness of the user experience step by step by testing for support for enhancements before applying them." In other words, start with a web page that displays well in most browsers and then add new design techniques, such as multiple background images, in a way that enhances the display for visitors who are using browsers that support the new technique.

To provide for progressive enhancement when using multiple background images, first configure a separate `background-image` property with a single image (rendered by most browsers) before the background property with multiple images (rendered by supporting browsers and ignored by nonsupporting browsers). Figure 30 shows the page displayed in Internet Explorer 8, which rendered the standard `background-image` property.

Figure 30 Progressive enhancement in action. Although only one background image displays, the web page has a similar display to Figure 29

Hands-On Practice 8

Let's practice configuring multiple background images. In this Hands-On Practice you will configure the body element selector to display multiple background images on the web page. Obtain the trilliumgradient.png and the trilliumfoot.gif images from the student files chapter4/starters folder. Save the images in your trilliumch4 folder. You'll update the index.html file from the previous Hands-On Practice. Launch a text editor, and open index.html.

1. Modify the style rule for the body element selector. Configure the `background-image` property to display trilliumgradient.png. This style rule will be applied by browsers that do not support multiple background images. Configure a `background` property to display both the trilliumgradient.png image and the trilliumfoot.gif image. The trilliumfoot.gif image should not repeat and should be displayed in the lower right corner. The body selector style rules are as follows:

```
body { background-color: #f4ffe4; color: #333333;
       font-family: Arial; Verdana, sans-serif;
       min-width: 700px;
       background-image: url(trilliumgradient.png);
       background: url(trilliumfoot.gif) no-repeat bottom right,
                   url(trilliumgradient.png); }
```

2. Save your page as index.html. Launch a browser, and test your page. It will look different, depending on which browser you use—similar to either Figure 29 (in a browser that supports multiple background images) or Figure 30 (in a browser that does not support multiple background images). *Note*: The W3C CSS validator currently defaults to CSS level 2.1, but the `background` property is part of CSS level 3 (CSS3). You need to choose the appropriate CSS level when validating. Visit http://jigsaw.w3.org/css-validator and select "CSS level 3" for the Profile value.

3. There is usually more than one way to design a web page. Let's consider the placement of the flower image in the footer area of the web page. Why not configure the gradient image

as the body element selector background and the flower image as the footer background? This configuration will provide for a similar display on all currently popular browsers. Let's try this out. Edit the index.html file. Remove the background property from the body selector. A code sample is

```
body { background-color: #f4ffe4; color: #333333;
       background-image: url(trilliumgradient.png); }
```

Next, configure the trilliumfoot.gif image as the background for the #footer selector. Configure a height value that will be large enough to display the image. The code is

```
#footer { font-size: .75em; font-style: italic;
          background-image: url(trilliumfoot.gif);
          background-repeat: no-repeat;
          background-position: right;
          height: 90px; }
```

4. Save your page as index2.html. Launch a browser, and test your page. It should look similar to Figure 29 on all popular modern browsers. See the chapter4/4.8 folder in the student files for solutions to this Hands-On Practice.

CSS3 Rounded Corners

VideoNote
Rounded Corners with CSS

As you've worked with borders and the box model, you may have begun to notice a lot of rectangles on your web pages! CSS3 introduces the **`border-radius` property**, which can be used to create rounded corners and soften up those rectangles. Valid values for the border-radius property include one to four numeric values (using pixel or em units) or percentages that configure the radius of the corner. If a single value is provided, it configures all four corners. If four values are provided the corners are configured in order of top left, top right, bottom right, and bottom left. You can configure corners individually with the `border-bottom-left-radius`, `border-bottom-right-radius`, `border-top-left-radius`, and `border-top-right-radius` properties.

There is a complication when configuring rounded corners, though. Developers of browser-rendering engines, such as **WebKit** (used by Safari and Google Chrome) and **Gecko** (used by Firefox and other Mozilla-based browsers), have created proprietary properties to implement rounded corners. In addition, Internet Explorer 9 is the first version of IE to support the `border-radius` property. So, you need to code three different style declarations to round those corners:

- `-webkit-border-radius` (for WebKit browsers)
- `-moz-border-radius` (for Gecko browsers)
- `border-radius` (W3C Draft Syntax)

Eventually, all browsers will support CSS3 and the border-radius property, so code this property last in the list. CSS declarations to set a border with rounded corners are shown in the next segment of code. If you would like a visible border to display, configure the border property. Then set the value of the three `border-radius` properties to a value below 20px for best results. For example:

```
border: 3px ridge #330000;
-webkit-border-radius: 15px;
-moz-border-radius: 15px;
border-radius: 15px;
```

See Figure 31 (chapter4/box.html in the student files) for an example of this code in action. With progressive enhancement in mind, note that your visitors using older versions of Internet Explorer will see right-angle rather than rounded corners. However, the functionality and usability of the web page will not be affected.

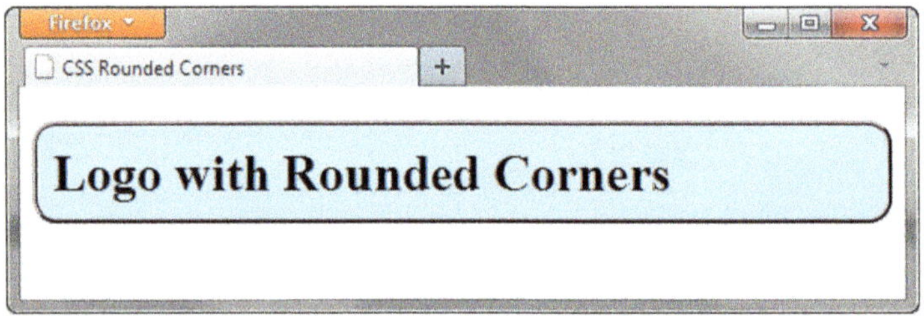

Figure 31 Rounded corners were configured with CSS

Be aware that when you code the nonstandard properties, your CSS will not pass W3C validation. Also, keep in mind that another approach to getting a rounded look is to create a rounded rectangle background image with a graphics application. However, once CSS3 becomes a well-supported standard, the box model will be easy to "round out" and is a much more efficient way to accomplish rounded corners.

Hands-On Practice 9

You'll configure a logo header area that uses a background image and rounded borders in this Hands-On Practice. When complete, your web page will look similar to the one shown in Figure 32.

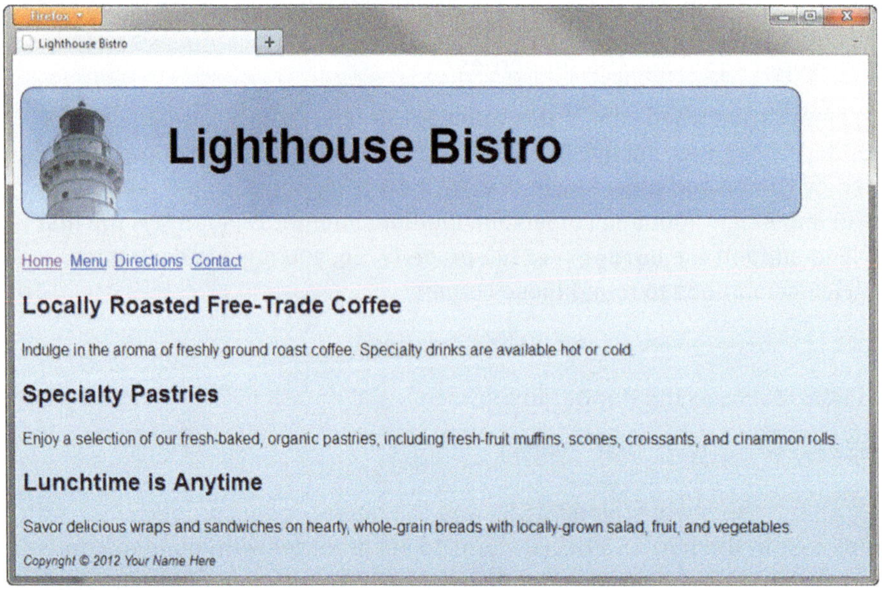

Figure 32 The web page with the logo area configured

1. Create a new folder called borderch4. Copy the lighthouselogo.jpg and the background.jpg files in the chapter4/starters folder to your borderch4 folder. A starter file is ready for you in the student files. Save the chapter4/starter3.html file to your borderch4 folder. Launch a browser to display the starter3.html web page shown in Figure 33.

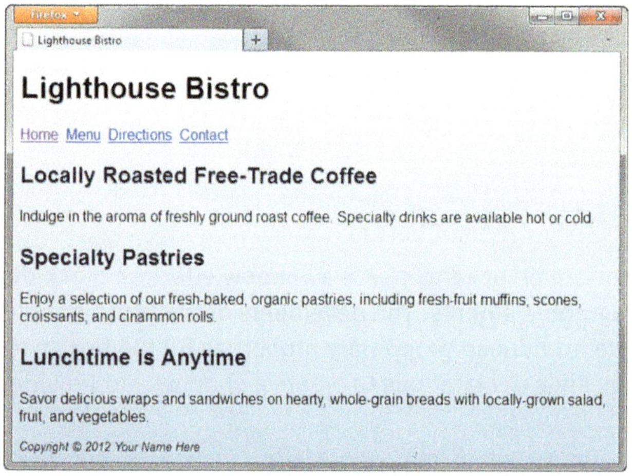

Figure 33 The starter3.html file

2. Launch a text editor, and open the starter3.html file. Save the file as index.html. Edit the embedded CSS, and add the following style declarations to the h1 selector that will configure the lighthouselogo.jpg image as a background image that does not repeat: height set to 100px, width set to 700px, font size set to 3em, 150px of left padding, 30px of top padding, and a solid dark-blue border (#000033) with a border radius of 15px. The style declarations are as follows:

```
h1 { background-image: url(lighthouselogo.jpg);
     background-repeat: no-repeat;
     height: 100px; width: 700px; font-size: 3em;
     padding-left: 150px; padding-top: 30px;
     border: 1px solid #000033;
     -webkit-border-radius: 15px;
     -moz-border-radius: 15px;
     border-radius: 15px; }
```

3. Save the file. When you test your index.html file in a browser, it should look similar to the one shown in Figure 32 if you are using a browser that supports rounded corners. Otherwise the logo will have right-angle corners, but the web page will still be usable. Compare your work with the solution in the student files (chapter4/lighthouse/index.html).

FAQ After I added the new properties, my CSS no longer passes W3C validation. What should I do?

Because you are using the browser-proprietary properties `-webkit-border-radius` and `-moz-border-radius` in addition to the CSS3 `border-radius` property, your CSS code will not pass validation, but your pages will display in modern browsers with the visual aesthetic you envisioned. In this case, it's a deliberate decision to choose the visual display over the use of absolutely correct syntax. In time, all browsers will support the border-radius property, you'll be able to remove the proprietary code, and your CSS will pass W3C CSS Level 3 validation testing. In the meantime, if you are intentionally using nonstandard properties to enhance your web pages, don't worry when your CSS validation test generates errors related to those properties.

FAQ **Why do some browsers use proprietary properties?**

When adding early support for a CSS effect or proposed property, browser vendors typically use a prefix to identify the property as a browser extension. As time goes by and the W3C specification for the property becomes stable, the browser vendor will eventually support the official property. Since CSS is rendered top down, a standard practice is to code your style rules with the browser-specific properties listed before the W3C standard property.

The CSS3 box-shadow Property

The CSS3 **`box-shadow` property** can be used to create a shadow effect on block-display elements such as div and paragraph elements. The developers of the WebKit and Gecko browser rendering engines have introduced proprietary properties for the box shadow effect. You'll need to code three style declarations to create a shadow and provide three to five values for each:

- Numeric pixel value for the shadow's horizontal offset:

  Positive value configures a shadow on the right. Negative value configures a shadow on the left.
- Numeric pixel value for the shadow's vertical offset:

  Positive value configures a shadow below. Negative value configures a shadow above.
- Optional: Numeric pixel value for the blur radius:

  Higher values configure more blur for a softer shadow. `0` configures a sharp shadow.
- Optional: Numeric pixel value for the spread distance:

  Positive values cause the shadow to expand. Negative values cause the shadow to contract.
- Valid color value

Here's an example that configures a dark-gray drop shadow with 5px horizontal offset, 5px vertical offset, and a 5px blur radius:

```
-webkit-box-shadow: 5px 5px 5px #828282;
-moz-box-shadow: 5px 5px 5px #828282;
box-shadow: 5px 5px 5px #828282;
```

Eventually, all browsers will support CSS3 and the official `box-shadow` property, so code this property last in the list. Note that when you include the nonstandard properties, your CSS will not pass W3C validation.

Include the optional `inset` value to configure an inner shadow. For example:

```
-webkit-box-shadow: inset 5px 5px 5px #828282;
-moz-box-shadow: inset 5px 5px 5px #828282;
box-shadow: inset 5px 5px 5px #828282;
```

The CSS3 `text-shadow` Property

The CSS3 **`text-shadow` property** configures a shadow effect on text and is supported by most recent versions of modern browsers, except for Internet Explorer 9. The property requires four values:

- Numeric pixel value for the shadow's horizontal offset:

  Positive value configures a shadow on the right. Negative value configures a shadow on the left.

- Numeric pixel value for the shadow's vertical offset:

  Positive value configures a shadow below. Negative value configures a shadow below.

- Numerical pixel value for the blur radius:

  Higher values configure more blur. 0 configures a sharp shadow.

- Valid color value

Here's an example:

```
text-shadow: 3px 3px 3px #666;
```

Hands-On Practice 10

You'll configure a centered content area and apply the `text-shadow` and `box-shadow` properties in this Hands-On Practice. When complete, your web page will look similar to the one shown in Figure 34.

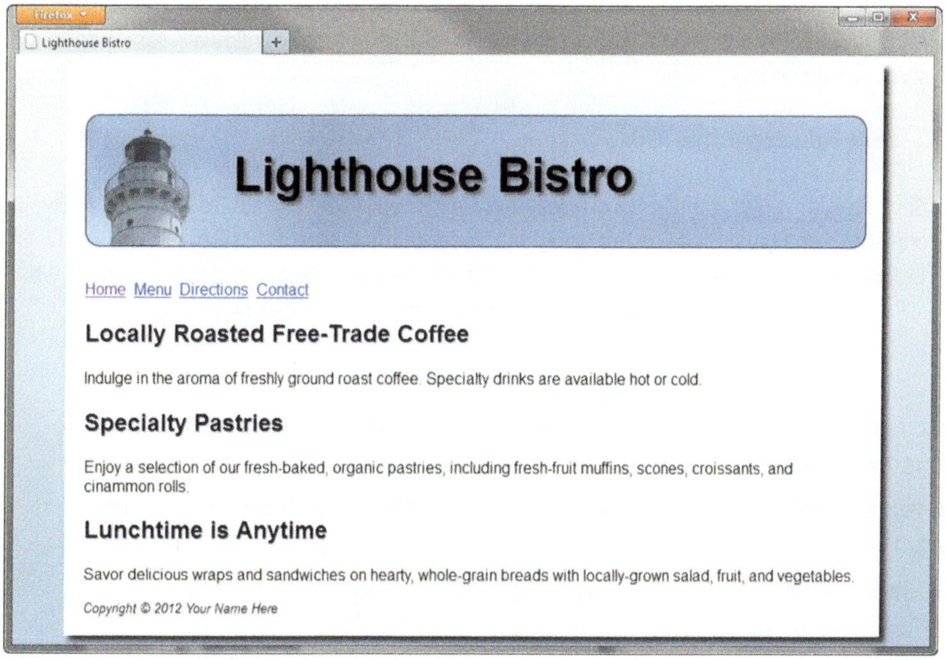

Figure 34 The centered neutral background along with shadow properties add dimension

Create a new folder called shadowch4. Copy the lighthouselogo.jpg and the background.jpg files from the chapter4/starters folder to your shadowch4 folder. Launch a text editor, and open the chapter4/lighthouse/index.html file (shown in Figure 32). Save the file in your shadowch4 folder.

1. Configure the page content to be centered, with an 800-pixel width, a white background, and some padding.

   a. Edit the HTML. Configure a div element assigned to the id named container that wraps the code within the body section. Code the opening `<div>` tag on a new line after the opening body tag. Code a closing div tag on a new line before the closing body tag.

   b. Edit the embedded CSS to configure a new selector, an id named container. Configure a white background color and 20 pixels of padding. Use the `width`, `margin-left`, and `margin-right` properties as follows:

```
#container { background-color: #ffffff;
             padding: 20px;
             width: 800px;
             margin-right: auto;
             margin-left: auto; }
```

2. Edit the embedded CSS to add the following style declarations to the #container selector to configure a box shadow:

```
-webkit-box-shadow: 5px 5px 5px #1e1e1e;
-moz-box-shadow: 5px 5px 5px #1e1e1e;
box-shadow: 5px 5px 5px #1e1e1e;
```

3. Add the following style declaration to the h1 element selector to configure a dark-gray text shadow:

```
text-shadow: 3px 3px 3px #666;
```

4. Add the following style declaration to the h2 element selector to configure a light-gray text shadow with no blur:

```
text-shadow: 1px 1px 0 #ccc;
```

5. Save the file. When you test your index.html file in a browser, it should look similar to the one shown in Figure 34 if you are using a browser that supports the `box-shadow` and `text-shadow` properties. Otherwise the shadows will not display, but the web page will still be usable. See the student files for a solution (chapter4/lighthouse/shadow.html).

Browser support changes with each new browser version. There is no substitute for thoroughly testing your web pages.

However, several resources provide support lists. The following websites provide this information:

- http://westciv.com/wiki/Experimental_CSS_compatibility_table
- http://www.findmebyip.com/litmus
- http://www.quirksmode.org/css/contents.html
- http://www.impressivewebs.com/css3-click-chart

The CSS3 opacity Property

The CSS3 `opacity` **property** configures the transparency of the background color. Opacity values range from 0 (which is completely transparent) to 1 (which is completely opaque and has no transparency). See Figure 35 for an example of using the opacity property to configure a white background that is only 60% opaque.

Figure 35 The background of the h1 area is transparent

Hands-On Practice 11

In this Hands-On Practice you'll work with the opacity property as you configure the web page shown in Figure 35.

1. Create a new folder called opacitych4. Copy fall.jpg file from the chapter4/starters folder to your opacitych4 folder. Launch a text editor and open the chapter2/template.html file. Save it in your opacitych4 folder with the name index.html. Change the page title to "Fall Nature Hikes".
2. Let's create the structure of the web page with a div that contains an h1 element. Add the following code to your web page in the body section:

```
<div id="content">
 <h1>Fall Nature Hikes</h1>
</div>
```

3. Now, add style tags to the head section, and configure the embedded CSS. You'll create an id named content to display the fall.jpg as a background image that does not repeat. The content id also has a width of 640 pixels, a height of 480 pixels, left and right auto margins (which will center the object in the browser viewport), and 20 pixels of top padding. The code is

```
#content { background-image: url(fall.jpg);
           background-repeat: no-repeat;
           margin-left: auto;
           margin-right: auto;
           width: 640px;
           height: 480px;
           padding-top: 20px;}
```

4. Now configure the h1 element selector to have a white background color with opacity set to 0.6, font size set to 4em, and 10 pixels of padding. Sample code is

```
h1 { background-color: #FFFFFF;
     opacity: 0.6;
     font-size: 4em;
     padding: 10px; }
```

5. Save the file. When you test your index.html file in a browser that supports opacity (such as Chrome, Firefox, Safari, or Internet Explorer 9), it should look similar to the page shown in Figure 35. See the student files for a solution (chapter4/opacity/index.html). If you look very carefully at the web page, you'll see that the opacity property configured both the background color and the text color of the h1 element to be partially transparent. The opacity property is inherited and would also affect any elements contained within the h1 element. Experiment by changing the opacity property to different values, and observe the results.

Figure 36 shows the web page displayed in Internet Explorer 8, which does not support the opacity property. Notice that the visual aesthetic is not exactly the same, but the page is still usable. While Internet Explorer 9 supports opacity, earlier versions support the proprietary `filter` property with an opacity level configured between 1 (transparent) and 100 (opaque). A sample is found in the student files (chapter4/opacity/opacityie.html). The CSS for the filter property is

```
filter: alpha(opacity=60);
```

Figure 36 Internet Explorer 8 does not support the opacity property and displays an opaque background color

CSS3 RGBA Color

CSS3 supports new syntax for the color property that configures transparent color, called **RGBA color**. Four values are required: red color, green color, blue color, and alpha (transparency). RGBA color does not use hexadecimal color values. Instead, decimal color values are configured; see the partial color chart in Figure 37 and the Web-Safe Color Palette in the appendix for examples.

#FFFFFF
rgb (255, 255, 255)
	#FFFFCC
	rgb(255, 255, 204)
		#FFFF99
		rgb(255,255,153)
			#FFFF66
			rgb(255,255,102)

#FFFF33
rgb(255,255,51)
	#FFFF00
	rgb(255,255,0)
		#FFCCFF
		rgb(255, 204, 255)
			#FFCCCC
			rgb(255,204,204)

#FFCC99
rgb(255,204,153)
	#FFCC66
	rgb(255,204,102)
		#FFCC33
		rgb(255,204,51)
			#FFCC00
			rgb(255,204,0)

#FF99FF
rgb(255,153,255)
	#FF99CC
	rgb(255,153,204)
		#FF9999
		rgb(255,153,153)
			#FF9966
			rgb(255,153,102)

Figure 37 Hexadecimal and RGB decimal color values

The values for red, green, and blue must be decimal values from 0 to 255. The alpha value must be a number between 0 (transparent) and 1 (opaque). Figure 38 shows a web page with the text configured to be slightly transparent.

Figure 38 CSS3 RGBA color configures the transparent text

Hands-On Practice 12

In this Hands-On Practice you'll configure transparent text as you code the web page shown in Figure 38.

1. Launch a text editor, and open the file you created in the previous Hands-On Practice (also located in the student files chapter4/opacity/index.html). Save the file with the name rgba.html.
2. Delete the current style declarations for the h1 element selector. You will create new style rules for the h1 selector to configure 10 pixels of right padding and right-aligned sans-serif white text that is 70% opaque, with a font size of 5em. Since not all browsers support RBGA color, you'll configure the color property twice. The first instance will be the standard color value that is supported by all modern browsers; the second instance will configure the RGBA color. Older browsers will not understand the RGBA color and will ignore it. Newer browsers will "see" both of the color style declarations and will apply them in the order they are coded, so the result will be transparent color. The CSS code is

```
h1 { color: #ffffff;
     color: rgba(255, 255, 255, 0.7);
     font-family: Verdana, Helvetica, sans-serif;
     font-size: 5em;
     padding-right: 10px;
     text-align: right; }
```

3. Save the file. When you test your rgba.html file in a browser that supports RGBA color (such as Chrome, Firefox, Safari, or Internet Explorer 9), it should look similar to the page shown in Figure 38. See the student files for a solution (chapter4/opacity/rgba.html). If you are using a nonsupporting browser such as Internet Explorer 8 (or earlier), you'll see white text instead of transparent text. While Internet Explorer 9 supports RGBA color, earlier versions support the proprietary filter property; an example is in the student files (chapter4/opacity/rbgaie.html).

FAQ What's HSLA color all about?

There is another new method to configure color when using CSS3, called HSLA color. The letters in HSLA stand for hue, saturation, lightness, and alpha. It's a different way of thinking about color than the RGB system that web designers typically use. HSLA color is not yet supported on all browsers. Check out the following resources for more information:

- http://www.w3.org/TR/2003/CR-css3-color-20030514/#hsla-color
- http://www.useragentman.com/blog/2010/08/28/coding-colors-easily-using-css3-hsl-notation
- http://css-tricks.com/yay-for-hsla

CSS3 Gradients

CSS3 provides a method to configure color as a **gradient**, which is a smooth blending of shades from one color to another color. A CSS3 gradient background color is defined purely with CSS; no image file is needed! This provides flexibility for web designers, along with a savings in the bandwidth required to serve out gradient background image files.

Sound great? Yes, it does, but there is a catch: The WebKit and Gecko browser rendering engines use a proprietary coding syntax to process CSS gradients. The W3C has added gradient support to the CSS Image Value and Replaced Content Module (in draft status), but at the time this text was written, this syntax had not yet been adopted by browsers. This section will provide an example of a CSS3 gradient, along with links to resources for further study.

Figure 34 displays a web page with a JPG gradient background image that was configured in a graphics application. The web page shown in Figure 39 (available in the student files chapter4/lighthouse/gradient.html) does not use a JPG for the background; CSS3 gradient properties re-created the look of the linear gradient image.

CSS3 Gradients and Progressive Enhancement

It's very important to keep progressive enhancement in mind when using CSS3 gradients. Configure a "fallback" background-color property or background-image property which will be rendered by browsers that do not support CSS3 gradients. In Figure 39 the background color was configured to be same value as the ending gradient color.

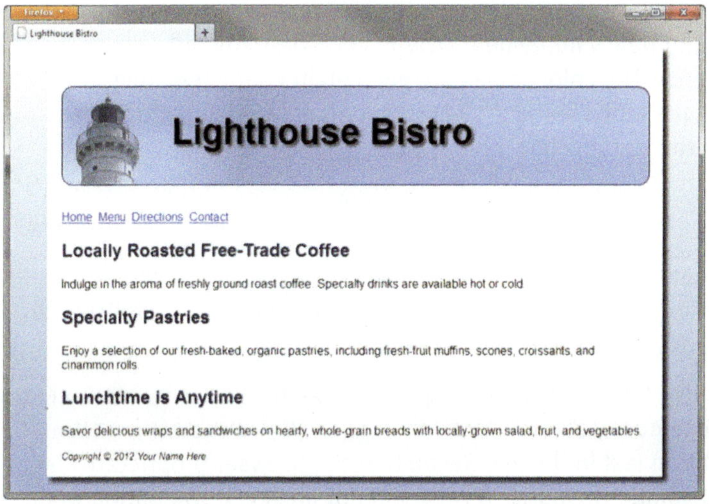

Figure 39 The gradient in the background was configured with CSS3 without an image file.

Configuring CSS3 Gradients

Code four style declarations to configure a gradient background:

- `-webkit-gradient` (for Webkit browsers)
- `-moz-linear-gradient` (for Gecko browsers)
- `filter` (for Internet Explorer)
- `linear-gradient` (W3C draft syntax)

Configure the gradient as the value of the background-image property (except for Internet Explorer, which uses its `filter` property). The following CSS code first configures a background color (for nonsupporting browsers) and then configures a linear gradient that blends from white (#FFFFFF) to a medium blue (#8FA5CE):

```
background-color: #8FA5CE;
background-image: -webkit-gradient(linear, left top, left bottom,
                  from(#FFFFFF), to(#8FA5CE));
background-image: -moz-linear-gradient(top, #FFFFFF, #8FA5CE);
filter: progid:DXImageTransform.Microsoft.gradient
      (startColorstr=#FFFFFFFF, endColorstr=#FF8FA5CE);
background-image: linear-gradient(#FFFFFF, #8FA5CE);
```

WebKit Syntax

Examine the WebKit code syntax which is used by the Safari and Google Chrome browsers. In its most basic form, the value of `–webkit-gradient` lists the type of gradient (linear or radial), starting point, ending point, starting color, and ending color.

Gecko Syntax

Review the Gecko code syntax which is used by browsers such as Firefox and Flock. The value of `–moz-linear-gradient` lists the starting point and color-stops (in this case there are two colors: #FFFFFF and #8FA5CE).

Internet Explorer Syntax

Internet Explorer version 9 and below implements the `filter` property rather than the `background-image property`. The color values are each eight characters long. The first two characters indicate the alpha value (#00 is transparent; #FF is opaque). The next six characters indicate the hexadecimal color value.

W3C Syntax

The W3C syntax uses different functions for linear (`linear-gradient`) and radial (`radial-gradient`) gradients. The basic format for a two-color linear gradient lists the value for each color (in this example, #FFFFFF and #8FA5CE).

As shown in the code samples, the syntax for configuring gradients varies by browser engine. It is expected that eventually all browsers will support W3C `linear-gradient` syntax, so code this declaration last in the list. Recall that the browser-proprietary CSS syntax in this section is nonstandard. Your CSS code will not pass W3C validation when you use these properties.

Experiment with generating CSS3 gradient code at http://www.westciv.com/tools/gradients, http://www.colorzilla.com/gradient-editor, and http://gradients.glrzad.com. For more information about CSS3 gradient syntax, visit the corresponding websites:

- **Webkit**: http://webkit.org/blog/175/introducing-css-gradients
- **Mozilla**: http://developer.mozilla.org/en/CSS/-moz-linear-gradient
- **Internet Explorer:** http://msdn.microsoft.com/en-us/library/ms532997(VS.85,loband).aspx
- **W3C:** http://dev.w3.org/csswg/css3-images/#gradients

Chapter Summary

This chapter has introduced the use of visual elements and graphics on web pages. The number-one reason visitors leave web pages is long download times. When using images, be careful to optimize the images for the Web, reducing both the size of the file and the dimensions of the image, in order to minimize download time.

You explored new HTML5 elements and many CSS properties in this chapter. When using the new CSS3 properties and HTML5 elements, be mindful of the concepts of progressive enhancement and accessibility. Verify that the pages display in an acceptable manner even if new techniques are not supported by the browser. Provide text alternatives to images with the alt attribute.

Visit the text's website at http://www.webdevfoundations.net for examples, the links listed in this chapter, and updated information.

Key Terms

`<area>`
`<figcaption>`
`<figure>`
`<hr>`
`<img>`
`<map>`
`<meter>`
`<progress>`
`alt` attribute
animated GIFs
`background-attachment` property
`background-clip` property
`background-image` property
`background-origin` property
`background-position` property
`background-repeat` property
`background-size` property
`border` property
`border-color` property
`border-radius` property
`border-style` property
`border-width` property
`box-shadow` property
favicon
filter property
gamma
Gecko
GIF
gradient
`height` attribute
hotspots
HSLA color
`hspace` attribute
image link
image map
image optimization
image slicing
interlaced image
JPEG
`longdesc` attribute
lossless compression
lossy compression
min-width property
opacity property
padding property
PNG
progressive enhancement
progressive JPEG
RGBA color
resolution
`src` attribute
text-shadow property
thumbnail image
transparency
`usemap` attribute
`vspace` attribute
Webkit
WebP
`width` attribute

Review Questions

Multiple Choice

1. Which CSS property configures the background color?
   a. bgcolor
   b. background-color
   c. color
   d. none of the above

2. Which HTML tag configures a horizontal line on a web page?
   a. `<line>`
   b. `<br>`
   c. `<hr>`
   d. `<border>`

3. Which of the following creates an image link to the index.html page when the home.gif graphic is clicked?
   a. `<a href="index.html" src="home.gif" alt="Home"></a>`
   b. `<a href="index.html"><img src="home.gif" alt="Home"></a>`
   c. `<img src="home.gif" href="index.html" alt="Home">`
   d. `<a href="index.html"><img href="home.gif" alt="Home"></a>`
4. Why should you include height and width attributes on an <img> tag?
   a. They are required attributes and must always be included.
   b. They help the browser render the page faster because it reserves the appropriate space for the image.
   c. They help the browser display the image in its own window.
   d. none of the above
5. Which attribute specifies text that is available to browsers and other user agents that do not support graphics?
   a. alt
   b. text
   c. src
   d. none of the above
6. What is the term used to describe a square icon that is associated with a web page and is displayed in the browser address bar or tab?
   a. background
   b. bookmark icon
   c. favicon
   d. logo
7. Which of the following graphic types is best suited to photographs?
   a. GIF
   b. JPG
   c. BMP
   d. PHOTO
8. Which of the following graphic types can be made transparent?
   a. GIF
   b. JPG
   c. BMP
   d. PHOTO
9. Which of the following configures empty space between the content of the HTML element (usually text) and the border?
   a. vspace property
   b. padding property
   c. margin property
   d. none of the above
10. Which of the following configures a graphic to repeat vertically down the side of a web page?
    a. `hspace="10"`
    b. `background-repeat:repeat;`
    c. `valign="left"`
    d. `background-repeat: repeat-y;`

Fill in the Blank

11. A background image will automatically be repeated, or ________________, by a web browser.
12. If your web page uses graphic links, include ________________ at the bottom of the page to increase accessibility.
13. A ________________ image is a smaller version of a larger image that usually links to the larger image.
14. The ______________ CSS3 property configures a drop-shadow effect on text.
15. The ___________element displays a visual gauge of a numeric value within a known range.

Apply Your Knowledge

1. **Predict the Result.** Draw and write a brief description of the web page that will be created with the following HTML code:

```
<!DOCTYPE html>
<html lang="en">
<head>
<title>Predict the Result</title>
<meta charset="utf-8">
</head>
<body>
<img src="logo.gif" alt="CircleSoft Design" height="150"
width="600"> <br>
Home <a href="about.html">About</a>
<a href="services.html">Services</a>
<p><img src="people.jpg" alt="Professionals at CircleSoft Design"
height="300" width="300"> Our professional staff takes pride
in its working relationship with our clients by offering
personalized services that take their needs into account, develop
their target areas, and incorporate these items into a website
that works.</p>
</div>
</body>
</html>
```

2. **Fill in the Missing Code.** This web page contains an image link and should be configured so that the background and text colors have good contrast. The image used on this web page should link to a page called services.html. Some HTML attribute values, indicated by "_", are missing. Some CSS style rules, indicated by "_", are incomplete. The code follows:

```
<!DOCTYPE html>
<html lang="en">
<head>
<title>CircleSoft Design</title>
<meta charset="utf-8">
<style>
body { "_": "_";
       color: "_";
}
</style>
</head>
<body>
  <div>
  <a href="_"><img src="logo.gif" alt="_" height="100"
  width="600">
  <br>Enter CircleSoft Design</a>
</div>
</body>
</html>
```

3. **Find the Error.** This page displays an image called trillium.jpg. The image is 100 pixels wide by 200 pixels high. When this page is displayed, the image does not look

right. Find the error. Describe the attributes that you would code in the `<img >` tag to provide accessibility. The code follows:

```
<!DOCTYPE html>
<html lang="en">
<head>
<title>Find the Error<title>
<meta charset="utf-8">
</head>
<body>
<img src="trillium.jpg" height="100" width="100" alt="Trillium
flower">
</body>
</html>
```

Hands-On Exercises

1. Write the HTML to place an image called primelogo.gif on a web page. The image is 100 pixels high by 650 pixels wide.
2. Write the HTML to create an image hyperlink. The image is called schaumburgthumb.jpg. It is 100 pixels high by 150 pixels wide. The image should link to a larger image called schaumburg.jpg. There should be no border on the image.
3. Write the HTML to create a div that contains three images used as navigation links. Table 5 provides information about the images and their associated links.

Table 5

Image Name	Link Page Name	Image Height	Image Width
home.gif	index.html	50	200
products.gif	products.html	50	200
order.gif	order.html	50	200

4. Experiment with page backgrounds. Locate the twocolor.gif file in the student files chapter4/starters folder. Design a web page that uses this file as a background image that repeats down the left side of the browser window. Save your file as bg1.html.
5. Experiment with page backgrounds. Locate the twocolor1.gif file in the student files chapter4/starters folder. Design a web page that uses this file as a background image that repeats across the top of the browser window. Save your file as bg2.html.
6. Visit one of your favorite websites. Note the colors used for background, text, headings, images, and so on. Write a paragraph that describes how the site uses color for these elements and if the Web-Safe Color Palette is used. Code a web page that uses colors in a similar manner. Save your file as color.html.
7. Practice with CSS.
   a. Write the CSS for a class named footer with the following characteristics: a light-blue background color, Arial font, dark-blue text color, 10 pixels of padding, and a narrow, dashed border in a dark-blue color.
   b. Write the CSS for an id named notice that is configured to 80% width and centered.

c. Write the CSS to configure a class that will produce a headline with a dotted line underneath it. Choose a color that you like for the text and dotted line.

d. Write the CSS to configure an h1 element selector with drop-shadow text, a 50% transparent background color, and sans-serif font that is 4em in size.

e. Write the CSS to configure an id named section with small, red, Arial font; a white background; a width of 80%; and a drop shadow.

8. Design a new web page about you. Use CSS to configure a background color and text color for the page. Include the following on your web page:

- Your name
- A description of your favorite hobbies and activities
- A photo of yourself (be sure to optimize the image for display on the Web)

Save the page as yourlastname.html.

9. Design a web page that provides a list of resources for free clip art and free photographs. The list should contain at least five different websites. Use your favorite graphic sites, the sites suggested in this chapter, or sites you have found on the Web. Save the page as freegraphics.html.

10. Visit the text's website at http://webdevfoundations.net/6e/chapter4.html and follow the link to the Adobe Fireworks or Adobe Photoshop tutorial. Follow the instructions to create a logo banner. Hand in the printouts described in the tutorial to your instructor.

Web Research

1. Providing access to the Web for all people is an important issue. Visit the W3C's Web Accessibility Initiative and explore its WCAG 2.0 Quick Reference at http://www.w3.org/WAI/WCAG20/quickref. View additional pages at the W3C's site as necessary. Explore the checkpoints that are related to the use of color and images on web pages. Create a web page that uses color, uses images, and includes the information that you discovered.

2. This chapter has introduced you to several new CSS3 properties. Choose one of them to research further. Create an example web page that demonstrates the use of the property. Use one of the following sites to determine the current browser support of the property, and include a summary of this information (along with the URLs of the resources you used) in your web page:

- http://www.quirksmode.org/css/contents.html
- http://westciv.com/wiki/Experimental_CSS_compatibility_table
- http://www.findmebyip.com/litmus
- http://www.impressivewebs.com/css3-click-chart

Focus on Web Design

Visit a website that interests you. Print the home page or one other pertinent page from the site. Write a one-page summary and reaction to the website you chose to visit. Address the following topics:

a. What is the purpose of the site?

b. Who is the intended audience?

c. Do you believe the site reaches its audience?

d. Was this site useful to you? Why or why not?

e. List the colors and/or graphics that are used on the home page of this website: background, backgrounds of page sections, text, logo, navigation buttons, and so on.

f. How does the use of color and graphics enhance the website?

WEBSITE CASE STUDY

Using Graphics & Visual Elements

JavaJam Coffee House

Figure 25 in the chapter "HTML Basics" shows a site map for the JavaJam website. The Home page and Menu page were created in other chapters. Using the existing website as a starting point, you will modify the design of the pages and create a new page, the Music page. You have five tasks in this case study:

1. Create a new folder for this JavaJam case study, and obtain the starter image files.
2. Modify the Home page to display a logo image, a JPEG image, and a content div as shown in Figure 40.
3. Modify the Menu page to be consistent with the Home page.
4. Create a new Music page, as shown in Figure 41.
5. Modify the style rules in the javajam.css file as needed.

Figure 40 New JavaJam Home page

Hands-On Practice Case

Task 1: Create a folder on your hard drive or portable storage device called javajam4. Copy all the files from your Chapter 3 javajamcss folder into the javajam4 folder. Obtain the images used in this case study from the student files. The images are located in the chapter4/casestudystarters/javajam folder. The images are background.gif, greg.jpg, gregthumb.jpg, javalogo.gif, melanie.jpg, melaniethumb.jpg, and windingroad.jpg. Save them in your javajam4 folder.

Task 2: The Home Page. Launch a text editor, and open the index.html file from your javajam4 folder. Modify the index.html file to look similar to the web page shown in Figure 40.

1. Replace the "JavaJam Coffee House" text contained within the h1 element with the javalogo.gif. Be sure to include the alt, height, and width attributes on the `<img>` tag for the graphic.
2. Configure a div element that will contain all the web page content between the navigation area and the footer area.
   - Add a new blank line below the navigation div. Code an opening div tag that is assigned to the id named content.
   - Add a new blank line above the footer div. Code a closing div tag.
3. Add a new blank line below the opening div tag for the content id. Configure the windingroad.jpg image to display. Be sure to include the alt, height, and width attributes. Also configure the image to appear to the right of the unordered list by coding the `align="right"` attribute on the `<img>` tag.

Save and test your new index.html page. It will be similar to Figure 40, but you'll notice that a few final touches (like the background image) are missing; you'll configure these with CSS in Task 5.

Task 3: The Menu Page. Launch a text editor, and open the menu.html page from your javajam4 folder. Replace the JavaJam Coffee House heading with the javalogo.gif. Configure the content div in the same manner as on the home page. Save and test your new menu.html page.

Task 4: The Music Page. Use the Menu page as the starting point for the Music page. Launch a text editor, and open the menu.html file in the javajam4 folder. Save the file as music.html. Modify the music.html file to look similar to the Music page, as shown in Figure 41:

1. Change the page title to an appropriate phrase.
2. Delete the description list from the page.
3. The main content in the page will consist of a paragraph below the navigation and two sections describing music performances.
   - The text of the paragraph follows:

     The first Friday night each month at JavaJam is a special night. Join us from 8pm to 11pm for some music you won't want to miss!
   - *Hint*: Use the special character `’` for the apostrophe character.
   - The section describing each music performance consists of an h2 element, a paragraph assigned to the class named details, and an image link.

Figure 41 JavaJam music.html

January Music Performance:

- Configure an h2 element with the following text: January
- Code an opening paragraph tag. Assign the paragraph to the class named details.
- Configure the melaniethumb.jpg as an image link to melanie.jpg. Code appropriate attributes on the <img> tag.
- Configure the following text within the paragraph after the image:

  Melanie Morris entertains with her melodic folk style. Check out the podcast! CDs are now available.

February Music Performance:

- Configure an h2 element with the following text: February
- Code an opening paragraph tag. Assign the paragraph to the class named details.
- Configure the gregthumb.jpg as an image link to greg.jpg. Code appropriate attributes on the <img> tag.
- Configure the following text within the paragraph after the image:

  Tahoe Greg's back from his tour. New songs. New stories. CDs are now available.
- *Hint*: Use the special character ’ for the apostrophe character.

Save the music.html file. If you test your page in a browser, you'll notice that it looks different from Figure 41—you still need to configure style rules.

Task 5: Configure the CSS. Open javajam.css in a text editor. Edit the style rules as follows:

1. Modify the body element selector style rules. Configure background.gif as the background image.
2. Modify the style rules for the wrapper id. Configure the background color to be #ffffcc. Configure a minimum width of 700px (use `min-width`). Use the `box-shadow` property to configure a drop-shadow effect.
3. Modify the h1 element selector. Remove the line-height style rule.
4. Add a new style rule for the h2 selector that configures a background color (#ccaa66), font size (1.2em), left padding (10px) and bottom padding (5px). The style rules follow:

```
background-color: #ccaa66;
font-size: 1.2em;
padding-left: 10px;
padding-bottom: 5px;
```

5. Modify the footer id. Configure 10 pixels of padding.
6. Add a new style rule for the id named content to configure 25 pixels of padding.
7. Add a new style rule for the class named details to add 20% left and right padding (use `padding-left` and `padding-right`). Notice how this rule adds empty space on either side of the music performance description and image.
8. Add a new style rule for the img element selector not to display a border.

Save the javajam.css file. Test your pages (index.html, menu.html, and music.html) in a browser. If your images do not appear or your image links do not work, examine your work carefully. Use Windows Explorer or Mac Finder to verify that the images are saved in your javajam4 folder. Examine the src attribute on the `<img>` tags to be sure you spelled the image names correctly. Another useful troubleshooting technique is to validate the HTML and CSS code.

Fish Creek Animal Hospital

Figure 29 in the chapter "HTML Basics" shows a site map for Fish Creek. The Home page and Services page were created in other chapters. Using the existing website as a starting point, you will modify the design of the pages and create a new page, the Ask the Vet page. You have five tasks in this case study:

1. Create a new folder for this Fish Creek case study, and obtain the starter image files.
2. Modify the Home page to display a logo image and navigation image links as shown in Figure 42.
3. Modify the Services page to be consistent with the Home page.
4. Create a new Ask the Vet page, as shown in Figure 43.
5. Modify the style rules in the fishcreek.css file as needed.

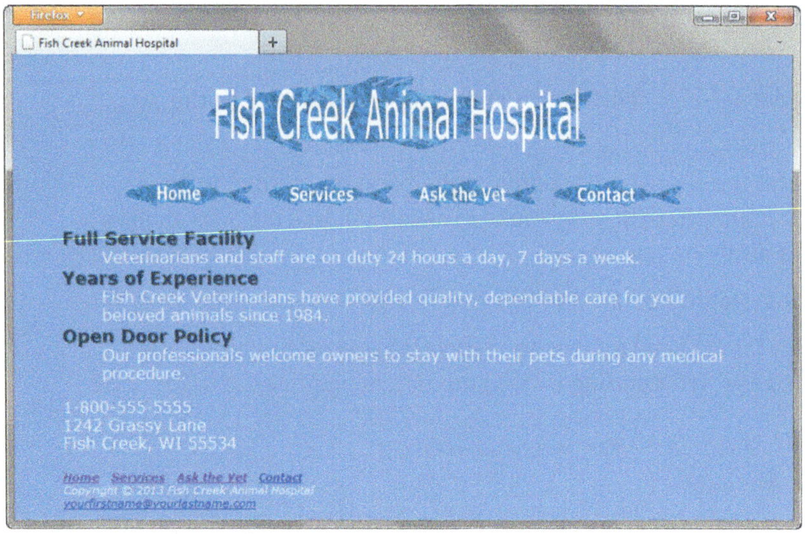

Figure 42 New Fish Creek Home page

Hands-On Practice Case

Task 1: Create a folder on your hard drive or portable storage device called fishcreek4. Copy all the files from your Chapter 3 fishcreekcss folder into the fishcreek4 folder. Obtain the images used in this case study from the student files. The images are located in the chapter4/casestudystarters/fishcreek folder. The images are fishcreeklogo.gif, home.gif, services.gif, askthevet.gif, and contact.gif. Save the files in your fishcreek4 folder.

Task 2: The Home Page. Launch a text editor, and open the index.html file from your fishcreek4 folder. Modify the index.html file to look similar to the web page shown in Figure 42.

1. Replace the "Fish Creek Animal Hospital" text contained within the h1 element with the fishcreeklogo.gif. Be sure to include the alt, height, and width attributes on the `<img>` tag for the graphic.
2. Update the navigation area.
   - Since you will be replacing the main navigation with image links, it's a good idea to provide for accessibility by including a set of text navigation links in the footer section of the web page. Copy the nav div, and paste it inside the footer area above the copyright line.
   - Refer to Figure 42, and replace the main navigation text hyperlinks with image links. The home.gif should link to index.html. The services.gif should link to services.html. The askthevet.gif should link to askvet.html. The contact.gif should link to contact.html. Use appropriate attributes on the `<img>` tag: alt, height, and width. Assign the div that contains the main navigation to the id named main. The div tag is coded as follows:

```
<div class="nav" id="main">
```

Save and test your new index.html page. It will be similar to Figure 42, but you'll notice that a few final touches (like the text shadow on the categories) are missing; you'll configure these with CSS in Task 5.

Task 3: The Services Page. Launch a text editor, and open the services.html page from your fishcreek4 folder. Replace the "Fish Creek Animal Hospital" heading with the fishcreeklogo.gif. Configure the navigation areas in a similar way as the home page. Save and test your new services.html page.

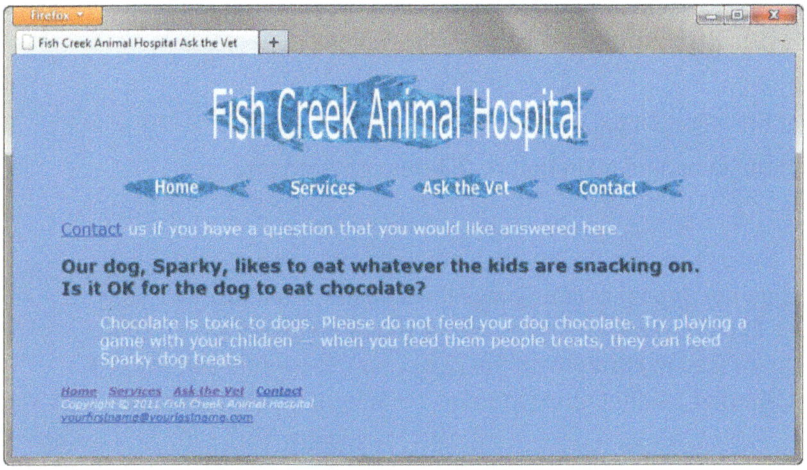

Figure 43 Fish Creek askvet.html

Task 4: The Ask the Vet Page. Use the Services page as the starting point for the Ask the Vet page. Launch a text editor, and open the services.html file in the fishcreek4 folder. Save the file as askvet.html. Modify the askvet.html file to look similar to the Ask the Vet page, as shown in Figure 43:

1. Change the page title to an appropriate phrase.
2. Delete the unordered list from the page.
3. The page content consists of a paragraph of text followed by a definition list that contains a question and an answer.
   a. Replace the text in the paragraph as follows:

      Contact us if you have a question that you would like answered here.

   b. The word "Contact" should link to the contact.html page.
   c. The description list displays the question and answer. The `<dt>` element configures the question. Assign the `<dt>` element to the category class used on the Services page. The `<dd>` element configures the answer. The content of the description list follows:

      Question: Our dog, Sparky, likes to eat whatever the kids are snacking on. Is it OK for the dog to eat chocolate?"

      Answer: Chocolate is toxic to dogs. Please do not feed your dog chocolate. Try playing a game with your children—when you feed them people treats, they can feed Sparky dog treats.

   d. *Hint*: See the appendix "Special Entity Characters," for the character code to display the em dash (—).

Save the askvet.html file. If you test your page in a browser, you'll notice that it looks different from Figure 43—you still need to configure style rules.

Task 5: Configure the CSS. Open fishcreek.css in in a text editor. Edit the style rules as follows:

1. The fish navigation image area is quite wide. Modify the style rules to change the width of the page content container id from 80% to 700 pixels.
2. Modify the style rules for the h1 element selector. Delete the existing style rules. Add a new style rule to center the image (use `text-align:center`).
3. Modify the category class to display text with a drop shadow (use `text-shadow: 1px 1px 1px #666`).
4. Add a new style rule for the img element selector to display no border.
5. Add a new style rule for the id named main that configures centered text (use `text-align: center`).

Save the fishcreek.css file. Test your pages (index.html, services.html, and askvet.html) in a browser. If your images do not appear or your image links do not work, examine your work carefully. Use Windows Explorer or Mac Finder to verify that the images are saved in your fishcreek4 folder. Examine the src attribute on the `<img>` tags to be sure you spelled the image names correctly. Another useful troubleshooting technique is to validate the HTML and CSS code.

Pacific Trails

Figure 33 in the chapter "HTML Basics" shows a site map for Pacific Trails. The Home page and Yurts page were created. Using the existing website as a starting point, you will modify the design of the pages and create a new page, the Activities page. You have five tasks in this case study:

1. Create a new folder for this Pacific Trails case study, and obtain the starter image files.
2. Modify the Home page to display a logo image and scenic photograph as shown in Figure 44.
3. Modify the Yurts page to be consistent with the Home page.
4. Create a new Activities page, as shown in Figure 45.
5. Modify the style rules in the pacific.css file as needed.

Hands-On Practice Case

Task 1: Create a folder on your hard drive or portable storage device called pacific4. Copy all the files from your Chapter 3 pacificcss folder into the pacific4 folder. Obtain the images used in this case study from the student files. The images are located in the chapter4/casestudystarters/pacific folder. The images are sunset.jpg, coast.jpg, yurt.jpg, trail.jpg, and background.jpg. Save the files in your pacific4 folder.

Task 2: The Home Page. Launch a text editor, and open the index.html file from your pacific4 folder. Modify the index.html file to look similar to the web page shown in Figure 44.

1. Configure a div that will contain all the web page content between the navigation area and the footer area.
   - Add a new blank line below the navigation div. Code an opening div tag that is assigned to the id named content.
   - Add a new blank line above the footer div. Code a closing div tag.
2. Add a new blank line below the h2 element. Configure the coast.jpg image to display. Be sure to include the alt, height, and width attributes.

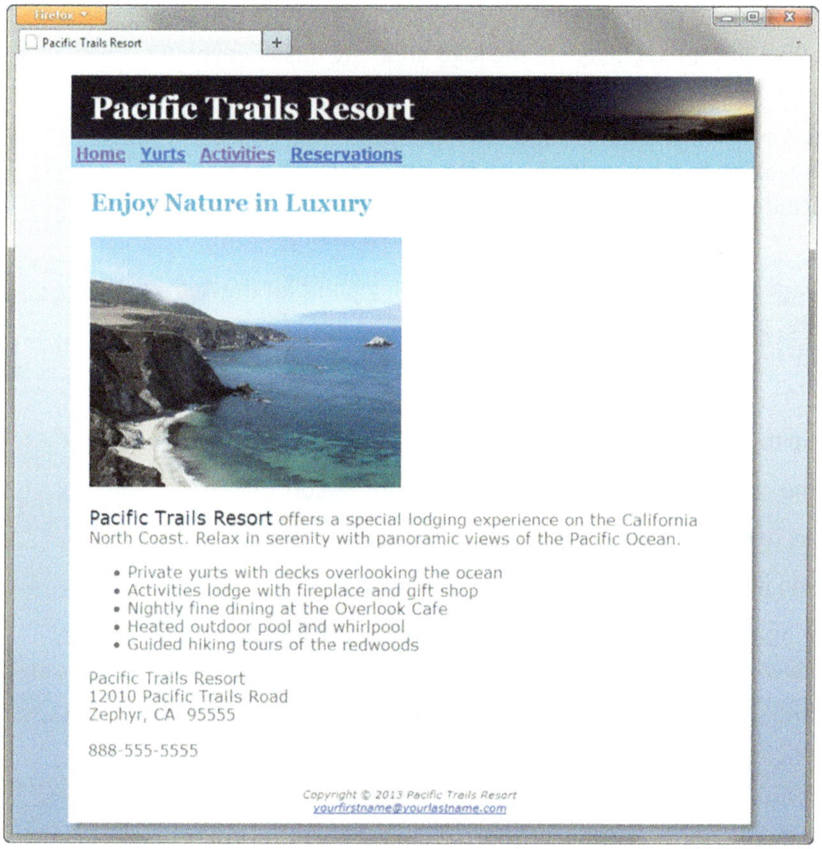

Figure 44 New Pacific Trails Resort Home page

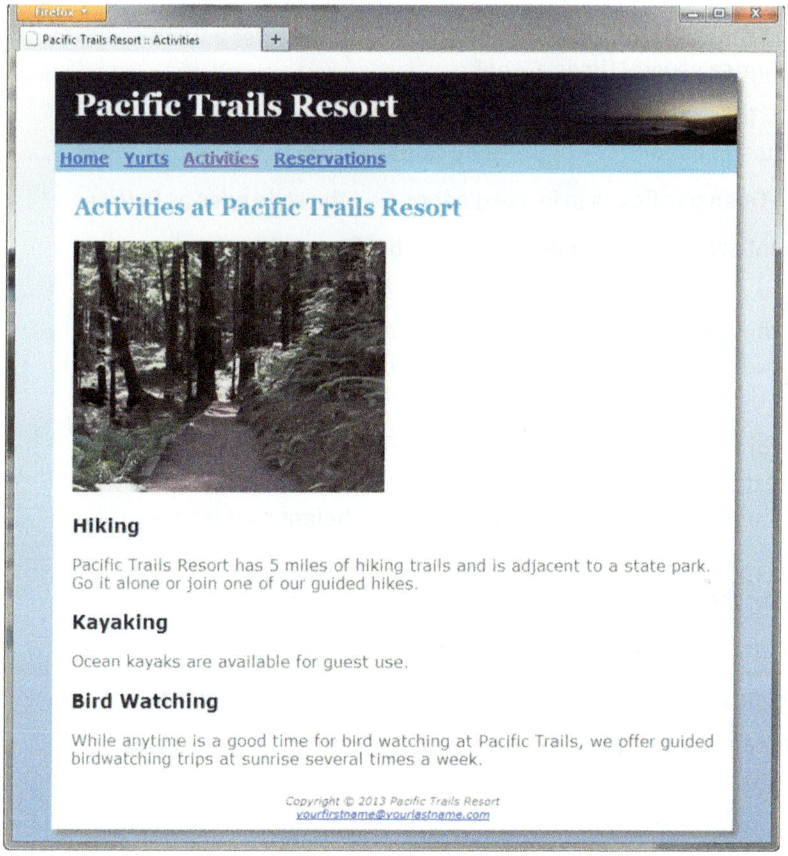

Figure 45 Pacific Trails activities.html

Save and test your new index.html page. It will be similar to Figure 44, but you'll notice that a few final touches (like the sunset image in the logo area) are missing; you'll configure these with CSS in Task 5.

Task 3: The Yurts Page. Launch a text editor, and open the yurts.html page from your pacific4 folder. Add a new blank line below the h2 element. Configure the yurt.jpg image to display. Be sure to include the alt, height, and width attributes. Save and test your new yurts.html page.

Task 4: The Activities Page. Use the Yurts page as the starting point for the Activities page. Launch a text editor, and open the yurts.html file in the pacific4 folder. Save the file as activities.html. Modify the activities.html file to look similar to the Activities page, as shown in Figure 45:

1. Change the page title to an appropriate phrase.
2. Change the text in the `<h2>` to be "Activities at Pacific Trails Resort".
3. Modify the `<img>` tag to display the trail.jpg image.
4. Delete the description list from the page.
5. Configure the following text, using h3 tags for the headings and paragraph tags for the sentences:

   Hiking

   Pacific Trails Resort has 5 miles of hiking trails and is adjacent to a state park. Go it alone or join one of our guided hikes.

   Kayaking

   Ocean kayaks are available for guest use.

   Bird Watching

   While anytime is a good time for bird watching at Pacific Trails, we offer guided birdwatching trips at sunrise several times a week.

Save the activities.html file. If you test your page in a browser, you'll notice that it looks different from Figure 45; you still need to configure style rules.

Task 5: Configure the CSS. Open pacific.css in in a text editor. Edit the style rules as follows:

1. Modify the body element selector style rules. Configure background.jpg as the background image.
2. Modify the style rules for the wrapper id. Configure the background color to be #ffffff. Configure a minimum width of 700px (use `min-width`). Use the `box-shadow` property to configure a drop-shadow effect.
3. Modify the style rules for the h1 element selector. Configure the sunset.jpg as a background image that displays on the right and does not repeat. Also configure 20 pixels of left padding. Configure a 72-pixel height (the same height as the background image).
4. Modify the style rules for the nav id. Configure 5 pixels of padding.
5. Modify the style rules for the footer id. Configure 10 pixels of padding.
6. Add a new style rule for the h3 element selector to display #000033 text color.
7. Add a new style rule for an id named content that configures 20 pixels of left and right padding.

8. Have you noticed extra empty space between the logo header area and the navigation? Let's do something about that. Modify the style rules for the h1 selector to set the bottom margin to 0 with the following code:

```
margin-bottom: 0;
```

Save the pacific.css file. Test your pages (index.html, yurts.html, and activities.html) in a browser. If your images do not appear or your image links do not work, examine your work carefully. Use Windows Explorer or Mac Finder to verify that the images are saved in your pacific4 folder. Examine the src attribute on the <img> tags to be sure you spelled the image names correctly. Another useful troubleshooting technique is to validate the HTML and CSS code.

Prime Properties

Figure 37 in the chapter "HTML Basics" shows a site map for Prime Properties. The Home page and Financing page were created. Using the existing website as a starting point, you will modify the design of the pages and create a new page, the Listings page. You have five tasks in this case study:

1. Create a new folder for this Prime Properties case study, and obtain the starter image files.
2. Modify the Home page to display a logo image and navigation buttons as shown in Figure 46.
3. Modify the Financing page to be consistent with the Home page.
4. Create a new Listings page, as shown in Figure 47.
5. Modify the style rules in the prime.css file as needed.

Hands-On Practice Case

Task 1: Create a folder on your hard drive or portable storage device called prime4. Copy all the files from your Chapter 3 primecss folder into the prime4 folder. Obtain the images used in this case study from the student files. The images are located in the chapter4/casestudystarters/prime folder. The images are primelogo.gif, primehomenav.gif, primehomebtn.gif, primelistingsnav.gif, primelistingsbtn.gif, primefinancingnav.gif, primefinancingbtn.gif, primecontactnav.gif, primecontactbtn.gif, schaumburg.jpg, schaumburgthumb.jpg, libertyville.jpg, libertyvillethumb.jpg, primevertical.png, primehorizontal.png, and primediagonal.png. Save the files in your prime4 folder.

Task 2: The Home Page. Launch a text editor, and open the index.html file from your prime4 folder. Modify the index.html file to look similar to the web page shown in Figure 46.

1. Replace the "Prime Properties" text contained within the h1 element with the primelogo.gif. Be sure to include the alt, height, and width attributes on the <img> tag for the graphic.
2. Update the navigation area.

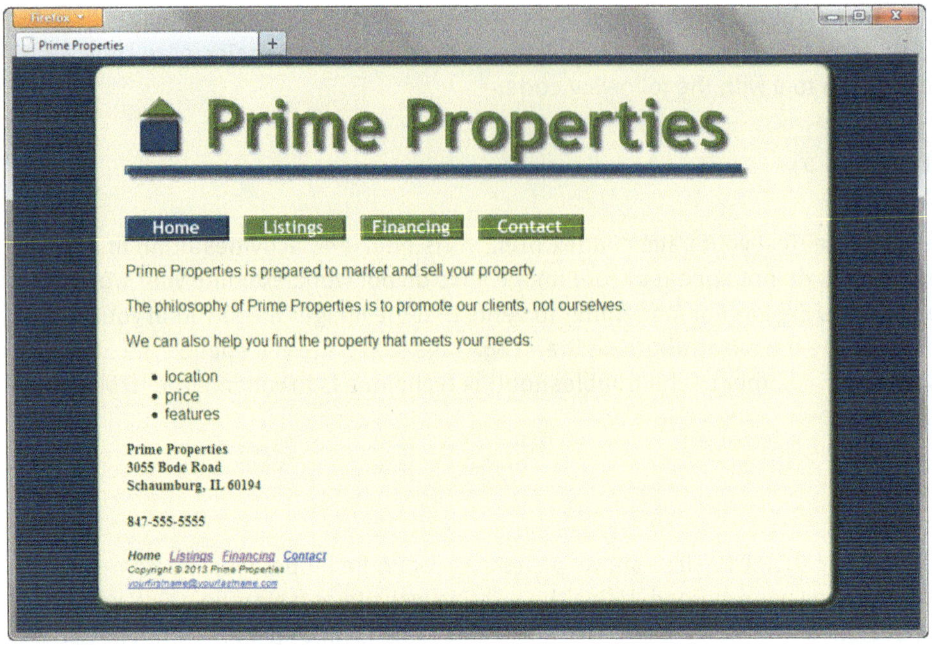

Figure 46 Prime Properties Home page

- Since you will be replacing the main navigation with image links, it's a good idea to provide for accessibility by including a set of text navigation links in the footer section of the web page. Copy the navigation div, and paste it inside the footer area above the copyright line.
- Refer to Figure 46, and replace the main navigation text hyperlinks with image links. The navigation buttons use color as a visual cue for visitors. The navigation button for the current page has a blue background. The navigation buttons for other pages have a green background. To configure this area for the Home page, use primehomebtn.gif (link to index.html), primelistingsnav.gif (link to listings.html), primefinancingnav.gif (link to financing.html), and primecontactnav.gif (link to contact.html). Use appropriate attributes on the `<img>` tag: alt, height, and width.

Save and test your new index.html page. It will be similar to Figure 46 but you'll notice that a few final touches (like the dark-blue page background) are missing; you'll configure these with CSS in Task 5.

Task 3: The Financing Page. Launch a text editor, and open the financing.html page from your prime4 folder. Replace the "Prime Properties" heading with the primelogo.gif. Configure the navigation areas in a similar way as in the home page. In the top navigation, use primehomenav.gif (link to index.html), primelistingsnav.gif (link to listings.html), primefinancingbtn.gif (link to financing.html), and primecontactnav.gif (link to contact.html). Save and test your new financing.html page.

Task 4: The Listings Page. Use the Financing page as the starting point for the Listings page. Launch a text editor, and open the financing.html file in the prime4 folder. Save the file as listings.html. Modify your file to look similar to the Listings page, as shown in Figure 47.

1. Change the title to an appropriate phrase.
2. Configure the top navigation area to display primehomenav.gif (link to index.html), primelistingsbtn.gif (link to listings.html), primefinancingnav.gif (link to financing.html), and primecontactnav.gif (link to contact.html).

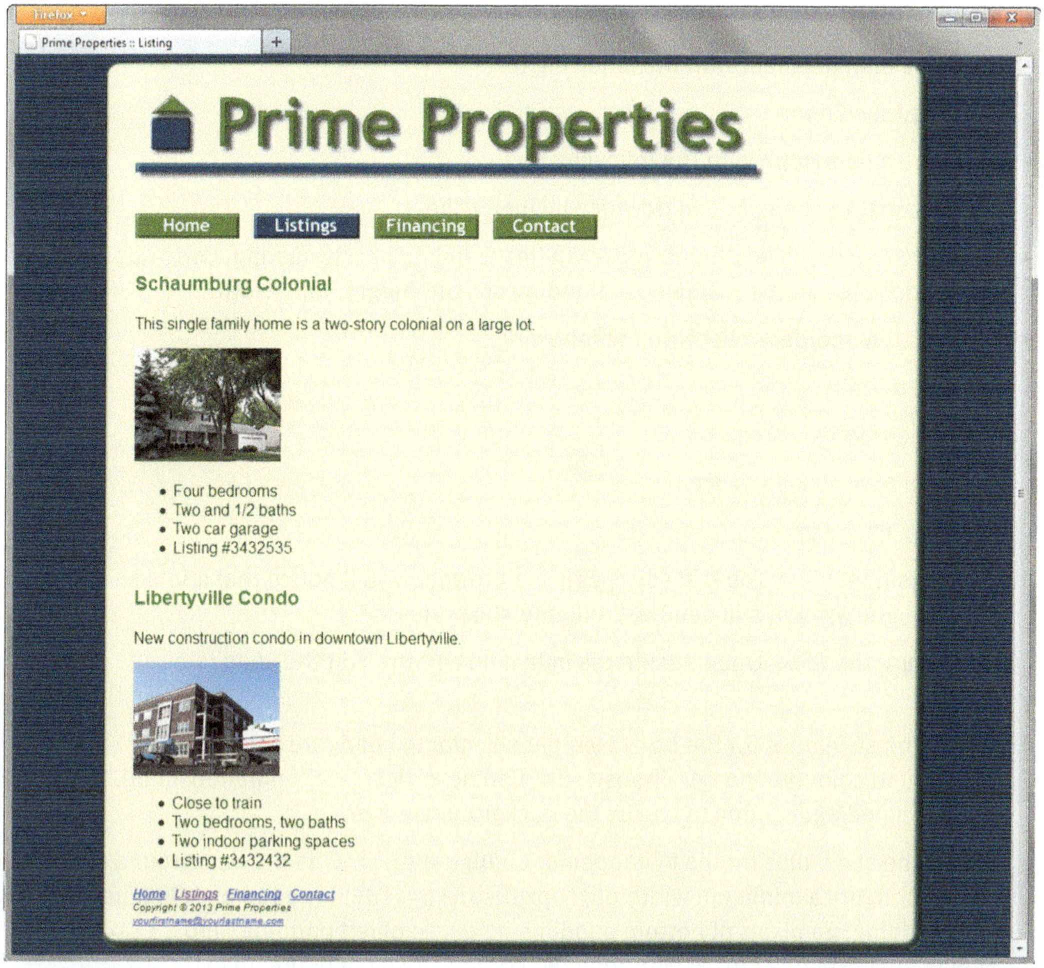

Figure 47 Prime Properties listings.html

3. Replace the h2 element text “Financing” with “Listings”.
4. Delete the text between the Listings heading and the footer section of the web page.
5. The section describing each listing consists of an h3 element, an image link, a paragraph, and an unordered list.

   Schaumburg Colonial Listing

   - Configure an h3 element with the following text:

     Schaumburg Colonial

   - Configure a paragraph with the following text:

     This single family home is a two-story colonial on a large lot.

   - Configure the schaumburgthumb.jpg as an image link to schaumburg.jpg. Code appropriate attributes on the `<img>` tag, including src, alt, height, and width.
   - Configure an unordered list with the following text:

     Four bedrooms

     Two and 1/2 baths

     Two car garage

     Listing #3432535

Libertyville Condo Listing

- Configure an h3element with the following text:

  Libertyville Condo
- Configure a paragraph with the following text:

  New construction condo in downtown Libertyville.
- Configure the libertyvillethumb.jpg as an image link to libertyville.jpg. Code appropriate attributes on the `<img>` tag, including src, alt, height, and width.
- Configure an unordered list with the following text:

  Close to train

  Two bedrooms, two baths

  Two indoor parking spaces

  Listing #3432432

Save the listings.html file. If you test your page in a browser, you'll notice that it looks different from Figure 47; you still need to configure style rules.

Task 5: Configure the CSS. Open pacific.css in in a text editor. Edit the style rules as follows:

- Modify the style rules for the body element selector to configure a very dark background color (#000033). Choose either primevertical.png, primehorizontal.png or primediagonal.png to use as the background image.
- Modify the style rules for the #wrapper id. Configure #FFFFCC as the background color. Configure a minimum width of 700px (use `min-width`), no top padding, no right padding, 20 pixels of bottom padding, 30 pixels of left padding, and a 1 pixel blue (#00332B) ridge border with rounded corners. Also configure an inset box shadow with the following CSS:

```
-webkit-box-shadow: inset -3px -3px 3px 3px #00332B;
-moz-box-shadow: inset -3px -3px 3px 3px #00332B;
box-shadow: inset -3px -3px 3px 3px #00332B;
```

- Modify the style rules for the h3 element selector to have 10 pixels of top padding.
- The background properties on the header id selector, h2 element selector, and h3 element selector interfere with the inset box shadow in some browsers. Remove the `background-property` style rule from these selectors.
- Configure the img element selector to display no border.

Save the prime.css file. Test your pages (index.html, financing.html, and listing.html) in a browser. If your images do not appear or your image links do not function, examine your work carefully. Use Windows Explorer or Mac Finder to verify that the images are saved in your prime folder. Examine the src attributes on the `<img>` tags to be sure you spelled the image names correctly. Another useful troubleshooting technique is to validate the HTML and CSS code.

Answers

Checkpoint 1

1. It is reasonable to code pages that look similar on various browsers; it is not reasonable to try to code pages that look exactly the same on various browsers and operating systems. As shown in this chapter, even a simple horizontal rule displays differently. Modern web developers code pages to look satisfactory in commonly used browsers and may add enhancements that are applied by the most recent browser versions. This approach is called "progressive enhancement."
2. The first style rule is missing an ending semicolon (;).
3. True. CSS can be utilized to configure color, text, and even visual elements such as rectangular shapes (with the background-color property) and lines (with the border property).

Checkpoint 2

1. The CSS background-image property configures the file that is displayed. The CSS background-repeat property configures the way the image is displayed on the page.

   Suggested solution:

```
h1 { background-image: url(circle.jpg);
     background-repeat: no-repeat;
}
```

2. The CSS background-image property configures the file that is displayed. The CSS background-repeat property configures the way the image is displayed on the page.

   Suggested solution:

```
body { background-image: url(bg.gif);
       background-repeat: repeat-y;
}
```

3. The browser will display the background color immediately. Then, the browser will render the background image and repeat the image as specified in the CSS. The background color will appear in areas not covered by the background image.

Checkpoint 3

1. Answers will vary with the site that you choose to review. Suggested solution: The page reviewed is the home page of a travel soccer league. The URL is http://www.alithsa.org. Image links are used for the main navigation of the site. Each image link contains a rectangle with text and a soccer ball. There is good

contrast between the black text and the background color of either yellow or green. Yellow background is used to indicate the current page. Because of the alt attribute values used, this page would not be accessible to a visitor who cannot see the images. Currently, every graphic has the same value for the alt attribute "Picture". To improve accessibility, the alt attribute values on each image tag should be modified to contain brief descriptive phrases. On the plus side, the page does display plain text links in the footer section. The images used as navigation links on this page contribute to the fun, sporty attitude of the site. The accessibility of the page needs to be improved.

2. The image, map, and area elements work together to create a functioning image map. The `<img>` tag configures the image that will be used for the map and contains a usemap attribute whose value corresponds to the id value on the `<map>` tag associated with the image. The `<map>` tag is a container tag and surrounds one or more `<area>` tags. There is one self-contained `<area>` tag for each clickable hotspot on the image map. See the working example on the text website at http://webdevfoundations.net/6e/chapter4.html.

3. False. There is a trade-off between the quality of the image and the file size. The goal should be to save images that use the smallest file size which provides acceptable display quality.

Review Questions

1. b
2. c
3. b
4. b
5. a
6. c
7. b
8. a
9. b
10. d
11. tiled
12. text links
13. thumbnail
14. text-shadow
15. meter

Credits

All photographs except those noted below © Terry Ann Morris

"Checkpoint" icon (green check mark), "Web Site Case Study" icon (blue "WWW"), "FAQ" icon (orange caption bubble), "Focus on Accessibility" icon (orange key) © Fotolia LLC

"Hands-On Practice" icon (green hand); empty green, yellow, purple, red, and blue icons © Piotr M./Fotolia LLC

"Focus on Ethics" icon (black scales) © so47/Fotolia LLC

Figures 4, 10 (screen captures depicting author's own material within Microsoft Internet Explorer) © Microsoft Corporation. MICROSOFT AND/OR ITS RESPECTIVE SUPPLIERS MAKE NO REPRESENTATIONS ABOUT THE SUITABILITY OF THE INFORMATION CONTAINED IN THE DOCUMENTS

Special Entity Characters

The table that follows lists a selection of special entity characters in order of numeric code. The most commonly used special characters are shown in bold. The W3C's list of special characters is found at http://www.w3.org/MarkUp/html-spec/html-spec_13.html.

Entity Name	Numeric Code	Descriptive Code	Character
Quotation mark	**"**	**"**	"
Ampersand	**&**	**&**	**&**
Apostrophe	**'**		'
Less than sign	**<**	**<**	<
Greater than sign	**>**	**>**	>
Vertical bar					
Left single quotation mark	**‘**	**‘**	‘
Right single quotation mark	**’**	**’**	’
Nonbreaking space	** **	** **	**a blank space**
Inverted exclamation	¡	¡	¡
Cent sign	¢	¢	¢
Pound sterling sign	£	£	£
General currency sign	¤	¤	†
Yen sign	¥	¥	¥
Broken vertical bar	¦	¦	¦
Section sign	§	§	§
Umlaut	¨	¨	¨
Copyright symbol	**©**	**©**	**©**
Feminine ordinal	ª	ª	a
Left angle quote	«	«	<<
Not sign	¬	¬	¬
Soft hyphen			-

(Continued)

Special Entity Characters

Entity Name	Numeric Code	Descriptive Code	Character
Registered trademark symbol	**®**	**®**	®
Macron	¯	¯	¯
Degree sign	°	°	°
Plus or minus	±	±	±
Superscript two	²	²	^{2}
Superscript three	³	³	^{3}
Acute accent	´	´	´
Micro (Mu)	µ	µ	µ
Paragraph sign	¶	¶	¶
Middle dot	·	·	·
Cedilla	¸	¸	¸
Superscript one	¹	¹	^{1}
Masculine ordinal	º	º	º
Right angle quote	»	»	>>
Fraction one-fourth	¼	¼	¼
Fraction one-half	½	½	½
Fraction three-fourths	¾	¾	¾
Inverted question mark	¿	¿	¿
Small e, grave accent	è	è	è
Small e, acute accent	é	é	é
En dash	–	–	–
Em dash	**—**	**—**	—

FTP Tutorial

Publish with File Transfer Protocol (FTP)

Once you obtain your web hosting space, you'll need to upload your files. Although your web host may offer a web-based file manager application for client use, a common method of transferring files is to use File Transfer Protocol (FTP). A protocol is a convention or standard that enables computers to speak to one another. FTP is used to copy and manage files and folders over the Internet. FTP uses two ports to communicate over a network—one for the data (typically port 20) and one for control commands (typically port 21). See http://www.iana.org/assignments/port-numbers for a list port numbers used on the Internet.

FTP Applications

There are many FTP applications available for download or purchase on the Web, including the following:

- **Filezilla**
  - Windows, Mac, Linux Platform
  - http://filezilla-project.org
  - Free download
- **SmartFTP**
  - Windows
  - http://www.smartftp.com
  - Free download
- **CuteFTP**
  - Windows, Mac
  - http://www.cuteftp.com
  - Free trial download, academic pricing available

- **WS_FTP**
  - Windows
  - http://www.ipswitch.com
  - Free trial download

Connecting with FTP

Your web host will provide you with the following information along with any other specifications, such as whether the FTP server requires the use of active mode or passive mode:

FTP Host: Your FTP Host

Username: Your Account Username

Password: Your Account Password

Overview of Using an FTP Application

This section focuses on FileZilla, a free FTP application with versions for the Windows, Mac, and Linux platforms. A free download of FileZilla is available at http://filezilla-project.org/download.php?type=client. After you download an FTP application of your choice, install the program on your computer, using the instructions provided.

Launch and Login

Launch Filezilla or another FTP application. Enter the information required by your web host (such as FTP host, username, and password) and initiate the connection. An example screenshot of FileZilla after a connection is shown in Figure 1.

As you examine Figure 1, notice the text boxes near the top of the application for the Host, Username, and Password information. Under this area is a display of messages from the FTP server. Review the area to confirm a successful connection and the results of file transfers. Next, notice that the application is divided into a left panel and a right panel. The left panel is the local site—it displays information about your local computer and allows you to navigate to your drives, folders, and files. The right panel is the remote site—it displays information about your website and provides a way to navigate to its folders and files.

Uploading a File

It's really easy to transfer a file from your local computer to your remote website: Just select the file with your mouse in the left panel (local site list) and drag it to the right panel (remote site list).

Downloading a File

If you need to download a file from your website to your local computer, just drag the file with your mouse from the right panel (remote site list) to the left panel (local site list).

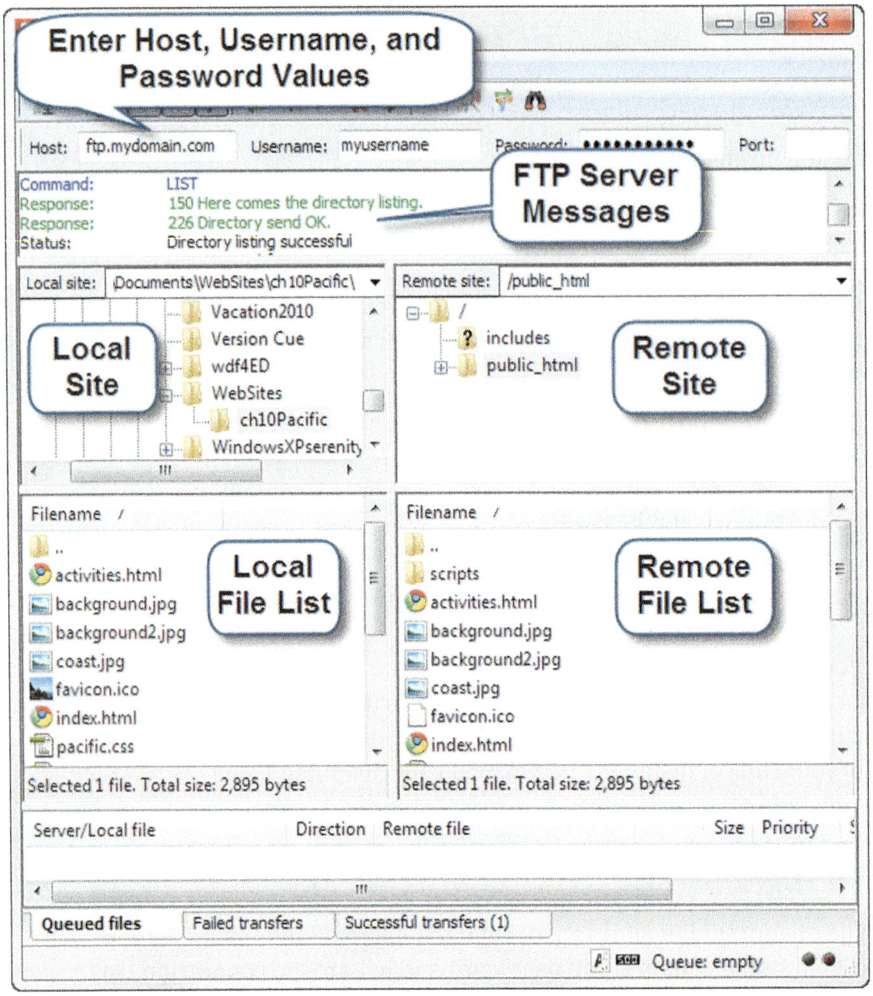

Figure F.1 The FileZilla FTP application

Deleting a File

To delete a file on your website, right-click on the file name (in the right panel) and select Delete from the context-sensitive menu.

And There's More!

Feel free to explore the other functions offered by FileZilla (and most FTP applications). Right-click on a file in the remote site list to display a context-sensitive menu with several options, including renaming a file, creating a new directory (also known as a folder), and viewing a file.

Web Design

Chapter Objectives

In this chapter, you will learn how to . . .

- Describe the most common types of website organization
- Describe the principles of visual design
- Design for your target audience
- Design clear, easy-to-use navigation
- Improve the readability of the text on your web pages
- Use graphics appropriately on web pages
- Apply the concept of universal design to web pages
- Describe web page layout design techniques
- Apply best practices of web design

As a website visitor, you have probably found that certain websites are appealing and easy to use while others seem awkward or just plain annoying. What separates the good from the bad? This chapter discusses recommended web design practices. The topics include site organization, navigation design, page layout design, text design, graphic design, and accessibility considerations.

1 Design for Your Target Audience

Whatever your personal preferences, design your website to appeal to your **target audience**—the people who will use your site. Your intended target audience may be specific, such as kids, college students, young couples, or seniors, or you may intend your site to appeal to everyone. The purpose and goals of your visitors will vary—they may be casually seeking information, performing research for school or work, comparison shopping, job hunting, and so on. The design of a website should appeal to and meet the needs of the target audience.

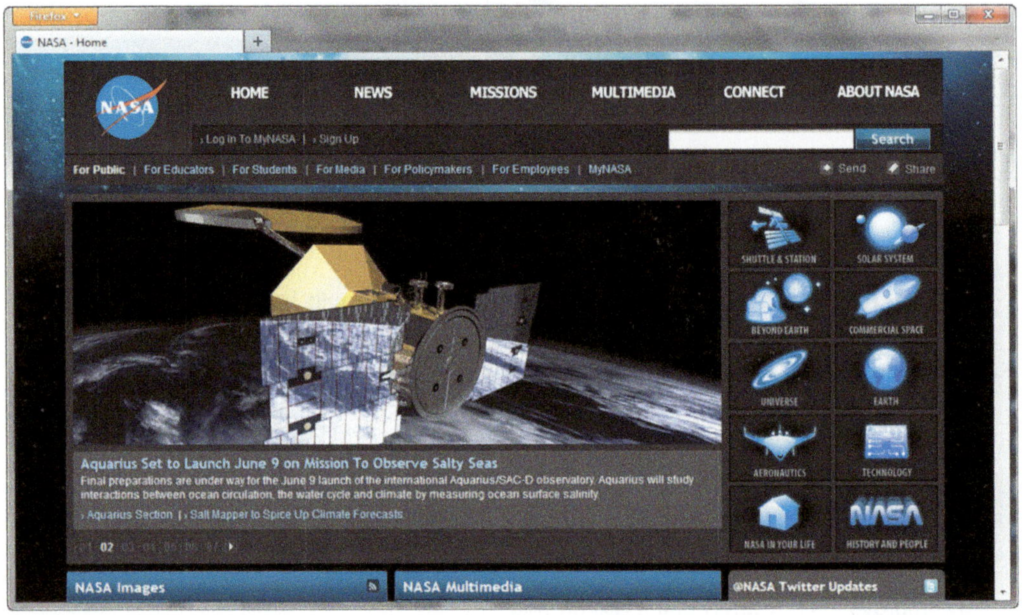

Figure 1
The compelling graphic draws you in

For example, NASA's website, http://www.nasa.gov, as shown in Figure 1, features compelling graphics and has a different look and feel from the text-based, link-intensive Bureau of Labor Statistics Consumer Price Index web page, http://www.bls.gov/cpi, in Figure 2.

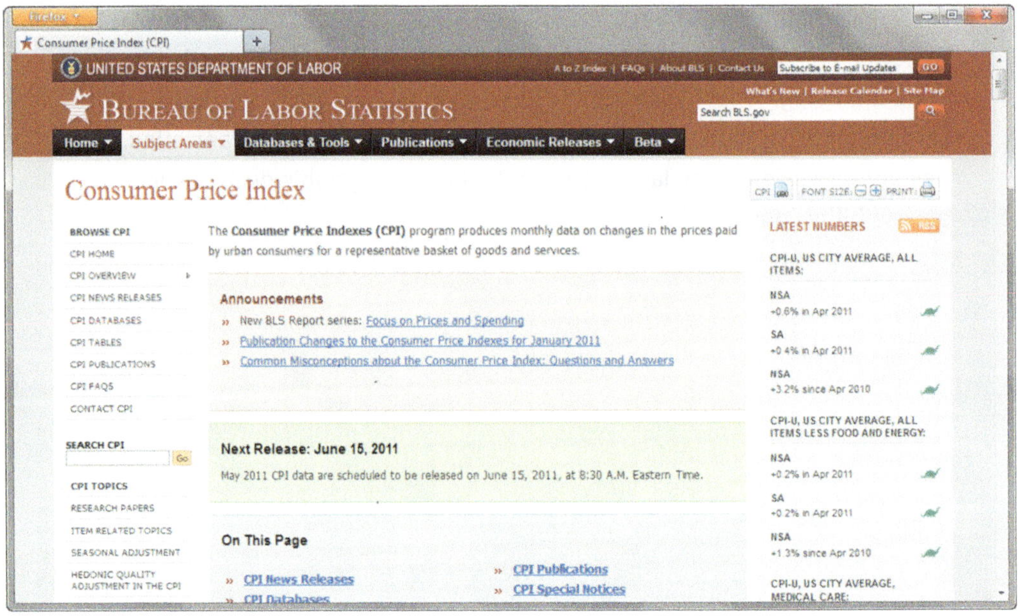

Figure 2
This text-intensive web page offers numerous choices

The first site engages you, draws you in, and invites exploration. The second site provides you with a wide range of choices so that you can quickly get down to work. The layout, navigation, and even the use of color and text can work together to appeal to your target audience. Keep your target audience in mind as you explore the web design practices in this chapter.

2 Website Organization

How will visitors move around your site? How will they find what they need? This is largely determined by the website's organization or architecture. There are three common types of website organization:

- Hierarchical
- Linear
- Random (sometimes called Web organization)

A diagram of the organization of a website is called a **site map**. Creating the site map is one of the initial steps in developing a website.

Hierarchical Organization

Most websites use **hierarchical organization**. A site map for hierarchical organization, such as the one shown in Figure 3, is characterized by a clearly defined home page with links to major site sections. Web pages within sections are placed as needed. The home page and the first level of pages in a hierarchical site map typically indicate the hyperlinks on the main navigation bar of each web page.

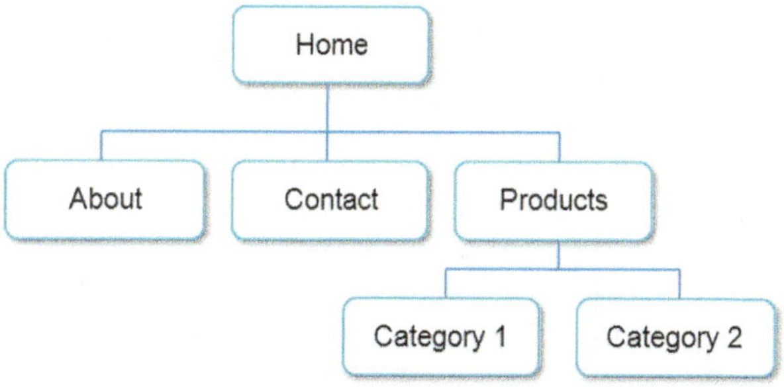

Figure 3 Hierarchical site organization

It is important to be aware of the pitfalls of hierarchical organization. Figure 4 shows a site design that is too shallow—there are too many major site sections.

This site design needs to be organized into fewer, easily managed topics or units of information, a process called **chunking**. In the case of web page design, each unit

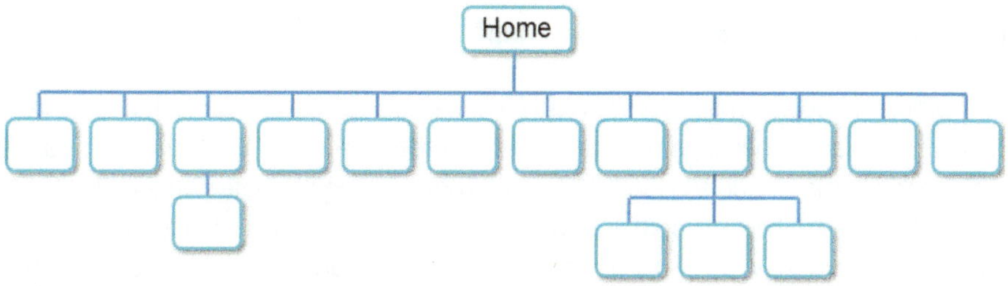

Figure 4 This site design uses a shallow hierarchy

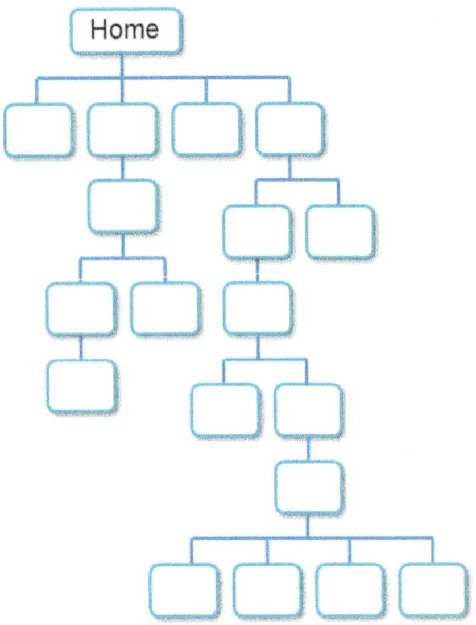

Figure 5 This site design uses a deep hierarchy

of information is a page. Nelson Cowan, a research psychologist at the University of Missouri, found that adults typically can keep about four items or chunks of items (such as the three parts of a phone number 888-555-5555) in their short-term memory (http://web.missouri.edu/~cowann/research.html). Following this principle, be aware of the number of major navigation links and try to group them into visually separate sections on the page with each group having no more than about four links.

Another pitfall is designing a site that is too deep. Figure 5 shows an example of this. The interface design "three click rule" says that a web page visitor should be able to get from any page on your site to any other page on your site with a maximum of three hyperlinks. In other words, a visitor who cannot get what they want in three mouse clicks will begin to feel frustrated and may leave your site. This rule may be very difficult to satisfy on a large site, but in general, the goal is to organize your site so that your visitors can easily navigate from page to page within the site structure.

Linear Organization

When the purpose of a site or series of pages on a site is to provide a tutorial, tour, or presentation that needs to be viewed sequentially, **linear organization**, as shown in Figure 6, is useful.

Figure 6 Linear site organization

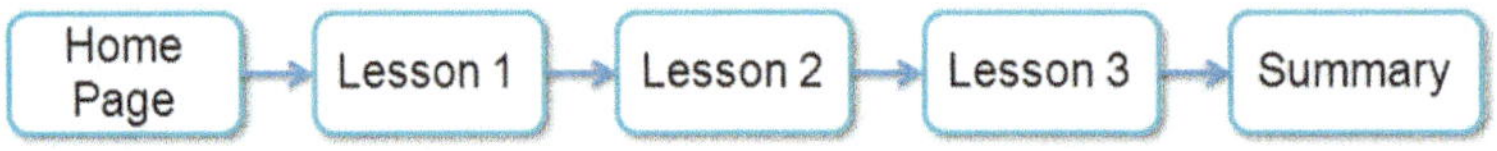

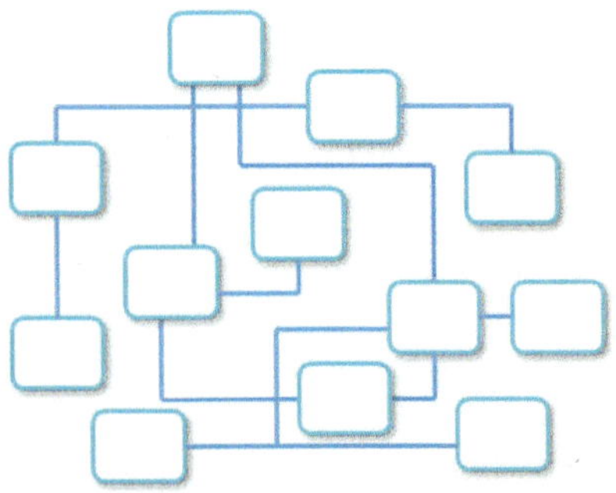

Figure 7 Random site organization

In linear organization, the pages are viewed one after another. Some websites use hierarchical organization in general, but with linear organization in a few small areas.

Random Organization

Random organization (sometimes called Web organization) offers no clear path through the site, as shown in Figure 7. There is often no clear home page and no discernable structure. Random organization is not as common as hierarchical or linear organization and is usually found only on artistic sites or sites that strive to be especially different and original. This type of organization is typically not used for commercial websites.

FAQ What's a good way to build my site map?

Sometimes it is difficult to begin creating a site map for a website. Some design teams meet in a room with a blank wall and a package of large Post-it® Notes. They write the titles of topics and subtopics needed in the site on the Post-it® Notes. They arrange the notes on the wall and discuss them until the site structure becomes clear and there is consensus within the group. If you are not working in a group, you can try this on your own and then discuss the organization of the website with a friend or fellow student.

3 Principles of Visual Design

There are four visual design principles that you can apply to the design of just about anything: repetition, contrast, proximity, and alignment. Whether you are designing a web page, a button, a logo, a DVD cover, a brochure, or a software interface, the four design principles will help to create the "look," or visual aesthetic, of your project and will determine whether your message is effectively communicated.

VideoNote
Principles of Visual Design

Repetition: Repeat Visual Elements Throughout the Design

When applying the principle of **repetition**, the designer repeats one or more elements throughout the product. The repeating aspect ties the work together. Whether it is color, shape, font, or image, the repetition of elements helps to unify a design.

Contrast: Add Visual Excitement and Draw Attention

To apply the principle of **contrast**, the designer should make the elements very different (add contrast) in order to make the design interesting and to direct attention. When designing web pages, there should be good contrast between the background color and the text.

Proximity: Group Related Items

When designers apply the principle of **proximity**, related items are placed physically close together. Unrelated items should have space separating them. The placing of items close together gives visual clues to the logical organization of the information or functionality.

Alignment: Align Elements to Create Visual Unity

Another principle that helps to create a cohesive web page is **alignment**. When applying this principle, the designer organizes the page so that each element placed has some alignment (vertical or horizontal) with another element on the page.

Repetition, contrast, proximity, and alignment are four principles that can greatly improve your web page designs. If you apply these principles effectively, your web pages will look more professional and you will communicate your message more clearly. Keep these visual design principles in mind as you design and build websites.

4 Design to Provide Accessibility

The Center for Universal Design defines **universal design** as "the design of products and environments to be usable by all people, to the greatest extent possible, without the need for adaptation or specialized design."

Focus on Accessibility

Who Benefits from Universal Design and Increased Accessibility?

Consider the following scenarios:

- Maria, a young woman in her twenties with physical challenges who cannot manipulate a mouse and who uses a keyboard with much effort: Accessible web pages designed to function without a mouse will help Maria to access content.
- Leotis, a college student who is deaf and wants to be a web developer: Captions for audio/video content and transcripts will provide Leotis access to content.
- Jim, a middle-aged man who has a dial-up Internet connection and is using the Web for personal enjoyment: Alternate text for images and transcripts for multimedia will provide Jim improved access to content.
- Nadine, a mature woman with age-related macular degeneration who has difficulty reading small print: Web pages that are designed so that text can be enlarged in the browser will make it easier for Nadine to read.
- Karen, a college student using a smartphone to access the Web: Accessible content organized with headings and lists will make it easier for Karen to surf the Web on a mobile device.
- Prakesh, a man in his thirties who is legally blind and needs access to the Web in order to do his job: Web pages that are designed to be accessible (which are organized with headings and lists, display descriptive text for hyperlinks, provide alternate text descriptions for images, and are usable without a mouse) will help Prakesh to access content.

Figure 8 Everyone benefits from an accessible web page

All of these individuals benefit from web pages that are designed with accessibility in mind. A web page that is designed to be accessible is typically more usable for all—even a person who has no physical challenges and is using a broadband connection benefits from the improved presentation and organization of a well-designed web page (Figure 8).

Accessible Design Can Benefit Search Engine Listing

Search engine programs (commonly referred to as bots or spiders) walk the Web and follow hyperlinks on websites. An accessible website with descriptive page titles that is well organized with headings, lists, descriptive text for hyperlinks, and alternate text for images is more visible to search engine robots and may result in a better ranking.

Accessibility Is the Right Thing to Do

The Internet and the World Wide Web are such a pervasive part of our culture that accessibility is mandated by law in the United States. Section 508 of the Rehabilitation Act requires electronic and information technology, including web pages, used by federal agencies to be accessible to people with disabilities. At the time this was written, the Section 508 standards were undergoing revision; see http://www.access-board.gov for current information. The accessibility recommendations presented in this text are intended to satisfy the Section 508 standards and the Web Content Accessibility Guidelines 2.0 (WCAG 2.0) recommended by the W3C's Web Accessibility Initiative (WAI). The following four principles are essential to conformance with WCAG 2.0: **P**erceivable, **O**perable, **U**nderstandable, and **R**obust, referred to by the acronym **POUR**.

1. Content must be **Perceivable**. Perceivable content is easy to see or hear. Any graphic or multimedia content should be available in a text format, such as text descriptions for images, closed captions for videos, and transcripts for audio.
2. Interface components in the content must be **Operable**. Operable content has navigation forms, or other interactive features that can be used or operated with either a mouse or a keyboard. Multimedia content should be designed to avoid flashing, which may cause a seizure.
3. Content and controls must be **Understandable**. Understandable content is easy to read, organized in a consistent manner, and provides helpful error messages when appropriate.
4. Content should be **Robust** enough to work with current and future user agents, including assistive technologies. Robust content is written to follow W3C recommendations and should be compatible with multiple operating systems, browsers, and assistive technologies such as screen reader applications.

The WCAG 2.0 Quick Reference in the appendix contains a brief list of guidelines for designing accessible web pages. See http://www.w3.org/TR/WCAG20/Overview for a detailed description of the WCAG 2.0 guidelines. These guidelines are segmented into three levels of conformance: Level A, Level AA, and Level AAA. In addition to satisfying the Section 508 guidelines, the accessibility recommendations discussed in this text are also intended to fully satisfy the WCAG 2.0 Level AA (includes Level A) guidelines and partially satisfy the Level AAA guidelines. Visit http://www.w3.org/WAI/WCAG20/quickref for an interactive checklist of these guidelines. Developing accessible web pages is an important aspect of web design. WebAIM has created a WCAG 2.0 checklist with helpful tips at http://webaim.org/standards/wcag/checklist. The University of Toronto (http://achecker.ca/checker/index.php) provides a free accessibility validation service.

As you work through this text, you'll learn to include accessibility features as you create practice pages. You've already discovered the importance of the title tag, heading tags, descriptive text for hyperlinks, and alternate text. You're well on your way to creating accessible web pages!

5 Writing for the Web

Long-winded sentences and explanations are often found in academic textbooks and romance novels, but they really are not appropriate on a web page. Large blocks of text and long paragraphs are difficult to read on the Web. The following suggestions will help to increase the readability of your web pages.

Organize Your Content

According to web usability expert Jakob Neilsen, people don't really read web pages; they scan them. Organize the text content on your pages to be quickly scanned. Be concise. Use headings, subheadings, brief paragraphs, and unordered lists to organize web page content so that it is easy to read and visitors can quickly find what they need.

Also be aware of line length—use white space and multiple columns if possible. Look ahead to Figure 15 for examples of text placement on a web page. While it's fine to center headings and navigation areas, avoid centering all of your text—a paragraph of centered text is more difficult to read than left-aligned text.

Text in Hyperlinks

Hyperlink key words or descriptive phrases; do not hyperlink entire sentences. Avoid use of the words "Click here" in hyperlinks because users know what to do by now. Also, be aware that an increasing number of people are using touch screens so they'll be selecting or tapping rather than clicking.

Reading Level

Match the reading level and style of writing to your target audience. Use vocabulary that they will be comfortable with. Juicy Studio offers a free online readability test at http://juicystudio.com/services/readability.php.

Use Common Fonts

Use common font typefaces such as Arial, Verdana, Georgia, or Times New Roman. Remember that the web page visitor must have the font installed on his or her computer in order for that particular font to appear. Your page may look great with Gill Sans Ultra Bold Condensed, but if your visitor doesn't have the font, the browser's default font will be displayed. Explore the list of "browser safe fonts" at http://www.ampsoft.net/webdesign-l/WindowsMacFonts.html.

Font Size and Weight

Be aware that fonts display smaller on a Mac than on a PC. Even within the PC platform, the default font size displayed by browsers may not be the same. Consider creating prototype pages of your font size settings to test on a variety of browsers and screen resolution settings. **Bold** or *emphasize* important text. However, be careful not to bold everything—that has the same effect as bolding nothing.

Font Color Contrast

Use appropriate color combinations. Newbie web designers sometimes choose color combinations for web pages that they would never dream of using in their wardrobe. An easy way to choose colors that contrast well and look good together is to select colors from an image or logo that you will use for your site.

Spelling and Grammar

Unfortunately, many websites contain misspelled words. Most web authoring tools such as Adobe Dreamweaver have built-in spell checkers; consider using this feature. Finally, be sure that you proofread and test your site thoroughly. It's very helpful if you can find web developer buddies—you check their sites and they check yours. It's always easier to see someone else's mistake than your own.

6 Use of Color

Choosing Colors

You may be wondering how to select colors to display on web pages. One easy way to choose colors is to use a monochromatic color scheme—all shades or tints of the same color along with neutrals such as white, black, and/or gray. Try the Color Blender at http://meyerweb.com/eric/tools/color-blend to select colors for a monochromatic color scheme. Another way to create a color scheme is to base it on a photograph or image. If you have a favorite color and would like to create a color scheme around it, visit one of the following sites that suggest color schemes:

- Colors on the Web: http://colorsontheweb.com/colorwizard.asp
- Kuler: http://kuler.adobe.com
- Lee Street Management: http://www.leestreet.com/QuickColor.swf
- Color Scheme Designer: http://colorschemedesigner.com
- ColorJack: http://www.colorjack.com/articles/color_formulas.html

Accessibility and Color

While color can help you create a compelling web page, keep in mind that not all of your visitors will see or be able to distinguish between colors. Some visitors will use a screen reader and will not experience your colors, so your information must be clearly conveyed even if the colors cannot be viewed.

Focus on Accessibility

Your color choices can be crucial. For example, red text on a blue background, as shown in Figure 9, is usually difficult for everyone to read. Also avoid using a red and green color scheme or a brown and purple color scheme because individuals with color-deficient vision may have difficulty differentiating the colors. According to Vischeck (http://www.vischeck.com/vischeck), about 1 out of 20 people experience some type of color perception deficiency. Visit http://www.vischeck.com/vischeck/vischeckURL.php to simulate how a person with a color deficiency experiences the colors on a web page. White, black, and shades of blue and yellow are easier for most people to discern.

Figure 9
Some color combinations are difficult to read

Choose background and text colors with a high amount of contrast. The WCAG 2.0 guidelines recommend a contrast ratio of 4.5:1 for standard text. If the text has a large font, the contrast ratio can be as low as 3:1. Jonathan Snook's online Colour Contrast Check at http://snook.ca/technical/colour_contrast/colour.html can help you to verify the contrast level of your text and background colors.

See Lighthouse International's website (http://lighthouse.org/accessibility/design/accessible-print-design/effective-color-contrast) for more information on the effective use of color. When choosing color, it's important to consider the preferences of your target audience. The next sections focus on this aspect of web design.

Colors and Your Target Audience

Choose colors that will appeal to your target audience. Younger audiences, such as children and preteens, prefer bright, lively colors along with animation and interactivity. Individuals in their late teens and early twenties generally prefer dark background colors with occasional use of bright contrast, music, and dynamic navigation. For an older target audience, light backgrounds, well-defined images, and large text are appropriate.

If your goal is to appeal to everyone, follow the example of the popular Amazon.com and eBay websites in their use of color. These sites use a neutral white background with splashes of color to add interest and highlight page areas. Use of white as a background color was also reported by Jakob Nielsen and Marie Tahir in *Homepage Usability: 50 Websites Deconstructed*, a book that includes analyses of 50 top websites. According to this study, 84% of the sites used white as the background color and 72% used black as the text color. This maximized the contrast between text and background, providing maximum ease of reading.

You'll also notice that websites targeting "everyone" often include compelling visual graphics while providing the main content on a white background for maximum contrast.

Checkpoint 1

1. List the four basic principles of design. View the home page of your school and describe how each principle is applied.
2. List three best practices used when writing text for the Web. The following text was found on an actual website. The company name and city have been changed. Apply the best practices used when writing for the Web and rewrite the following content:

   Acme, Inc. is a new laboratory instrument repair and service company. Our staff at this time has a combined total of 30 plus years of specimen preparation instrumentation service and repair.

   Our technicians are EPA refrigeration certified. We are fully insured and all of our workers are fully covered by workman's compensation insurance. A proof of insurance certificate can be provided upon request.

   We are located in Chicago, Illinois. Which houses shop repair facilities and offices. Acme, Inc. technicians are factory trained and equipped with the best diagnostic and repair equipment available.

We keep a separate file on every piece of equipment we work on. When a technician is sent on a repair, he has a file which lists the whole repair history on that piece of equipment. These files also help us answer any of your questions about past repairs.

Our rates are $100.00 per hour for Labor and Travel with a 2 hour minimum. $0.40 per mile and all related expenses PARTS are not included.

3. View the following three websites: Walmart (http://www.walmart.com), MuggleNet (http://www.mugglenet.com), and Sesame Street (http://www.sesamestreet.org/muppet). Describe the target audience for each site. How do their designs differ? Do the sites meet the needs of their target audiences?

7 Use of Graphics and Multimedia

As shown in Figure 1, a compelling graphic can be an engaging element on a web page. However, avoid relying on images to convey meaning. Some individuals may not be able to see your images and multimedia—they may be accessing your site with a mobile device or using an assistive technology such as a screen reader to visit your page. You may need to include text descriptions of important concepts or key points that a graphic image or multimedia file conveys. In this section, you'll explore recommended techniques for the use of graphics and multimedia on web pages.

File Size and Image Dimensions Matter

Keep both the file size and the dimensions of images as small as possible. Try to display only exactly what is needed to get your point across. Use a graphic application to crop an image or create a thumbnail image that links to a larger version of the image.

Antialiased/Aliased Text in Media

Antialiasing introduces intermediate colors to smooth jagged edges in digital images. Graphic applications such as Adobe Photoshop and Adobe Fireworks can be used to create antialiased text images. The graphic shown in Figure 10 was created using antialiasing. Figure 11 displays an image created without antialiasing; notice the jagged edges.

Figure 10 Antialiased text

Use Only Necessary Multimedia

Use animation and multimedia only if it will add value to your site. Don't include an animated GIF or a Flash animation just because you have one. Limit the use of animated items. Only use animation if it makes the page more effective. Consider limiting how long an animation plays.

In general, younger audiences find animation more appealing than older audiences. However, a well-done navigation animation or an animation that describes a product or service could be appealing to almost any target group. Adobe Flash is frequently used on the Web to add visual interest and interactivity to web pages.

Figure 11 This graphic was not antialiased: The letter "A" has a jagged look

Focus on Accessibility

Provide Alternate Text

Each image on your web page should be configured with alternate text. Alternate text may be displayed by mobile devices, displayed briefly when an image is slow to load, and displayed when a browser is configured to not show images. Alternate text is also read aloud when a person with a disability uses a screen reader to access your website. In Figure 12, the Firefox Web Developer extension was used to display the alt text for an image on the National Park Service website (http://nps.gov).

Figure 12 The alt text is displayed above the image by the Firefox Web Developer extension

To satisfy accessibility requirements, also provide alternate text equivalents for multimedia, such as video and audio. A text transcript of an audio recording can be useful not only to those with hearing challenges, but also to individuals who prefer to read when accessing new information. In addition, the text transcript may be accessed by a search engine and used when your site is categorized and indexed. Captions help to provide accessibility for video files.

8 Navigation Design

Ease of Navigation

Sometimes web developers are so close to their sites that they can't see the forest for the trees. A new visitor will wander onto the site and not know what to click or how to find the information he or she seeks. Clearly labeled navigation on each page is helpful. For maximum usability, the navigation should be in the same location on each page.

Navigation Bars

Clear **navigation bars**, either graphic or text based, make it obvious to website users where they are and where they can go next. It's quite common for site-wide navigation to be located either in a horizontal navigation bar placed under the logo or in a vertical navigation bar on the left side of the page. Less common is a vertical navigation bar on the right side of the page because this area can be cut off at lower screen resolutions.

Breadcrumb Navigation

Jakob Nielsen, a well-known usability and web design professional, favors what he calls a breadcrumb trail for larger sites, which indicates the path of web pages a visitor has viewed during the current session. A common design technique is to place the breadcrumb trail navigation at the top of the main content area that indicates the pages the visitor has viewed during a visit.

Using Graphics for Navigation

Focus on Accessibility

Sometimes graphics are used instead of text to provide navigation. When image hyperlinks instead of text hyperlinks provide the main navigation for the site, two techniques provide for accessibility:

- Each image element is configured with an alternate text description.
- The page is configured with text hyperlinks in the footer section.

Skip Repetitive Navigation

Focus on Accessibility

Provide a method to skip repetitive navigation links. It is easy for visitors without vision and mobility challenges to scan a web page and quickly focus on the page content. However, long, repetitive navigation bars quickly become tedious to access when utilizing a screen reader or a keyboard to visit a web page. Consider adding a "Skip navigation" or "Skip to content" hyperlink before your main navigation bar that links to a named fragment at the beginning of the content section of your page. Figure 13 presents another way to implement the skip navigation feature. Although not immediately visible in the browser, visitors using a screen reader or a keyboard to tab through the page will immediately encounter the "Skip to main content" hyperlink in the upper-left side of the U.S. Department of Transportation web page (http://www.dot.gov).

Figure 13 Press the tab key to access the "Skip to content" link on the U.S. Department of Transportation website

Dynamic Navigation

In your experiences visiting websites you've probably encountered navigation menus that display additional options when your mouse cursor moves over an item. This is dynamic navigation, which provides a way to offer many choices to visitors while at the same time avoid overwhelming them. Instead of showing all the navigation links all the time, menu items are dynamically displayed (typically using a combination of HTML and CSS) as appropriate. The additional items are made available when a related top-level menu item has focus or is selected. Visit Dynamic Drive (http://www.dynamicdrive.com/dynamicindex1) for sample code that you can use to create dynamic navigation for your own web pages.

Site Map

Even with clear and consistent navigation, visitors sometimes may lose their way on large websites. A site map provides an outline of the organization of the website with hyperlinks to each major page. This can help visitors find another route to get to the information they seek, as shown in the Ready.gov website in Figure 14.

Site Search Feature

Note the search feature in the upper-right corner of the web page in Figure 14. This site search feature helps visitors to find information that is not apparent from the navigation or the site map.

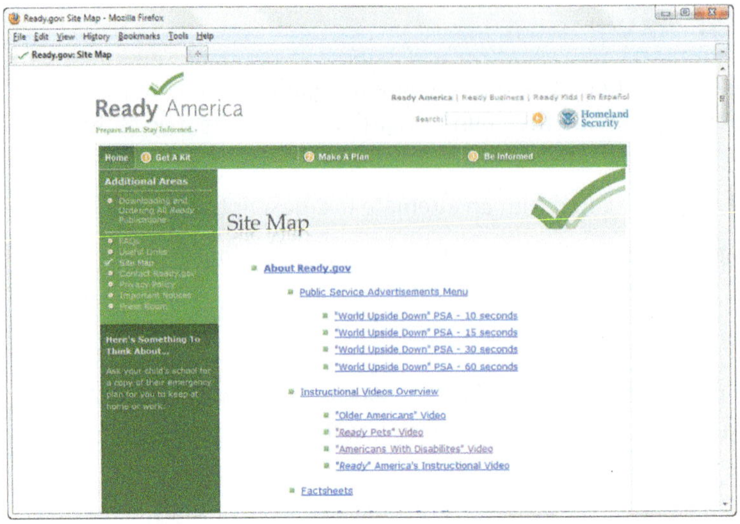

Figure 14 This large site offers a site search feature and a site map to visitors

9 Page Layout Design

Wireframes and Page Layout

A **wireframe** is a sketch or blueprint of a web page that shows the structure (but not the detailed design) of basic page elements such as the logo, navigation, content, and footer. Wireframes are used as part of the design process to experiment with various page layouts, develop the structure and navigation of the site, and provide a basis for communication among project members. Note that the exact content (text, images, logo, and navigation) does not need to be placed in the wireframe diagram. Figure 15 depicts a diagram of a web page with a logo, navigation area, content area (with headings, subheadings, images, paragraphs, and unordered lists), and a footer area.

Cascading Style Sheets (CSS) are used to configure web pages with multiple columns. Sometimes the page layout for the home page is different from the page layout used for the content pages. Even when this is the case, a consistent logo and color scheme will produce a more cohesive website.

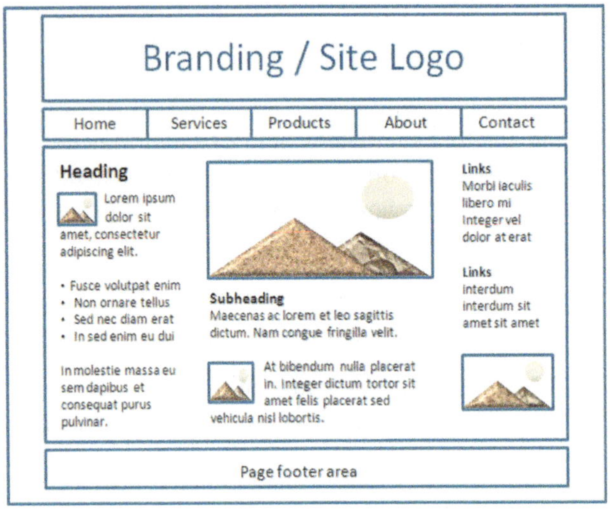

Figure 15 This wireframe page layout uses images and columns of various widths

Page Layout Design Techniques

Now that you have been introduced to page layout, it's time to consider three popular techniques for web page layout design: ice, jello, and liquid.

Ice Design

The **ice design** technique is sometimes referred to as a solid or fixed design. The page hugs the left margin and has a fixed width. Websites that use this technique include Federal Student Aid website (http://studentaid.ed.gov) and the League for Innovation in the Community College website (http://www.league.org).

Jello Design

The **jello design** technique configures content that is centered and may be of a fixed width or a percentage width, such as 80%. Regardless of the screen resolution, the content is centered in the page with even margins on both sides. Websites that use this technique include Public Broadcasting Service (http://www.pbs.org), Office Depot (http://www.officedepot.com), and the State of California (http://www.ca.gov).

The **liquid design** technique results in a fluid web page with content that takes up 100% of the browser window regardless of the screen resolution. There is no empty margin on the left or right—the multicolumn content will flow to fill whatever size of window is used to display it. A disadvantage of this page layout is that at high screen resolutions the lines of text may extend quite far across the browser viewport and become more difficult to read. Websites using this technique include Amazon.com (http://www.amazon.com) and Moodle™ (http://moodle.org).

Websites designed using ice, jello, and liquid techniques can be found throughout the Web. Ice designs using a fixed-width layout give the web developer the most control over the page configuration but result in pages with large empty areas when viewed at higher screen resolutions. Liquid designs may become less readable when viewed at high screen resolutions because the page stretches to fill a wider area than originally intended by the developer. Jello designs are often used because the web pages are typically most pleasing to view on a variety of screen resolutions.

Design for the Mobile Web

Access to the Web from cell phones, smartphones, and tablets makes it possible to always be online. The research firm eMarketer (http://emarketer.com) predicts significant growth for mobile access to the Web, with a projected 134.3 million mobile Internet users by 2013. With this growth in mind, it's becoming more important to design web pages that are accessible and usable for your mobile visitors.

There are a few schools of thought on the best way to accomplish this, including developing a new mobile site with a .mobi top-level domain, creating a separate website hosted within your current domain that is targeted for mobile users, and using CSS to create a style sheet along with new CSS3 media queries to configure your current website for display on mobile devices. Whichever method you choose to use, be mindful of the following considerations when designing mobile websites.

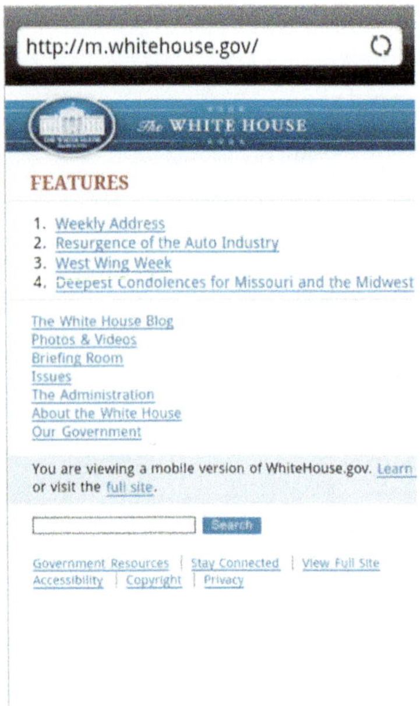

Figure 16 A text-intensive mobile site features hyperlinks to frequently accessed information

- **Small screen size.** Common mobile phone screen sizes include 320×240, 320×480, 480×800, and 640×960 (Apple iPhone 4). Even on one of the large phones, that's not a lot of pixels to work with!
- **Low bandwidth (slow connection speed).** Although the use of faster 3G and 4G networks is becoming more widespread, many mobile users experience slow connection speeds. Images usually take up quite a bit of bandwidth on a typical website. Depending on the service plan, some mobile web visitors may be paying per kilobyte. Be aware of this and eliminate unnecessary images.
- **Font, color, and media issues.** Mobile devices may have very limited font support. Configure font size using ems or percentages. Include generic font family names in your stylesheet. Mobile devices may have very limited color support. Choose colors carefully to maximize contrast. Many mobile devices do not support Adobe Flash media.
- **Awkward controls; limited processor and memory.** While smartphones with touch controls are becoming more popular, many mobile users will not have access to mouse-like controls. Provide keyboard access to assist these users. Although mobile device processing speed and available memory are improving, they still cannot compare to the resources of a desktop computer. While this won't be an issue for the websites you create for exercises in this text, be mindful of this issue in the future as you continue to develop your skills and create web applications.
- **Functionality.** Provide easy access to your website's features with prominent hyperlinks or a prominent search button. The mobile site for the White House (Figure 16) is quite text-intensive with links to featured content, a search feature, and a prominent link to the regular (full) website.

10 More Design Considerations

Load Time

The last thing you want to happen is for your visitors to leave your page before it has even finished loading! Make sure your pages load as quickly as possible. Web usability expert Jakob Nielsen reports that visitors will often leave a page after waiting more than 10 seconds. It takes just less than 9 seconds at 56Kbps for a browser to display a web page and associated files of 60KB. It's a good practice to try to limit the total file size of a website's home page and all of its associated images and media files to less than 60KB. However, it's common to go over this recommended limit for content pages when you're sure that your visitors will be interested enough to wait to see what your site is presenting.

According to a recent study by the PEW Research Center's Internet and American Life Project, the percentage of U.S. Internet users with a broadband (cable, DSL, and so on) connection at home or at work is rising. Sixty-six percent of adult Americans have access to broadband at home. Even with the trend of increasing bandwidth available to your visitors, keep in mind that 34% of households do not have broadband Internet access. Visit Pew Internet (http://www.pewinternet.org) for the most up-to-date statistics. The chart shown in Figure 17 compares file sizes and connection speed download

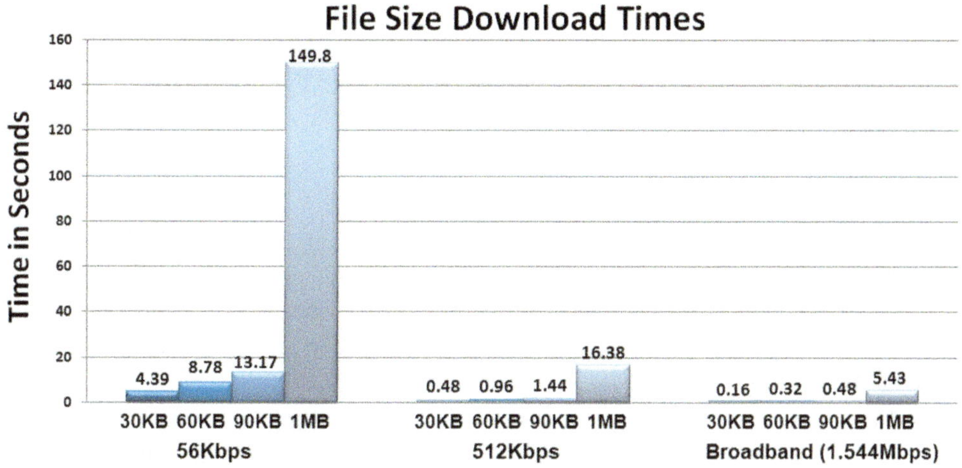

Figure 17 File size download times and Internet connection speeds

times, and was created using a File Transfer Time–Data Transfer Speed Calculator (http://www.t1shopper.com/tools/calculate/downloadcalculator.php).

One method to help determine whether the load time of your page is acceptable is to view the size of your website files in Windows Explorer or Mac Finder. Calculate the total file size of your web page plus all of its associated images and media. If the total file size for a single page and its associated files is more than 60KB and it is likely that your target audience may not be using broadband access, take a closer look at your design. Consider whether you really need to use all of the images to convey your message. The **perceived load time** is the amount of time that a web page visitor is aware of waiting while your page is loading. Because visitors often leave a website if a page takes too long to load, it is important to shorten their perception of waiting. A common technique is to shorten the perceived loading time by optimizing images, using CSS Sprites, and breaking a long page into multiple smaller pages. Popular web authoring tools such as Microsoft Expression Web and Adobe Dreamweaver will calculate load time at various transmission speeds.

Above the Fold

Placing important information **above the fold** is a technique borrowed from the newspaper industry. When newspapers are placed on counters and in vending machines to be sold, the portion above the fold on the page is viewable. Publishers noticed that more papers were sold when the most important, attention-getting information was placed in this location. You may use this technique to attract visitors to your web pages and to keep them there. At the most popular screen resolution of 1024×768, the amount of screen viewable above the fold (after accounting for browser menus and controls) is about 600 pixels. Avoid placing important information and navigation on the far right side because this area may not be initially displayed by browsers at some screen resolutions.

White Space

This term **white space** is also borrowed from the publishing industry. Placing blank or white space (because paper is usually white) in areas around blocks of text increases the readability of the page. Placing white space around graphics helps them to stand out. Allow for some blank space between blocks of text and images. How much is adequate? It depends—experiment until the page is likely to look appealing to your target audience.

Avoid Horizontal Scrolling

In order to make it easy for visitors to view and use your web pages, avoid creating pages that are too wide to be displayed in the browser window. These pages require the user to scroll horizontally. Currently, the most popular screen resolution is 1024×768. Cameron Moll (http://www.cameronmoll.com/archives/001220.html) suggests that the optimal web page width for display at 1024×768 screen resolution is 960 pixels. Be mindful that not all of your web page visitors will maximize their browser viewport.

Browsers

Unless you are designing for an intranet within an organization, expect your website to be visited using a wide variety of browsers. Just because your web page looks great in your favorite browser doesn't automatically mean that all browsers will render it well. A recent survey by Net Market Share (http://marketshare.hitslink.com/browser-market-share.aspx?qprid=0&qpcustomd=0) indicates that while Microsoft Internet Explorer is still the most popular web browser, the Firefox open-source browser and the Google Chrome browser have been gaining ground. The survey reports that about 54% of website visitors use Internet Explorer (including versions 6 through 9), 22% use Firefox, 13% use Google Chrome, 7% use Safari, 2% use Opera, 1% use the Opera Mini mobile browser, and the remaining 1% use a variety of browsers, including Blackberry, Playstation, and Konqueror.

Apply the principle of **progressive enhancement**. Design the site so that it looks good in browsers commonly used by your target audience and then add enhancements with CSS3 and/or HTML5 for display in modern browsers. Always try to test your pages with the most popular versions of browsers on desktop PC and Mac operating systems. At the time of this writing, these are Internet Explorer 8, Internet Explorer 7, Firefox 4, Google Chrome 11, and Safari. Many web page components, including default text size and default margin size, are different among browsers, browser versions, and operating systems. Also try to test your site on other types of devices such as tablets and smartphones. Opera offers free simulators for the Opera Mini mobile browser at http://www.opera.com/mobile/demo.

Screen Resolution

Your website visitors will use a variety of screen resolutions. A recent survey by Net Market Share (http://marketshare.hitslink.com/report.aspx?qprid=17) reported the use of more than 90 different screen resolutions, with the top four being 1024×768 (with 19.6%), 1280×800 (15%), 1366×768 (13%), and 1280×1024 (8%). A typical smartphone screen resolution of 320×480 was in use by about 2% of web visitors. Mobile use will vary with the purpose of the website, but it is expected to grow as the use of smartphones and tablets increases. Be aware that mobile devices have low screen resolution, such as 240×320, 320×480, or 480×800. Popular tablet devices offer a higher screen resolution: Apple iPad (1024×768), Motorola Xoom (1280×800), Samsun Galaxy Tab (1200×800), and Blackberry Playbook (1024×600). CSS media queries are a technique for configuring a web page to display well on various screen resolutions.

11 Web Design Best Practices Checklist

Table 1 contains a checklist of recommended web design practices. Use this as a guide to help you create easy-to-read, usable, and accessible web pages.

Table 1 Web design best practices checklist

Page Layout		
❑	1.	Appealing to target audience
❑	2.	Consistent site header/logo
❑	3.	Consistent navigation area
❑	4.	Informative page title that includes the company/organization/site name
❑	5.	Page footer area—copyright, last update, contact e-mail address
❑	6.	Good use of basic design principles: repetition, contrast, proximity, and alignment
❑	7.	Displays without horizontal scrolling at 1024×768 and higher resolutions
❑	8.	Balance of text/graphics/white space on page
❑	9.	Good contrast between text and background
❑	10.	Repetitive information (header/logo and navigation) takes up no more than one-quarter to one-third of the browser window at 1024×768 resolution
❑	11.	Home page has compelling, interesting information above the fold (before scrolling down) at 1024×768 resolution
❑	12.	Home page downloads within 10 seconds on dial-up connection
Browser Compatibility		
❑	1.	Displays on current versions of Internet Explorer (8+)
❑	2.	Displays on current versions of Firefox (4+)
❑	3.	Displays on current versions of Google Chrome
❑	4.	Displays on current versions of Safari (both Mac and Windows)
❑	5.	Displays on current versions of Opera (10+)
❑	6.	Displays on mobile devices
Navigation		
❑	1.	Main navigation links are clearly and consistently labeled
❑	2.	Navigation is easy to use for target audience
❑	3.	When the main navigation consists of images and/or multimedia, the page footer area contains plain-text hyperlinks (accessibility)
❑	4.	Navigation aids (such as site map, skip to content link, and/or breadcrumbs) are used
❑	5.	All navigation hyperlinks work

(Continued)

Table 1 (*Continued*)

Color and Graphics		
❑	1.	Use of different colors in page background/text is limited to a maximum of three or four plus neutrals
❑	2.	Color is used consistently
❑	3.	Background and text colors have good contrast
❑	4.	Color is not used alone to convey meaning (accessibility)
❑	5.	Use of color and graphics enhances rather than detracts from the site
❑	6.	Graphics are optimized and do not slow download significantly
❑	7.	Each graphic used serves a clear purpose
❑	8.	Image tags use the alt attribute to configure alternate text replacement (accessibility)
❑	9.	Animated images do not distract from the site and either do not repeat or only repeat a few times
Multimedia		
❑	1.	Each audio/video/Flash file used serves a clear purpose
❑	2.	The audio/video/Flash files used enhance rather than distract from the site
❑	3.	Captions or transcripts are provided for each audio or video file used (accessibility)
❑	4.	The file size is indicated for audio or video file downloads
❑	5.	Hyperlinks to downloads for media plug-ins are provided
Content Presentation		
❑	1.	Common fonts such as Arial, Verdana, Georgia, or Times New Roman are used
❑	2.	Writing techniques for the Web are used: headings, bullet points, short paragraphs, and so on
❑	3.	Fonts, font sizes, and font colors are consistently used
❑	4.	Content provides meaningful, useful information
❑	5.	Content is organized in a consistent manner
❑	6.	Information is easy to find (minimal clicks)
❑	7.	Timeliness: The date of the last revision and/or copyright date is accurate
❑	8.	Content does not include outdated material
❑	9.	Content is free of typographical and grammatical errors
❑	10.	Avoids the use of "Click here" when writing text for hyperlinks
❑	11.	Hyperlinks use a consistent set of colors to indicate visited/nonvisited status
❑	12.	Alternate text equivalent to content is provided for graphics and media (accessibility)
Functionality		
❑	1.	All internal hyperlinks work
❑	2.	All external hyperlinks work
❑	3.	All forms function as expected
❑	4.	No JavaScript errors are generated by the pages

Table 1 (*Continued*)

		Accessibility
❑	1.	When the main navigation consists of images and/or multimedia, the page footer area contains plain-text hyperlinks
❑	2.	Color is not used alone to convey meaning
❑	3.	Image tags use the alt attribute to configure alternate text replacement
❑	4.	Captions or transcripts are provided for each audio or video file used
❑	5.	Attributes designed to improve accessibility, such as alt, title, and summary, are used where appropriate
❑	6.	If the site uses frames, frame titles are configured and meaningful content is placed in the no-frames area
❑	7.	To assist screen readers, the spoken language of the page is indicated with the HTML element's lang attribute

Note: Web Design Best Practices Checklist is copyrighted by Terry Morris (http://terrymorris.net). Used by permission.

Checkpoint 2

1. View the home page of your school. Use the Web Design Best Practices Checklist (Table 1) to evaluate the page. Describe the results.
2. View your favorite website (or a URL provided by your instructor). Maximize and resize the browser window. Decide whether the site uses ice, jello, or liquid design. Adjust the screen resolution on your monitor to a different resolution than you normally use. Does the website look similar or very different? Offer two recommendations for improving the design of the site.
3. List three best practices used when placing graphics on web pages. View the home page of your school. Describe the use of web graphic design best practices on this page.

Chapter Summary

This chapter introduced recommended web design practices. The choices you make in the use of page layout, color, graphics, text, and media depend on your particular target audience. Developing an accessible web site should be the goal of every web developer. Visit the text's website at http://www.webdevfoundations.net for examples, the links listed in this chapter, and updated information.

Key Terms

above the fold
alignment
antialiased text
breadcrumb trails
chunking
contrast
hierarchical organization
horizontal scrolling
ice design
jello design
linear organization
liquid design
load time
navigation bar
page layout
perceived load time
POUR
progressive enhancement
proximity
random organization
repetition
screen resolution
site map
site search
skip to content
target audience
WAI (Web Accessibility Initiative)
WCAG 2.0 (Web Content Accessibility Guidelines 2.0)
white space
wireframe

Review Questions

Multiple Choice

1. Which of the following would a consistent website design *not* have?
   a. a similar navigation area on each content page
   b. the same fonts on each content page
   c. a different background color on each page
   d. the same logo in the same location on each content page

2. Which of the following are the three most common methods for organizing websites?
   a. horizontal, vertical, and diagonal
   b. hierarchical, linear, and random
   c. accessible, readable, and maintainable
   d. none of the above

3. Which of the following is not a web design recommended practice?
   a. Design your site to be easy to navigate.
   b. Colorful pages appeal to everyone.
   c. Design your pages to load quickly.
   d. Limit the use of animated items.

4. Which of the following are the four principles of the Web Content Accessibility Guidelines?
   a. repetition, contrast, proximity, and alignment
   b. perceivable, operable, understandable, and robust
   c. accessible, readable, maintainable, and reliable
   d. hierarchical, linear, random, and sequential

5. Which of the following is a sketch or blueprint of a web page that shows the structure (but not the detailed design) of basic page elements?
   a. drawing
   b. HTML code
   c. site map
   d. wireframe

6. Which of the following are influenced by the intended or target audience of a site?
   a. the amount of color used on the site
   b. the font size and styles used on the site
   c. the overall look and feel of the site
   d. all of the above

7. Which of the following recommended design practices apply to a website that uses images for its main site navigation?
   a. Provide alternative text for the images.
   b. Place text links at the bottom of the page.
   c. Both a and b.
   d. No special considerations are needed.
8. Which of the following is known as white space?
   a. the empty screen area around blocks of text and images
   b. the background color of white used for a page
   c. configuring the color of the text to be white
   d. none of the above
9. Which of the following should you do when creating text hyperlinks?
   a. Create the entire sentence as a hyperlink.
   b. Include the words "Click here" in your text.
   c. Use a key phrase as a hyperlink.
   d. none of the above
10. Which of the following is the design technique used to create pages that stretch to fill the browser window?
    a. ice
    b. liquid
    c. jello
    d. none of the above

Fill in the Blank

11. The most common structure used for commercial websites is ___________ organization.
12. All browsers and browser versions ___________ display web pages in exactly the same way.
13. The ___________ is a group whose mission is to create guidelines and standards for web accessibility.

Short Answer

14. Describe an issue to consider when designing for the mobile Web.
15. Describe one of the four principles of WCAG 2.0.

Hands-On Exercises

1. **Web Design Evaluation.** As you read this chapter, you explored web page design, including navigation design techniques and the design principles of repetition, contrast, proximity, and alignment. You'll review and evaluate screenshots of web pages in this hands-on exercise.

   Select a website to review. Provide the following information:
   a. Indicate the type(s) of navigation evident.
   b. Describe how the design principles of repetition, contrast, proximity, and alignment are applied. Be specific.
   c. Complete the Web Design Best Practices Checklist (see Table 1).
2. Practice creating site maps for the following situations.
   a. Doug Kowalski is a freelance photographer who specializes in nature photography. He often gets contract work shooting photos for textbooks and journals. Doug would like a website that showcases his talents and provides publishers with an easy way to contact him. He would like a home page, a few pages with samples of his nature photographs, and a contact page. Create a site map based on this scenario.
   b. Mary Ruarez owns a business, named Just Throw Me, which sells handcrafted specialty pillows. She currently sells at craft fairs and local gift shops, but would like to expand her business to the Web. She would like a website with a home page, a page that describes her products, a page for each of her seven pillow

styles, and an order page. She has been advised that because she is collecting information from individuals, a page describing her privacy policy would be a good idea. Create a site map based on this scenario.

c. Prakesh Khan owns a dog-grooming business named A Dog's Life. He would like a website that includes a home page, a page about grooming services, a page with a map to his shop, a contact page, and a section that explains how to select a good pet. The content for the part of the website on selecting a pet will be a step-by-step presentation. Create a site map based on this scenario.

3. Practice creating wireframe page layouts for the following situations. Use the style for page layout composition shown in Figure 15 where places for logo, navigation, text, and images are indicated. Do not worry about exact wording or exact images.
   a. Create sample wireframe page layouts for Doug Kowalski's photography business, described in 2(a). Create a wireframe layout for the home page. Create another wireframe page layout for the content pages.
   b. Create sample wireframe page layouts for the Just Throw Me website described in 2(b). Create a wireframe layout for the home page. Create another wireframe page layout for the content pages.
   c. Create sample wireframe page layouts for the A Dog's Life website described in 2(c). Create a wireframe layout for the home page and the regular content pages. Create another wireframe page layout for the presentation pages.

4. Choose two sites that are similar in nature or have a similar target audience, such as the following:

   - Amazon.com (http://www.amazon.com) and Barnes & Noble (http://www.bn.com)
   - Kohl's (http://www.kohls.com) and JCPenney (http://www.jcpenney.com)
   - CNN (http://www.cnn.com) and MSNBC (http://www.msnbc.com)

   Describe how the two sites you chose to review exhibit the design principles of repetition, contrast, proximity, and alignment.

5. Choose two sites that are similar in nature or have a similar target audience, such as the following:

   - Crate & Barrel (http://www.crateandbarrel.com) and Pottery Barn (http://www.potterybarn.com)
   - Harper College (http://goforward.harpercollege.edu) and College of Lake County (http://www.clcillinois.edu)
   - Chicago Bears (http://www.chicagobears.com) and Green Bay Packers (http://www.packers.com)

   Describe how the two sites you chose to review exhibit web design best practices. How would you improve these sites? Recommend three improvements for each site.

6. How would you design a home page for the following businesses using the ice design technique? Create a wireframe page layout for the home page.
   a. See 2(a) for the description of Doug Kowalski's photography business.
   b. See 2(b) for the description of Just Throw Me.
   c. See 2(c) for the description of A Dog's Life.

7. How would you design a home page for the following businesses using the jello design technique? Create a wireframe page layout for the home page.

a. See 2(a) for the description of Doug Kowalski's photography business.
b. See 2(b) for the description of Just Throw Me.
c. See 2(c) for the description of A Dog's Life.

8. How would you design a home page for the following businesses using the liquid design technique? Create a wireframe page layout for the home page.
a. See 2(a) for the description of Doug Kowalski's photography business.
b. See 2(b) for the description of Just Throw Me.
c. See 2(c) for the description of A Dog's Life.

Web Research

This chapter introduced techniques that are useful when writing for the Web. Explore this topic further. Visit the resources listed below to get started.

- Writing for the Web: http://www.useit.com/papers/webwriting
- Writing Well for the Web: http://www.webreference.com/content/writing
- Web Writing that Works!: http://www.webwritingthatworks.com/CGuideJOBAID.htm
- A List Apart: 10 Tips on Writing the Living Web: http://www.alistapart.com/articles/writeliving
- The Yahoo! Style Guide: http://styleguide.yahoo.com/writing

If these resources are no longer available, search the Web for information on "writing for the Web." Read one or more articles. Select five techniques that you would like to share with others. Write a one-page summary of your findings. Include the URLs of your resources.

Focus on Web Design

1. This chapter discusses recommended web design practices. Sometimes it is helpful to learn about good design by examining poor design. Visit Web Pages that Suck (http://www.webpagesthatsuck.com) and read about their examples of poor design. Think about some websites that you have visited. Do any of them have similar qualities? Find two websites that use poor web design practices. Write a one-page report that includes an introduction about the design practices that are not followed at the websites, a link to each site, and a description of how each site has practiced poor website design.

2. Visit any of the websites referenced in this chapter that interest you. Write a one-page summary and reaction to the website you chose to visit. Address the following topics:

- What is the purpose of the site?
- Who is the intended audience?
- Do you think the site reaches the intended audience?
- List three examples of how this website uses recommended web design guidelines.
- How could this site be improved?

WEBSITE CASE STUDY
Web Design Best Practices

In this section, you are asked to analyze the design of four websites.

JavaJam Coffee House

Figure 25 in the chapter "HTML Basics" shows a site map for the JavaJam website. Three pages for this site were created in other chapters. In this case study, you will review the site for recommended web design practices.

Hands-On Practice Case

1. Examine the site map in Figure 25 of Chapter 2. What type of site organization is used for the JavaJam website? Is it the most appropriate organization for the site? Why or why not?
2. Review the recommended web design practices from this chapter. Use the Web Design Best Practices Checklist (Table 1) to evaluate the JavaJam site. Cite three design practices that have been well implemented. Cite three design practices that could be implemented in a better way. How else would you improve the website?

Fish Creek Animal Hospital

Figure 29 in the chapter "HTML Basics" shows a site map for the Fish Creek website. Three pages for the site were created. In this case study, you will review the site for recommended web design practices.

Hands-On Practice Case

1. Examine the site map in Figure 29 in Chapter 2. What type of site organization is used for the Fish Creek website? Is it the most appropriate organization for the site? Why or why not?
2. Review the recommended web design practices from this chapter. Use the Web Design Best Practices Checklist (Table 1) to evaluate the Fish Creek site. Cite three design practices that have been well implemented. Cite three design practices that could be implemented in a better way. How else would you improve the website?

Pacific Trails Resort

Figure 33 in the chapter "HTML Basics" shows a site map for the Pacific Trails Resort website. Three pages for the site were created. During this case study, you will review the site for recommended web design practices.

Hands-On Practice Case

1. Examine the site map in Figure 33 in Chapter 2. What type of site organization is used for the Pacific Trails Resort website? Is it the most appropriate organization for the site? Why or why not?
2. Review the recommended web design practices from this chapter. Use the Web Design Best Practices Checklist (Table 1) to evaluate the Pacific Trails Resort site. Cite three design practices that have been well implemented. Cite three design practices that could be implemented in a better way. How else would you improve the website?

Prime Properties

Figure 37 in the chapter "HTML Basics" shows a site map for the Prime Properties website. Three pages for the site were created. During this case study, you will review the site for recommended web design practices.

Hands-On Practice Case

1. Examine the site map in Figure 37 in Chapte 2. What type of site organization is used for the Prime Properties website? Is it the most appropriate organization for the site? Why or why not?
2. Review the recommended web design practices from this chapter. Use the Web Design Best Practices Checklist (Table 1) to evaluate the Prime Properties site. Cite three design practices that have been well implemented. Cite three design practices that could be implemented in a better way. How else would you improve the website?

Web Project

The purpose of this Web Project case study is to design a website using recommended design practices. Your website might be about a favorite hobby or subject, your family, a church or club you belong to, a company a friend owns, or the company you work for. Your website will contain a home page and at least six (but no more than ten) content pages. Complete the following documents: Topic Approval, Site Map, and Page Layout Design. You will not develop web pages at this point.

Hands-On Practice Case

1. **Web Project Topic Approval.** The topic of your website must be approved by your instructor. Provide the following information:
   - What is the purpose of the website?

     List the reason you are creating the website.
   - What do you want the website to accomplish?

     List the goals you have for the website.

     Describe what needs to happen for you to consider your website a success.

- Who is your target audience?

  Describe your target audience by age, gender, socioeconomic characteristics, and so on.

- What opportunity or issue is your website addressing?

  For example, your website might address the opportunity to provide information about a topic to others or create an initial web presence for a company.

- What type of content might be included in your website?

  Describe the type of text, graphics, and media you will need for the website.

- List the URLs for at least two related or similar websites found on the Web.

2. **Web Project Site Map.** Use the drawing feature of a word processing program, a graphics application, or a paper and pencil to create a site map of your website that shows the hierarchy of pages and relationships between pages.
3. **Web Project Page Layout Design.** Use the drawing feature of a word processing program, a graphics application, or paper and pencil to create wireframe page layouts for the home page and content pages of your site. Unless otherwise directed by your instructor, use the style for page layout composition shown in Figure 15. Indicate where the logo, navigation, text, and images will be located. Do not worry about exact wording or exact images.

Answers

Checkpoint 1

1. The four basic principles of design are repetition, contrast, proximity, and alignment. Descriptions of school home pages and how these principles are applied will vary.
2. Best practices for writing for the Web include the following: short paragraphs, bullet points, common fonts, white space, multiple columns if possible, bold or emphasized important text, and correct spelling and grammar.

   Answers will vary. The following suggested solution adds interest with bullet points, places emphasis on important phrases, and includes editing of the original text:

   Acme, Inc., is a new laboratory instrument repair and service company. At this time, our staff has a combined total of 30-plus years of specimen preparation instrumentation service and repair.

   - **EPA Refrigeration Certified**
     Acme, Inc., technicians are factory trained and equipped with the best diagnostic and repair equipment available.
   - **Fully Insured**
     Our workers are fully covered by workman's compensation insurance. A proof-of-insurance certificate can be provided upon request.

- **Convenient Location**
  Repair shop facilities and offices are located in Chicago, Illinois.
- **Service History**
  Your equipment is important to us. A detailed repair history is kept and is available to our service technicians.
- **Rates**
  - Labor and travel, $100.00 per hour
  - 2-hour minimum
  - $0.40 per mile and all related expenses
  - Parts are not included

3. http://www.walmart.com is an e-commerce site. It is designed to appeal to the general public—note the white background and high contrast and the use of tabbed navigation, product hierarchy, and site search. This design meets the needs of its target audience: teen and adult shoppers. http://www.sesameworkshop.org/sesamestreet is geared toward young children and their parents. It is bright and colorful with much interactivity and animation, all of which is appealing to the target audience. http://www.mugglenet.com is a fan site designed to appeal to teens and young adults. It is a dark, mysterious site with much interaction—the forums are very busy. This site appeals to its niche audience.

Checkpoint 2

1. Answers will vary.
2. Answers will vary.
3. Best practices for using graphics on web pages include the following: careful choice of colors (the appendix "Web-Safe Color Palette" is recommended for the most similar cross-platform display), use of necessary images only, use of images as small as possible, a usable site even if images are not displayed, and use of the alt attribute to configure text descriptions for images. Recommendations for school home pages will vary.

Review Questions

1. c
2. b
3. b
4. b
5. d
6. d
7. c
8. a
9. c
10. b
11. hierarchical
12. do not
13. Web Accessibility Initiative (WAI)
14. Student answers will vary. Issues to be aware of in designing for the mobile web include small screen size, low bandwidth, awkward controls, limited processor and memory, and reduced support of font typefaces and color.

15. Student answers will vary. The four principles that are essential to complying with WCAG 2.0 are as follows: **P**erceivable, **O**perable, **U**nderstandable, and **R**obust.
    1. Content must be **P**erceivable
    2. Interface components in the content must be **O**perable
    3. Content and controls must be **U**nderstandable
    4. Content should be **R**obust enough to work with current and future user agents, including assistive technologies

Credits

All photographs except those noted below © Terry Ann Morris

"Checkpoint" icon (green check mark), "Web Site Case Study" icon (blue "WWW"), "FAQ" icon (orange caption bubble), "Focus on Accessibility" icon (orange key) © Fotolia LLC

Figure 9 © Dmitriy Shironosov/Shutterstock Images LLC

The Web Design Best Practices Checklist (Table 1) © Terry Ann Morris (http://www.terrymorris.net)

Page 7, Web Content Accessibility Guidelines 2.0 (WCAG 2.0) recommended by the W3C's Web Accessibility Initiative (WAI) © W3C (World Wide Web Consortium)

Appendix, "WCAG 2.0 Quick Reference" © W3C (World Wide Web Consortium)

WCAG 2.0 Quick Reference

Perceivable

- **1.1 Text Alternatives:** Provide text alternatives for any nontext content so that it can be changed into other forms people need, such as large print, Braille, speech, symbols, or simpler language. *You configure images and multimedia on web pages and provide for alternative text content.*
- **1.2 Time-Based Media:** Provide alternatives for time-based media. *You don't create time-based media in this text, but keep this option in mind for the future if you create animation or use client-side scripting for features such as interactive slide shows.*
- **1.3 Adaptable:** Create content that can be presented in different ways (for example, simpler layout) without losing information or structure. *You use block elements (such as headings, paragraphs, and lists) to create single-column web pages. You create multicolumn web pages. You use HTML tables to configure information.*
- **1.4 Distinguishable:** Make it easier for users to see and hear content, including separating foreground from background. *You are aware of the importance of good contrast between text and background.*

Operable

- **2.1 Keyboard Accessible:** Make all functionality available from a keyboard. *You configure hyperlinks to named fragment identifiers on a web page. The label element is introduced.*
- **2.2 Enough Time:** Provide users enough time to read and use content. *You don't create time-based media in this text, but keep this option in mind for the future if you create animation or use client-side scripting for features such as interactive slide shows.*

- **2.3 Seizures:** Do not design content in a way that is known to cause seizures. *Be careful when you use animation created by others; web pages should not contain elements that flash more than three times in a one-second period.*
- **2.4 Navigable:** Provide ways to help users navigate, find content, and determine where they are. *Block elements (such as headings and lists) to organize web page content. Navigation links can be within an unordered list. In Chapter 7, you configure hyperlinks to named fragment identifiers on a web page.*

Understandable

- **3.1 Readable:** Make text content readable and understandable. *You explore techniques used in writing for the Web.*
- **3.2 Predictable:** Make web pages appear and operate in predictable ways. *The web pages you create are predictable, with clearly labeled and functioning hyperlinks.*
- **3.3 Input Assistance:** Help users avoid and correct mistakes. *You learn to use HTML form controls that cause a supporting browser to validate basic form information and display error messages. Note that client-side scripting can be used to edit web page forms and provide additional feedback to users.*

Robust

- **4.1 Compatible:** Maximize compatibility with current and future user agents, including assistive technologies. *You provide for future compatibility by writing code that follows W3C Recommendations (standards).*

Resources

You'll find the most up-to-date information about WCAG 2.0 at the following resources:

- Overview of WCAG 2.0 http://www.w3.org/TR/WCAG20/Overview
- Understanding WCAG 2.0 http://www.w3.org/TR/UNDERSTANDING-WCAG20
- How to Meet WCAG 2.0 http://www.w3.org/WAI/WCAG20/quickref
- Techniques for WCAG 2.0 http://www.w3.org/TR/WCAG-TECHS

Credits

Appendix E, "WCAG 2.0 Quick Reference" © W3C (World Wide Web Consortium)

Page Layout

Chapter Objectives

In this chapter, you will learn how to . . .

- Describe and apply the CSS Box Model
- Configure margins with CSS
- Configure float with CSS
- Configure relative and absolute positioning with CSS
- Create two-column page layouts using CSS
- Configure navigation in unordered lists and style with CSS
- Add interactivity to hyperlinks with CSS pseudo-classes
- Configure web pages with HTML5 structural elements, including section, header, hgroup, nav, aside, and footer

We'll add to your toolbox of CSS page layout techniques in this chapter, starting with the box model. You'll explore floating and positioning elements with CSS. You'll be introduced to using CSS to add interactivity to hyperlinks with pseudo-classes and use CSS to style navigation in unordered lists. You will practice coding new HTML5 elements that structure web page content.

1 The Box Model

Each element in a document is considered to be a rectangular box. As shown in Figure 1, this box consists of a content area surrounded by padding, a border, and margins. This is known as the **box model**.

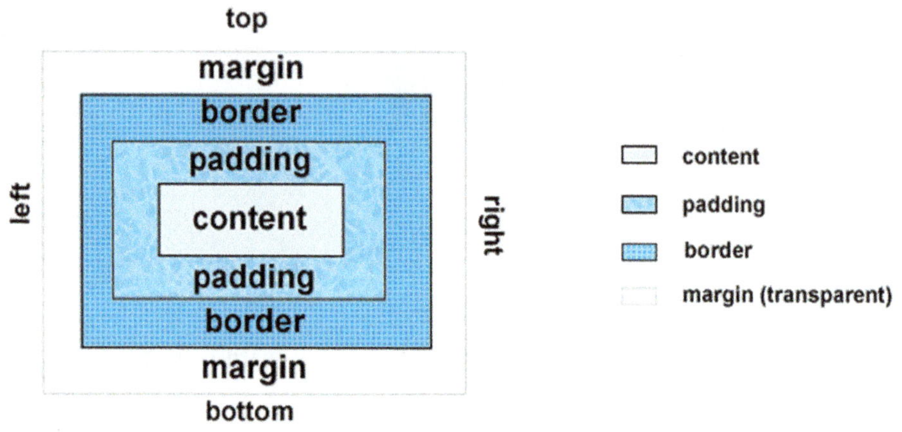

Figure 1 The CSS box model

Content

The content area can consist of a combination of text and web page elements such as images, paragraphs, headings, lists, and so on. The visible width of the element on a web page is the total of the content width, the padding width, and the border width. However, the **`width` property** only configures the actual width of the content; it does not include any padding, border, or margin.

Padding

The padding area is between the content and the border. The default padding value is zero. When the background of an element is configured, the background is applied to both the padding and the content areas. Use the `padding` property to configure an element's padding.

Border

The border area is between the padding and the margin. The default border has a value of 0 and does not display. Use the `border` property to configure an element's border.

Margin

The margin determines the empty space between the element and any adjacent elements. The solid line in Figure 1 that contains the margin area does not display on a web page.

The `margin` Property

Use the **`margin` property** to configure margins on all sides of an element. The margin is always transparent—the background color of the web page or parent element shows in this area. Browsers have default margin values set for the web page document and for certain elements such as paragraphs, headings, forms, and so on. Use the margin property to override the default browser values.

To configure the size of the margin, use a numeric value (px or em). To eliminate the margin, configure it to 0 (with no unit). Use the value `auto` to indicate that the browser should calculate the margin. You may have already used `margin-left: auto;` and `margin-right: auto;` to configure a centered page layout. Table 1 shows CSS properties that configure margins.

Table 1 Configuring margins with CSS

Property	Description and Common Values
`margin`	Shorthand notation to configure the margin surrounding an element A numeric value (px or em) or percentage; for example, `margin: 10px;` The value `auto` causes the browser to automatically calculate the margin for the element Two numeric values (px or em) or percentages: The first value configures the top margin and bottom margin, and the second value configures the left margin and right margin; for example, `margin: 20px 10px;` Three numeric values (px or em) or percentages: The first value configures the top margin, the second value configures the left margin and right margin, and the third value configures the bottom margin; for example, `margin: 10px 20px 5px;` Four numeric values (px or em) or percentages; the values configure the margin in the following order: `margin-top`, `margin-right`, `margin-bottom`, and `margin-left`; for example, `margin: 10px 30px 20px 5px;`
`margin-bottom`	Bottom margin; a numeric value (px or em), percentage, or `auto`
`margin-left`	Left margin; a numeric value (px or em), percentage, or `auto`
`margin-right`	Right margin; a numeric value (px or em), percentage, or `auto`
`margin-top`	Top margin; a numeric value (px or em), percentage, or `auto`

The Box Model in Action

The web page shown in Figure 2 (chapter6/box.html[1] in the student files) depicts the box model in action with an h1 and a div element.

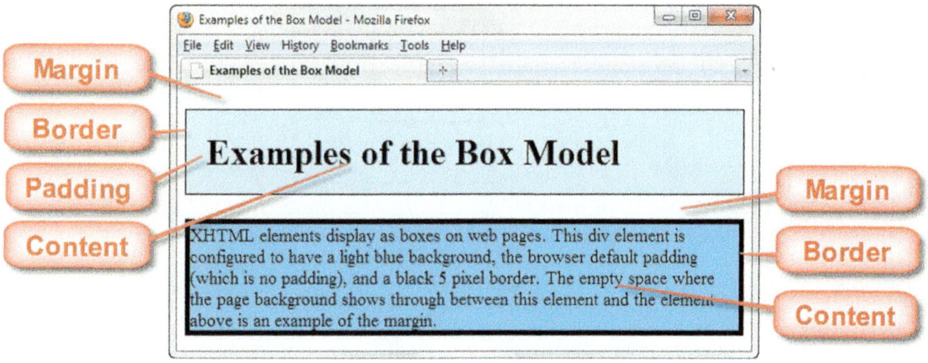

Figure 2 Examples of the box model

[1]Website Case Study starter files are available for download from Pearson's CS Support website at http://cssupport.pearsoncmg.com.

- The h1 element is configured to have a light-blue background, 20 pixels of padding (the space between the content and the border), and a black, 1 pixel border.
- The empty space where the white web page background shows through is the margin. When two vertical margins meet (such as between the h1 element and the div element), the browser collapses the margin size to be the larger of the two margin values instead of applying both margins.
- The div element has a medium-blue background; the browser default padding (which is no padding); and a black, 5 pixel border.

You will get more practice using the box model in this chapter. Feel free to experiment with the box model and the chapter6/box.html file.

2 Normal Flow

Browsers render your web page code line by line in the order it appears in the .html document. This processing is called normal flow. **Normal flow** displays the elements on the page in the order they appear in the web page source code.

Figures 3 and 4 each display two div elements that contain text content. Let's take a closer look. Figure 3 shows a screenshot of two div elements placed one after another on a web page. In Figure 4, the boxes are nested inside each other. In both cases, the browser used normal flow (the default) and displayed the elements in the order that they appeared in the source code.

You'll practice this a bit more in the next Hands-On Practice. Then, later in the chapter, you'll experiment with CSS positioning and float to configure the flow, or placement, of elements on a web page.

Figure 3 Two div elements

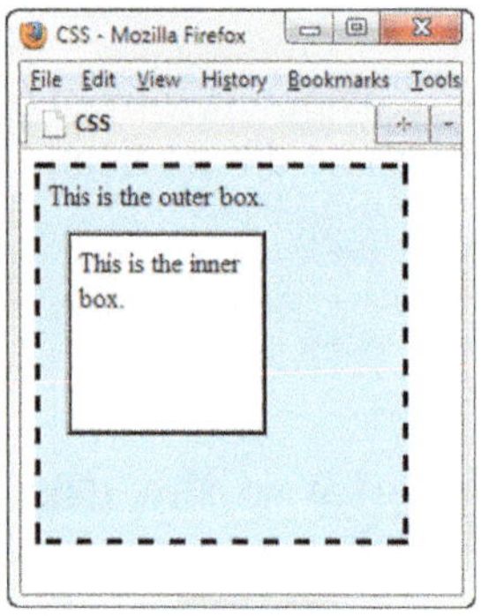

Figure 4 Nested div elements

Hands-On Practice 1

You will explore the box model and normal flow in this Hands-On Practice as you work with the web pages shown in Figure 3 and Figure 4.

Practice with Normal Flow

Launch a text editor and open chapter6/starter1.html in the student files. Save the file with the name box1.html. Edit the body of the web page and add the following code to configure two div elements:

```
<div class="div1">
This is the first box.
</div>
<div class="div2">
This is the second box.
</div>
```

Now let's add embedded CSS in the head section to configure the "boxes." Add a new style rule for a class named **div1** to configure a light-blue background, dashed border, width of 200 pixels, height of 200 pixels, and 5 pixels of padding. The code is

```
.div1 { width: 200px;
        height: 200px;
        background-color: #D1ECFF;
        border: 3px dashed #000000;
        padding: 5px; }
```

Create a style rule for a class named **div2** to configure a width and height of 100 pixels, white background color, ridged border, 10 pixel margin, and 5 pixels of padding. The code is

```
.div2 { width: 100px;
        height: 100px;
        background-color: #ffffff;
        border: 3px ridge #000000;
        margin: 10px
        padding: 5px; }
```

Save the file. Launch a browser and test your page. It should look similar to the one shown in Figure 3. The student files contain a sample solution (see chapter6/box1.html).

Practice with Normal Flow and Nested Elements

Launch a text editor and open your box1.html file. Save the file with the name box2.html.

Edit the code. Delete the content from the body section of the web page. Add the following code to configure two div elements—one nested inside the other.

```
<div class="div1">
This is the outer box.
   <div class="div2">
   This is the inner box.
   </div>
</div>
```

Save the file. Launch a browser and test your page. It should look similar to the one shown in Figure 4. Notice how the browser renders the nested div elements: The second box is nested inside the first box because it is coded inside the first div element in the web page source code. This is an example of normal flow. The student files contain a sample solution (see chapter6/box2.html).

The examples in this Hands-On Practice happened to use two div elements. However, the box model applies to block display HTML elements in general, not just to div elements. You will get more practice using the box model in this chapter.

A Look Ahead: CSS Layout Properties

You've seen how normal flow causes the browser to render the elements in the order that they appear in the HTML source code. When using CSS for page layout, there are situations in which you will want to specify the location of an element on the page—either the absolute pixel location, the location relative to where the element would normally display, or floating on the page. The CSS properties that configure the placement of elements on a web page are discussed in the following sections.

3 CSS Positioning

You've seen how normal flow causes the browser to render the elements in the order that they appear in the HTML source code. When using CSS for page layout, there are situations when you may want more control over the position of an element. This section introduces relative and absolute positioning.

Relative Positioning

Use **relative positioning** to change the location of an element slightly, relative to where it would otherwise appear with normal flow. Configure relative positioning with the `position: relative;` property along with one or more of the following properties: `left`, `right`, `top`, and `bottom`. Table 2 lists CSS position and offset properties.

Figure 5 shows a web page (see chapter6/relative.html in the student files) that uses relative positioning along with the `left` property to configure the placement of an element in relation to the normal flow. In this case, the container element is the body of the web page.

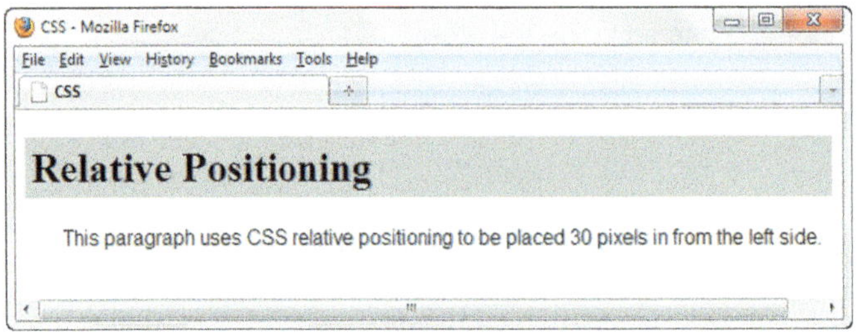

Figure 5 The paragraph is configured using relative positioning

Table 2 CSS properties for relative and absolute position

Property	Value	Purpose
`position`	`static`	Default value; the element is rendered in normal flow
	`relative`	Configures the location of an element relative to where it would otherwise render in normal flow
	`absolute`	Configures the location of an element outside of normal flow precisely in its container element
	`fixed`	Configures the location of an element within the browser viewport; the element does not move when the page is scrolled
`left`	Numeric value or percentage	The position of the element offset from the left side of the container element
`right`	Numeric value or percentage	The position of the element offset from the right side of the container element
`top`	Numeric value or percentage	The position of the element offset from the top of the container element
`bottom`	Numeric value or percentage	The position of the element offset from the bottom of the container element

The result is that the content of the element is rendered as being offset or shifted 30 pixels from the left, where it would normally be placed at the browser's left margin. Notice also how the padding and background-color properties configure the heading element. The CSS is

```
#myContent { position: relative;
             left: 30px;
             font-family: Arial, sans-serif; }
h1 { background-color: #cccccc;
     padding: 5px;
     color: #000000; }
```

The HTML source code is

```
<h1>Relative Positioning</h1>
<div id="myContent">
<p>This paragraph uses CSS relative positioning to be placed 30 pixels
in from the left side.</p>
</div>
```

Absolute Positioning

Use **absolute positioning** to specify the precise location of an element outside of the normal flow in its container element. Configure absolute positioning with the `position: absolute;` property along with one or more of the following offset properties: `left`, `right`, `top`, and `bottom`. See Table 2 for a list of CSS position and offset properties.

Figure 6 depicts a web page that configures a div element using absolute positioning to display the content 200 pixels in from the left margin and 100 pixels down from the top

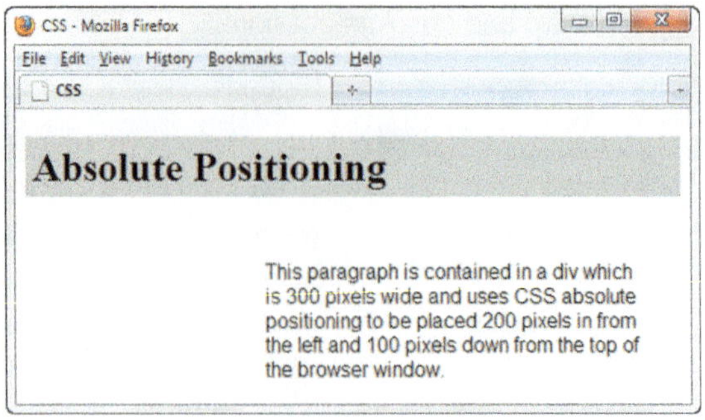

Figure 6 The div element is configured using absolute positioning

of its container element, which is the body of the document. The padding and background-color properties configure the heading element. See the student files (chapter8/absolute.html) for an example.

The CSS is

```
#content { position: absolute;
           left: 200px;
           top: 100px;
           font-family: Arial, sans-serif;
           width: 300px; }
h1 { background-color: #cccccc;
     padding: 5px;
     color: #000000; }
```

The HTML source code is

```
<h1>Absolute Positioning</h1>
<div id="content">
<p>This paragraph is contained in a div which is 300 pixels wide and
uses CSS absolute positioning to be placed 200 pixels in from the left
and 100 pixels down from the top of the browser window.</p>
</div>
```

When working with absolute positioning, it is important to be aware that elements not absolutely positioned will be rendered using normal flow by the browser. Elements that are absolutely positioned are rendered outside of normal flow. You'll explore this behavior in the next Hands-On Practice.

Hands-On Practice 2

Figure 7 shows screenshots of two web pages with similar HTML content. The web page in the upper screenshot does not have any CSS applied. The web page in the lower screenshot uses CSS to configure text, color, and the absolute position of a paragraph element. Launch a text editor and open chapter6/starter2.html in the student files. When a browser renders the page, it will use normal flow and display the HTML elements in the order in which they are coded: `<h1>`, `<div>`, `<p>`, and `<ul>`. Launch a browser and display the page to verify.

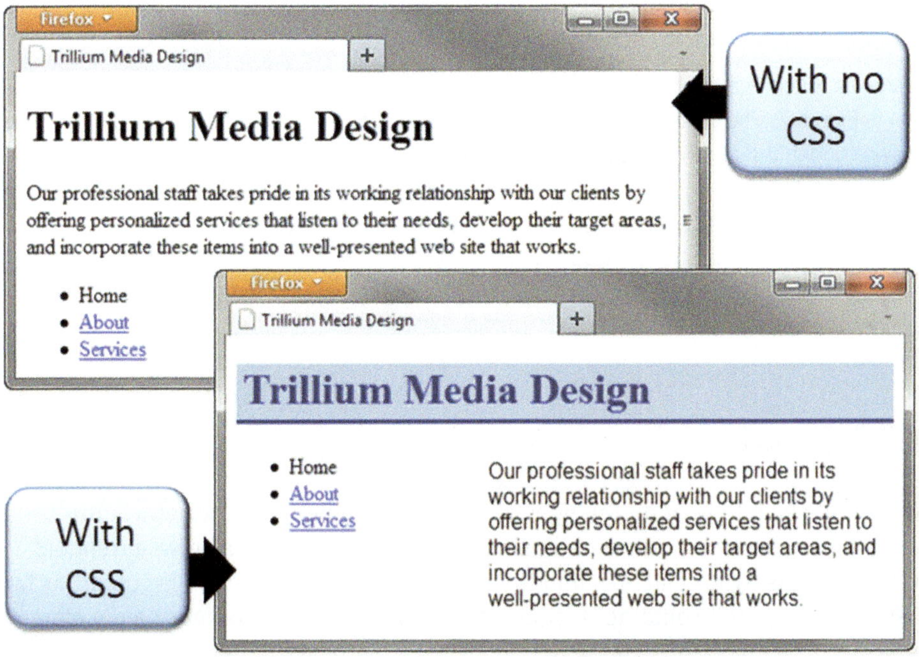

Figure 7 The lower web page uses CSS absolute positioning

Let's add the CSS to make this page more engaging, like the lower screenshot in Figure 7. Save the file with the name trillium.html. With trillium.html open in a text editor, modify the code as follows:

1. This page uses embedded styles. Code opening and closing `<style>` tags in the head section.

```
<style>
</style>
```

2. Create style rules for the h1 element selector. Configure a background color (#B0C4DE), text color (#000080), a 3 pixel solid bottom border in the color #000080, and 5 pixels of padding on the bottom and left sides.

```
h1 { border-bottom: 3px solid #000080;
     color: #000080;
     background-color: #B0C4DE;
     padding: 0 0 5px 5px; }
```

3. Create style rules for a class named `content`. Configure the position to be absolute, 200 pixels from the left, 75 pixels from the top, a width of 300 pixels, and Arial or sans-serif font typeface.

```
.content { position: absolute;
           left: 200px;
           top: 75px;
           font-family: Arial, sans-serif;
           width: 300px; }
```

4. Assign the paragraph to the `content` class. Add `class="content"` to the opening paragraph tag in the body of the web page.

Save the file. Launch a browser and test your page. It should look similar to the lower web page shown in Figure 7. The student files contain a sample solution (see chapter6/trillium.html). Note that even though the unordered list is coded in the page after the paragraph, it's displayed immediately after the heading. This is because the paragraph is absolutely positioned (`position: absolute`). Browsers render absolutely positioned elements outside of normal flow.

Note: This Hands-On Practice used embedded CSS for ease of editing. However, for an actual website with more than one page, the most efficient solution is to use an external CSS file. You'll use external style sheets later in this chapter.

4 CSS Float

Elements that seem to float on the right or left side of either the browser window or another element are often configured using the **float property.** The browser renders these elements using normal flow and then shifts them to either the right or left as far as possible within their container (usually either the browser viewport or a div element).

- Use `float: right;` to float the element on the right side of the container.
- Use `float: left;` to float the element on the left side of the container.
- Specify a width for a floated element unless the element already has an implicit width, such as an img element.
- Other elements and web page content will flow around the floated element.

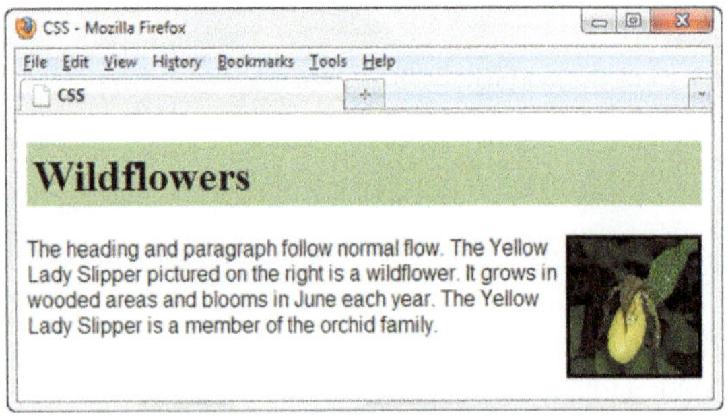

Figure 8 The image is configured to float

Figure 8 shows a web page with an image configured with `float: right;` to float on the right side of the browser viewport (see chapter6/float.html in the student files). When floating an image, the margin property is useful to configure empty space between the image and text on the page.

View Figure 8 and notice how the image stays on the right side of the browser viewport. An id called `yls` was created that applies the `float`, `margin`, and `border` properties. The attribute `id="yls"` was placed on the image tag. The CSS is

```
h1 { background-color: #A8C682;
     padding: 5px;
     color: #000000; }
p { font-family: Arial, sans-serif; }
#yls { float: right;
       margin: 0 0 5px 5px;
       border: 1px solid #000000; }
```

The HTML source code is

```
<h1>Wildflowers</h1>
<img id="yls" src="yls.jpg" alt="Yellow Lady Slipper" height="100"
width="100">
```

```
<p>The heading and paragraph follow normal flow. The Yellow Lady
Slipper pictured on the right is a wildflower. It grows in wooded
areas and blooms in June each year. The Yellow Lady Slipper is a
member of the orchid family.</p>
```

Hands-On Practice 3

In this Hands-On Practice, you'll use the CSS float property as you configure the web page shown in Figure 9.

Figure 9 The CSS float property left-aligns the image

Create a folder named ch6float. Copy the starter3.html and yls.jpg files from the chapter6 folder in the student files into your ch6float folder. Launch a text editor and open starter3.html. Notice the order of the images and paragraphs. Note that there is no CSS configuration for floating the images. Display starter3.html in a browser. The browser renders the page using normal flow and displays the HTML elements in the order they are coded.

Let's add CSS to float the image. Save the file as floatyls.html in your ch6float folder. With floatyls.html open in a text editor, modify the code as follows:

1. Add a style rule for a class name `float` that configures float, margin, and border properties.

```
.float { float: left;
         margin-right: 10px;
         border: 3px ridge #000000; }
```

2. Assign the image element to the class named float (use `class="float"`).

Save the file as index.html. Launch a browser and test your page. It should look similar to the web page shown in Figure 9. The student files contain a sample solution (see chapter6/floatyls.html).

The Floated Element and Normal Flow

Take a moment to examine your file in a browser (see Figure 9) and consider how the browser rendered the page. The div element is configured with a light background color to demonstrate how floated elements are rendered outside of normal flow. Observe that the image and the first paragraph are contained within the div element. The h2 element follows the div. If all the elements were rendered using normal flow, the area with the light background color would contain both child elements of the div: the image and the first paragraph. In addition, the h2 element would be placed on its own line under the div element.

However, once the image is placed vertically on the page, it is floated outside of normal flow—that's why the light background color only appears behind the first paragraph and why the h2 element's text begins immediately after the first paragraph and appears next to the floated image. In the following sections, you'll explore properties that can "clear" this float and improve the display.

5 CSS: Clearing a Float

The `clear` Property

The **`clear` property** is often used to terminate, or clear, a float. You can set the value of the clear property to `left`, `right`, or `both`, depending on the type of float you need to clear.

Review Figure 9 and the code sample (see chapter6/floatyls.html in the student files). Notice that although the div element contains both an image and the first paragraph, the light background color of the div only displays behind the screen area occupied by the first paragraph—it stops a bit earlier than expected. Clearing the float will help take care of this display issue.

Clear a Float with a Line Break

A common technique to clear a float within a container element is to add a line break element configured with the `clear` property. See chapter6/floatylsclear1.html in the student files for an example. Observe that a CSS class is configured to clear the left float:

```
.clearleft { clear: left; }
```

Also, a line break tag assigned to the `clearleft` class is coded before the closing `div` tag. The code for the div element is

```
<div>
<img class="float" src="yls.jpg" alt="Yellow Lady Slipper"
height="100" width="100">
<p>The Yellow Lady Slipper grows in wooded areas and blooms in June
each year. The flower is a member of the orchid family.</p>
<br class="clearleft">
</div>
```

Figure 10 displays a screen shot of this page. Review Figure 9 and note two changes: the light background color of the div element extends farther down the page and the h2 element's text begins on its own line under the image.

Another Technique to Clear a Float

If you are not concerned about the light background color display, another option is to omit the line break tag and, instead, apply the `clearleft` class to the h2 element, which is the first block display element after the div. This does not change the display of the light background color, but it does force the h2 element's text to begin on its own line, as shown in Figure 11 (see chapter6/floatylsclear2.html in the student files).

Figure 10 The clear property is applied to a line break tag

Figure 11 The clear property is applied to the h2 element

The `overflow` Property

The **`overflow` property** is often used to clear a float, although its intended purpose is to configure how content should display if it is too large for the area allocated. See Table 3 for a list of commonly used values for the overflow property.

Table 3 The `overflow` property

Value	Purpose
`visible`	Default value; the content is displayed, and if it's too large, the content will overflow and extend outside the area allocated to it
`hidden`	The content is clipped to fit the area allocated to the element in the browser viewport
`auto`	The content fills the area allocated to it and, if needed, scrollbars are displayed to allow access to the remaining content
`scroll`	The content is rendered in the area allocated to it and scrollbars are displayed

Clear a Float

Review Figure 9 and the code sample (chapter6/floatyls.html in the student files). Observe the div element, which contains the floated image and first paragraph on the page. Notice that although the div element contains both an image and the first paragraph, the light background color of the div element does not extend as far as expected; it is only visible in the area occupied by the first paragraph. You can use the `overflow` property assigned to the container element to resolve this display issue and clear the float. In this case, we'll apply the `overflow` and `width` properties to the div selector. The CSS to configure the div in this manner is

```
div { background-color: #F3F1BF;
      overflow: auto;
      width: 100%; }
```

This will clear the float. The web page will display as shown in Figure 12 (see chapter6/floatylsoverflow.html in the student files).

Figure 12 The overflow property is applied to the div selector

Figure 13 The browser displays scrollbars

Notice that using the `overflow` property (see Figure 12) and applying the `clear` property to a line break tag (see Figure 10) result in a similar web page display. You may be wondering about which CSS property (`clear` or `overflow`) is the best one to use when you need to clear a float.

Although the `clear` property is widely used, in this example, it is more efficient to apply the `overflow` property to the container element (for example, a div element). This will clear the float, avoid adding an extra line break tag, and ensure that the container element expands to enclose the entire floated element. You'll get more practice with the `float`, `clear`, and `overflow` properties as you continue working through this text. Floating elements is a key technique for designing multicolumn page layouts with CSS.

Configure Scrollbars

The web page in Figure 13 demonstrates the use of `overflow: auto;` to automatically display scrollbars if the content exceeds the space allocated to it. In this case, the div that contains the paragraph and the floated image was configured with a width of 300px and a height of 100px.

See the example web page (chapter6/floatylsscroll.html in the student files). The CSS for the div is shown below:

```
div { background-color: #F3F1BF;
      overflow: scroll;
      width: 300px;
      height: 100px; }
```

Checkpoint 1

1. List the components of the box model from innermost to outermost.
2. Describe the difference between relative and absolute positioning.
3. Describe the purpose of the CSS float property.

6 CSS Two-Column Page Layout

A common design for a web page is a two-column layout. This can be accomplished with CSS by configuring one of the columns to float on the web page. This section introduces you to two formats for the two-column page layout.

Two Columns with Left Navigation

See Figure 14 for a wireframe for a two-column web page. The left column will contain navigation.

The HTML template for the page layout is

```
<div id="wrapper">
   <div id="leftcolumn">
   </div>
   <div id="rightcolumn">
      <div id="header">
      </div>
      <div id="content">
      </div>
      <div id="footer">
      </div>
   </div>
</div>
```

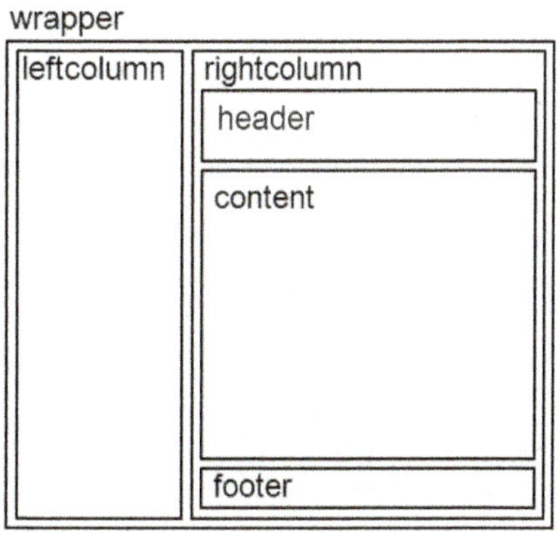

Figure 14
Wireframe for a two-column layout with left navigation

The web page in Figure 15 implements a two-column layout with the navigation on the left (see chapter6/twocolumn1.html in the student files). The key to this layout is that the left column is coded to float to the left with the `float` property. The browser renders the other content on the page using normal flow.

- The wrapper is centered and takes up 80% of the web page width. This area is assigned a medium-blue background color that will display behind the left column:

```
#wrapper { width: 80%;
           margin-left: auto;
           margin-right: auto;
           background-color: #b3c7e6; }
```

Figure 15
A two-column page layout with left navigation

- The left column is assigned a fixed width and configured to float to the left. Because no background color is configured, the background color of the container element (the wrapper div) displays:

```
#leftcolumn { float: left;
              width: 150px; }
```

- The right column is assigned a margin on the left that is equal to or greater than the width of the left column. This margin creates the look of two columns (often called faux columns). A white background color is assigned to the right column, which overrides the background color configured in the wrapper:

```
#rightcolumn { margin-left: 155px;
               background-color: #ffffff; }
```

Two Columns with Top Header and Left Navigation

See Figure 16 for a wireframe for a web page with that has a top logo header spanning two columns with a navigation area in the left column.

The HTML template for the page layout is

```
<div id="wrapper">
   <div id="header">
   </div>
   <div id="leftcolumn">
   </div>
   <div id="rightcolumn">
      <div id="content">
      </div>
      <div id="footer">
      </div>
   </div>
</div>
```

The web page shown in Figure 17 implements a two-column layout with a top header (see chapter6/twocolumn2.html in the student files). The CSS that configures the

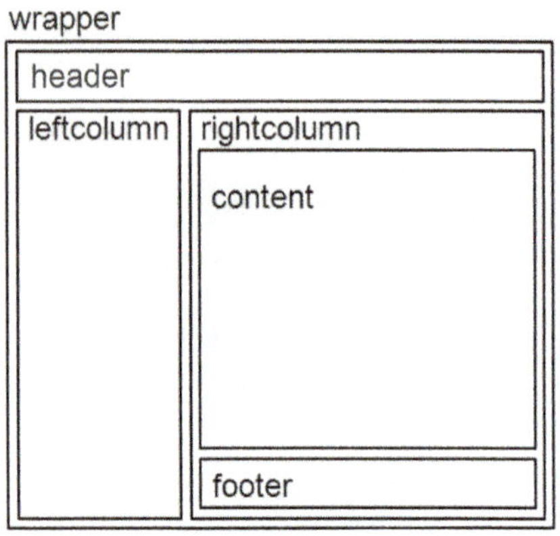

Figure 16 Wireframe for a two-column layout with a top logo area

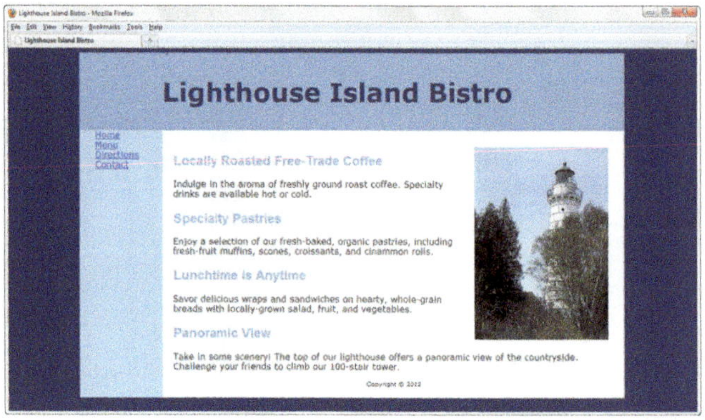

Figure 17 A two-column page layout with a top logo and left navigation

`wrapper`, `leftcolumn`, and `rightcolumn` areas is the same as for the web page shown in Figure 15. However, notice that the location of the div assigned to the `header` id is different. It is now coded as the first div element within the wrapper and displays before the left and right columns.

FAQ Do I have to use a wrapper?

No, you are not required to use a wrapper or container for a web page layout. However, it does make it easier to get the two-column look because the background color of the wrapper div will display behind any of its child elements that do not have their own background color configured. This technique also provides you with the option of configuring a different background color or background image for the page (as shown in Figure 17) using the body element selector.

Not Yet Ready for Prime Time

There is one more aspect of the two-column layout web page design to consider before it is ready for "prime time." The navigation area is a list of hyperlinks. In order to more closely semantically describe the navigation area, the hyperlinks should be configured in an unordered list. In the next section, you'll learn techniques to configure horizontal and vertical navigation hyperlinks in unordered lists.

7 Hyperlinks in an Unordered List

One of the advantages of using CSS for page layout involves the use of semantically correct code. Writing semantically correct code means choosing the markup tag that most accurately reflects the purpose of the content. Using the various levels of heading tags for content headings and subheadings or placing paragraphs of text within paragraph tags (rather than using line breaks) are examples of writing semantically correct code. This type of coding is a step in the direction of supporting the Semantic Web. Leading Web developers such as Eric Meyer, Mark Newhouse, Jeffrey Zeldman, and others have promoted the idea of using unordered lists to configure navigation menus. After all, a navigation menu is a list of hyperlinks.

Configuring navigation with a list also helps to provide accessibility. Screen reader applications offer easy keyboard access and verbal cues for information organized in lists, such as the number of items in the list.

Focus on Accessibility

Configure List Markers with CSS

Recall that the default display for an unordered list is to show a disc marker (often referred to as a bullet) in front of each list item. The default display for an ordered list is to show a decimal number in front of each list item. When you configure navigation hyperlinks in an unordered list, you may not always want to see those list markers. It's easy to configure them with CSS. Use the `list-style-type` property to configure the marker for an unordered or ordered list. See Table 4 for common property values.

Table 4 CSS properties for ordered and unordered list markers

Property	Description	Value	List Marker Display
`list-style-type`	Configures the style of the list marker	`none`	No list markers display
		`disc`	Circle
		`circle`	Open circle
		`square`	Square
		`decimal`	Decimal numbers
		`upper-alpha`	Uppercase letters
		`lower-alpha`	Lowercase letters
		`lower-roman`	Lowercase Roman numerals
`list-style-image`	Image replacement for the list marker	The `url` keyword with parentheses surrounding the file name or path for the image	Image displays in front of each list item
`list-style-position`	Configures placement of the list marker	`inside`	Markers are indented; text wraps under the markers
		`outside` (default)	Markers have default placement

Figure 18 shows an unordered list configured with square markers using the following CSS:

```
ul { list-style-type: square; }
```

Figure 19 shows an ordered list configured with uppercase letter markers using the following CSS:

```
ol { list-style-type: upper-alpha; }
```

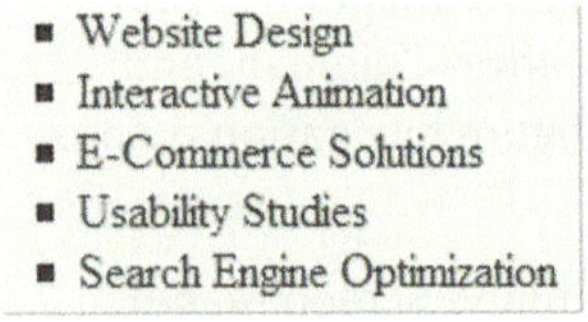

Figure 18 The unordered list markers are square

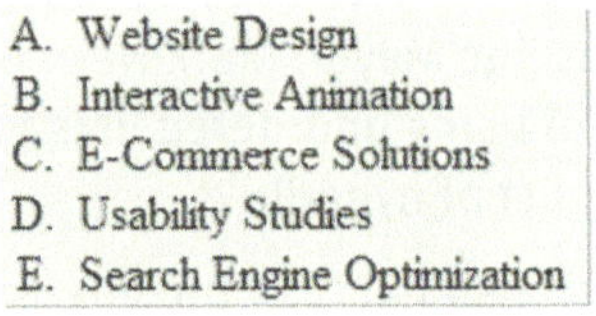

Figure 19 The ordered list markers use uppercase letters

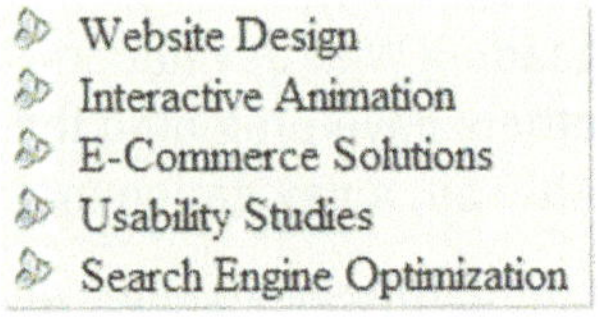

Figure 20 The list markers are replaced with an image

Configure an Image as a List Marker

Use the `list-style-image` property to configure an image as the marker in an unordered or ordered list. In Figure 20, an image named trillium.gif was configured to replace the list markers using the following CSS:

```
ul {list-style-image: url(trillium.gif); }
```

Vertical Navigation with an Unordered List

Figure 21 shows the navigation area of a web page (see chapter6/twocolumn3.html in the student files) that uses an unordered list to organize the navigation links. The HTML is

Figure 21 Navigation in an unordered list

```
<ul>
<li><a href="index.html">Home</a></li>
<li><a href="menu.html">Menu</a></li>
<li><a href="directions.html">Directions</a></li>
<li><a href="contact.html">Contact</a></li>
</ul>
```

Configure with CSS

OK, so now that we're semantically correct, how about improving the visual aesthetic? Let's use CSS to eliminate the list marker. We also need to make sure that our special styles only apply to the unordered list in the navigation area (within the `leftcolumn` id), so we'll use a contextual selector. The CSS to configure the list in Figure 22 is

Figure 22 The list markers have been eliminated with CSS

```
#leftcolumn ul { list-style-type: none; }
```

Remove the Underline with CSS

The **`text-decoration` property** modifies the display of text in the browser. This property is most often used to eliminate the underline from the navigation hyperlinks with `text-decoration: none;`.

The CSS to configure the list in Figure 23 (see chapter6/twocolumn4.html in the student files) that eliminates the underline on the hyperlinks in the navigation area (within the `leftcolumn` id) is

Figure 23 The CSS text-decoration property has been applied

```
#leftcolumn a { text-decoration: none; }
```

Horizontal Navigation with an Unordered List

You may be wondering how to use an unordered list for a horizontal navigation menu. The answer is CSS! List items are block display elements. They need to be configured as inline display elements to display in a single line. The CSS `display` **property** configures how the browser renders, or displays, an element on a web page. See Table 5 for a list of commonly used values.

Table 5 The `display` property

Value	Purpose
`none`	The element will not display
`inline`	The element will display as an inline element in the same line as the surrounding text and/or elements
`block`	The element will display as a block element with a margin above and below

Figure 24
Navigation in an unordered list

Figure 24 shows the navigation area of a web page (see chapter6/navigation.html in the student files) with a horizontal navigation area organized in an unordered list. The HTML is

```
<div id="nav">
<ul>
   <li><a href="index.html">Home</a></li>
   <li><a href="menu.html">Menu</a></li>
   <li><a href="directions.html">Directions</a></li>
   <li><a href="contact.html">Contact</a></li>
</ul>
</div>
```

Configure with CSS

The following CSS was applied in this example:

- To eliminate the list marker, apply `list-style-type: none;` to the ul element selector:

  ```
  #nav ul { list-style-type: none; }
  ```

- To render the list items horizontally instead of vertically, apply `display: inline;` to the li element selector:

  ```
  #nav li { display: inline; }
  ```

- To eliminate the underline from the hyperlinks, apply `text-decoration: none;` to the a element selector. Also, to add some space between the hyperlinks, apply `padding-right: 10px;` to the a element selector:

  ```
  #nav a { text-decoration: none; padding-right: 10px; }
  ```

8 CSS Interactivity with Pseudo-Classes

VideoNote
Interactivity with CSS pseudo-classes

Have you ever visited a website and found that the text hyperlinks changed color when you moved the mouse pointer over them? Often, this is accomplished using a CSS **pseudo-class**, which can be used to apply a special effect to a selector. The five pseudo-classes that can be applied to the anchor element are shown in Table 6.

Table 6 Commonly used CSS pseudo-classes

Pseudo-Class	When Applied
`:link`	Default state for a hyperlink that has not been clicked (visited)
`:visited`	Default state for a visited hyperlink
`:focus`	Triggered when the hyperlink has keyboard focus
`:hover`	Triggered when the mouse pointer moves over the hyperlink
`:active`	Triggered when the hyperlink is actually clicked

Notice the order in which the pseudo-classes are listed in Table 6. Anchor element pseudo-classes *must be coded in this order* (although it's OK to omit one or more of those listed). If you code the pseudo-classes in a different order, the styles will not be reliably applied. It's common practice to configure the `:hover`, `:focus`, and `:active` pseudo-classes with the same styles.

To apply a pseudo-class, write it after the selector. The following code sample will configure text hyperlinks to be red initially. The sample also uses the `:hover` pseudo-class to configure the hyperlinks to change their appearance when the visitor places the mouse pointer over them so that the underline disappears and the color changes.

```
a:link { color: #ff0000; }
a:hover { text-decoration: none;
          color: #000066; }
```

Figure 25 shows part of a web page that uses a similar technique. Note the position of the mouse pointer over the Print This Page hyperlink. The text color has changed and has no underline. Most modern browsers support CSS pseudo-classes.

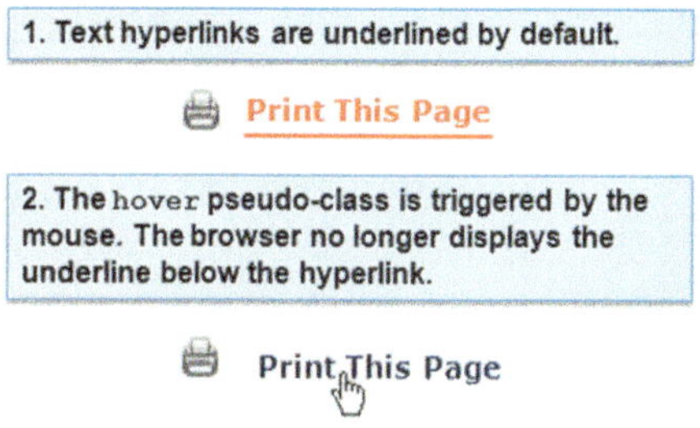

Figure 25 Using the `hover` pseudo-class

Hands-On Practice 4

You will use pseudo-classes to create interactive hyperlinks in this Hands-On Practice. Create a folder named ch6hover. Copy the lighthouseisland.jpg, lighthouselogo.jpg, and starter3.html files from the chapter6 folder in the student files into your ch6hover folder. Display the web page in a browser. It should look similar to Figure 26. Notice that the navigation area needs to be configured.

Launch a text editor and open starter3.html. Save the file as index.html in your ch6hover folder.

Figure 26 The navigation area needs to be styled in this two-column page layout

1. Review the code for this page, which uses a two-column layout. Examine the `leftcolumn` id and modify the code to configure the navigation in an unordered list.

```
<ul>
   <li><a href="index.html">Home</a></li>
   <li><a href="menu.html">Menu</a></li>
   <li><a href="directions.html">Directions</a></li>
   <li><a href="contact.html">Contact</a></li>
</ul>
```

   Let's add CSS to the embedded styles to configure the unordered list elements in the `leftcolumn` id. Eliminate the list marker and set the padding to 10 pixels.

```
#leftcolumn ul { list-style-type: none;
                 padding: 10px; }
```

2. Next, configure basic interactivity with pseudo-classes.
   - Configure the anchor tags in the `leftcolumn` id to have 10 pixels of padding, use bold font, and display no underline.

```
#leftcolumn a { text-decoration: none;
                padding: 10px;
                font-weight: bold; }
```

   - Use pseudo-classes to configure anchor tags in the `leftcolumn` id to display white (#ffffff) text for unvisited hyperlinks, light-gray (#eaeaea) text for visited hyperlinks, and dark-blue (#000066) text when the mouse pointer hovers over hyperlinks:

```
#leftcolumn a:link { color: #ffffff; }
#leftcolumn a:visited { color: #eaeaea; }
#leftcolumn a:hover { color: #000066; }
```

Save your page and test in a browser. Move your mouse pointer over the navigation area and notice the change in the text color. Your page should look similar to Figure 27 (see chapter6/hover/index.html in the student files).

Figure 27 CSS pseudo-classes add interactivity to the navigation

9 Practice with CSS Two-Column Layout

You've had some experience with a two-column layout, organizing navigation links in an unordered list, and configuring CSS pseudo-classes. Let's reinforce these skills with a Hands-On Practice.

Hands-On Practice 5

In this Hands-On Practice, you'll create a new version of the Lighthouse Island Bistro home page with a top header section spanning two columns, content in the left column, navigation in the right column, and a footer section below the two columns. See Figure 28 for a wireframe. You will configure the CSS in an external style sheet. Create a new folder named ch6practice. Copy the starter4.html, lighthouseisland.jpg, and lighthouselogo.jpg files from the chapter6 folder in the student files into your ch6practice folder.

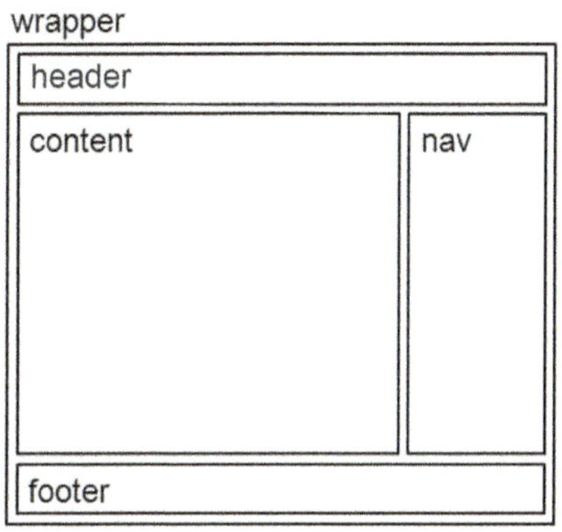

Figure 28 Wireframe for a two-column layout with a top header area

1. Launch a text editor and open starter4.html. Save the file as index.html. Add a link element to the head section of the web page that associates this file with an external style sheet named lighthouse.css. A code sample follows.

```
<link href="lighthouse.css" rel="stylesheet">
```

2. Save the index.html file. Launch a text editor and create a new file named lighthouse.css in your ch6practice folder. Configure the CSS for the wireframe sections as follows:
   - The body element selector: very-dark-blue background (#00005D) and Verdana, Arial, or the default sans-serif font typeface

   ```
   body { background-color: #00005D;
          font-family: Verdana, Arial, sans-serif; }
   ```

   - The `wrapper` id: centered, width set to 80% of the browser viewport, minimum width of 960px, display text in a dark-blue color (#000066), and display a medium-blue (#B3C7E6) background color (*this color will display behind the nav section*)

   ```
   #wrapper { margin: 0 auto;
              width: 80%;
              min-width: 960px;
              background-color: #B3C7E6;
              color: #000066; }
   ```

- The **header** id: slate-blue (#869DC7) background color; very-dark-blue (#00005D) text color; 150% font size; top, right, and bottom padding of 10px; 155 pixels of left padding; and the lighthouselogo.jpg background image

```
#header { background-color: #869DC7;
          color: #00005D;
          font-size: 150%;
          padding: 10px 10px 10px 155px;
          background-repeat: no-repeat;
          background-image: url(lighthouselogo.jpg); }
```

- The h1 element selector: Configure 20 pixels of bottom margin to prevent an Internet Explorer display issue.

```
h1 { margin-bottom: 20px; }
```

- The **nav** id: float on the right, width set to 150px, display bold text, letter spacing of 0.1 em

```
#nav { float: right;
       width: 150px;
       font-weight: bold;
       letter-spacing: 0.1em; }
```

- The **content** id: white background color (#FFFFFF), black text color (#000000), 10 pixels of padding on the top and bottom, 20 pixels of padding on the left and right, and overflow set to auto

```
#content { background-color: #ffffff;
           color: #000000;
           padding: 10px 20px;
           overflow: auto; }
```

- The **footer** id: 70% font size, centered text, 10 pixels of padding, slate-blue background color (#869DC7), and clear set to both

```
#footer { font-size: 70%;
          text-align: center;
          padding: 10px;
          background-color: #869DC7;
          clear: both;}
```

Save the file and display it in a browser. Your display should be similar to Figure 29.

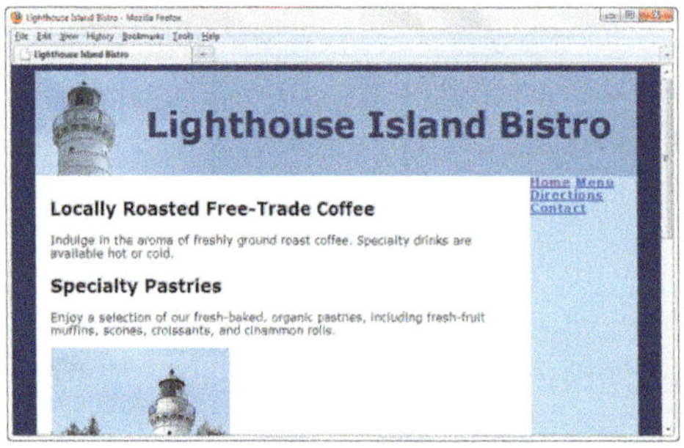

Figure 29 Home page with major sections configured using CSS

3. Continue editing the lighthouse.css file to style the h2 element selector and floating image. Configure the h2 element selector with slate-blue text color (#869DC7) and Arial or sans-serif font typeface. Configure the `floatright` id to float on the right side with 10 pixels of margin.

```
h2 { color: #869DC7;
     font-family: Arial, sans-serif; }
#floatright { float: right;
              margin: 10px; }
```

4. Continue editing the lighthouse.css file and configure the navigation bar.
   - The ul element selector: Eliminate the list markers. Set a zero margin and zero padding.

   ```
   #nav ul { list-style-type: none; margin: 0; padding: 0; }
   ```

   - The a element selector: no underline, 20 pixels of padding, medium-blue background color (#B3C7E6), and 1 pixel solid white bottom border

     Use `display: block;` to allow the web page visitor to click anywhere on the anchor "button" to activate the hyperlink.

   ```
   #nav a { text-decoration: none;
            padding: 20px;
            display: block;
            background-color: #B3C7E6;
            border-bottom: 1px solid #FFFFFF; }
   ```

   Configure the `:link`, `:visited`, and `:hover` pseudo-classes as follows:

   ```
   #nav a:link { color: #FFFFFF; }
   #nav a:visited { color: #EAEAEA; }
   #nav a:hover { color: #869DC7;
                  background-color: #EAEAEA; }
   ```

Save your files. Open your index.html file in a browser. Move your mouse pointer over the navigation area and notice the interactivity, as shown in Figure 30 (see chapter6/practice/index.html in the student files).

Figure 30 CSS pseudo-classes add interactivity to the page

10 CSS Resources

CSS Debugging Techniques

Using CSS for page layout requires some patience. It takes a while to get used to it. Fixing problems in code is called **debugging**. This term dates back to the early days of programming when an insect (a bug) lodged inside the computer and caused a malfunction. Debugging CSS can be frustrating and requires patience. One of the biggest issues is that even modern browsers implement CSS in slightly different ways. Browser support changes with each new browser version. Testing is crucial. Expect your pages to look slightly different in various browsers. Although Internet Explorer's support of the CSS standard is improving, there still are differences in compliance. The following are helpful techniques to use when your CSS isn't behaving properly:

Verify Correct HTML Syntax

Invalid HTML code can cause issues with CSS. Use the W3C Markup Validation Service at http://validator.w3.org to verify the correct HTML syntax.

Verify Correct CSS Syntax

Sometimes a CSS style does not apply because of a syntax error. Use the W3C CSS Validation Service at http://jigsaw.w3.org/css-validator to verify your CSS syntax. Carefully check your code. Many times, the error is in the line *above* the style that is not correctly applied.

Configure Temporary Background Colors

Sometimes your code is valid but the page is not rendered in the way that you would expect. If you temporarily assign distinctive background colors such as red or yellow and test again, it should be easier to see where the boxes are ending up.

Configure Temporary Borders

Similar to the temporary background colors, you could temporarily configure an element with a 3 pixel red solid border. This will really jump out at you and help you recognize the issue quickly.

Use Comments to Find the Unexpected Cascade

Style rules and HTML attributes configured farther down the page can override earlier style rules. If your styles are misbehaving, try "commenting out" (see below) some styles and test with a smaller group of statements. Then add the styles back in one by one to see where or when the breakdown occurs. Work patiently and test the entire style sheet in this manner.

Browsers ignore code and text that is contained between comment markers. A CSS comment begins with `/*` and ends with `*/`. The comment below is an example of documentation that explains the purpose of a style rule.

```
/* Set Page Margins to Zero */
body { margin: 0; }
```

Comments can span multiple lines. The comment on next page begins on the line above the `nav` class and ends on the line below the `nav` class. This causes the browser to skip the `nav` class when applying the style sheet. This technique can be useful for testing when you are experimenting with a number of properties and may need to temporarily disable a style rule.

```
/* temporarily commented out during testing
.nav { text-decoration: none; }
*/
```

A common mistake when using comments is to type the beginning `/*` without subsequently typing `*/` to end the comment. As a result, *everything* after the `/*` is treated as a comment by the browser.

CSS Web Resources

This chapter introduces you to CSS for page layout configuration and should get you started in your exploration of this technology. It may help you to know that you are not alone in your quest to learn CSS. There are many resources with documentation, tutorials, and support for this technology. The page layout techniques discussed in this text are just an introduction to using this technology. There are many websites that offer additional insight and techniques for configuring page layout with CSS. The following are a few that you may find useful:

- CSS Layout Techniques: For Fun and Profit: Large collection of CSS page layouts and links to tutorials http://glish.com/css
- The Layout Reservoir: A collection of CSS page layouts http://www.bluerobot.com/web/layouts
- Listamatic: Vertical and horizontal lists with CSS http://css.maxdesign.com.au/listamatic
- W3C Cascading Style Sheets http://www.w3.org/Style/CSS
- Experimental CSS Compatibility Table http://westciv.com/wiki/Experimental_CSS_compatibility_table
- HTML5 and CSS3 Browser Support Chart http://www.findmebyip.com/litmus
- CSS Contents and Browser Compatibility: Peter-Paul Koch's site is dedicated to studying and defeating browser incompatibility related to CSS and JavaScript. http://www.quirksmode.org/css/contents.html
- Position Is Everything: John and Holly Bergevin's site focuses on CSS bugs in modern browsers. It contains some great sample CSS page layouts. http://www.positioniseverything.net
- CSS3 Click Chart http://www.impressivewebs.com/css3-click-chart
- SitePoint CSS Reference http://reference.sitepoint.com/css

Checkpoint 2

1. Open chapter6/practice/index.html from Hands-On Practice 5 in a browser. Resize the browser window. Describe what happens. What type of page design layout (ice, jello, or liquid) is being used?
2. Describe one CSS debugging tip that you have found to be helpful.
3. Describe how to choose whether to configure an HTML element selector, create a class, or create an id when working with CSS.

11 HTML5 Structural Elements

HTML5 introduces a number of semantic structural elements that you can use to configure areas on a web page. These new block display elements are not intended to completely replace the div element, but are intended to be used along with div and other elements to structure web page documents in a more meaningful manner that indicates the purpose of the structural areas.

Standard HTML4 and XHTML coding practice is to use only one h1 element on a web page and configure the heading-level elements in outline format. Outlining is different in HTML5. Instead of a heading-level outline, the outline is also configured by sectioning elements (such as section, article, nav, and aside) with heading levels within each section. Try out an HTML5 outliner at http://gsnedders.html5.org/outliner. We'll explore the HTML5 header, hgroup, nav, footer, section, article, aside, and time elements in this section. Let's first take a closer look at the header, hgroup, nav, and footer elements.

Header Element

The **header element** contains the headings of either a web page document or an area in the document such as a section or article. The header element begins with the `<header>` tag and ends with the `</header>` tag. The header element is block display and will typically contain one or more heading-level elements (h1 through h6) and, optionally, the hgroup element.

Hgroup Element

The **hgroup element** groups heading-level tags and is useful if the logo header area of a web page contains both the website name and a **tagline** (a phrase that identifies and captures the essence of a business, e.g., the tagline of L. L. Bean [http://www.llbean.com] is "GUARANTEED TO LAST"). The hgroup element is block display and begins with the `<hgroup>` tag and ends with the `</hgroup>` tag. When there is more than one heading-level element in an hgroup, only the first heading element is placed in the page outline.

Nav Element

The **nav element** contains a section of navigation hyperlinks. The block display nav element begins with the `<nav>` tag and ends with the `</nav>` tag.

Footer Element

The **footer element** contains the footer content of a web page, section, article, paragraph, or even the blockquote element. The block display footer element begins with the `<footer>` tag and ends with the `</footer>` tag.

Remember that these new HTML5 elements are not supported by all browsers. However, you can begin to practice with them today.

Hands-On Practice 6

In this Hands-On Practice, you'll start with the two-column Lighthouse Island Bistro home page from Hands-On Practice 5 (shown in Figure 30) and modify it to use HTML5 structural elements. You'll also add a tagline to the header area. Create a new folder named ch6structure. Copy the index.html, lighthouse.css, lighthouseisland.jpg, and lighthouselogo.jpg files from the chapter6/practice folder in the student files and save them in your ch6structure folder.

1. Launch a text editor and open index.html. Replace the div assigned to the **`header`** id with an HTML5 header element that contains an hgroup. Also add the tagline "the best coffee on the coast" with an h2 element. The new code is

```
<header>
  <hgroup>
    <h1>Lighthouse Island Bistro</h1>
    <h2>the best coffee on the coast</h2>
  </hgroup>
</header>
```

2. Replace the opening and closing tags for the div assigned to the **`nav`** id with the HTML5 nav element.
3. Replace the opening and closing tags for the div assigned to the **`footer`** id with the HTML5 footer element.
4. Code a figure element that contains an image. Code a figcaption element that displays the text "Island Lighthouse, Built in 1870" within the figure container below the image. Remove **`id="floatright"`** from the image element. You'll configure the entire figure element to float in step 9. The code is shown below:

```
<figure>
   <img src="lighthouseisland.jpg" width="250" height="355"
alt="Lighthouse Island">
   <figcaption>Island Lighthouse, Built in 1870</figcaption>
</figure>
```

5. Save the index.html file.
6. Open lighthouse.css in a text editor. Edit the CSS to use HTML element selectors for the header, nav, and footer elements. Replace the **`#header`** selector with the HTML header element selector. Replace all instances of the **`#nav`** selector with the HTML nav element selector. Replace the **`#footer`** selector with the HTML footer element selector.
7. Configure CSS for the h1 and h2 elements in the header. Use contextual HTML selectors. Set the h1 bottom margin to 0. Set the h2 with 20 pixels of right padding; no margins; and .80em italic, right-aligned, #00005D color text. The CSS is

```
header h1 { margin-bottom: 0; }
header h2 { margin: 0;
            padding-right: 20px;
            font-size: .80em;
            font-style: italic;
            text-align: right;
            color: #00005D; }
```

8. Clean up some leftover CSS. Remove the `#floatright` style rule and the h1 element style rule from the CSS.

9. Configure the style rules for the figure and figcaption element selectors. The figure element selector is set as follows: float to the right, 260 pixels in width, and 10 pixel margin. The figcaption element selector is set to render small, italic, centered text. The CSS is

```
figure { float: right;
         width: 260px;
         margin: 10px; }
figcaption { text-align: center;
             font-size: .80em;
             font-style: italic; }
```

10. The most recent versions of Internet Explorer, Firefox, Safari, Chrome, and Opera support the HTML5 elements that you have coded. But how can you help older browsers understand the HTML5 code? One technique is to use CSS to configure the HTML5 element selectors as block display elements. At the time that this was written, popular browsers (except Internet Explorer 8 and earlier versions) correctly applied this style declaration. Add the following CSS:

```
header, nav, footer, figure, figcaption { display: block; }
```

11. Save your lighthouse.css file.

12. Display your index.html page in a modern browser. It should look similar to the page shown in Figure 31 (see chapter6/structure/index.html in the student files).

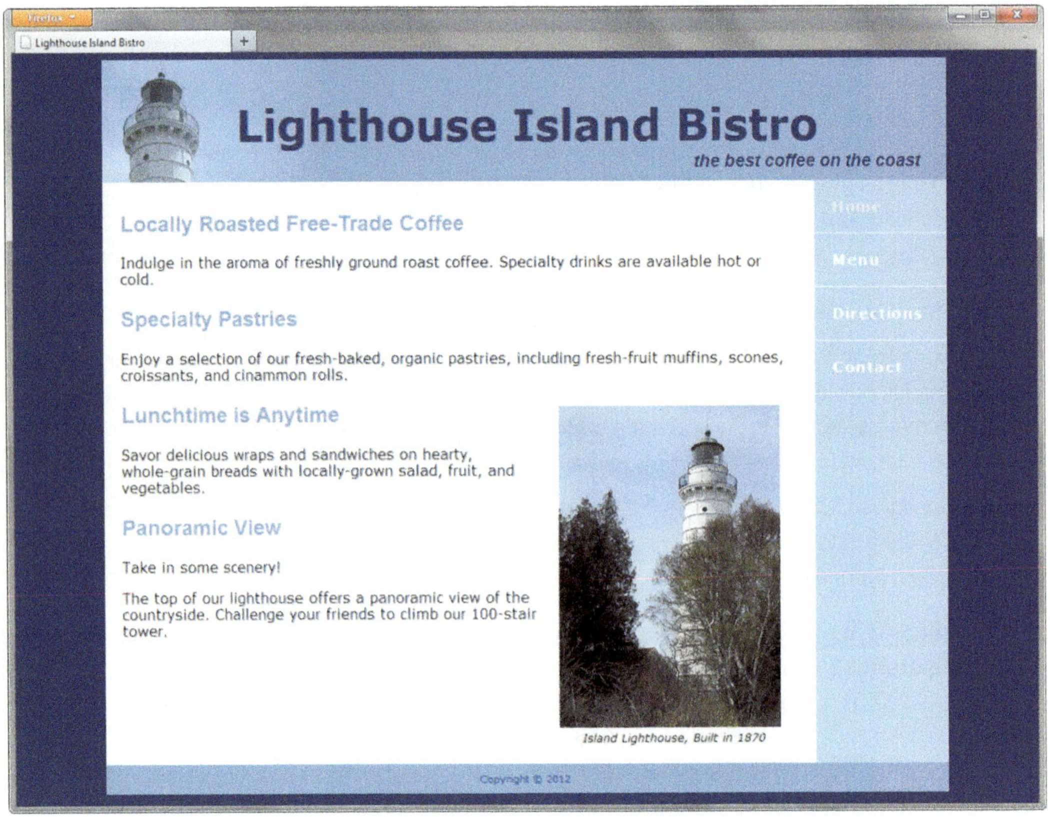

Figure 31 HTML5 structural elements were used on this web page

As you completed the Hands-On Practice, you might have noticed that some of the id names used for standard page areas, such as `header`, `nav`, and `footer`, were also the names of new HTML5 structural elements. This is a great way to prepare for HTML5, even if you are still coding XHTML! Become accustomed to the new HTML5 element names by configuring divs with these names as id or class values. Then, later, when it's time to always code in HTML5 syntax, you've got a head start! The HTML5 Gallery at http://html5gallery.com contains many examples of how HTML5 is being used on the Web today. Next, we'll explore the HTML5 section, article, aside, and time elements.

Section Element

The section element contains a "section" of a document, such as a chapter or topic. The block display section element begins with the `<section>` tag and ends with the `</section>` tag. A section element might contain header, footer, article, aside, div, and other elements needed to display the content. Section elements can contain other section elements.

Article Element

The article element contains an independent entry, such as a blog posting, comment, or e-zine article that could stand on its own. The block display article element begins with the `<article>` tag and ends with the `</article>` tag. An article element is block display and might contain header, footer, section, aside, div, and other elements needed to display the content.

Aside Element

The aside element is block display and contains a sidebar, a note, or other tangential content. The aside element begins with the `<aside>` tag and ends with the `</aside>` tag.

Time Element

The time element represents a date or a time and could be useful to date articles or blog postings. The inline display time element begins with the `<time>` tag and ends with the `</time>` tag. An optional `datetime` attribute can be used to specify a calendar date and/or time in machine-readable format. Use YYYY-MM-DD for a date. Use a 24-hour clock and HH:MM for time. See HTML: The Markup Language at http://www.w3.org/TR/html-markup/time.html for additional `datetime` syntax options.

Hands-On Practice 7

In this Hands-On Practice, you'll begin with the HTML5 Lighthouse Island Bistro home page (shown in Figure 31) and modify the content to use a blog format that is structured with the new HTML5 elements article, header, aside, and time. Create a new folder named ch6blog. Copy the index.html, lighthouseisland.jpg, and lighthouselogo.jpg files from the chapter6/structure folder in the student files into your ch6blog folder.

1. Launch a text editor and open index.html. Delete the text and elements contained within the div assigned to the `content` id. Replace them with an HTML5 section element (assigned to

the `content` id) that contains an h1 element with "Bistro Blog" and two blog articles. Use the section, article, header, aside, and time elements to create two blog postings for the home page. Configure the new section as follows and save the file.

```
<section id="content">
  <h1>Bistro Blog</h1>
  <article>
      <header><h1>Valentine Wrap</h1></header>
      <time datetime="2011-02-02">February 2, 2011</time>
      <aside>Watch for the March Madness Wrap next month!</aside>
      <p>The February special sandwich is the Valentine Wrap &mdash;
      heart-healthy organic chicken with roasted red peppers on a
      whole wheat wrap.</p>
  </article>
  <article>
     <header><h1>New Coffee of the Day Promotion</h1></header>
     <time datetime="2011-01-11">January 11, 2011</time>
     <p>Enjoy the best coffee on the coast in the comfort of your
     home. We will feature a different flavor of our gourmet,
     locally roasted coffee each day with free bistro tastings
     and a discount on one-pound bags.</p>
  </article>
</section>
```

2. Open lighthouse.css in a text editor. Recall that the aside element contains content that is tangential to the main content. Configure CSS to display the aside element on the right (use float) in a light-gray rectangle about 120 pixels wide, a 10 pixel left margin, 5 pixels of padding, 80% font size, and a drop-shadow effect.

```
aside { float: right;
        background-color: #eaeaea;
        width: 120px;
        padding: 5px;
        margin-left: 10px;
        font-size: 80%;
        -webkit-box-shadow: 5px 5px 5px #828282;
        -moz-box-shadow: 5px 5px 5px #828282;
        box-shadow: 5px 5px 5px #828282; }
```

Save the lighthouse.css file. Launch a modern browser and test your index.html page. You might be surprised by the way that the section and article headings display. We'll need to code CSS declarations specifically for the article header and for the h1 in the `content` id. Use contextual selectors. Launch a text editor and open lighthouse.css again. Add the following new CSS code:

```
article header { background-color: #FFFFFF;
                 background-image: none;
                 padding: 0;
                 font-size: 80%;}
```

```
#content h1 { color: #869dc7;
              font-family: Arial, sans-serif;
              font-size: 1.5em;}
```

3. Recall from Hands-On Practice 6 the CSS technique that helps older browsers to render HTML5 elements as expected. Add the section, article, and aside HTML element selectors to the CSS. The new style rule is

```
header, nav, footer, figure, figcaption, section, article, aside
{ display: block; }
```

4. Save the lighthouse.css file. Display your index.html page in a modern browser. It should look similar to the page shown in Figure 32 (see chapter6/blog/index.html in the student files).

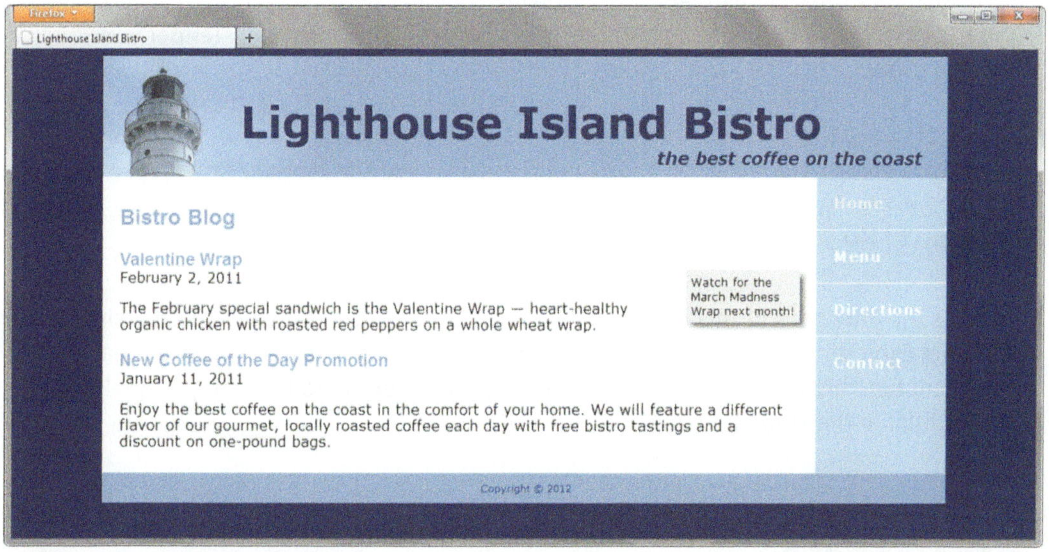

Figure 32 The HTML5 section, article, and aside elements were used on this page

HTML5 and Today's Browsers

Internet Explorer 9 and current versions of Safari, Chrome, Firefox, and Opera offer good support of HTML5 structural elements. The issue is that many people still use earlier versions of browsers. There are two different approaches that you can follow if you'd like to begin using HTML5 today: a conservative, straightforward approach and a progressive, enthusiastic approach that is more involved and requires JavaScript.

Conservative Approach to Using HTML5 Today

For the best chance at compatibility, code using either HTML5 or XHTML syntax and avoid using the new HTML5 elements. Instead, use the new element names as class names or id names. In this way, you'll become acquainted with the new element names and it will be easier to update the pages to all HTML5 later on. See chapter6/blog/all.html for an example of this technique. As time goes by and older browsers are used less and less, you'll be all set!

Progressive Approach to Using HTML5 Today

For starters, use Hands-On Practice 6 and 7 as an example: Code using the new HTML5 elements and include CSS that configures older non-supporting browsers to render the HTML5 header, figure, figcaption, footer, nav, section, article, and aside elements as block display (use `display: block;`). This will work well in all browsers except for Internet Explorer 8 and earlier versions.

So, what to do about Internet Explorer 8 and earlier versions? Remy Sharp offers a solution to enhance the support of Internet Explorer 8 and earlier versions (see http://remysharp.com/2009/01/07/html5-enabling-script). The technique uses conditional comments that are only supported by Internet Explorer and are ignored by other browsers. The conditional comments cause Internet Explorer to interpret JavaScript statements that configure it to recognize and process CSS for the new HTML5 element selectors. Sharp has uploaded the script to Google's code project and has made it available for anyone to use. Add the following code to the head section of a web page after CSS to cause Internet Explorer 8 and earlier versions to correctly render your HTML5 code:

```
<!--[if lt IE 9]>
<script src="http://html5shim.googlecode.com/svn/trunk/html5.js">
</script>
<![endif]-->
```

What's the drawback to this approach? Be aware that your web page visitors using Internet Explorer 8 and earlier versions may see a warning message and must have JavaScript enabled for this method to work. Try out an example (see chapter6/blog/today.html in the student files).

Checkpoint 3

1. Why should you use HTML5 structural elements instead of div elements for some page areas?
2. What is the purpose of the article element?
3. What is the purpose of the hgroup element?

Chapter Summary

This chapter introduced CSS page layout techniques and HTML5 structural elements. Techniques for positioning and floating elements and configuring two-column page layouts were demonstrated. This topic is very deep and you have much to explore. Visit the resources cited in the chapter to continue learning about this technology.

Visit the text website at http://www.webdevfoundations.net for examples, the links listed in this chapter, and updated information.

Key Terms

:active
:focus
:hover
:link
:visited
`<article>`
`<aside>`
`<footer>`
`<header>`
`<hgroup>`
`<nav>`
`<section>`
`<time>`
absolute positioning
border
box model
clear property
content
`display` property
`float` property
`left` property
list marker
`list-style-image` property
`list-style-type` property
margin
margin property
normal flow
`overflow` property
padding
`position` property
pseudo-class
relative positioning
`right` property
`top` property
visible width
`width` property

Review Questions

Multiple Choice

1. Which of the following is used to change the location of an element slightly in relation to where it would otherwise appear on the page?
   a. relative positioning
   b. the float property
   c. absolute positioning
   d. this cannot be done with CSS

2. Which of the following, from outermost to innermost, are components of the box model?
   a. margin, border, padding, content
   b. content, padding, border, margin
   c. content, margin, padding, border
   d. margin, padding, border, content

3. Which HTML5 element has the purpose of providing tangential content?
   a. article
   b. aside
   c. sidebar
   d. section

4. Which of the following configures a class called nav to float to the left?
   a. `.nav { left: float; }`
   b. `.nav { float: left; }`
   c. `.nav { float-left: 200px; }`
   d. `.nav { position: left; }`

5. Which of the following is the rendering flow used by a browser by default?
   a. XHTML flow
   b. normal display
   c. browser flow
   d. normal flow

6. Which of the following is an example of using a contextual selector to configure the anchor tags within the .nav class?
   a. `nav. a`
   b. `a nav.`
   c. `.nav a`
   d. `a#nav`

7. Which property and value are used to configure an unordered list item with a square list marker?
   a. `list-bullet: none;`
   b. `list-style-type: square;`
   c. `list-style-image: square;`
   d. `list-marker: square;`
8. Which of the following causes an element to display as a block of content with white space above and below?
   a. `display: none;`
   b. `block: display;`
   c. `display: block;`
   d. `display: inline;`
9. Which of the following pseudo-classes is the default state for a hyperlink that has been clicked?
   a. `:hover`
   b. `:link`
   c. `:onclick`
   d. `:visited`
10. Which of the following properties can be used to clear a float?
   a. float or clear
   b. clear or overflow
   c. position or clear
   d. overflow or float

Fill in the Blank

11. Configure a style with a(n) ____________ if the style will only apply to one element on a page.
12. If an element is configured with `float: right;`, the other content on the page will appear to its ____________.
13. The ______________ is always transparent.
14. The __________ pseudo-class can be used to modify the display of a hyperlink when a mouse pointer passes over it.
15. Use the HTML5 _______ element to configure a web page heading area.

Apply Your Knowledge

1. **Predict the Result.** Draw and write a brief description of the web page that will be created with the following HTML code:

```
<!DOCTYPE html>
<html lang="en">
<head>
<title>CircleSoft Web Design</title>
<meta charset="utf-8">
<style>
  h1 { border-bottom: 1px groove #333333;
       color: #006600;
       background-color: #cccccc }
  #content { position: absolute;
             left: 200px;
             top: 75px;
             font-family: Arial, sans-serif;
             width: 300px; }
  .nav a { font-weight: bold; }
</style>
</head>
<body>
<h1>CircleSoft Web Design</h1>
<div id="content">
<p>Our professional staff takes pride in its working relationship
with our clients by offering personalized services that listen to
```

```
their needs, develop their target areas, and incorporate these
items into a website that works.</p>
</div>
<ul class="nav">
  <li>Home</li>
  <li><a href="about.html">About</a></li>
  <li><a href="services.html">Services</a></li>
</ul>
</body>
</html>
```

2. **Fill in the Missing Code.** This web page should be configured as a two-column page layout with a right column that is 150 pixels wide. The right column should have a 1 pixel border. The margin in the left-column content area needs to allow for space that will be used by the right column. Some CSS selectors, properties, and values, indicated by "_", are missing. Fill in the missing code.

```
<!DOCTYPE html>
<html lang="en">
<head>
<title>Trillium Media Design</title>
<meta charset="utf-8">
<style>
#rightcolumn { "_": "_";
               width: "_";
               background-color: #cccccc;
               border: "_"; }
#logo { background-color: #cccccc;
        color: #663333;
        font-size: x-large;
        border-bottom: 1px solid #333333; }
.content { margin-right: "_"; }
.footer { font-size: x-small;
          text-align: center;
          clear: "_"; }
#"_" a { color: #000066;
         text-decoration: none; }
ul {list-style-type: "_"; }
</style>
</head>
<body>
<div id="rightcolumn">
<ul>
  <li><a href="index.html">Home</a></li>
  <li><a href="products.html">Products</a></li>
  <li><a href="services.html">Services</a></li>
  <li><a href="about.html">About</a></li>
</ul>
</div>
```

```
<div class="content">
<div id="logo">
<h1>Trillium Media Design</h1>
</div>
<p>Our professional staff takes pride in its working relationship
with our clients by offering personalized services that listen to
their needs, develop their target areas, and incorporate these
items into a website that works.</p>
</div>
<div class="footer">
Copyright &copy; 2012 Trillium Media Design<br>
Last Updated on 06/08/12
</div>
</body>
</html>
```

3. **Find the Error.** When this page is displayed in a browser, the heading information obscures the floating image and paragraph text. Correct the errors and describe the process that you followed.

```
<!DOCTYPE html>
<html lang="en">
<head>
<title>CSS Float</title>
<meta charset="utf-8">
<style>
body { width: 500px; }
h1 { background-color: #eeeeee;
     padding: 5px;
     color: #666633;
     position: absolute;
     left: 200px;
     top: 20px; }
p { font-family: Arial, sans-serif;
    position; absolute;
    left: 100px;
    top: 100px; }
#yls { float: right;
       margin: 0 0 5px 5px;
       border: solid; }
</style>
</head>
<body>
<h1>Floating an Image</h1>
<img id="yls" src="yls.jpg" alt="Yellow Lady Slipper" height="100"
width="100">
<p>The Yellow Lady Slipper pictured on the right is a wildflower.
It grows in wooded areas and blooms in June each year. The Yellow
Lady Slipper is a member of the orchid family.</p>
</body>
</html>
```

Hands-On Exercises

1. Write the CSS for an id with the following attributes: float to the left of the page, light-beige background, Verdana or sans-serif large font, and 20 pixels of padding.
2. Write the CSS to configure a class that will produce a headline with a dotted line underneath it. Choose a color that you like for the text and dotted line.
3. Write the CSS for an id that will be absolutely positioned on a page 20 pixels from the top and 40 pixels from the right. This area should have a light-gray background and a solid border.
4. Write the CSS for a class that is relatively positioned. This class should appear 15 pixels in from the left. Configure the class to have a light-green background.
5. Write the CSS to configure an image file named myimage.gif as the list marker in an unordered list.
6. Write the CSS to configure an unordered list to display a square list marker.
7. Write the HTML to configure a header element that contains an hgroup element with an h1 element, h2 element, and h3 element. Configure your school name as the h1 element. Configure your major as the h2 element. Configure the name of your current web development course as the h3 element.
8. Configure a web page with a list of hyperlinks to your favorite sites. Use an unordered list without any list markers to organize the hyperlinks. Choose a background color for the web page and a background color for the following states: unvisited hyperlink, hyperlink with a mouse pointer passing over it, and visited hyperlink. Use embedded CSS to configure the background and text colors. Also use CSS to configure the hyperlink's underline to not display when the mouse pointer is passing over it. Save the file as mylinks.html.
9. Use the mylinks.html file you created in 8 as a starting point. Modify the web page to use external rather than embedded CSS. Save the CSS file as links.css.
10. Create an HTML5 web page about one of your favorite hobbies. Choose a hobby and either take a relevant photo or select a relevant royalty-free photo from the Web. Decide on a heading for your page. Write one or two brief paragraphs about the hobby. The page must use valid HTML5 syntax and include the following HTML5 elements: header, article, and footer. Include a hyperlink to a website that is relevant to the hobby. Include your name in an e-mail address in the page footer area. Configure the text, color, and layout with embedded CSS. Refer to the section "HTML5 and Today's Browser" and review the techniques for configuring HTML5 pages to display in both modern and older versions of browsers. Modify the CSS and HTML of your page for cross-browser display. Save the file as myhobby.html.
11. Use the myhobby.html file you created in 10 as a starting point. Modify the web page to use external rather than embedded CSS. Save the file as hobby.css.

Web Research

This chapter introduced using CSS to configure web page layout. Use the resources listed in the text as a starting point. You can also use a search engine to search for CSS resources. Create a web page that provides a list of at least five CSS resources on the Web. For each CSS resource, provide the URL (configured as a hyperlink), the name of the website, a brief description, and a rating that indicates how helpful it is to beginning web developers.

Focus on Web Design

There is still much for you to learn about CSS. A great place to learn about web technology is on the Web itself. Use a search engine to search for CSS page layout tutorials. Choose a tutorial that is easy to read. Select a section that discusses a CSS technique that was not covered in this chapter. Create a web page that uses this new technique. Consider how the suggested page layout follows (or does not follow) principles of design such as contrast, repetition, alignment, and proximity. The web page should provide the URL of your tutorial (configured as a hyperlink), the name of the website, a description of the new technique you discovered, and a discussion of how the technique follows (or does not follow) principles of design.

WWW WEBSITE CASE STUDY

Implementing a CSS Two-Column Page Layout

Each of the following case studies implements a CSS two-column page layout in the websites.

JavaJam Coffee House

Figure 25 in the chapter "HTML Basics" shows a site map for the JavaJam. In this case study, you will implement a new two-column CSS page layout for JavaJam. Figure 33 shows a wireframe for a two-column page layout with wrapper, header, left column, right column, floating, and footer areas.

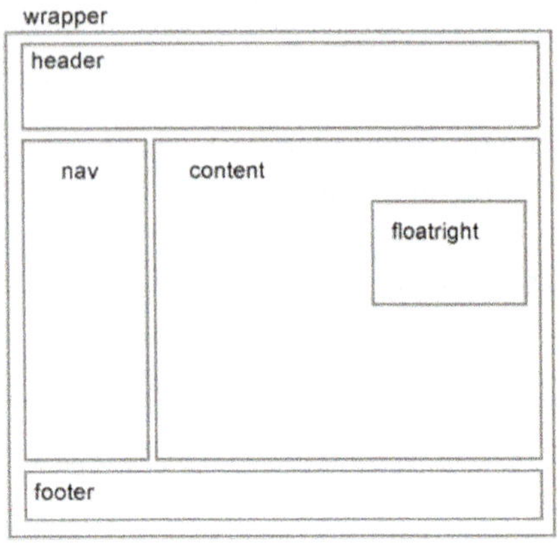

Figure 33 Wireframe for a two-column page layout for the JavaJam website

You will modify the external style sheet and the Home, Menu, and Music pages. You have five tasks in this case study:

1. Create a new folder for this JavaJam case study.
2. Modify the style rules in the javajam.css file to configure a two-column page layout, as shown in Figure 33.

Figure 34 The new JavaJam two-column layout (index.html)

3. Modify the Home page to implement the two-column page layout, as shown in Figure 34.
4. Modify the Menu page to be consistent with the Home page.
5. Modify the Music page (Figure 35) to be consistent with the Home page.

Hands-On Practice Case

Task 1: Create a Folder. Create a folder called javajam6. Copy all of the files from the Chapter 4 javajam4 folder into the javajam6 folder. You will modify the javajam.css file and each web page file (index.html, menu.html, and music.html) to implement the two-column page layout shown in Figure 33. See the new JavaJam Home page, as shown in Figure 34.

Task 2: Configure the CSS. Open javajam.css in a text editor. Edit the style rules as follows:

1. Configure the header area. Create a new id named `header` with a background (#ccaa66) and text (`#000000`) color, center alignment (`text-align: center;`), and no margin (`margin: 0;`). Remove the h1 element selector and style rules.
2. Configure the left-column navigation area. Add style rules to the `nav` id to configure an area that floats to the left, is `100` pixels wide, displays centered text, and has `10` pixels of padding on the top.
3. Configure the navigation hyperlinks. Use a contextual selector to add a new style rule for the anchor tags within the `nav` id. Configure this selector with 15 pixels of bottom padding and no underline on hyperlinks.

```
#nav a { text-decoration: none;
         padding-bottom: 15px; }
```

4. Configure the `:link`, `:visted`, and `:hover` pseudo-classes for the navigation hyperlinks. Use the following text colors: #996633 (unvisited hyperlinks), #ccaa66 (visited hyperlinks), and #330000 (hyperlinks with `:hover`). For example,

```
#nav a:link { color: #996633; }
```

5. You will organize the navigation hyperlinks within an unordered list in later tasks. The navigation area in Figure 33 does not show list markers. Use a contextual selector to configure unordered lists in the navigation area to display without list markers.

```
#nav ul { list-style-type: none; }
```

6. Modify the `content` id style rules for the right column. Change the padding to 10 pixels top, 30 pixels bottom, 20 pixels left, and 20 pixels right. Configure a 150 pixel left margin, background (#f2eab7) color, and text (#000000) color.

7. Configure an area that floats to the right. Notice how the winding road graphic shown in Figure 33 floats on the right side—this is configured with the `floatright` class. Images are more compelling when they are separated from other elements (such as text) by empty space. Add 20 pixels of padding to the left side of this area.

8. Modify the `footer` id style rules. Change the padding to 20 pixels top and bottom. Configure the footer to clear all floats.

9. Configure the `:link`, `:visited`, and `:hover` pseudo-classes for the footer hyperlink. Use the following text colors: #ffffcc (unvisited hyperlink), #f2eab7 (visited hyperlink), and #330000 (hyperlink with `:hover`).

10. Modify the h2 element selector style rules. View the Music page shown in Figure 35 and notice that the `<h2>` tags are styled differently, with all uppercase text (using a new property, `text-transform`) and different background and text colors, font size, bottom border, padding, and margin. Also configure styles to clear floats on the left. Replace the h2 element selector style rules with the following:

```
h2 { text-transform: uppercase;
     background-color: #ffffcc;
     color: #663300;
     font-size: 1.2em;
     border-bottom: 1px solid #000000;
     padding: 5px 0 0 5px;
     margin-right: 20px;
     clear: left; }
```

11. Refer to the Music page shown in Figure 35 and notice how the images float on the left side of the paragraph description. Configure a new class named `floatleft` that floats to the left with 20 pixels of right and bottom padding.

12. Configure a new class named `clear` that clears the left float.

Save the javajam.css file.

Task 3: The Home Page. Open index.html in a text editor. Edit the code as follows:

1. Configure the header area. Assign the `<h1>` element to the `header` id.

2. Configure the left-column navigation area, which is the div assigned to the `nav` id. Remove any ` ` characters that may be present. Code an unordered

list to organize the navigation hyperlinks. Each hyperlink should be contained within `<li>` tags.

3. Configure the image that floats to the right. Modify the winding road image element. Remove the `align="right"` attribute and add `class="floatright"` to the winding road image element.

Save the index.html file. It should look similar to the web page shown in Figure 34. Remember that validating your HTML and CSS can help you find syntax errors. Test and correct this page before you continue.

Task 4: The Menu Page. Open menu.html in a text editor. Configure the header area, left-column navigation area, and navigation hyperlinks in the same manner as the home page. Save your new menu.html page and test it in a browser. Use the CSS and HTML validators to help you find syntax errors.

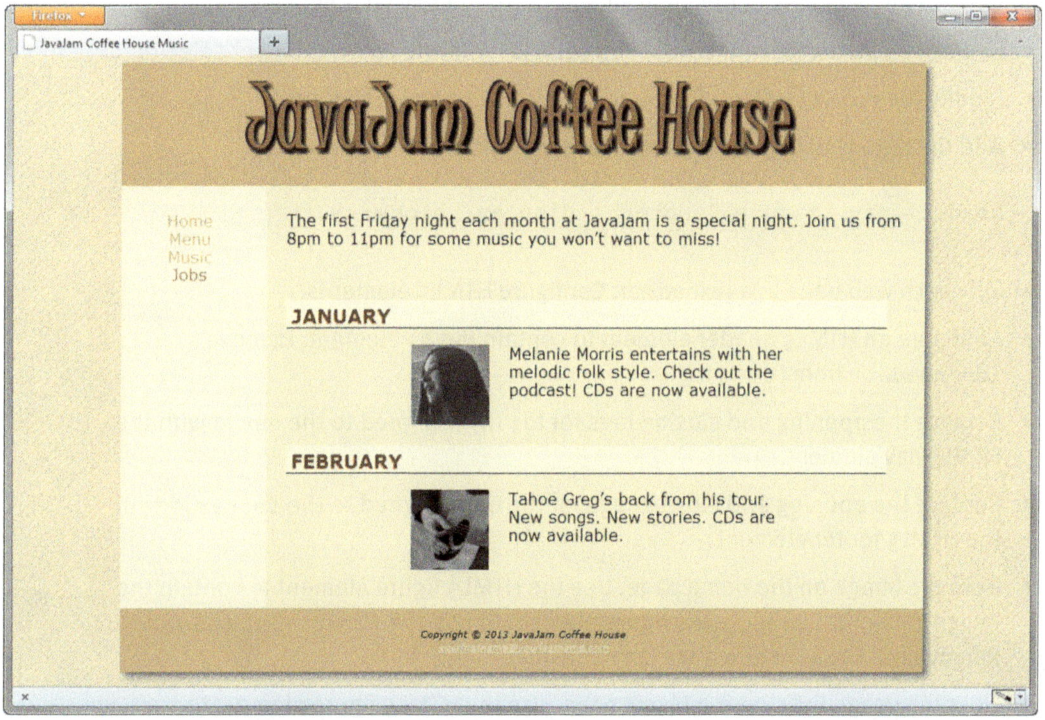

Figure 35 The new JavaJam Music page

Task 5: The Music Page. Open music.html in a text editor. Configure the header area, left-column navigation area, and navigation hyperlinks in the same manner as the home page.

1. Configure the thumbnail images to float to the left. Add `class="floatleft"` to the image tag for each thumbnail image.
2. Add a blank line above the closing div tag for the `content` id. Clear the last floated thumbnail image by coding a line break tag that is assigned to the `clearleft` class.

Save your new menu.html page and test it in a browser. Use the CSS and XHTML validators to help you find syntax errors.

In this case study, you changed the page layout of the JavaJam website. Notice that with just a few changes in the CSS and HTML code, you configured a two-column page layout.

OPTIONAL: JavaJam Case Study: HTML5 Extension

Get more practice with the new HTML5 structural elements by creating a new version of the JavaJam website. Create a folder called javajam6HTML5 to contain your JavaJam website files. Copy the files from the javajam6 folder.

1. Modify the javajam.css file in a text editor. Configure new styles and use HTML element selectors for the header, nav, and footer elements.
   - All style declarations previously associated with the `header` id will apply to the header element selector. Replace the `header` id with the header element selector.
   - Configure an h1 element selector with a zero margin.
   - Replace all instances of the `#nav` selector with the nav element selector.
   - Replace all instances of the `#footer` selector with the footer element selector.
   - Modify the `details` class. Configure 35 pixels of bottom padding.
   - Add the following CSS to be compatible with most older browsers:

     ```
     header, nav, figure, footer { display: block; }
     ```

2. Modify each web page in a text editor. Configure HTML5 elements.
   - Configure an HTML5 header element to contain the h1 element. Remove `id="header"` from the h1 tag.
   - Replace the opening and closing tags for the div assigned to the `nav` id with the HTML5 nav element.
   - Replace the opening and closing tags for the div assigned to the `footer` id with the HTML5 footer element.
   - Note the image on the home page. Use the HTML5 figure element to contain the image element. Configure the figure element to use the `floatright` class. Remove the `floatright` class from the image tag.
   - Note the image links on the Music page. Use the HTML5 figure element to contain each image link. Configure the figure element to use the `floatleft` class. Remove the `floatleft` class from the image tags. Also replace the paragraph tags assigned to the `details` class with div tags assigned to the `details` class.
   - Add the following code in the head section of the web page after the link element to assist Internet Explorer 8 and earlier versions):

     ```
     <!--[if lt IE 9]>
     <script src="http://html5shim.googlecode.com/svn/trunk/html5.js">
     </script>
     <![endif]-->
     ```

Save your files. Display your pages in a modern browser. Your new case study web pages should look similar to the previous version. This optional exercise provided you with additional practice using new HTML5 elements.

Fish Creek Animal Hospital

Figure 29 in the chapter "HTML Basics" shows a site map for Fish Creek Animal Hospital. In this case study, you will implement a redesign with a new two-column CSS page layout. Figure 36 displays a wireframe for a two-column page layout with wrapper, logo header, left column, right column, and footer areas.

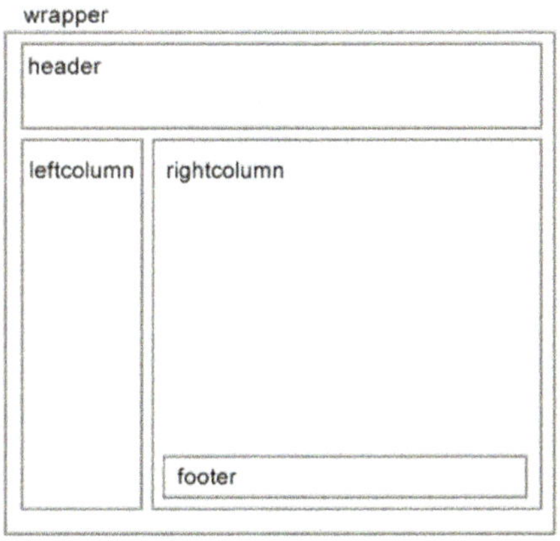

Figure 36 Wireframe for a two-column page layout for the Fish Creek website

You will modify the external style sheet and the Home, Services, and Ask the Vet pages. You have five tasks in this case study:

1. Create a new folder for this Fish Creek case study.
2. Modify the style rules in the fishcreek.css file to configure a two-column page layout, as shown in Figure 36.
3. Modify the Home page to implement the two-column page layout, as shown in Figure 37.
4. Modify the Services page to be consistent with the Home page.
5. Modify the Ask the Vet page to be consistent with the Home page.

Hands-On Practice Case

Task 1: Create a Folder. Create a folder called fishcreek6. Copy all of the files from the Chapter 4 fishcreek4 folder (except the fish navigation images home.gif, services.gif, askvet.gif, and contact.gif) into the fishcreek6 folder. You will modify the fishcreek.css file and each web page file (index.html, services.html, and askvet.html) to implement the two-column page layout, as shown in Figure 36. See the new Fish Creek home page, as shown in Figure 37.

Task 2: Configure the CSS. Open fishcreek.css in a text editor. Edit the style rules as follows:

1. Configure a background image for the body element selector. Use the chapter6/gradientblue.jpg file found in the student files.
2. Modify the `wrapper` id. Configure a white background color (#FFFFFF) and dark-blue text color (#000066) for this area. Change the width to 80%. Set the minimum width to 700 pixels.

Figure 37 The new Fish Creek two-column home page (index.html)

3. Configure the header area. Remove the h1 element selector and style rules. Create a new id named `header` with centered text, a dark-blue background color (#000066), and 10 pixels of padding.
4. Configure the left column area. Add a new style rule for the `leftcolumn` id to configure an area that floats to the left and is 150 pixels wide.
5. You will organize the navigation hyperlinks within an unordered list in later tasks. The navigation area in Figure 37 does not show list markers. Use a contextual selector to configure unordered lists in the left column area to display without list markers and no padding.

```
#leftcolumn ul { list-style-type: none;
                 padding-left: 0;}
```

6. Configure the anchor tags in the `leftcolumn` id to display no underline.

```
#leftcolumn a { text-decoration: none; }
```

7. Configure the `:link`, `:visited`, and `:hover` pseudo-classes for the `leftcolumn` hyperlinks. Use the following text colors: #3262A3 (unvisited hyperlinks), #6699FF (visited hyperlinks), and #CCCCCC (hyperlinks with `:hover`). For example,

```
#leftcolumn a:link { color: #3262A3; }
```

8. Configure the right column area. Add a new style rule for the `rightcolumn` id to configure an area with a 180 pixel left margin, 10 pixels of right padding, and 20 pixels of bottom padding.
9. Remove the `main` id. It is no longer used.
10. Modify the `category` class. Remove the background color style rule.

Save the fishcreek.css file.

Task 3: Modify the Home Page. Open index.html in a text editor and modify the code as follows:

1. Configure the header area. Assign the `<h1>` to the id `header`.
2. Configure the left column. Modify the div tag that contains this area. Change `id="main"` to `id="leftcolumn"`.
3. Rework the navigation area. Remove any ` ` characters that may be present. Replace the fish image links with text image links. Then, code an unordered list to organize the navigation hyperlinks. Each hyperlink should be contained within `<li>` tags.
4. Configure the right column. This area contains the description list, the div with the contact information, and the footer div. Code a div element to contain this area. Assign the div to the id `rightcolumn`.

Save the index.html file. It should look similar to the web page shown in Figure 37. Remember that validating your HTML and CSS can help you find syntax errors. Test and correct this page before you continue.

Task 4: Modify the Services Page. Open services.html in a text editor. Configure the header area, left-column navigation area, navigation hyperlinks, and right-column content area in the same manner as the home page. Save your new services.html page and test it in a browser. Use the CSS and HTML validators to help you find syntax errors.

Task 5: Modify the Ask the Vet Page. Open askvet.html in a text editor. Configure the header area, left-column navigation area, and navigation hyperlinks in the same manner as the home page. Save your new askvet.html page and test it in a browser. Use the CSS and HTML validators to help you find syntax errors.

In this case study, you changed the page layout of the Fish Creek website. Notice that with just a few changes in the CSS and HTML code, you configured a two-column page layout with a completely new visual aesthetic.

OPTIONAL: Fish Creek Case Study: HTML5 Extension

Get more practice with the new HTML5 structural elements by creating a new version of the Fish Creek website. Create a folder called fishcreek6HTML5 to contain your Fish Creek website files. Copy the files from the fishcreek6 folder.

1. Modify the fishcreek.css file in a text editor. Configure new styles and use HTML element selectors for the header, nav, and footer elements.
    - All style declarations previously associated with the `header` id will apply to the header element selector. Replace the `header` id with the header element selector.
    - Replace all instances of the `#leftcolumn` selector with the nav element selector.
    - Replace all instances of the `#footer` selector with the footer element selector.
    - Add the following CSS to be compatible with most older browsers:

```
header, nav, footer { display: block; }
```

2. Modify each web page in a text editor. Configure HTML5 elements.
   - Configure an HTML5 header element to contain the h1 element. Remove `id="header"` from the h1 tag.
   - Replace the opening and closing tags for the first div assigned to the `nav` class with the HTML5 nav element.
   - Replace the opening and closing tags for the div assigned to the `footer` id with the HTML5 footer element.
   - Add the following code in the head section of the web page after the link element to assist Internet Explorer 8 and earlier versions:

```
<!--[if lt IE 9]>
<script src="http://html5shim.googlecode.com/svn/trunk/html5.js">
</script>
<![endif]-->
```

Save your files. Display your pages in a modern browser. Your new case study web pages should look similar to the previous version. This optional exercise provided you with additional practice using new HTML5 elements.

Pacific Trails Resort

Figure 33 in the chapter "HTML Basics" shows a site map for Pacific Trails. The pages were created in other chapters. In this case study, you will implement a new two-column CSS page layout. Figure 38 displays a wireframe for a two-column page layout with wrapper, header, nav, content, and footer areas.

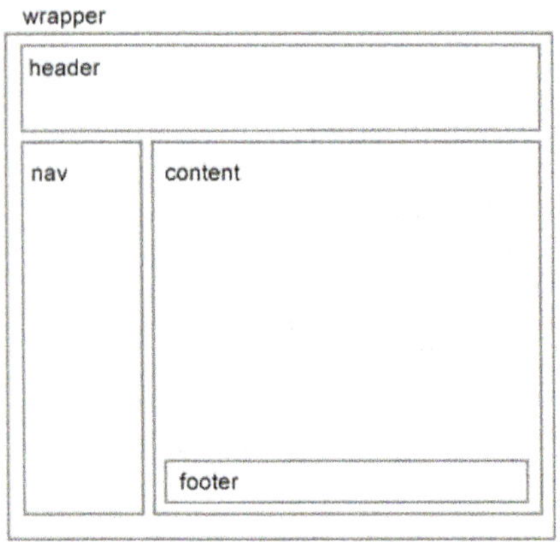

Figure 38 Wireframe for a two-column page layout for the Pacific Trails website

You will modify the external style sheet and the Home, Yurts, and Activities pages. You have five tasks in this case study:

1. Create a new folder for the Pacific Trails case study.
2. Modify the style rules in the pacific.css file to configure a two-column page layout, as shown in Figure 38.

3. Modify the Home page to implement the two-column page layout, as shown in Figure 39.
4. Modify the Yurts page to be consistent with the Home page.
5. Modify the Activities page to be consistent with the Home page.

Hands-On Practice Case

Task 1: Create a Folder. Create a folder called pacific6. Copy all of the files from the Chapter 4 pacific4 folder (except the navigation button images) into the pacific6 folder. You will modify the pacific.css file and each web page file (index.html, yurts.html, and activities.html) to implement the two-column page layout, as shown in Figure 38. See the new Pacific Trails home page, as shown in Figure 39.

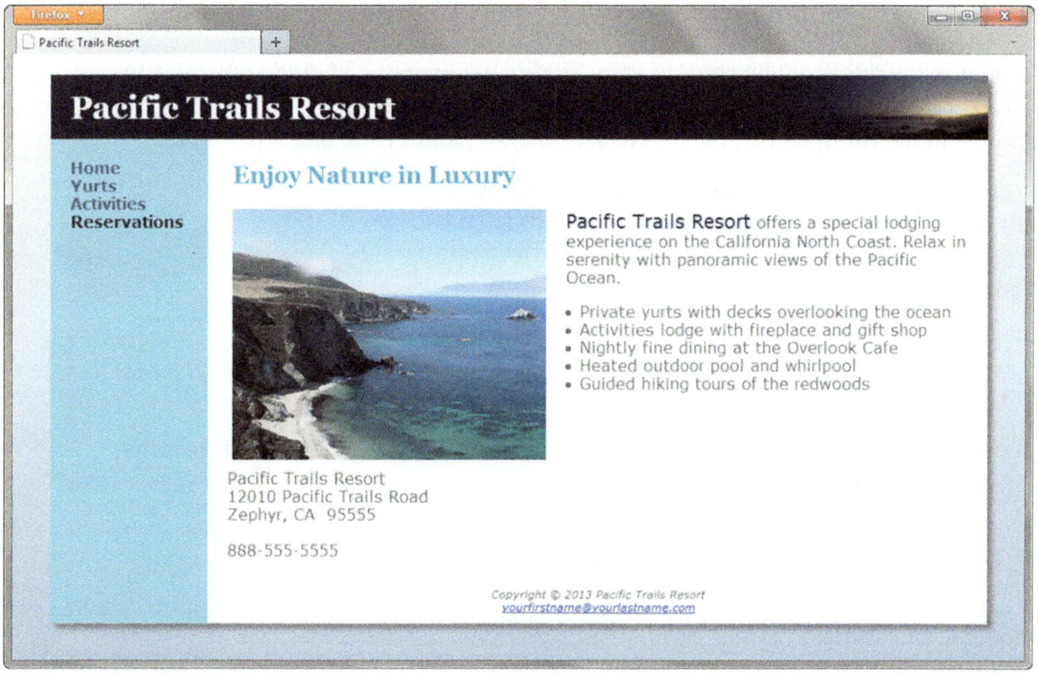

Figure 39 The new Pacific Trails two-column home page (index.html)

Task 2: Configure the CSS. Open pacific.css in a text editor. Edit the style rules as follows:

1. Modify the `wrapper` id. Change the background color to blue (#90C7E3), which will be the background behind the navigation area. Configure a minimum width of 960 pixels.
2. Configure the left-column navigation area. Modify the `nav` id. Keep the style rule that configures bold text. Remove the background color property. The nav area will inherit the background color of the `wrapper` id. Add style rules to configure this area to float to the left with a width of 160 pixels. Also configure 20 pixels top padding, 5 pixels right padding, 5 pixels bottom padding, and 20 pixels left padding.
3. Configure the navigation hyperlinks. Use a contextual selector to add a new style rule for the anchor tags within the `nav` id that removes the underline from hyperlinks.

```
#nav a { text-decoration: none; }
```

4. Configure the `:link`, `:visited`, and `:hover` pseudo-classes for the navigation hyperlinks. Use the following text colors: #000033 (unvisited hyperlinks), #344873 (visited hyperlinks), and #FFFFFF (hyperlinks with `:hover`). For example,

```
#nav a:link { color: #000033; }
```

5. You will organize the navigation hyperlinks within an unordered list in later tasks. The navigation area in Figure 39 does not show list markers. Use a contextual selector to configure unordered lists in the navigation area to display without list markers. Also configure the unordered list to have no margin and no left padding.

```
#nav ul { list-style-type: none;
          margin: 0;
          padding-left: 0; }
```

6. Configure the right-column content area. Modify the `content` id. Add style rules to configure a white (#FFFFFF) background, 160 pixels of left margin (this value corresponds to the width of the floated navigation area), and 1 pixel of top padding.
7. Create a new style rule to configure images displayed in the `content` id to float to the left with 20 pixels of right padding. Use a contextual selector.

```
#content img { float: left;
               padding-right: 20px }
```

8. Create a new class named `clear` that clears a float.
9. Configure the unordered lists in the `content` id to display list markers inside rather than outside of the list.

```
#content ul {list-style-position: inside; }
```

Save the pacific.css file.

Task 3: Modify the Home Page. Open index.html in a text editor and modify the code as follows:

1. Configure the left-column navigation area, which is the div assigned to the `nav` id. Remove any ` ` characters that may be present. Code an unordered list to organize the navigation hyperlinks. Each hyperlink should be contained within `<li>` tags.
2. Locate the div that contains the address information. Assign this div to the class named `clear`.
3. The page layout in Figure 38 shows the `footer` id contained within the `content` id. Move the closing div tag for the `content` id and place it on a new line after the closing div tag for the `footer` id.

Save the index.html file. It should look similar to the web page shown in Figure 39. Remember that validating your HTML and CSS can help you find syntax errors. Test and correct this page before you continue.

Task 4: Modify the Yurts Page. Open yurts.html in a text editor. Configure the left-column navigation area, navigation hyperlinks, and footer location in the same manner as the home page. Save your new yurts.html page and test it in a browser. Use the CSS and HTML validators to help you find syntax errors.

Task 5: Modify the Activities Page. Open yurts.html in a text editor. Configure the left-column navigation area, navigation hyperlinks, and footer location in the same manner as the home page. Save your new activities.html page and test it in a browser. Use the CSS and HTML validators to help you find syntax errors.

In this case study, you changed the page layout of the Pacific Trails Resort website. Notice that with just a few changes in the CSS and HTML code, you configured a two-column page layout.

OPTIONAL: Pacific Trails Case Study: HTML5 Extension

Get more practice with the new HTML5 structural elements by creating a new version of the Pacific Trails website. Create a folder called pacific6HTML5 to contain your Pacific Trails website files. Copy the files from the pacific6 folder.

1. Modify the pacific.css file in a text editor. Configure new styles and use HTML element selectors for the header, nav, and footer elements.
   - Replace all instances of the `#nav` selector with the nav element selector.
   - Replace all instances of the `#footer` selector with the footer element selector.
   - Replace the `#content img` selector with a `#content figure` selector. Add a style rule to configure a zero margin.
   - Add the following CSS to be compatible with most older browsers:

   ```
   header, nav, figure, footer { display: block; }
   ```

2. Modify each web page in a text editor. Configure HTML5 elements.
   - Configure an HTML5 header element to contain the h1 element.
   - Replace the opening and closing tags for the div assigned to the `nav` id with the HTML5 nav element.
   - Replace the opening and closing tags for the div assigned to the `footer` id with the HTML5 footer element.
   - Note the image on each page in the content area. Use the HTML5 figure element to contain the image element. Configure the figure element to use the `floatleft` class. Remove the `floatleft` class from the image tag.
   - Add the following code in the head section of the web page after the link element to assist Internet Explorer 8 and earlier versions):

   ```
   <!--[if lt IE 9]>
   <script src="http://html5shim.googlecode.com/svn/trunk/html5.js">
   </script>
   <![endif]-->
   ```

Save your files. Display your pages in a modern browser. Your new case study web pages should look similar to the previous version. This optional exercise provided you with additional practice using new HTML5 elements.

Prime Properties

Figure 37 in the chapter "HTML Basics" shows a site map for Prime Properties. In this case study, you will implement a new two-column CSS page layout for Prime Properties. Figure 40 displays a wireframe for a two-column page layout with a wrapper, header, left column, right column, and footer area.

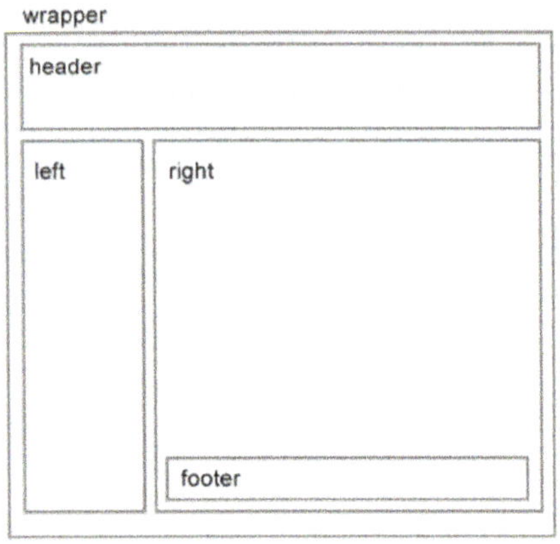

Figure 40 Wireframe for a two-column page layout for the Prime Properties website

You will modify the external style sheet and the Home, Listings, and Financing pages. You have five tasks in this case study:

1. Create a new folder for the Prime Properties case study.
2. Modify the style rules in the prime.css file to configure a two-column page layout, as shown in Figure 40.
3. Modify the Home page to implement the two-column page layout, as shown in Figure 41.
4. Modify the Listings page to be consistent with the Home page.
5. Modify the Financing page to be consistent with the Home page.

Hands-On Practice Case

Task 1: Create a Folder. Create a folder called prime6. Copy all of the files from the Chapter 4 prime4 folder into the prime6 folder. You will modify the prime.css file and each web page file (index.html, listings.html, and financing.html) to implement the two-column page layout shown in Figure 40. See the new Prime Properties home page in Figure 41.

Task 2: Configure the CSS. Open prime.css in a text editor. Edit the style rules as follows:

1. Configure the left column area. Add a new style rule for the `left` id to configure an area that floats to the left and is 150 pixels wide.
2. Configure the navigation hyperlinks to use CSS for the background color and border instead of using image links. We'll set up the CSS in this step.
   a. Use a contextual selector to add a new style rule for the anchor tags within the `nav` id that removes the underline from hyperlinks. Also configure the anchor tags to

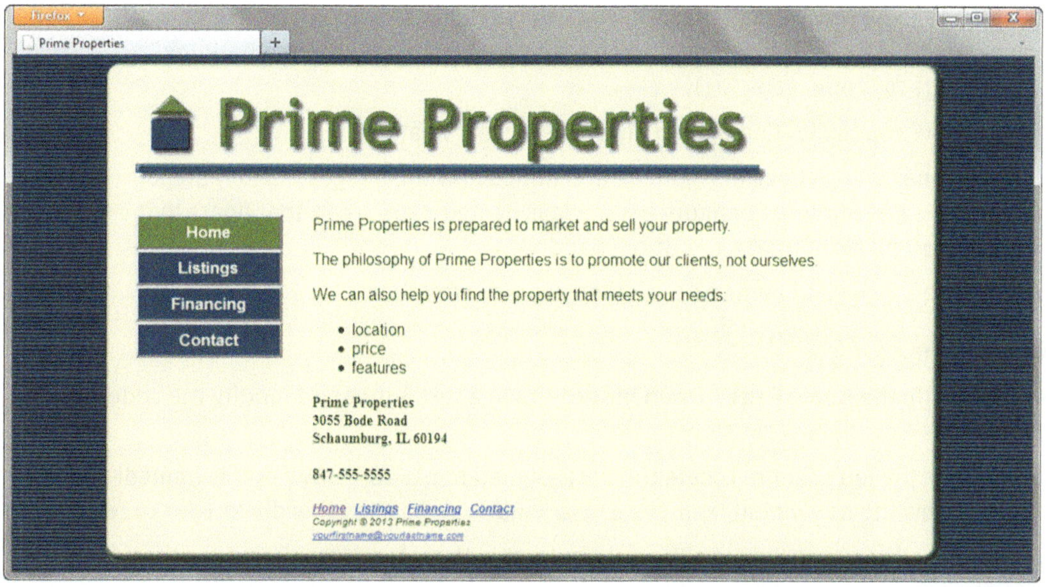

Figure 41 The new Prime Properties two-column home page (index.html)

use block display, centered text, bold font, text color #FFFFCC, a 3 pixel gray (#CCCCCC) outset border, and 5 pixels of padding.

```
#left a { text-decoration: none;
          display: block:
          text-align: center;
          color: #FFFFCC;
          font-weight: bold;
          border: 3px outset #CCCCCC;
          padding: 5px;}
```

b. Configure the `:link`, `:visited`, and `:hover` pseudo-classes for the navigation hyperlinks. Use the following background colors: #003366 (unvisited hyperlinks) and #48751A (visited hyperlinks). Configure a 3 pixel inset #333333 border for hyperlinks in the hover state.

```
#left a:link { background-color: #003366; }
#left a:visited { background-color: #48751A; }
#left a:hover { border: 3px inset #333333; }
```

3. You will organize the navigation hyperlinks within an unordered list in later tasks. The navigation area in Figure 41 does not show list markers. Use a contextual selector to configure unordered lists in the navigation area to display without list markers. Also configure the unordered list to have no margin and no left padding.

```
#left ul { list-style-type: none;
           margin: 0;
           padding-left: 0; }
```

4. Configure the right column area. Add a new style rule for the `right` id to configure an area with a 180 pixel left margin and 20 pixels of right and bottom padding (`padding: 0 20px 20px 0;`).
5. Modify the `footer` id. Configure a style rule to clear floats.
6. Refer to the Listings page in Figure 42 and notice how the images float on the left side of the description. Configure a new class named `floatleft` that floats to the left with 20 pixels of right and bottom padding.
7. Configure a new class named `clear` that clears the left float.

Save the prime.css file.

Task 3: Modify the Home Page. Open index.html in a text editor and modify the code as follows:

1. Configure the left column. Locate the div assigned to `class="nav"` that is immediately below the h1 element. Remove `class="nav"` and assign this div to `id="left"`.
2. The navigation image links are the only content in the left column. Remove other code, including any ` ` characters that may be present. Replace the image links with text image links. Then, code an unordered list to organize the navigation hyperlinks. Each hyperlink should be contained within `<li>` tags.
3. Configure the right column. This area contains the content (paragraphs, unordered list, and contact information) and the footer section. Code a `<div>` that surrounds this area. Assign the <div> to `id="right"`.

Save the index.html file. It should look similar to the web page shown in Figure 41. Remember that validating your HTML and CSS can help you find syntax errors. Test and correct this page before you continue.

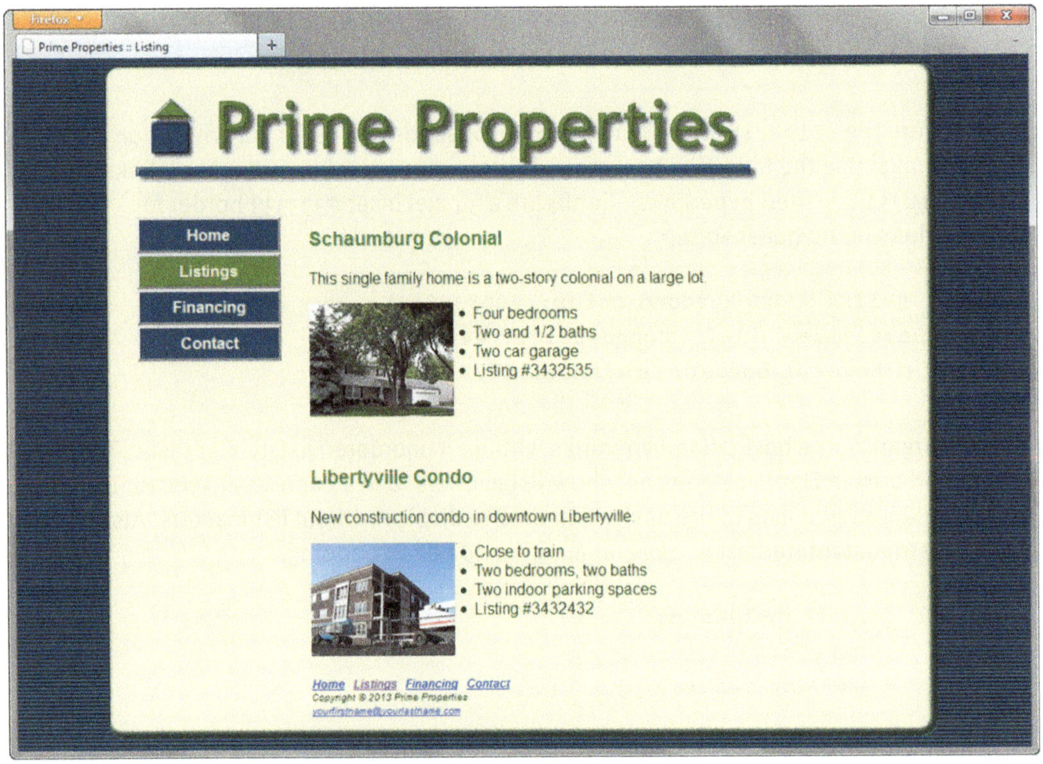

Figure 42 The new Prime Properties two-column Listings page

Task 4: Modify the Listings Page. Open listings.html in a text editor.

1. Configure the left-column navigation area, navigation hyperlinks, and right column in the same manner as the home page.
2. Configure the house and condo images to float to the left. Add `class="floatleft"` to these image elements.
3. Add a blank line above the second h3 element on the page. Clear the first floated thumbnail image by coding a line break tag that is assigned to the `clear` class.

Save your new listings.html page and test it in a browser. Use the CSS and HTML validators to help you find syntax errors.

Task 5: Modify the Financing Page. Open financing.html in a text editor. Configure the left-column navigation area, navigation hyperlinks, and right column in the same manner as the home page. Save your new financing.html page and test it in a browser. Use the CSS and HTML validators to help you find syntax errors.

In this case study, you changed the page layout of the Prime Properties website. Notice that with just a few changes in the CSS and HTML code, you configured a two-column page layout.

OPTIONAL: Prime Properties Case Study: HTML5 Extension

Get more practice with the new HTML5 structural elements by creating a new version of the Prime Properties website. Create a folder called prime6HTML5 to contain your Prime Properties website files. Copy the files from the prime6 folder.

1. Modify the prime.css file in a text editor. Configure new styles and use HTML element selectors for the header, nav, and footer elements.
   - All style declarations previously associated with the `header` id will apply to the header element selector. Replace the `header` id with the header element selector.
   - Replace all instances of the `#left` selector with the nav element selector.
   - Replace all instances of the `#footer` selector with the footer element selector.
   - Add the following CSS to be compatible with most older browsers:

     ```
     header, nav, figure, footer { display: block; }
     ```

2. Modify each web page in a text editor. Configure the HTML5 elements.
   - Configure an HTML5 header element to contain the h1 element. Remove `id="header"` from the h1 tag.
   - Replace the opening and closing tags for the div assigned to the `left` id with the HTML5 nav element.
   - Replace the opening and closing tags for the div assigned to the `footer` id with the HTML5 footer element.
   - Note the image links on the Listings page. Use the HTML5 figure element to contain each image link. Configure the figure element to use the `floatleft` class. Remove the `floatleft` class from the image tags. Code a line break above the footer element that is assigned to the `clear` class.

- Add the following code in the head section of the web page after the link element to assist Internet Explorer 8 and earlier versions:

```
<!--[if lt IE 9]>
<script src="http://html5shim.googlecode.com/svn/trunk/html5.js">
</script>
<![endif]-->
```

Save your files. Display your pages in a modern browser. Your new case study web pages should look similar to the previous version. This optional exercise provided you with additional practice using the new HTML5 elements.

Web Project

In this case study, you will use your design documents as a guide as you develop the pages for your Web Project using CSS in an external style sheet for both formatting and page layout.

Hands-On Practice Case

1. Create a folder called project. All of your project files and graphics will be organized in this folder and in subfolders as needed.
2. Refer to your Site Map to view the pages that you need to create. Jot down a list of the file names. Add these to the Site Map.
3. Refer to the Page Layout Design. Make a list of the common fonts and colors used on the pages. These may become the CSS you configure for the body element. Note where typical elements used for organization (such as headings, lists, paragraphs, and so on) may be used. You may want to configure CSS for these elements. Identify various page areas such as header, navigation, footer, and so on, and list any special configurations needed for these areas. These will be configured as classes in your CSS. Create an external style sheet, called project.css, which contains these configurations.
4. Using your design documents as a guide, code a representative page for your site. Use CSS to format text, color, and layout. Apply classes and ids where appropriate. Associate the web page to the external style sheet.

   Save and test the page. Modify both the web page and the project.css file as needed. Test and modify them until you have achieved the look you want.
5. Using the completed page as a template wherever possible, code the rest of the pages on your site. Test and modify them as needed.
6. Experiment with modifying the project.css file. Change the page background color, the font family, and so on. Test your pages in a browser. Notice how a change in a single file can affect multiple files when external style sheets are used.

Answers

Checkpoint 1

1. The components of the box model, from innermost to outermost, are the content, padding, border, and margin.
2. Relative positioning allows you to alter the position of an element in relation to where it would be displayed when normal flow is used. Absolute positioning allows you to specify by pixels the exact location of an element in a web page.
3. The purpose of the float property is to shift the display of an element to the right or left side of the container element.

Checkpoint 2

1. The page layout is jello. The content has a percentage width with a centered layout that takes up 80% of the browser viewport. A minimum width is configured to avoid awkward wrapping of text when the browser is resized.
2. Answers will vary. Some of the suggestions listed in the debugging section may be used.
3. Configure an HTML element selector if the style is expected to be applied every time that tag is used. Configure an id if the style is for a specific element that is expected to occur only once on a page. Configure a class if the style is expected to be applied to a variety of different HTML elements.

Checkpoint 3

1. The div element is a multipurpose generic element that configures a section or division of a web page. HTML5 introduces new elements for configuring web page areas intended to be more specific in their semantic purpose. Depending on the target audience for a website, it may be appropriate to use new HTML5 elements instead of div elements to configure page areas for navigation (the nav element), logo header (header and hgroup elements), footer (footer element), sidebar (aside element), articles (article element), images/charts (figure and figcaption elements), and page sections (section element). As time goes on and browser support increases, use of these new HTML5 elements is expected to be the norm.
2. The article element is intended to contain an independent entry, such as a blog posting, comment, or e-zine article that could stand on its own and be syndicated or distributed.
3. The hgroup element is intended to group multiple heading elements.

Review Questions

1. a
2. a
3. b
4. b
5. d
6. c
7. b
8. c
9. d
10. b
11. id
12. left
13. margin
14. :hover
15. header

Credits

All photographs except those noted below © Terry Ann Morris

"Checkpoint" icon (green check mark), "Web Site Case Study" icon (blue "WWW"), "FAQ" icon (orange caption bubble), "Focus on Accessibility" icon (orange key) © Fotolia LLC

"Hands-On Practice" icon (green hand); empty green, yellow, purple, red, and blue icons © Piotr M./Fotolia LLC

More on Links, Layout, and Mobile

Chapter Objectives

In this chapter, you will learn how to . . .

- Code relative hyperlinks to web pages in folders within a website
- Configure a hyperlink to a named fragment internal to a web page
- Configure images with CSS sprites
- Configure a three-column page layout using CSS
- Configure CSS for printing
- Configure CSS for mobile display
- Utilize CSS3 media queries to target mobile devices

Now that you've had some experience coding HTML and CSS, you're ready to explore a variety of techniques in this chapter, including relative hyperlinks and named fragment hyperlinks, CSS sprites, three-column page layout, styling for print, styling for mobile browsers, and configuring CSS3 media queries to target mobile devices.

1 Another Look at Hyperlinks

Hyperlinks make the Web a "web" of interconnected information. In this section, you'll revisit the topic of hyperlinks and explore coding relative links using the target attribute to open web pages in a new browser window, as well as coding hyperlinks that are internal to a web page.

Figure 1 The dog groomer site contains the images, products, and services folders

More on Relative Linking

A relative hyperlink is used to link to web pages within your site. You've been coding relative links to display web pages within the same folder. There are times when you need to link to files in other folders on your website. Let's consider the example of a website for a dog groomer that highlights services and products. The web developer for this site created separate folders called services and products in order to organize the site. See the folder and file listing shown in Figure 1.

Relative Link Examples

To review, when linking to a file in the same folder or directory, the value of the href is the name of the file. For example, to link to the contact.html page from the home page (index.html), code the anchor element as follows:

```
<a href="contact.html">Contact</a>
```

When linking to a folder located within the current directory, use both the folder name and the file name in the relative link. For example, to link to the collars.html page in the products folder from the home page (index.html), code the anchor element as follows:

```
<a href="products/collars.html">Collars</a>
```

In Figure 1, the collars.html page is located in a subfolder of the groomer folder. The home page for the site (index.html) is located in the groomer folder. When linking to a file that is up one directory level from the current page, use the "`../`" notation. To link to the home page for the site from the collars.html page, code the anchor element as follows:

```
<a href="../index.html">Home</a>
```

When linking to a file that is in a folder on the same level as the current folder, the href value will use the "`../`" notation to indicate moving up one level and then down to the chosen folder. For example, to link to the bathing.html page in the services folder from the collars.html page in the products folder, code the anchor element as follows:

```
<a href="../services/bathing.html">Dog Bathing</a>
```

Don't worry if the use of "`../`" notation and linking to files in different folders seems new and different. In most of the exercises in this text, you will code either absolute links to other websites or relative links to files in the same folder.

Fragment Identifiers

Browsers begin the display of a web page at the top of the document. However, there are times when you need to provide the capability to link to a specific portion of a web page instead of the top. You can accomplish this by coding a hyperlink to a **fragment identifier** (sometimes called a named fragment or fragment id), which is simply an HTML element assigned to an id. Lists of frequently asked questions (FAQs) often use this technique.

VideoNote
Linking to a Named Fragment

There are two components to your coding when using fragment identifiers:

1. The tag that identifies the **named fragment** of a web page: The tag must be assigned to an id. For example, `<div id="content">`
2. The anchor tag that links to the named fragment on a web page.

Linking to a named fragment is often seen on long web pages. You might see a "Back to top" hyperlink that a visitor could select to cause the browser to quickly scroll the page back to the top of the page for easy site navigation.

Another use of fragment identifiers helps to provide for accessibility. Web pages may have a fragment identifier to indicate the beginning of the actual page content. When the visitor clicks on the "Skip to content" hyperlink, the browser links to the fragment identifier and shifts focus to the content area of the page. This "Skip to content" or "Skip navigation" link provides a way for screen reader users to skip repetitive navigation links (see Figure 2). This is accomplished in two steps as follows:

Focus on Accessibility

1. **Establish the Target.** Create the "Skip to content" fragment identifier by configuring a div that contains the page content with an id. For example,

```
<div id="content">
```

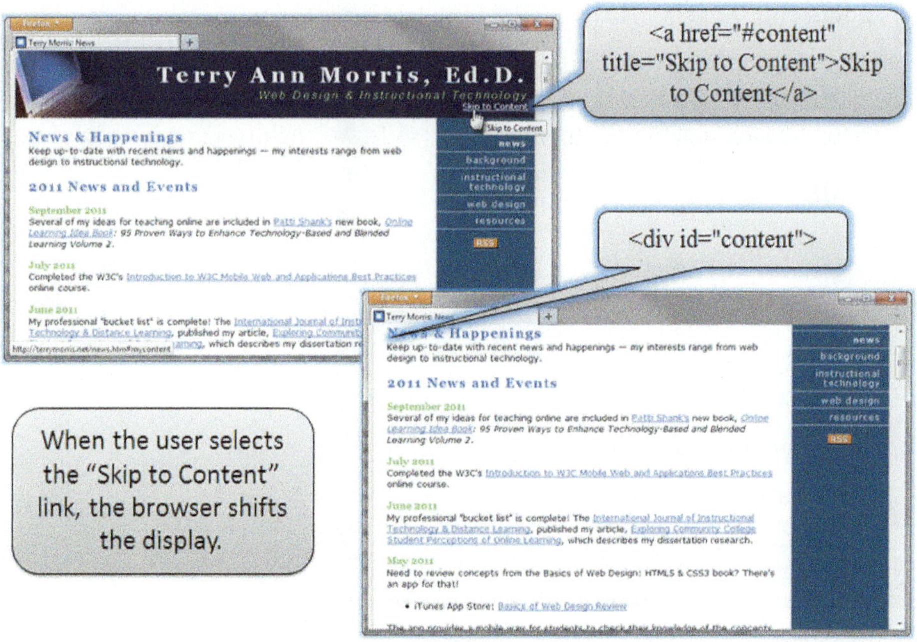

Figure 2 The "Skip to Content" link in action

2. **Reference the Target.** At the point of the page where you want to place a hyperlink to the content, type an anchor element. Use the href attribute and place a # (called a **hash mark**) before the name of the fragment identifier. The HTML for a hyperlink to the named fragment "content" is

```
<a href="#content">Skip to Content></a>
```

The hash mark indicates that the browser should search for an id on the same page. If you forget to type the hash mark, the browser will not look on the same web page; it will look for an external file.

Hands-On Practice 1

You will work with fragment identifiers in this Hands-On Practice. Locate chapter7/starter1.html[1] in the student files. Figure 3 shows a screenshot of this web page.

Launch a text editor and open starter1.html. Save the file as favorites.html. Examine the source code and notice that the top portion of the page contains an unordered list with categories of interest (such as Hobbies, HTML, Mobile Web Display, and Professional Organizations) that correspond to the text displayed in the h2 elements below. Each h2 element is followed by a definition list of topics and URLs related to that category. It might be helpful to web page visitors if they can click a category item and immediately jump to the page area that has information related to that item. This could be a useful application of linking to fragment identifiers!

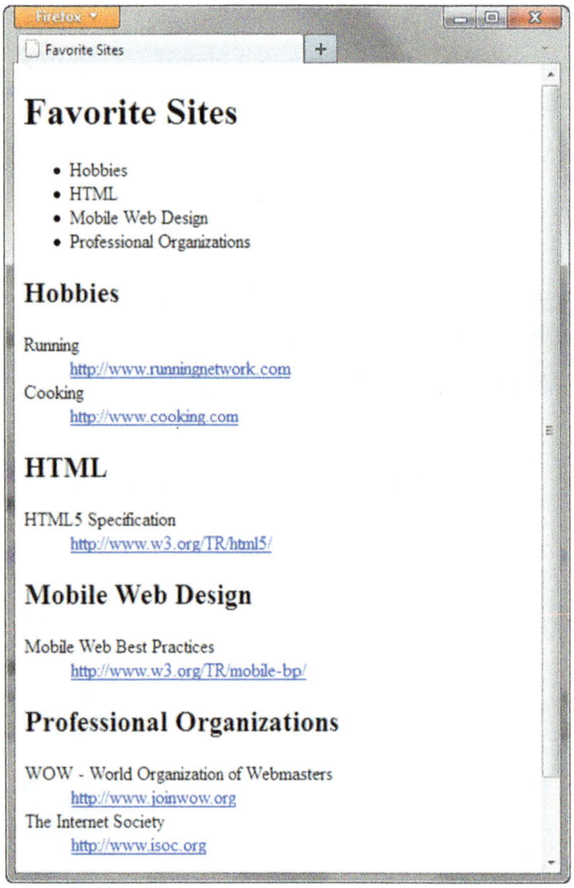

Figure 3 You will add hyperlinks to fragment identifiers

[1]Website Case Study starter files are available for download from Pearson's CS Support website at http://cssupport.pearsoncmg.com.

Modify the page as follows:

1. Code a named fragment for each h2 element in the definition list. For example,

```
<h2 id="hobbies">Hobbies</h2>
```

2. Add hyperlinks to the items in the unordered list so that each entry will link to its corresponding heading.
3. Add a named fragment near the top of the page.
4. Near the bottom of the favorites.html page, add a hyperlink to return to the top of the page.

Save the file and test it in a browser. Compare your work with the sample found in the student files (chapter7/favorites.html).

There may be times when you need to link to a named fragment on another web page. To accomplish this, place a "#" followed by the fragment identifier id value after the file name in the anchor tag. So, to link to the "Professional Organizations" (given that it is a named fragment called "prof") from any other page on the same website, you could use the following HTML:

```
<a href="favorites.html#prof">Professional Organizations</a>
```

FAQ Why don't some of my hyperlinks to fragment identifiers work?

The web browser fills the browser window (viewport) with the web page and will scroll to display the named fragment at the top of the viewport. However, if there is not enough "page" left below the named fragment, the content where the named fragment is located will not be displayed at the top of the browser viewport. The browser tries to do the best it can while still filling the viewport with the web page content. Try adding some blank lines (use the <br> tag) or padding to the lower portion of the web page. Save your work and test your hyperlinks again.

The Target Attribute

You may have noticed in Hands-On Practice 1 that when a visitor clicks on a hyperlink, the new web page will automatically open in the same browser window. You can configure the **target attribute** on an anchor tag with target="_blank" to open a hyperlink in a new browser window or browser tab. For example,

<a href="http://yahoo.com" target="_blank">Yahoo!</a> will open Yahoo! home page in a new browser window or tab.

Note that you cannot control whether the web page opens in a new window or opens in a new tab; this is dependent upon your visitor's browser configuration. Why not create a test page and try it? The target attribute with the value "_blank" configures the web page to open in a new browser window or tab.

Hands-On Practice 2

You will work with the target attribute in this Hands-On Practice. Locate chapter7/favorites.html in the student files. Launch a text editor and open favorites.html. Save the file as target.html. Let's practice using the target attribute. Choose one of the external hyperlinks to modify. And add `target="_blank"` so that the hyperlink opens in a new browser window or tab. The code is shown below:

```
<a href="http://www.isoc.org"
target="_blank">http://www.isoc.org</a>
```

Save the file. Launch a browser and test the file. When you click on the hyperlink that you modified, the new page will display in a new browser window or tab. You can compare your work to the solution in the student files (chapter7/target.html).

Block Anchor

It's typical to use anchor tags to configure phrases or even just a single word as a hyperlink. HTML5 provides a new function for the anchor tag—the block anchor. A block anchor can configure one or more elements (even those that display as a block, such as a div, h1, or paragraph) as a hyperlink. See an example in the student files (chapter7/block.html).

Telephone and Text Message Hyperlinks

If a web page displays a phone number, wouldn't it be handy for a person using a smartphone to be able to tap on the phone number and place a call or send an SMS (Short Message Service) text message? It's very easy to configure a telephone hyperlink or SMS hyperlink for use by smartphones.

According to RFC 3966, you can configure a telephone hyperlink by using a telephone scheme: Begin the href value with `tel:` followed by the phone number. For example, to configure a telephone hyperlink on a web page for use by mobile browsers, code as follows: `<a href="tel:888-555-5555">Call 888-555-5555</a>`.

RFC 5724 indicates that an SMS scheme hyperlink intended to send a text message can be configured by beginning the href value with `sms:` followed by the phone number, as shown in the following code:

```
<a href="sms:888-555-5555">Text 888-555-5555</a>.
```

Not all mobile browsers and devices support telephone and text hyperlinks, but expect increased use of this technology in the future. You'll get a chance to practice using the `tel:` scheme in the case study.

2 CSS Sprites

When browsers display web pages, they must make a separate http request for every file used by the page, including .css files and image files such as .gif, .jpg, and .png files. Each http request takes time and resources. A **sprite** is an image file that contains

multiple small graphics. Using CSS to configure the small graphics combined in the sprite as background images for various web page elements is called
CSS sprites, a technique made popular by David Shea (http://www.alistapart.com/articles/sprites).

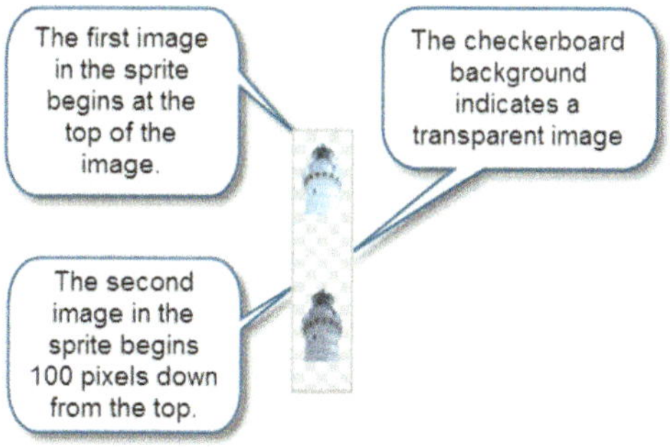

Figure 4 The sprite consists of two images in a single graphics file

The CSS sprites technique uses the CSS `background-image`, `background-repeat`, and `background-position` properties to manipulate the placement of the background image. The single graphics file saves download time because the browser only needs to make one http request for the combined image instead of many requests for the individual smaller images. Figure 4 shows a sprite with two lighthouse images on a transparent background. These images are configured as background images for the navigation hyperlinks with CSS as shown in Figure 5. You'll see this in action as you complete the next Hands-On Practice.

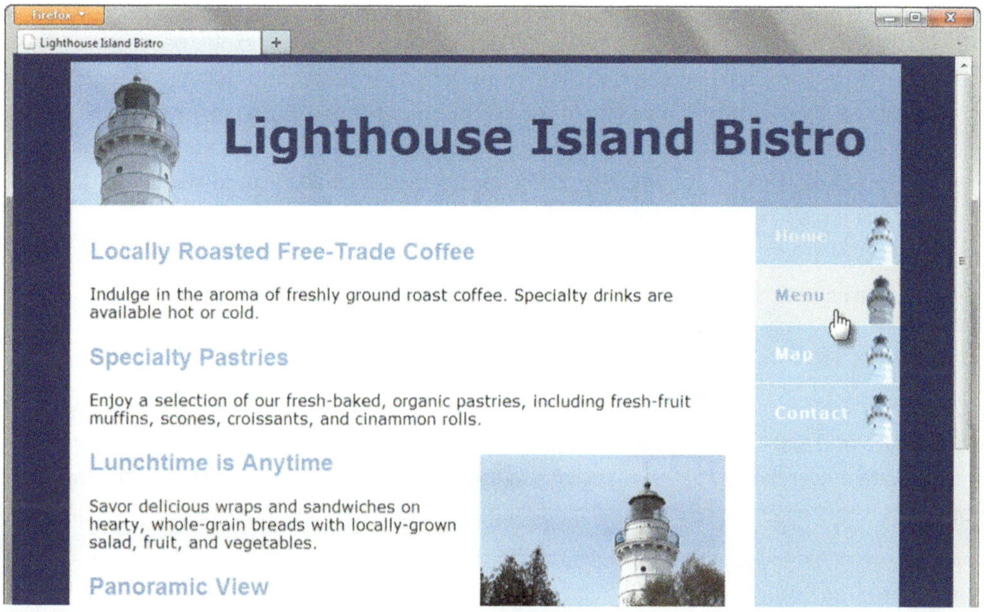

Figure 5 Sprites in action

Hands-On Practice 3

You will work with CSS sprites in this Hands-On Practice as you create the web page shown in Figure 5. Create a new folder named sprites. Locate chapter7/starter2.html in the student files. Copy starter2.html into your sprites folder. Copy the following files from chapter7/starters into your sprites folder: lighthouseisland.jpg, lighthouselogo.jpg, and sprites.gif. The sprites.gif, shown in Figure 4, contains two lighthouse images. The first lighthouse image starts at the top of the graphics file. The second lighthouse image begins 100 pixels down from the top of the graphics file. We'll use the value 100 when we configure the display of the second image.

Launch a text editor and open starter2.html. Save the file as index.html. You will edit the embedded styles to configure background images for the navigation hyperlinks.

1. Configure the background image for navigation hyperlinks. Add the following styles to the `#nav a` selector to set the background image to the sprites.gif with no repeat. The value `right` in the `background-position` property configures the lighthouse image to display at the right of the navigation element. The value `0` in the `background-position` property configures the display at offset 0 from the top (at the very top) so the first lighthouse image displays.

```
#nav a { text-decoration: none;
         display: block;
         padding: 20px;
         background-color: #b3c7e6;
         border-bottom: 1px solid #ffffff;
         background-image: url(sprites.gif);
         background-repeat: no-repeat;
         background-position: right 0; }
```

2. Configure the second lighthouse image to display when the mouse pointer passes over the hyperlink. Add the following styles to the `#nav a:hover` selector to display the second lighthouse image. The value `right` in the `background-position` property configures the lighthouse image to display at the right of the navigation element. The value `-100px` in the `background-position` property configures the display at an offset of 100 pixels down from the top so the second lighthouse image appears.

```
#nav a:hover { background-color: #eaeaea;
               color: #869dc7;
               background-position: right -100px; }
```

Save the file and test it in a browser. Your page should look similar to Figure 5. Move your mouse pointer over the navigation hyperlinks to see the background images change. Compare your work with the sample found in the student files (chapter7/sprites/index.html).

FAQ How can I create my own sprite graphics file?

Most web developers use a graphics application such as Adobe Photoshop, Adobe Fireworks, or GIMP to edit images and save them in a single graphics file for use as a sprite. Or, you could use a web-based sprite generator such as the ones listed below:

- CSS Sprites Generator: http://csssprites.com
- CSS Sprite Generator: http://spritegen.website-performance.org
- SpriteMe: http://spriteme.org

If you already have a sprite graphic, check out the online tool at Sprite Cow (http://www.spritecow.com) that can generate pixel-perfect `background-position` property values for a sprite.

Checkpoint 1

1. Why should you organize the files in a website using folders and subfolders?
2. Which attribute configures a hyperlink to open the file in a new browser window or tab?
3. State an advantage of using CSS sprites in a website.

3 Three-Column CSS Page Layout

Often a web page layout will consist of a header across the top of the page with three columns below: navigation, content, and sidebar. If you are thinking about this layout as a series of boxes—you're thinking correctly for configuring pages using CSS! Figure 6 shows a wireframe of this page layout design. Figure 7 shows a web page configured using this design. You will create this page in the next Hands-On Practice.

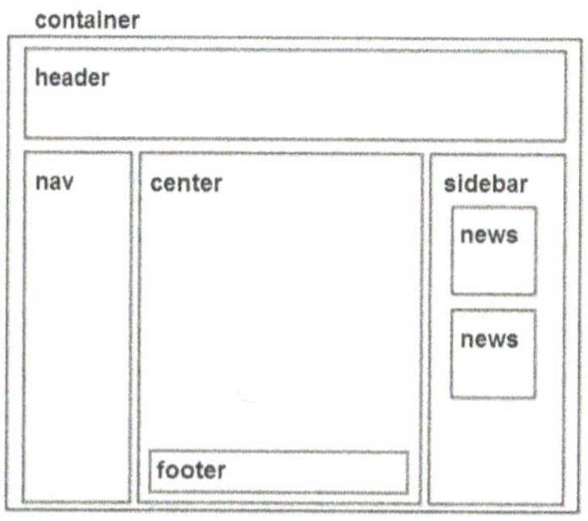

Figure 6 Wireframe for a three-column page layout

Figure 7 This three-column page layout is designed using CSS

Hands-On Practice 4

In this Hands-On Practice, you will develop your first three-column web page using CSS. The same techniques that you used to configure the two-column page will apply here. Think of the page as a series of elements or boxes. Using a wireframe as a guide, configure the basic page structure with HTML. Then code CSS to configure page areas; use ids or classes when appropriate. Recall that a key technique for creating a two-column web page with left-column navigation was to design the left column to float to the left. A key technique for our three-column page is to code the left column with `float:left` and the right column with `float:right`. The center column occupies the middle of the browser window. Refer to Figures 6 and 7 as you complete this Hands-On Practice.

Getting Started

Locate the showybg.jpg, plsthumb.jpg, and trillium.jpg files in the chapter7/starters folder in the student files. Create a new folder called wildflowers3. Copy the files to the folder.

Part 1: Code the HTML

Review Figures 6 and 7. Notice the page elements: a header area with a background image; a left column with a navigation area and an image; a center column with paragraphs of text, headings, and an image that floats to the right; a right column with two news items; and a footer. These will all be coded to use ids and classes that correspond to CSS, which configures a number of properties, including the float, margin, border, font-family, and so on. The navigation menu hyperlinks will be configured using an unordered list. As you code the HTML document, you will place the elements on the page and assign id and class values that correspond to the wireframe areas in Figure 6. Launch a text editor and type in the following HTML:

```
<!DOCTYPE html>
<html lang="en">
<head>
<title>Door County Wildflowers</title>
<meta charset="utf-8">
</head>
<body>
<div id="container">
  <div id="header">
     <span><a href="#center">Skip to Content</a></span>
     <h1>Door County Wildflowers</h1>
  </div>
  <div id="nav">
    <ul>
      <li><a href="index.html">Home</a></li>
      <li><a href="spring.html">Spring</a></li>
      <li><a href="summer.html">Summer</a></li>
      <li><a href="fall.html">Fall</a></li>
      <li><a href="winter.html">Winter</a></li>
  </ul>
  <img src="plsthumb.jpg" width="100" height="100" alt="Showy Lady
  Slipper">
</div>
<div id="sidebar">
    <h3>The Ridges</h3>
    <p class="news">The Ridges Nature Sanctuary offers wild orchid
hikes during the summer months. For more info, visit <a href=
"http://www.ridgesanctuary.org">The Ridges</a>.</p>
```

```
  <h3>Newport State Park</h3>
  <p class="news">The <a href="http://www.newportwildernesssociety.org">
Newport Wilderness Society</a> sponsors free meadow hikes at 9am
every Saturday. Stop by the park office to register.</p>
</div>
<div id="center">
    <h2>Door County</h2>
    <p>Wisconsin&rsquot;s Door County Peninsula is a unique,
ecologically diverse place with upland and boreal forest, bogs,
swamps, sand and rock beaches, limestone escarpments, and
farmlands.</p>
    <p>A wide array of wildflowers grow in the county because of this
variety of ecosystems.</p>
  <img src="trillium.jpg" width="200" height="150" alt="Trillium"
  id="floatright">
    <h3>Explore the beauty <br>of Door County Wildflowers. . . .</h3>
  <p>With five state parks, tons of county parks, and private nature
sanctuaries, Door County is teeming with natural areas for you to
stalk your favorite wildflowers.</p>
    <div id="footer"> Copyright &copy; 2012 Door County Wild Flowers<br>
    </div>
  </div>
</div>
</body>
</html>
```

Save your page as index.html in your wildflowers3 folder. Test the page in a browser. Your display will not look like Figure 7 because you have not yet configured the CSS. The top of your page should look similar to the page shown in Figure 8.

Figure 8 The three-column page before CSS is applied

Part 2: Code the Basic CSS

For ease of editing, in this Hands-On Practice, you will code the CSS as embedded styles in the header section of the web page. However, if you were creating an entire website, you would most likely use an external style sheet. Launch a text editor and open index.html. Let's take a moment to consider the main elements used on the page shown in Figure 6: header, left-column navigation area, right-column sidebar area, center column, and footer. The left column will contain a navigation area and a small image. The center column will contain paragraphs, a heading, and a right-floating image. The right column will contain a series of headings and news items. Locate these areas on the sketch in Figure 6. Notice also that the same font is used throughout the page and the page begins immediately at the browser margin.

With your file open in a text editor, modify the head section of your document and code a `<style>` tag. Now let's consider the CSS configuration. Type the CSS in your document as indicated below:

1. **Body Element Selector.** Set the margin to 0. Configure the background color to #ffffff.

```
body { margin:0;
       background-color: #ffffff; }
```

2. **Container.** Configure this area with background (#eeeeee) and text (#006600) colors, a minimum width of 960 pixels, and a font family of Verdana, Arial, or sans-serif.

```
#container { background-color: #eeeeee;
             color: #006600;
             min-width: 960px;
             font-family: Verdana, Arial, sans-serif; }
```

3. **Header.** Configure a background color (#636631) and a background image (position showybg.jpg at the bottom of the element to repeat horizontally). Set the height to 120 pixels, text color to #cc66cc, text alignment to right, no top padding, no bottom padding, 20 pixels left padding, and 20 pixels right padding. Configure a 2 pixel solid black border across the bottom of this area.

```
#header { background-color: #636631;
          background-image: url(showybg.jpg);
          background-position: bottom;
          background-repeat: repeat-x;
          height: 120px;
          color: #cc66cc;
          text-align: right;
          padding: 0 20px;
          border-bottom: 2px solid #000000; }
```

4. **Left Column.** One of the keys to this three-column page layout is that the left navigation column is designed to float to the left of the browser window. Configure a width of 150 pixels.

```
#nav { float: left;
width: 150px; }
```

5. **Right Column.** One of the keys to this three-column page layout is that the right sidebar column is designed to float to the right of the browser window. Configure a width of 200 pixels.

```
#sidebar { float: right;
           width: 200px; }
```

6. **Center.** The center column will take up all of the room that is available after the left and right columns float. The content area has a special need for margins because the left and right columns are floating on either side. Set the left margin to 160 pixels, the right margin to 210 pixels, and the remaining margins to 0. Also configure the padding for this area. Set the background (#ffffff) and text (#006600) colors.

```
#center { margin: 0 210px 0 160px;
          padding: 1px 10px 20px 10px;
          background-color: #ffffff;
          color: #006600; }
```

7. **Footer.** Configure the page footer with very small text that is centered. Configure the background (#ffffff) and text (#006600) colors for this area. Set the top padding to 10 pixels. Clear the floated image in the center content area.

```
#footer { font-size: .70em;
          text-align: center;
          color: #006600;
          background-color: #ffffff;
          padding-top: 10px;
          clear: both; }
```

At this point, you have configured the main elements of the three-column page layout. Code the closing HTML style tag with `</style>`. Save index.html in the wildflowers3 folder. It's a good idea to open your page in a browser to make sure you are on the right track. It should look similar to the one shown in Figure 9. Note that there is still some detail work to do, but you are well on your way!

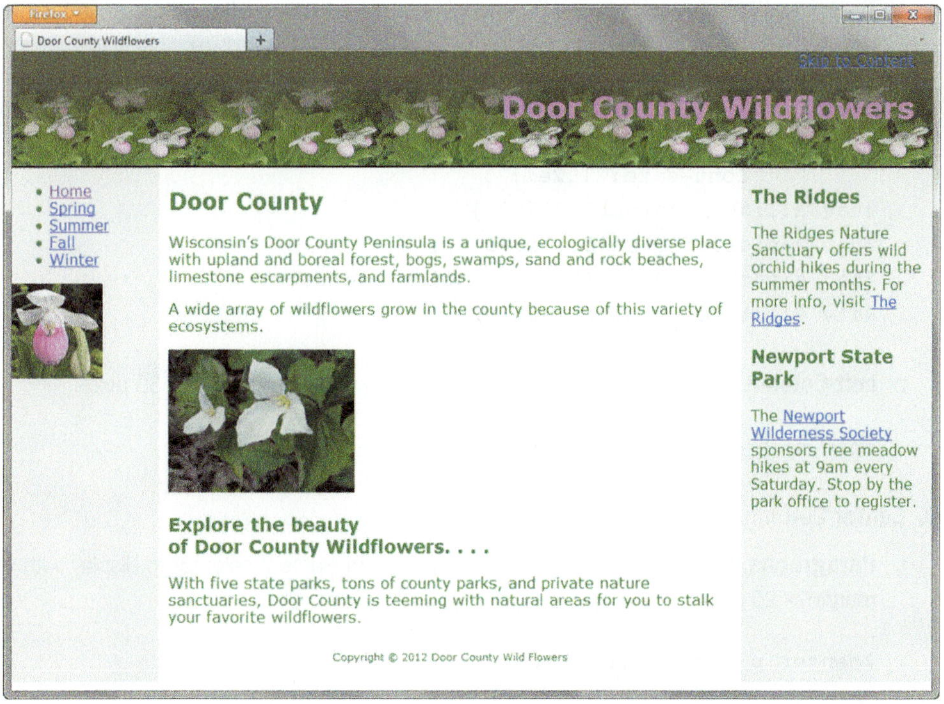

Figure 9 The CSS for the basic elements of the three-column layout has been completed

Part 3: Continue Coding CSS

Now you are ready to continue with your styles. Open index.html in a text editor and position your cursor on a blank line above the closing style tag.

1. **Header Area.**

   a. **The h1 Element Selector.** Notice the extra space above the "Door County Wildflowers" text, which is contained within the `<h1>` element in the header area. You can reduce this extra space by setting a 0 top margin for the h1 element selector. Also configure left alignment, text shadow, and a font size of 3em for the h1 selector.

```
h1 { margin-top: 0;
     font-size: 3em;
     text-align: left;
     text-shadow: 2px 2px 2px #000000; }
```

   b. **Skip to Content.** Configure the "Skip to Content" hyperlink in the header area with a 0.80em font size. Also configure pseudo-classes for `:link`, `:visited`, `:hover`, `:active`, and `:focus` with text color as shown below.

```
#header a {font-size: 0.80em; }
#header a:link, #header a:visited { color: #ffffff; }
#header a:focus, #header a:hover { color: #eeeeee; }
```

2. **Left Navigation Column.**

   a. **Navigation Menu.** Configure the unordered list in the `nav` id to provide for a 20 pixel top margin and not to display any list markers.

```
#nav ul { margin-top: 20px;
          list-style-type: none; }
```

   The navigation links should have no underline (`text-decoration: none`) and a 1.2em font size. Configure pseudo-classes for `:link`, `:visited`, `:hover`, `:active`, and `:focus` with text color as shown below.

```
#nav a { text-decoration: none;
         font-size: 1.2em; }
#nav a:link { color:#006600;}
#nav a:visited { color: #003300; }
#nav a:focus, #nav a:hover { color: #cc66cc; }
#nav a:active { color: #000000;}
```

   b. **Left Column Image.** Configure images in the `nav` id with a margin of 30 pixels.

```
#nav img { margin: 30px;}
```

3. **Center Column.**

   a. **Paragraphs.** Configure the center area's paragraph element selector to display with a margin of 20 pixels.

```
#center p { margin: 20px; }
```

b. **Headings.** Configure the h2 and h3 element selectors in the center area with the same text color as the logo header text and the same background color as the main body of the page.

```
#center h2, #center h3 { color: #cc66cc;
                         background-color: #ffffff; }
```

c. **Image Floating at the Right.** Create a `floatright` id to use a 10 pixel margin and float to the right.

```
#floatright { margin: 10px;
              float: right; }
```

4. Right Sidebar Column.

a. **Headings.** Configure the h2 element selector in this area with a 1 pixel black solid bottom border, 2 pixels of padding at the bottom, a 10 pixel margin, 0.90em font size, and the same text color as the logo header text.

```
#sidebar h3 { padding-bottom: 2px;
              border-bottom: 1px solid #000000;
              margin: 10px;
              font-size: 0.90em;
              color: #cc66cc;}
```

b. **News Items.** Configure a class called `news` that uses a small font and has a 10 pixel margin.

```
.news { font-size: 0.80em;
        margin: 10px; }
```

Save index.html in the wildflowers3 folder.

Part 4: Test the Page

Now that your styles are coded, test the index.html page again. Your page should look similar to the screenshot shown in Figure 7. Recall that Internet Explorer does not support the `text-shadow` property. If there are other differences, verify the id and class values in your HTML. Also check the syntax of your CSS. You may find the W3C CSS Validation Service at http://jigsaw.w3.org/css-validator to be helpful when verifying CSS syntax. The student files contain a copy of this page in the chapter7/wildflowers folder.

4 CSS Styling for Print

Even though the "paperless society" has been talked about for decades, the fact is that many people still love paper and you can expect your web pages to be printed. CSS offers you some control over what gets printed and how the printouts are configured. This is easy to do using external style sheets. Create one external style sheet with the configurations for browser display and a second external style sheet with the special printing configurations. Associate both of the external style sheets to the web page using two link elements. The link elements will utilize the **`media` attribute,** which indicates the media type for which the styles are intended, such as screen display or print display. See a list of media attribute values in Table 1.

Table 1 The media attribute

Value	Purpose
`screen`	Default value; Indicates the style sheet that configures the typical browser viewport display on a color computer screen
`print`	Indicates the style sheet that configures the printed formatting
`handheld`	Although this value is intended by the W3C to indicate the style sheet that configures display on handheld mobile devices, in practice, the attribute value is not reliably applied (see Return of the Mobile Stylesheet at http://www.alistapart.com/articles/return-of-the-mobile-stylesheet for more information). The next section will describe other methods for configuring the design of mobile web pages.

Modern browsers will use the correct screen or print style sheet, depending on whether they are rendering a screen display or preparing to print a document. Configure the link element for your browser display with `media="screen"`. Configure the link element for your printout with `media="print"`. An example of the HTML follows:

```
<link rel="stylesheet" href="wildflower.css" media="screen">
<link rel="stylesheet" href="wildflowerprint.css" media="print">
```

Print Styling Best Practices

You might be wondering how a print style sheet should differ from the CSS used to display the web page in a browser. Commonly used techniques for styling print are listed below.

Hide Non-Essential Content

It's common practice to prevent banner ads, navigation, or other extraneous areas from appearing on the printout. Use the `display: none;` style declaration to hide content that is not needed on a printout of the web page.

Configure Font Size and Color for Printing

Another common practice is to configure the font sizes on the print style sheet to use pt units. This will better control the text on the printout. You might also consider configuring the text color to black (`#000000`) if you envision the need for visitors to print your pages often. The default setting on most browsers prevent background colors and background images from printing, but you can also prevent background image display in your print style sheet.

Control Page Breaks

Use the CSS **`page-break-before`** or **`page-break-after`** properties to control page breaks when printing the web page. Well-supported values for these properties are `always` (the page break will always occur as designated), `avoid` (if possible, the page break will occur before or after, as designated), and `auto` (default). For example, to configure a page break at a specific point in the document (in this case, right before an element assigned to the class named `newpage`), configure the CSS as shown below:

```
.newpage { page-break-before: always; }
```

Print URLs for Hyperlinks

Consider whether a person would find it useful to see the actual URL for a resource when reading the printout of your web page. You can use CSS to display the value of the href attribute right on the page using two CSS coding techniques: a CSS pseudo-element and the CSS `content` property. The purpose of a CSS **pseudo-element** is to apply some type of effect to its selector. Table 2 lists pseudo-elements and their purpose.

Table 2 CSS 2.1 pseudo-elements

Pseudo-element	Purpose
`:after`	Inserts generated content after the selector: Configure the generated content with the content property
`:before`	Inserts generated content before the selector: Configure the generated content with the content property
`:first-letter`	Applies styles to the first letter of text
`:first-line`	Applies styles to the first line of text

Use the CSS `content` **property** along with the `:after` and `:before` pseudo-elements to generate content. A useful feature of the content property is the `attr(X)` function, which returns the value of the HTML attribute provided. You can use this to print the URL of a hyperlink (the value of the `href` attribute). Use quotation marks to contain additional text or characters, such as parentheses. The CSS below will display the URL for each hyperlink in the sidebar area within parentheses after the text hyperlink.

```
#sidebar a:after { content: " (" attr(href) ") "; }
```

Figure 10 shows the print preview of the content page you created in Hands-On Practice 4 (see Figure 7). Notice that the print preview includes the navigation area. Figure 11

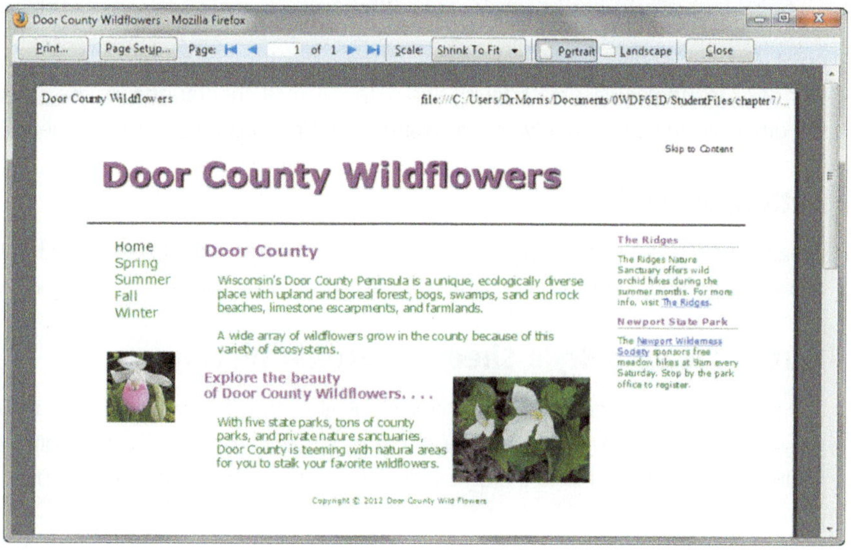

Figure 10 Print preview of the page displayed in Figure 7

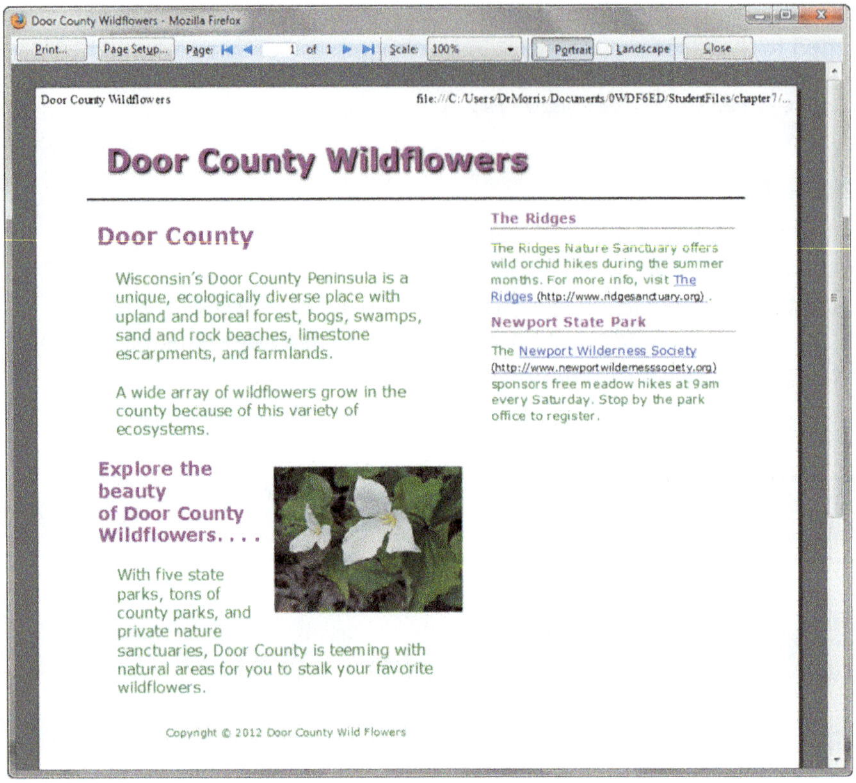

Figure 11 Print preview using CSS to configure for printing

displays an alternate version of the page that uses CSS to prevent the display of the navigation area, configures pt units for font sizes, and prints the URL for the hyperlinks in the sidebar area. You will explore these techniques in the next Hands-On Practice.

Hands-On Practice 5

In this Hands-On Practice, you will code special styles for use when printing a web page. We will use the Door County Wildflowers index.html page from Hands-On Practice 4 as a starting point. Figure 7 shows a browser display of the index.html page. You will create a new version of index.html that is associated with two external style sheets: one for the screen display and the other for printing. When you are finished, your printed page should resemble Figure 11.

Getting Started

Create a new folder named wildflowersPrint. Copy into your new folder index.html, plsthumb.jpg, showybg.jpg, and trillium.jpg from the chapter7/wildflowers folder in the student files.

Part 1: Create a Style Sheet for Screen Display

Launch a text editor and open index.html. Copy all of the style rules between the opening and closing style tags. Use your text editor to create a new file and save it as wildflower.css in your wildflowersPrint folder. Paste the style rules into wildflower.css and save the file.

Part 2: Edit the HTML

Edit index.html and remove the style tags. Code a link element to associate the web page with the external style sheet that you just created (wildflower.css). Add the `media` attribute with the value of `"screen"` to the link element for wildflower.css. Code a second link element to invoke an external style sheet called wildflowerprint.css for printing (`media="print"`). The HTML is as follows:

```
<link rel="stylesheet" href="wildflower.css" media="screen">
<link rel="stylesheet" href="wildflowerprint.css" media="print">
```

Save index.html in the wildflowersPrint folder.

Part 3: Code the New Style Sheet for Print Display

Launch a text editor and open wildflower.css. Because you want to keep most of the styles for printing, you will modify a copy of the screen display external style sheet. Save wildflower.css as wildflowerprint.css in the wildflowersPrint folder. You will modify several areas on this style sheet, including the `container` id, h1 element selector, `header` id, `nav` id, `center` id, and the hyperlinks located in the `header` and `sidebar` ids.

Remove the style declaration for minimum width (`min-width`) from the `container` id.

1. Modify the h1 element selector so that the printer will use 24 point font size. Remove the `text-align` property.

```
h1 { margin-top: 0;
     font-size: 24pt;
     text-shadow: 2px 2px 2px #000000; }
```

2. Modify the `header` id style rules. Configure a white background color (#ffffff). Remove the background image declaration. The height property is also not needed because there is no longer a background image. Also remove the text alignment and padding properties.

```
#header { color: #cc66cc;
          background-color: #ffffff;
          border-bottom: 2px solid #000000;
          padding: 0 20px; }
```

3. Configure the "Skip to Content" hyperlink in the `header` id to not display. Replace all style rules associated with `#header a` with the following:

```
#header a { display: none; }
```

4. Configure the navigation area to not display. Remove all style rules associated with `#nav` and add the following:

```
#nav { display: none; }
```

5. Configure the center area. Modify the style rule for `#center`. Set the left margin to 0, the right margin to 40%, and the font size to 12pt.

```
#center { margin: 0 40% 0 0;
          padding: 1px 10px 20px 10px;
          font-size: 12pt;
          background-color: #ffffff;
          color: #006600; }
```

6. Configure the width of the sidebar to 40%.

```
#sidebar { float: right;
           width: 40%; }
```

7. Configure the **news** class. Modify the style rule to configure the font size to 10pt.

```
.news { font-size: 10pt;
        margin: 10px; }
```

8. Configure the hyperlinks in the sidebar area so that the URLs are printed in 8pt black font. Add the following CSS:

```
#sidebar a:after { content " (" attr(href) ") ";
                   font-size: 8pt;
                   color: #000000; }
```

9. Look through the style rules and configure the **background-color** for each h2 and h3 element selector to be white (#ffffff).

Save your file in the wildflowersPrint folder.

Part 4: Test Your Work

Test index.html in a browser. Select File > Print > Preview. Your display should look similar to the page shown in Figure 11. The font sizes have been configured and the navigation does not display. The URLs appear after the hyperlink text in the sidebar area. The student files contain a solution in the chapter7/print folder.

Note that there is a change in CSS3 syntax, which requires two colons in front of each pseudo-element (for example, CSS3 uses **::after** instead of **:after**). However, we'll stick with the CSS2 pseudo-elements and syntax for now because there is broader browser support.

5 CSS Styling for the Mobile Web

There are three methods that can be used to provide access for website visitors who use mobile devices. One option is to design and publish a second website with a .mobi TLD. Visit JCPenney at http://jcp.com and http://jcp.mobi to see this in practice. Another option is to design and publish a separate website within your own domain that is optimized for mobile use. This technique is utilized by the White House at http://www.whitehouse.gov (Figure 12). The mobile version of the White House website can be viewed at http://m.whitehouse.gov (Figure 13). The third option is to configure one

Figure 12 The regular White House website (http://www.whitehouse.gov) viewed in a browser

website with separate styles for mobile and desktop browser display. Before we focus on coding, let's consider design techniques for the mobile web.

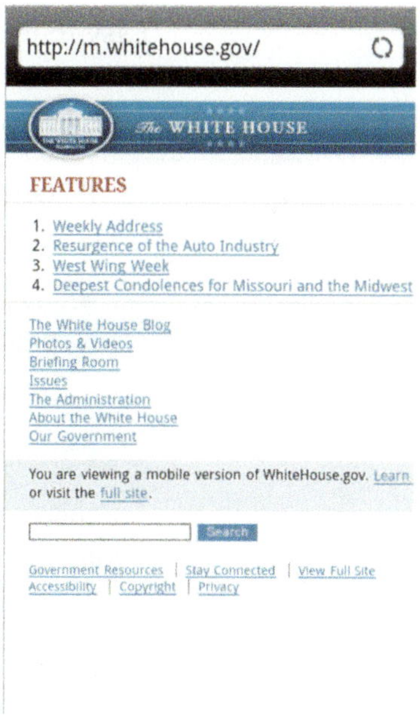

Figure 13 The mobile version of the White House website (http://m.whitehouse.gov)

Mobile Web Design Best Practices

Mobile web users are typically on-the-go, need information quickly, and may be easily distracted. A web page that is optimized for mobile access should try to serve these needs. Take a moment to review Figures 12 and 13 and observe how the design of the mobile website addresses the design considerations:

- **Small screen size.** The size of the header area is reduced to accommodate a small screen display.
- **Low bandwidth (slow connection speed).** Note that the large images visible in Figure 12 are not displayed on the mobile version of the web page.
- **Font, color, and media issues.** Common font typefaces are utilized. There is also good contrast between text and background color.
- **Awkward controls, and limited processor and memory.** The mobile website uses a single-column page layout that facilitates keyboard tabbing and will be easy to control by touch. The page is mostly text, which will be quickly rendered by a mobile browser.
- **Functionality.** Hyperlinks to popular site features display directly under the header. A search feature is also provided.

Let's build on this base of design considerations and expand them.

Optimize Layout for Mobile Use

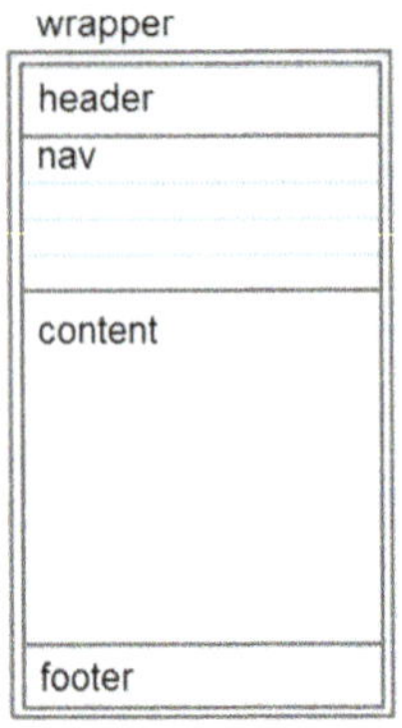

Figure 14
Wireframe for a typical single-column mobile page layout

A single-column page layout (Figure 14) with a small header, key navigation links, content, and page footer works well for a mobile device display. Mobile screen resolutions vary greatly (for example, 320×240 [BlackBerry Pearl], 320×480 [Apple iPhone3, Android HTC Dream], 360×640 [Nokia], 480×800 [Android HTC Desire, Windows HTC Pro], and 640×690 [Apple iPhone4, but with a higher pixel density than iPhone3]). W3C recommendations include the following:

- Limit scrolling to one direction.
- Use heading elements.
- Use lists to organize information (such as unordered lists, ordered lists, and definition lists).
- Avoid using tables because they typically force both horizontal and vertical scrolling on mobile devices.
- Provide labels for form controls.
- Avoid using pixel units in style sheets.
- Avoid absolute positioning in style sheets.
- Hide content that is not essential for mobile use.

Optimize Navigation for Mobile Use

Easy-to-use navigation is crucial on a mobile device. The W3C recommends the following:

- Provide minimal navigation near the top of the page.
- Provide consistent navigation.
- Avoid hyperlinks that open files in new windows or pop-up windows.
- Try to balance both the number of hyperlinks on a page and the number of levels of links needed to access information.

Optimize Graphics for Mobile Use

Graphics can help to engage visitors, but be aware of the following W3C recommendations for mobile use:

- Avoid displaying images that are wider than the screen width (assume a 320 pixel screen width on a smartphone display).
- Configure alternate small, optimized background images.
- Some mobile browsers will downsize all images, so images with text may become difficult to read.
- Avoid the use of large graphic images.
- Specify the size of images.
- Provide alternate text for graphics and other non-text elements.

Optimize Text for Mobile Use

It can be difficult to read text on a small mobile device. The following W3C recommendations will aid your mobile visitors.

- Configure good contrast between text and background colors.
- Use common font typefaces.
- Configure font size with em units or percentages.
- Use a short, descriptive page title.

The W3C has published Mobile Web Best Practices 1.0, a list of 60 mobile web design best practices, at http://www.w3.org/TR/mobile-bp. Visit http://www.w3.org/2007/02/mwbp_flip_cards.html for flipcards that summarize the Mobile Web Best Practices 1.0 document.

Figure 15 Mobile display of a web page

Design for One Web

The W3C mission of building **"One Web"** refers to the concept of providing a single resource that is configured for optimal display on multiple types of devices. This is more efficient than creating multiple versions of a web document. With the "One Web" in mind, we'll next explore using the viewport meta tag and CSS media queries to target and deliver style sheets that are optimized for mobile display to mobile devices.

Viewport Meta Tag

There are multiple uses for meta tags. It's often used to configure the character encoding on a web page. Now, we'll explore the new **viewport meta tag,** which was created as an Apple extension that helps with displays on mobile devices such as iPhones and Android smartphones by setting the width and scale of the viewport. Figure 15 displays a screen shot of a web page displayed on an Android smartphone without the viewport meta tag. Examine Figure 15 and notice that the mobile device zoomed out to display the entire web page on the tiny screen. The text on the web page is difficult to read.

Figure 16 shows the same web page after the viewport meta tag was added to the head section of the document. The code is shown below:

```
<meta name="viewport"
content="width=device-width, initial-scale=1.0">
```

Figure 16 The viewport meta tag helps with mobile displays

Code the viewport meta tag with the HTML `name="viewport"` and `content` attributes. The value of the HTML `content` attribute can be one or more **directives** (also referred to as properties by Apple), such as the `device-width` directive and directives that control zooming and scale. Table 3 lists viewport meta tag directives and their values.

Table 3 Viewport meta tag directives

Directive	Values	Purpose
`width`	Numeric value or `device-width` which indicates actual width of the device screen	The width of the viewport in pixels
`height`	Numeric value or `device-height` which indicates actual height of the device screen	The height of the viewport in pixels
`initial-scale`	Numeric multiplier; Set to 1 for 100% initial scale	Initial scale of the viewport
`minimum-scale`	Numeric multiplier; Mobile Safari default is 0.25	Minimum scale of the viewport
`maximum-scale`	Numeric multiplier; Mobile Safari default is 1.6	Maximum scale of the viewport
`user-scalable`	`yes` allows scaling, `no` disables scaling	Determines whether a user can zoom in or out

Now that you've scaled the page to be readable, what about styling it for optimal mobile use? That's where CSS comes into play.

CSS Media Queries

Earlier in the chapter, you used the link element along with `media="print"` to configure styles for printing web pages. The attribute value `media="handheld"` was originally intended to serve the same purpose, but it has not been well supported. So, with `media="handheld"` not working, what can you do? Use a **media query** (see http://www.w3.org/TR/css3-mediaqueries) to determine the capability of the mobile device, such as screen resolution and orientation (portrait or landscape), and direct browsers to styles configured specifically for those capabilities. Figure 17 shows the same web page as Figures 15 and 16 , but it looks quite different because of a link element that includes media queries and is associated with a style sheet configured for optimal mobile display. The HTML is shown below:

Figure 17 CSS media queries help to configure the page for mobile display

```
<link href="lighthousemobile.css" rel="stylesheet"
media="only screen and (max-device-width: 480px)">
```

The code sample above will configure an optimal display for the most popular smartphones. The value `only` is a keyword that will hide the media query from outdated browsers. The value `screen` targets devices with screens. The `max-device-width` **media feature** (see Table 4) is set to `480px`, which will target the most popular smartphone viewport dimensions. Commonly used **media types** and keywords include the following:

- `all` targets all devices
- `screen` targets screens
- `only` causes older nonsupporting browsers to ignore the media query
- `print` targets printout

Table 4 Commonly used media query features

Features	Values	Criteria
`max-device-height`	Numeric value	The height of the screen size of the output device in pixels is smaller than or equal to the value
`max-device-width`	Numeric value	The width of the screen size of the output device in pixels is smaller than or equal to the value
`min-device-height`	Numeric value	The height of the screen size of the output device in pixels is greater than or equal to the value
`min-device-width`	Numeric value	The width of the screen size of the output device in pixels is greater than or equal to the value
`max-height`	Numeric value	The height of the viewport in pixels is smaller than or equal to the value (reevaluated when screen is resized)
`min-height`	Numeric value	The height of the viewport in pixels is greater than or equal to the value (reevaluated when screen is resized)
`max-width`	Numeric value	The width of the viewport in pixels is smaller than or equal to the value (reevaluated when screen is resized)
`min-width`	Numeric value	The width of the viewport in pixels is greater than or equal to the value (reevaluated when screen is resized)
`orientation`	Portrait or landscape	The orientation of the device

Testing Mobile Display

The best way to test the mobile display of a web page is to publish it to the Web and access it from a mobile device. (See the appendix "FTP Tutorial" for an introduction to publishing a website with FTP.) However, not everyone has access to a smartphone. Several options for emulating a mobile display are listed below:

- **Opera Mobile Emulator** (Windows Only download and install)
  http://www.opera.com/developer/tools/mobile
  Supports media queries.
- **Mobilizer** (Windows and Mac download and install)
  http://www.springbox.com/mobilizer
  Supports media queries.
- **Web-Based Opera Mini 4.2 Simulator** (Runs in a browser window)
  http://www.opera.com/mobile/demo/?ver=4
  Disables background images; supports media queries.
- **Web-Based Opera Mini 6 Simulator** (Runs in a browser window)
  http://www.opera.com/mobile/demo
  Disables background images; supports media queries.
- **iPhone Emulator** (Runs in a browser window)
  http://www.testiphone.com
  Does not support media queries.
- **iPhoney** (Mac only download and install)
  http://www.marketcircle.com/iphoney
  Does not support media queries.

Figure 18 A desktop browser was used to approximate the mobile display

Testing with a Desktop Browser

What if you don't have a smartphone and are unable to publish your files to the Web? You can *approximate* the mobile display of your site using a desktop browser by using the following technique:

1. Modify the link element to point to your mobile CSS style sheet.
2. Display your page in a desktop browser and then reduce the width and height of the viewport until it approximates a mobile screen size (such as 320×480).

Figure 18 demonstrates this technique. The Firefox browser was used to display the same website using the mobile style sheet (see Figure 17).

For Serious Developers Only

If you are a software developer or information systems major, you may want to explore the SDKs (Software Developer Kits) for the iOS and Android platforms. Each SDK includes a mobile device emulator.

- **iOS SDK** (Mac only) http://developer.apple.com/programs/ios/develop.html
- **Android SDK** http://developer.android.com/sdk/index.html

Now that you're aware of some mobile design considerations, how to target a mobile device, and options for mobile testing and emulation, let's apply your new knowledge by configuring the web page shown in Figure 17.

Hands-On Practice 6

Create a new folder named mobile. Locate chapter7/starter2.html in the student files. Copy starter2.html into your mobile folder. Rename the starter2.html file as index.html. Copy the following files from chapter7/starters into your mobile folder: lighthouseisland.jpg, lighthouselogo.jpg, and mobilelogo.jpg. Launch a browser and view starter2.html as shown in Figure 19. You will configure the web page to use the viewport meta tag and media queries to target mobile devices. You'll configure CSS for both desktop and mobile display.

Part 1: Create a New Style Sheet

Launch a text editor and open index.html. Copy all the style rules between the opening and closing style tags. Use your text editor to create a new file and save it as lighthouse.css in your mobile folder. Paste the style rules into lighthouse.css and save the file.

Part 2: Edit the HTML

1. Edit index.html and remove the style tags. Code a link element to associate the web page with the external style sheet that you just created (lighthouse.css). Add the `media` attribute with the value of `screen` to the link element for lighthouse.css. Code a second link element to invoke an external style sheet called lighthousemobile.css for mobile display. The HTML code follows:

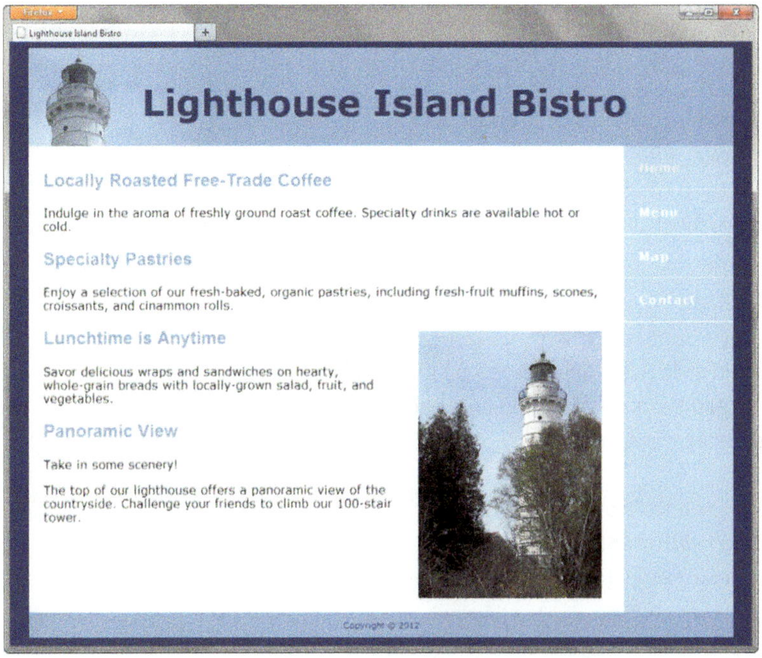

Figure 19 Web page displayed in a desktop browser

```
<link href="lighthouse.css" rel="stylesheet" media="screen">
<link href="lighthousemobile.css" rel="stylesheet"
      media="only screen and (max-device-width: 480px)">
```

2. Configure a viewport meta tag below the link elements. The HTML code follows:

```
<meta name="viewport"
content="width=device-width, initial-scale=1.0">
```

3. The mobile display will benefit from a "Back to Top" link at the bottom of the page. Add a div assigned to an id named `backtotop` at the bottom of the content area that contains a hyperlink to the `#header` id. The HTML code follows:

```
<div id="backtotop"><a href="#header">Back to Top</a></div>
```

Save the index.html file in the mobile folder.

Part 3: Code the New CSS

Launch a text editor and open lighthouse.css. Because you will want to keep most of the styles for mobile display, you will start by creating a new version of the external style sheet. Save the lighthouse.css file as lighhousemobile.css in the mobile folder. You will modify several areas on this style sheet, including the body element selector, `wrapper` id, h1 element selector, `header` id, `nav` id, `content` id, `footer` id, and the navigation hyperlinks.

1. Modify the body element selector. Add a style rule to configure no margins.

```
body { font-family: Verdana, Arial, sans-serif;
       background-color: #00005D;
       margin: 0; }
```

2. Modify the **wrapper** id style rules to also configure 100% width, no margin, no padding, and no minimum width.

```
#wrapper { background-color: #b3c7e6;
           color: #000066;
           width: 100%;
           margin: 0;
           padding: 0;
           min-width: 0; }
```

3. Modify the **header** id style rules. Change the padding as indicated below. Change the font size to 100%. Configure the mobilelogo.jpg as a background image that does not repeat. Set the position of the background image to display at the top on the right side.

```
#header { background-color: #869dc7;
          color: #00005D;
          font-size: 100%;
          padding: 0.5em 0 0 0.5em;
          background-image: url(mobilelogo.jpg);
          background-repeat: no-repeat;
          background-position: right top; }
```

4. Eliminate the margin configured for the h1 element selector.

```
h1 { margin: 0; }
```

5. Modify the **nav** id style rules. Remove the float. Set the width to 100% and the font size to 120%.

```
#nav { float: none;
       width: 100%;
       font-size: 120%;
       letter-spacing: 0.1em;
       font-weight: bold; }
```

6. Modify the **content** id style rules. Change the padding to 0.5em.

```
#content { background-color: #ffffff;
           color: #000000;
           padding: 0.5em;
           overflow: auto; }
```

7. Modify the **footer** id style rules. Set the padding to 0.

```
#footer { font-size: 70%;
          text-align: center;
          padding: 0;
          background-color: #869dc7;
          clear: both; }
```

8. Eliminate the margin for the h2 element selector.

```
h2 { color: #869dc7;
     font-family: Arial, sans-serif;
     margin: 0; }
```

9. Configure the paragraph element selector to have a 0.05em margin.

```
p {margin: 0.05em; }
```

10. Configure the `floatright` class to not float and to have no margin.

```
#floatright { margin: 0;
              float: none; }
```

11. Configure a new style rule for li elements in the `nav` id. Set the padding to 0.

```
#nav li { padding: 0; }
```

12. Modify the styles for hyperlinks in the `nav` id. Set the padding as shown below:

```
#nav a { text-decoration: none;
         display: block;
         padding: 0.5em;
         background-color: #b3c7e6;
         border-bottom: 1px solid #ffffff; }
```

13. Configure a new style rule for the `backtotop` id. Set the display to block.

```
#backtotop {display: block; }
```

Save your file in the mobile folder.

Part 4: Update the Desktop CSS

Open lighthouse.css in a text editor. Add CSS to configure the id named `backtotop` to not display.

```
#backtotop { display: none; }
```

Save the file.

Part 5: Test Your Work

Test your index.html file in a desktop browser. It should look similar to Figure 19. Then, test your index.html file in a mobile emulator. It should look similar to Figure 17 (Android smartphone) or Figure 18 (desktop browser approximation). The student files contain a suggested solution in the chapter7/mobile folder.

More on Media Queries

Modern web developers are using media queries to target not only smartphones but also to optimize display for other devices, including tablets and netbooks. The Media Queries website at http://mediaqueri.es displays a gallery of sites that demonstrate **responsive web design**, which Ethan Marcotte (http://www.alistapart.com/articles/responsive-web-design) describes as progressively enhancing a web page for different viewing contexts (such as smartphones and tablets) through the use of techniques, including media queries. The screen captures in the gallery at http://mediaqueri.es show web pages at the following screen widths: 320px (smartphone display), 768px (tablet display), 1024px (netbook display), and 1600px (desktop display). Visit Hardboiled CSS3 Media Queries at http://www.stuffandnonsense.co.uk/blog/about/hardboiled_css3_media_queries to explore sample media query code that targets a variety of device types and displays.

Although the examples in this text use separate style sheets for desktop and mobile display, you could include all of the styles in a single style sheet and write media queries directly in the CSS using the `@media` **rule**. The sample code below displays a different background image specifically for smartphone display.

```
@media only screen and (max-device-width: 480px) {
#header { background-image: url(mobile.gif); }
```

FAQ Does using media queries save on bandwidth?

While using media queries to target mobile devices creates a useful and functional web page for your mobile web visitors, the technique does not save bandwidth. While media queries should cause browsers to apply only specific styles, current browsers still download all of the style sheets and resources (such as background images) associated with your web page just in case they are needed. So, it's still a good idea to optimize all of your images to reduce the amount of bandwidth required by mobile devices. Hopefully, future versions of browsers will only download the resources that are initially needed when a page displays.

This section provided an introduction to mobile web design. You created a style sheet that configured a single-column mobile page layout for an existing website. If you are designing a new website, an alternate approach is to design the mobile style sheet first and then develop alternate style sheets for tablet and/or desktop browsers that progressively enhance the design with multiple columns and larger images. You can find out more about this "Mobile First" approach at http://www.lukew.com/ff/entry.asp?933. As mobile devices evolve and usage increases, there are sure to be new developments in this area of web design. If you are interested in exploring this topic further, you'll find the following resources to be helpful:

- Opera Mini: Web Content Authoring Guidelines: http://dev.opera.com/articles/view/opera-mini-web-content-authoring-guidelines
- W3C Mobile Web Best Practices 1.0: http://www.w3.org/TR/mobile-bp

- W3C Mobile Web Initiative: http://www.w3.org/Mobile
- Mobile Web Development: http://www.slideshare.net/estellevw/web-development-for-mobile
- Mobile First Helps with Big Issues: http://www.lukew.com/ff/entry.asp?1117

Checkpoint 2

1. State an advantage of using CSS to style for print.
2. Describe a design consideration when configuring a web page for mobile display.
3. True or False? The `media="handheld"` attribute reliably targets mobile devices.

Chapter Summary

This chapter explored a variety of web development topics, including relative hyperlinks and linking to fragment identifiers, CSS sprites, three-column page layout, styling for print, and styling for mobile devices. Visit the text website at http://www.webdevfoundations.net for examples, the links listed in this chapter, and updated information.

Key Terms

:after
:before
:first-letter
:first-line
content property
CSS sprite
directive
fragment identifier
media attribute
media feature
media query
media type
named fragment
One Web
`page-break-after` property
`page-break-before` property
pseudo-element
responsive web design
sprite
target attribute
viewport meta tag

Review Questions

Multiple Choice

1. Which of the following attributes define a fragment identifier on a page?
   a. id
   b. href
   c. fragment
   d. bookmark

2. How would you link to the named fragment `#jobs` on the page employ.html from the home page of the site?
   a. `<a href="employ.html#jobs">Jobs</a>`
   b. `<a name="employ.html#jobs">Jobs</a>`
   c. `<a link="employ.html#jobs">Jobs</a>`
   d. `<a href="#jobs">Jobs</a>`

3. Which of the following causes an element not to display?
   a. `display: block;`
   b. `display: 0px;`
   c. `display: none;`
   d. `display: 0;`

4. Which attribute below can be applied to an anchor tag to open a link in a new browser window?
   a. window
   b. target
   c. rel
   d. media

5. Which of the following is the attribute used to indicate whether the style sheet is for printing or screen display?
   a. rel
   b. type
   c. media
   d. content

6. Which meta tag is used to configure display for mobile devices?
   a. viewport
   b. handheld
   c. mobile
   d. screen

7. Which pseudo-element can be used to generate content that precedes an element?
   a. `:after`
   b. `:before`
   c. `:content`
   d. `:first-line`

8. Which of the following is a mobile web design best practice?
   a. Configure a multiple-column page layout.
   b. Avoid using lists to organize information.
   c. Configure a single-column page layout.
   d. Embed text in images wherever possible.

9. Which of the following font units is recommended for mobile display?
   a. pt unit
   b. px unit
   c. em unit
   d. cm unit

10. Which of the following is an image file that contains multiple small graphics?
    a. viewport
    b. sprite
    c. background-image
    d. media

Fill in the Blank

11. To indicate that an external style sheet is used to configure printing, code ____________ on the link element.

12. _______________ determine the capability of the mobile device, such as browser viewport dimensions and resolution.

13. The concept of _____________ relates to providing a single resource that is configured for optimal display on multiple types of devices.

14. Provide ____________ navigation near the top of the page when optimizing for mobile display.

15. When using CSS media queries, code the ______ keyword to hide the query from older nonsupporting browsers.

Apply Your Knowledge

1. **Predict the Result.** Draw and write a brief description of the web page that will be created with the following HTML code:

```
<!DOCTYPE html>
<html lang="en">
<head>
<title>Predict the Result</title>
<meta charset="utf-8">
<style>
body { background-color: #eaeaea;
       color: #000;
       font-family: Verdana, Arial, sans-serif; }
#wrapper { width: 80%;
           margin: auto;
           background-color: #d5edb3;}
#nav { float: left;
       width: 150px; }
#center { margin-left: 160px;
          margin-right: 160px;
          background-color: #ffffff;
          padding: 10px; }
#sidebar { float: right;
           width: 150px;
           color: #000000; }
</style>
</head>
<body>
<div id="wrapper">
```

```
<div id="nav">
<ul>
   <li><a href="index.html">Home</a></li>
   <li><a href="products.html">Products</a></li>
   <li><a href="services.html">Services</a></li>
   <li><a href="clients.html">Clients</a></li>
   <li><a href="contact.html">Contact</a></li>
</ul>
</div>
<div id="sidebar">
<h2>Newsletter</h2>
<p>Get monthly updates and free offers. Contact <a
  href="mailto:me@domainname.com">Trillium</a> to sign up for our
  newsletter.</p>
</div>
<div id="center">
<h1>Trillium Media Design</h1>
<p>Our professional staff takes pride in its working relationship
  with our clients by offering personalized services that listen to
  their needs, develop their target areas, and incorporate these
  items into a website that works. </p>
</div>
</div>
</body>
</html>
```

2. **Fill in the Missing Code.** This web page should be configured so that the left navigation column has a light green background color and floats on the left side of the browser window. Instead, the navigation displays with a white background color. CSS properties and values, indicated by "_" (underscore), are missing. Fill in the missing code to correct the error.

```
<!DOCTYPE html>
<html lang="en">
<head>
<title>Fill in the Missing Code</title>
<meta charset="utf-8">
<style>
   body { background-color: #d5edb3;
          color: #000066;
          font-family: Verdana, Arial, sans-serif; }
   #nav { float: left;
          width: 120px; }
   #content { "_": "_";
              background-color: #ffffff;
              color: #000000;
              padding: 20px; }
</style>
</head>
<body>
```

```
<div id="nav">
<ul>
   <li><a href="index.html">Home</a></li>
   <li><a href="products.html">Products</a></li>
   <li><a href="services.html">Services</a></li>
   <li><a href="clients.html">Clients</a></li>
   <li><a href="contact.html">Contact</a></li>
</ul>
</div>
<div id="content">
<h1>Trillium Media Design</h1>
<p>Our professional staff takes pride in its working relationship
with our clients by offering personalized services that listen to
their needs, develop their target areas, and incorporate these
items into a website that works. </p>
</div>
</body>
</html>
```

3. **Find the Error.** The page below is intended for the navigation area to display on the right side of the browser window. What needs to be changed to make this happen?

```
<!DOCTYPE html>
<html lang="en">
<head>
<title>Find the Error</title>
<meta charset="utf-8">
<style>
   body { background-color: #d5edb3;
          color: #000066;
          font-family: Verdana, Arial, sans-serif; }
   #nav { float: left;
          width: 120px; }
   #maincontent { padding: 20px 150px 20px 20px;
                  background-color: #ffffff;
                  color: #000000; }
</style>
</head>
<body>
<div id="nav">
   <ul>
      <li><a href="index.html">Home</a></li>
      <li><a href="services.html">Services</a></li>
      <li><a href="contact.html">Contact</a></li>
   </ul>
</div>
<div id="maincontent">
   <h1>Trillium Media Design</h1>
```

```
   <p>Our professional staff takes pride in its working
relationship with our clients by offering personalized services
that listen to their needs, develop their target areas, and
incorporate these items into a website that works.</p>
   </div>
</body>
</html>
```

Hands-On Exercises

1. Write the HTML to create a fragment identifier at the beginning of a web page designated by "top".
2. Write the HTML to create a hyperlink to the named fragment designated by "top".
3. Write the HTML to associate a web page with an external style sheet named myprint.css to configure a printout.
4. Write the HTML to associate a web page with an external style sheet named mobile.css to configure display for mobile devices.
5. Write the CSS to configure a graphic named mysprite.gif to display as a background image on the left side of a hyperlink. Note that mysprite.gif contains two different images. Configure the image that is located 72 pixels from the top of the sprites.gif graphic to display.
6. **Configure Printing for Hands-On Practice 3.** Configure special printing for the Lighthouse Island Bistro index.html file created in Hands-On Practice 3. This file is in the chapter7/sprites folder in the student files. Modify the web page so that it is associated with an external style sheet called lighthouse.css instead of using embedded styles. Save and test your page. Create a new style sheet called myprint.css, which will prevent the navigation from displaying when the page is printed. Modify the index.html page to be associated with this file. Review the use of the media attribute on the link element. Save all files and test your page. Select File › Print › Preview to test the print styles.
7. **Extending Hands-On Practice 4.** In Hands-On Practice 4, you created the home page for the Door County Wildflowers website. This file is also available in the chapter7/wildflowers folder in the student files. In this exercise, you will create two additional content pages for the Door County Wildflowers site (spring.html and summer.html). Make sure that all CSS is placed in an external style sheet (mywildflower.css). Modify index.html to use this style sheet. The following is some content to include on the new pages:

   Spring Page (spring.html):

   - Use the trillium.jpg image (see the chapter7/starters folder in the student files).
   - Trillium facts: 8–18 inches tall; perennial; native plant; grows in rich, moist deciduous woodlands; white flowers turn pink with age; fruit is a single red berry; protected flower species

   Summer Page (summer.html):

   - Use the yls.jpg image (see the chapter7/starters folder in the student files).
   - Yellow Lady's Slipper facts: 4–24 inches tall; perennial; native plant; grows in wet, shaded deciduous woods, swamps, and bogs; an orchid; official flower of Door County

8. **Modify the Design of Hands-On Practice 4.** Locate the index.html page you created in Hands-On Practice 4. This file is in the chapter7/wildflowers folder in the student files. A web page using jello design has content in the center of the web page with blank margins on either side. Configure the style rules for index.html to display the page in this manner.
9. **Create a Mobile Design for Hands-On Practice 4.** Locate the index.html page you created in Hands-On Practice 4. This file is in the chapter7/wildflowers folder in the student files. Modify the web page so that it links to an external style sheet (flowers.css) instead of using embedded styles. Save and test your page. Create a new style sheet (mymobile.css), which will configure the page for mobile display with a single-column layout (see Figure 14). Modify the index.html page to be associated with this file. Configure the viewport meta tag and CSS media queries for smartphone mobile display. Save all files and test your page with both a desktop browser and a mobile device or emulator.
10. **Practice Validating CSS.** Choose a CSS external style sheet file to validate (perhaps you have created one for your own website). Otherwise, use an external style sheet file that you worked on in this chapter. Use the free W3C CSS Validation Service (http://jigsaw.w3.org/css-validator). If your CSS does not immediately pass the validation test, modify it and test again. Repeat this process until W3C validates your CSS code. Write a one- or two-paragraph summary about the validation process. Answer the following questions: Was it easy to use? Did anything surprise you? Did you encounter a number of errors or just a few? How easy was it to determine how to correct the CSS file? Would you recommend this to other students? Why or why not?

Web Research

As you read about mobile web design best practices in this chapter, you may have noticed some overlap with techniques that provide for accessibility, such as alternate text and use of headings. Explore the Web Content Accessibility and Mobile Web document at http://www.w3.org/WAI/mobile. Explore related links that interest you. Write a one-page, double-spaced summary that describes areas of overlap and how web developers can support both accessibility and mobile devices.

Focus on Web Design

Take a few moments and visit the CSS Zen Garden at http://www.csszengarden.com. Explore the site and note the widely different designs. What thought processes and decisions are needed as a person creates a new design for this site? Visit Sheriar Designs (http://manisheriar.com/blog/anatomy-of-a-design-process) or Behind the Scenes of Garden Party (http://www.bobbyvandersluis.com/articles/gardenparty.php) for a behind-the-scenes look at how web developers have approached this task. Reflect on their stories and suggestions. Write a one-page, double-spaced essay that describes ideas about the design process that you'll be able to use as you begin to design websites for personal or professional use. Be sure to include the URL of the resources that you used.

WEBSITE CASE STUDY

Styling for the Mobile Web

Each of the following case studies configures the website for display on mobile devices.

JavaJam Coffee House

Figure 25 in the chapter "HTML Basics" shows a site map for the JavaJam website. In this case study, you will configure the website to display in mobile devices using the single-column layout shown in Figure 14. You will create a new mobile style sheet; modify the current styles; and update the Home, Menu, and Music pages. When you are finished, the mobile display should be similar to Figure 20 or 21. You have six tasks in this case study:

1. Create a new folder for this JavaJam case study.
2. Modify the Home page to target mobile devices and deliver a mobile style sheet.
3. Modify the Menu page to be consistent with the Home page.
4. Modify the Music page to be consistent with the Home page.
5. Create a new style sheet (javajammobile.css) that configures a single-column page layout.
6. Modify the desktop style sheet (javajam.css).

Figure 20 The new mobile home page displayed on smartphone

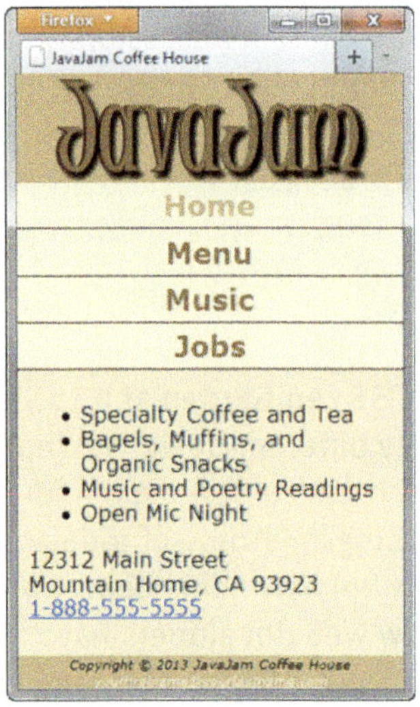

Figure 21 It's possible to approximate the mobile display of a web page using a desktop browser

Hands-On Practice Case Study

Task 1: Create a Folder. Create a folder called javajam7. Copy all the files from the Chapter 6 javajam6 folder into the javajam7 folder. Copy the javalogomobile.gif file from the chapter7/starters folder in the student files.

Task 2: Modify the Home Page. Open index.html in a text editor. Edit the code as follows:

1. Configure a new link element in the head section that associates the web page with javajammobile.css. Use CSS media queries to target smartphone mobile devices.
2. Configure a viewport meta tag that configures the width to the `device-width` and sets the `initial-scale` to 1.0.
3. The JavaJam logo image is too wide for display on a mobile device. If a mobile browser scales down the image, the text may be difficult to read. Your design strategy will be to remove the img tag from the web page and configure "JavaJam Coffee House" within the h1 element. You'll configure this area with CSS in Tasks 5 and 6. The HTML code is

```
<h1 id="header">JavaJam Coffee House</h1>
```

4. The home page displays a phone number in the contact information area. Wouldn't it be handy if a person using a smartphone could click on the phone number to call the coffee house? You can make that happen by using `tel:` in a hyperlink. Configure a hyperlink assigned to an id named `mobile` that contains the phone number as shown below:

```
<a id="mobile" href="tel:888-555-5555">1-888-555-5555</a>
```

But wait a minute, a telephone link could confuse those visiting the site with adesktop browser. Code another phone number directly after the hyperlink. Code a span element assigned to an id named `desktop` around the phone number as shown below:

```
<span id="desktop">1-888-555-5555</span>
```

Don't worry about the two phone numbers that are now on the page. You'll configure CSS in Tasks 5 and 6 to show the appropriate phone number (with or without the telephone link) to your website visitors.

Save the index.html file. It should look similar to the web page shown in Figure 22 when displayed in a desktop browser. Remember that validating your HTML can help you find syntax errors. Test and correct this page before you continue.

Task 3: Modify the Menu Page. Open menu.html in a text editor. Add the link element and viewport meta tag in a manner consistent with the home page. Reconfigure the header area and logo image in the same manner as the home page. Save and test your new menu.html page in a browser. Use the HTML validator to help you find syntax errors.

Task 4: Modify the Music Page. Open music.html in a text editor. Add the link element and viewport meta tag in a manner consistent with the home page. Reconfigure the header area and logo image in the same manner as the home page. Save and test your new music.html page in a browser. Use the HTML validator to help you find syntax errors.

Figure 22 Temporary desktop browser display before new styles are configured

Task 5: Configure the Mobile CSS. Create the mobile style sheet based on the desktop style sheet. Open javajam.css in a text editor. Save the file as javajammobile.css. Edit the style rules as follows:

1. Modify the body element selector. Set the margin and padding to 0. There's no need to display the background image. Set the `background-image` property to the value `none`.
2. Modify the `wrapper` id selector. Set left margin to 0, right margin to 0, width to 100%, and minimum width to 0.
3. Modify the `header` id selector. Set the text alignment to left. Recall that in Tasks 2, 3, and 4 you removed the logo image element from the web page background. Configure the small logo (javalogomobile.gif) as a background image with center `background-position` and no repeats, and height to 80px, which corresponds to the new background image height.
4. Configure an h1 element selector. Set the margin to 0. Recall that the h1 element contains the text "JavaJam Coffee House". Use the `text-indent` property to make this text available to screen readers but not display directly on the web page. The new style rule is

```
h1 { text-indent: -99999px;
     margin: 0; }
```

5. Configure the `nav` id selector. The mobile layout uses a single column. Set the float to `none`, 100% width, 0 top padding, and 0 top margin.
6. Configure the anchor tags in the `nav` id. Modify the style declaration for the `#nav a` selector. Set the display to `block`, padding to 0.2em, font size to 1.3em, font weight to bold. Also configure a 1 pixel bottom border (use #330000 for the border color).
7. Modify the `#nav ul` selector. Set padding and margin to 0.
8. Modify the `content` id selector. Set padding to 0.5em. Set margin to 0.
9. Modify the h2 element selector. Set 0.5em top padding, 0 right padding, 0 bottom padding, and 0.5em left padding. Set the right margin to 0.5em.
10. Modify the `details` class selector. Set left and right padding to 0.

11. Modify the `floatright` class selector. This selector is used by the winding road image on the home page, which will take up too much screen area on mobile devices. Add a new style rule to set display to `none`.
12. Modify the `floatleft` class selector. Set left and right padding to 0.5em.
13. Modify the `footer` id selector. Set top and bottom padding to zero.
14. Remember the telephone number hyperlink you created in Task 2? Configure the CSS for the phone number display as shown below:

```
#mobile { display: inline; }
#desktop { display: none; }
```

Save the javajammobile.css file. Use the CSS validator to help you find syntax errors.

Task 6: Modify the Desktop CSS. Open javajam.css in a text editor. Edit the style rules as follows:

1. Modify the `header` id selector. Set the text alignment to left. Recall that in Tasks 2, 3, and 4 you removed the logo image element from the web page background. Configure the desktop logo (javalogo.gif) as a background image with center `background-position` and no repeats, and height to 100px, which corresponds to the background image height.
2. Configure an h1 element selector. Use the `text-indent` property to make this text available to screen readers but not display directly on the web page. The new style rule is

```
h1 {text-indent: -99999px; }
```

3. Remember the telephone number hyperlink you created in Task 2? Configure the CSS for the phone number display as shown below:

```
#mobile { display: none; }
#desktop { display: inline; }
```

Save the javajam.css file. Use the CSS validator to help you find syntax errors.

Display your pages in a desktop browser. The pages should look the same as they did before you started this case study. Next, test the mobile display. Either publish your pages to the Web and display with a mobile device/emulator OR temporarily modify the href value (change javajam.css to javajammobile.css) on the first link element. Display your page and reduce the width of the browser. Your mobile display should be similar to Figure 20 or 21. Select the hyperlinks to view the Menu and Music pages. They should be similar to the home page. JavaJam is mobile!

Fish Creek Animal Hospital

Figure 29 in the chapter "HTML Basics" shows a site map for the Fish Creek website. In this case study, you configure the website to display in mobile devices using the single-column layout shown in Figure 14. You will create a new mobile style sheet; modify the current styles; and update the Home,

Services, and Ask the Vet pages. When you are finished, the mobile display should be similar to Figure 23 or 24. You have six tasks in this case study:

1. Create a new folder for this Fish Creek case study.
2. Modify the Home page to target mobile devices and deliver a mobile style sheet.
3. Modify the Services page to be consistent with the Home page.
4. Modify the Ask the Vet page to be consistent with the Home page.
5. Create a new style sheet (fishcreekmobile.css), which configures a single-column page layout.
6. Modify the desktop style sheet (fishcreek.css).

Figure 23 The new mobile home page displayed on smartphone

Figure 24 It's possible to approximate the mobile display of a web page using a desktop browser

Hands-On Practice Case Study

Task 1: Create a Folder. Create a folder called fishcreek7. Copy all of the files from the Chapter 6 fishcreek6 folder into the fishcreek7 folder. Copy the bigfish.gif and lilfish.gif files from the chapter7/starters folder in the student files.

Task 2: Modify the Home Page. Open index.html in a text editor. Edit the code as follows:

1. Configure a new link element in the head section that associates the web page with fishcreekmobile.css. Use CSS media queries to target smartphone mobile devices.
2. Configure a viewport meta tag that configures the width to the `device-width` and sets the `initial-scale` to 1.0.
3. The Fish Creek logo image is too wide for display on a mobile device. If a mobile browser scales down the image, the text may be difficult to read. Your design strategy will be to remove the img tag from the web page and configure "Fish Creek Animal

Hospital" text within the h1 element. You'll configure this area with CSS in Tasks 5 and 6. The HTML code is

```
<h1 id="header">Fish Creek Animal Hospital</h1>
```

4. The home page displays a phone number in the contact information area. Wouldn't it be handy if a person using a smartphone could click on the phone number to call the animal hospital? You can make that happen by using `tel:` in a hyperlink. Configure a hyperlink assigned to an id named `mobile` that contains the phone number as shown below:

```
<a id="mobile" href="tel:888-555-5555">1-888-555-5555</a>
```

But wait a minute, a telephone link could confuse those visiting the site with a desktop browser. Code another phone number directly after the hyperlink. Code a span element assigned to an id named `desktop` around the phone number as shown below:

```
<span id="desktop">1-888-555-5555</span>
```

Don't worry about the two phone numbers that are now on the page. You'll configure CSS in Tasks 5 and 6 to show the appropriate phone number (with or without the telephone link) to your website visitors.

Save the index.html file. It should look similar to the web page shown in Figure 25 when displayed in a desktop browser. Remember that validating your HTML can help you find syntax errors. Test and correct this page before you continue.

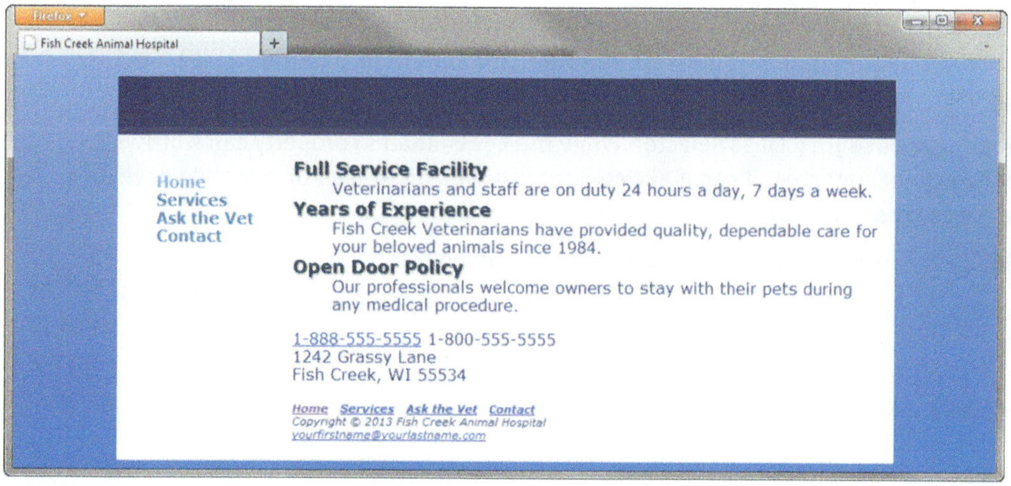

Figure 25 Temporary desktop browser display before new styles are configured

Task 3: Modify the Services Page. Open services.html in a text editor. Add the link element and viewport meta tag in a manner consistent with the home page. Reconfigure the header area and logo image in the same manner as the home page. Save and test your new services.html page in a browser. Use the HTML validator to help you find syntax errors.

Task 4: Modify the Ask the Vet Page. Open askvet.html in a text editor. Add the link element and viewport meta tag in a manner consistent with the home page. Reconfigure the header area and logo image in the same manner as the home page. Save and test your new askvet.html page in a browser. Use the HTML validator to help you find syntax errors.

Task 5: Configure the Mobile CSS. Create the mobile style sheet based on the desktop style sheet. Open fishcreek.css in a text editor. Save the file as fishcreekmobile.css. Edit the style rules as follows:

1. Modify the body element selector. Set margin and padding to 0. Set background color to white (#ffffff). There's no need to display the background image. Set the `background-image` property to the value `none`.
2. Modify the `wrapper` id selector. Set left margin to 0, right margin to 0, width to 100%, and minimum width to 0.
3. Modify the `header` id selector. Recall that in Tasks 2, 3, and 4 you removed the logo image element from the web page background. Configure the small fish logo (lilfish.gif) as a background image with center `background-position` and no repeats, and height to 40px, which corresponds to the new background image height. Configure white text color, 2em font size, 120% line height, and a gray (#CCCCCC) `text-shadow`. Set the padding to 0.2em.
4. Configure the `leftcolumn` id selector. The mobile layout uses a single column. Set the float to `none`, 100% width, 0 top padding, and 0 top margin.
5. Configure the anchor tags in the `leftcolumn` id. Modify the style declaration for the `#leftcolumn a` selector. Set display to `block`, padding to 0.2em, and font size to 1.3em. Also configure a 1 pixel bottom border (use #330000 for the border color).
6. Modify the `#leftcolumn ul` selector. Set padding and margin to 0.
7. Modify the `rightcolumn` id selector. Set 0 top padding, 0 right padding, 0 bottom padding, and 0.4em left padding. Set margin to 0 and font size to 90%.
8. Modify the `category` class selector. While the `text-shadow` property can work well in the logo header area, it can make content text difficult to read on a mobile device. Set `text-shadow` to `none`.
9. Modify the `footer` id selector. Set padding and margin to 0.
10. Configure the navigation links in the footer section to not display. The code is shown below:

```
#footer .nav { display: none; }
```

11. Remember the telephone number hyperlink you created in Task 2? Configure the CSS for the phone number display as shown below:

```
#mobile { display: inline; }
#desktop { display: none; }
```

Save the fishcreekmobile.css file. Use the CSS validator to help you find syntax errors.

Task 6: Modify the Desktop CSS. Open fishcreek.css in a text editor. Edit the style rules as follows:

1. Modify the `header` id selector. Set the text alignment to left. Recall that in Tasks 2, 3, and 4 you removed the logo image element from the web page background. Configure the big fish logo (bigfish.gif) as a background image with center `background-position` and no repeats, and height to 80px, which corresponds to the background image height. Configure white text color, 3em font size, 150% line height, and a gray (#CCCCCC) `text-shadow`.
2. Modify the `wrapper` id selector. Change the minimum width to 960px.
3. Remember the telephone number hyperlink you created in Task 2? Configure the CSS for the phone number display as shown below:

```
#mobile { display: none; }
#desktop { display: inline; }
```

Save the fishcreek.css file. Use the CSS validator to help you find syntax errors.

Display your pages in a desktop browser. The home page should look similar to Figure 26. Next, test the mobile display. Either publish your pages to the Web and display with a mobile device/emulator OR temporarily modify the href value (change fishcreek.css to fishcreekmobile.css) on the first link element. Display your page and reduce the width of the browser. Your mobile display should be similar to Figure 23 or 24. Select the hyperlinks to view the Services and Ask the Vet pages. They should be similar to the home page. Fish Creek is mobile!

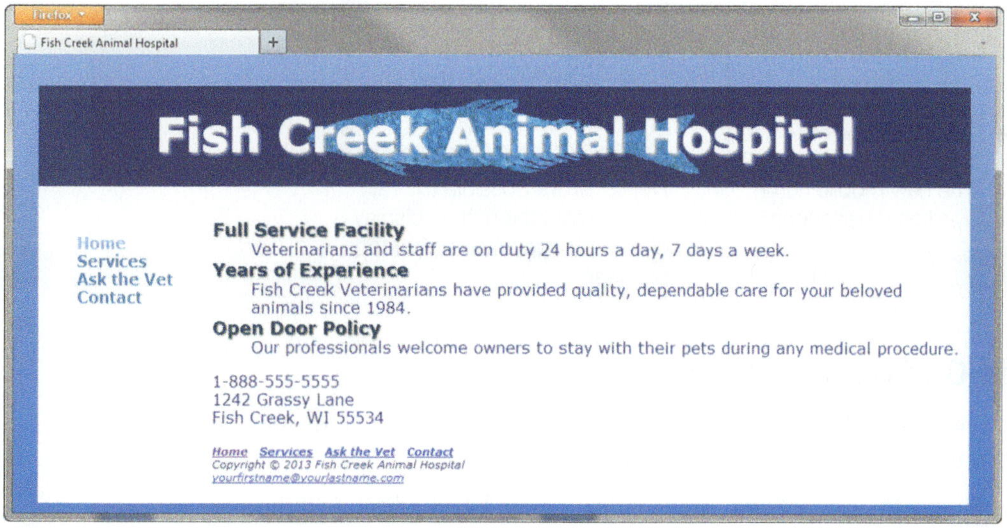

Figure 26 The new header area displayed on a desktop browser

Pacific Trails Resort

Figure 33 in the chapter "HTML Basics" shows a site map for the Pacific Trails website. In this case study, you will configure the website to display on mobile devices using the single-column layout shown in Figure 14. You will create a new mobile style sheet; modify the current styles; and update the Home, Yurts, and Activities pages.

When you have finished, the mobile display should be similar to Figure 27 or 28. You have six tasks in this case study:

1. Create a new folder for this Pacific Trails case study.
2. Modify the Home page to target mobile devices and deliver a mobile style sheet.
3. Modify the Yurts page to be consistent with the Home page.
4. Modify the Activities page to be consistent with the Home page.
5. Create a new style sheet (pacificmobile.css), which will configure a single-column page layout.
6. Modify the desktop style sheet (pacific.css).

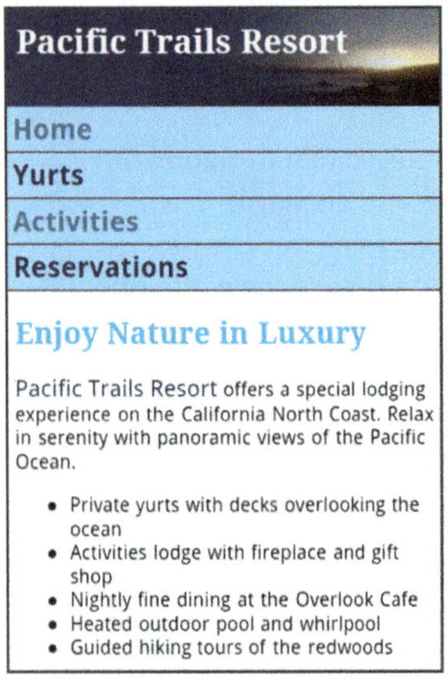

Figure 27 The new mobile home page displayed on smartphone

Figure 28 It's possible to approximate the mobile display of a web page using a desktop browser

Hands-On Practice Case Study

Task 1: Create a Folder. Create a folder called pacific7. Copy all of the files from the Chapter 6 pacific6 folder into the pacific7 folder.

Task 2: Modify the Home Page. Open index.html in a text editor. Edit the code as follows:

1. Configure a new link element in the head section that associates the web page with pacificmobile.css. Use CSS media queries to target smartphone mobile devices. Refer to Section 5.
2. Configure a viewport meta tag that configures the width to the `device-width` and sets the `initial-scale` to 1.0. Refer to Section 5.
3. The home page displays a phone number in the contact information area. Wouldn't it be handy if a person using a smartphone could click on the phone number to call the

resort? You can make that happen by using `tel:` in a hyperlink. Configure a hyperlink assigned to an id named `mobile` that contains the phone number as shown below:

```
<a id="mobile" href="tel:888-555-5555">888-555-5555</a>
```

But wait a minute, a telephone link could confuse those visiting the site with a desktop browser. Code another phone number directly after the hyperlink. Code a span element assigned to an id named `desktop` around the phone number as shown here:

```
<span id="desktop">888-555-5555</span>
```

Don't worry about the two phone numbers that are now on the page. You'll configure CSS in Tasks 5 and 6 to show the appropriate phone number (with or without the telephone link) to your website visitors.

Save the index.html file. Remember that validating your HTML can help you find syntax errors. Test and correct this page before you continue.

Task 3: Modify the Yurts Page. Open yurts.html in a text editor. Add the link element and viewport meta tag in a manner consistent with the home page. Save and test your new yurts.html page in a browser. Use the HTML validator to help you find syntax errors.

Task 4: Modify the Activities Page. Open activities.html in a text editor. Add the link element and viewport meta tag in a manner consistent with the home page. Save and test your new activities.html page in a browser. Use the HTML validator to help you find syntax errors.

Task 5: Configure the Mobile CSS. Create the mobile style sheet based on the desktop style sheet. Open pacific.css in a text editor. Save the file as pacificmobile.css. Edit the style rules as follows:

1. Modify the body element selector. Set the margin and padding to 0. Set text color to black (#000000). There's no need to display the background image. Set the `background-image` property to the value `none`.
2. Modify the `wrapper` id selector. Set left margin to 0, right margin to 0, width to 100%, and minimum width to 0.
3. Configure the h1 element selector. Set margin to 0, font size to 1.5em, and left padding to 0.3em.
4. Configure the `nav` id selector. The mobile layout uses a single column. Set float to `none`, 100% width, 0 padding, and 0 margin.
5. Configure the anchor tags in the `nav` id. Modify the style declaration for the `#nav a` selector. Set display to `block`, padding to 0.2em, and font size to 1.3em. Also configure a 1 pixel bottom border (use #330000 for the border color).
6. Modify the `#nav ul` selector. Set padding to 0.
7. Modify the `content` id selector. Set 0.1em top padding, 0 right padding, 0 bottom padding, and 0.4em left padding. Set margin to 0 and font size to 90%.
8. Modify the `#content img` selector to not display. Add a new style rule to set display to `none`. Set float to `none`. Set `padding-right` to 0.

9. Modify the `#content ul` selector to use `list-style-position: outside;`.
10. Modify the h1 element selector. Set left padding to 0.3em, height to 20 pixels, and line height to 120%.
11. Modify the `footer` id selector. Set padding and margin to 0.
12. Modify the `clear` class. Set top padding to 0.
13. Remember the telephone number hyperlink you created in Task 2? Configure the CSS for the phone number display as shown below:

```
#mobile { display: inline; }
#desktop { display: none; }
```

Save the pacificmobile.css file.

Task 6: Modify the Desktop CSS. Open pacific.css in a text editor. Edit the style rules. Remember the telephone number hyperlink you created in Task 2? Configure the CSS for the phone number display as shown below:

```
#mobile { display: none; }
#desktop { display: inline; }
```

Display your pages in a desktop browser. The pages should look the same as they did before you started this case study. Next, test the mobile display. Either publish your pages to the Web and display with a mobile device/emulator OR temporarily modify the href value (change pacific.css to pacificmobile.css) on the first link element. Display your page and reduce the width of the browser. Your mobile display should be similar to Figure 27 or 28. Select the hyperlinks to view the Yurts and Activities pages. They should be similar to the home page. Pacific Trails is mobile!

Prime Properties

Figure 37 in the chapter "HTML Basics" shows a site map for the Prime Properties website. In this case study, you will configure the website to display on mobile devices using the single-column layout shown in Figure 14. You will create a new mobile style sheet, modify the current styles, and update the Home, Financing, and Listings pages. When you are finished, the mobile display should be similar to Figure 29 or 30. You have six tasks in this case study:

1. Create a new folder for this Prime Properties case study.
2. Modify the Home page to target mobile devices and deliver a mobile style sheet.
3. Modify the Financing page to be consistent with the Home page.
4. Modify the Listings page to be consistent with the Home page.
5. Create a new style sheet (primemobile.css), which will configure a single-column page layout.
6. Modify the desktop style sheet (prime.css).

Figure 29 The new mobile home page displayed on smartphone

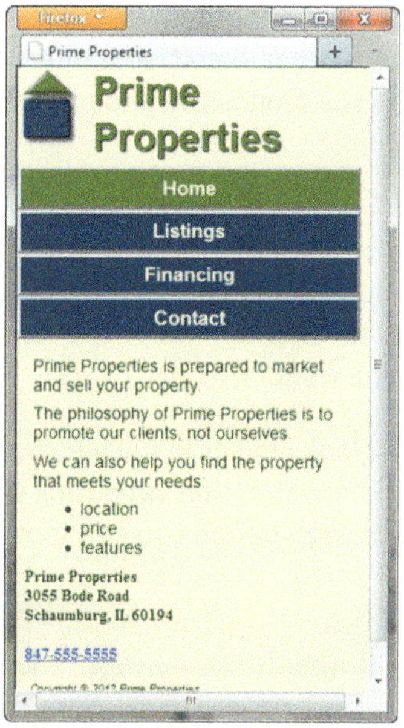

Figure 30 It's possible to approximate the mobile display of a web page using a desktop browser

Hands-On Practice Case Study

Task 1: Create a Folder. Create a folder called prime7. Copy all of the files from the Chapter 6 prime6 folder into the prime7 folder. Copy the primemobile.gif file from the chapter7/starters folder in the student files.

Task 2: Modify the Home Page. Open index.html in a text editor. Edit the code as follows:

1. Configure a new link element in the head section that associates the web page with primemobile.css. Use CSS media queries to target smartphone mobile devices. Refer to Section 5.

2. Configure a viewport meta tag that configures the width to the `device-width` and sets the `initial-scale` to 1.0. Refer to Section 5.

3. The Prime Properties logo image is too wide for display on a mobile device. If a mobile browser scales down the image, the text may be difficult to read. Your design strategy will be to remove the img tag from the web page and configure "Prime Properties" text within the h1 element. You'll configure this area with CSS in Tasks 5 and 6. The HTML code is

```
<h1 id="header">Prime Properties</h1>
```

4. The home page displays a phone number in the contact information area. Wouldn't it be handy if a person using a smartphone could click on the phone number to call the company? You can make that happen by using `tel:` in a hyperlink. Configure a hyperlink assigned to an id named `mobile` that contains the phone number as shown below:

```
<a id="mobile" href="tel:847-555-5555">847-555-5555</a>
```

But wait a minute, a telephone link could confuse those visiting the site with a desktop browser. Code another phone number directly after the hyperlink. Code a span element assigned to an id named `desktop` around the phone number as shown below:

```
<span id="desktop">847-555-5555</span>
```

Don't worry about the two phone numbers that are now on the page. You'll configure CSS in Tasks 5 and 6 to show the appropriate phone number (with or without the telephone link) to your website visitors.

Save the index.html file. It should look similar to the web page shown in Figure 31 when displayed in a desktop browser. Remember that validating your HTML can help you find syntax errors. Test and correct this page before you continue.

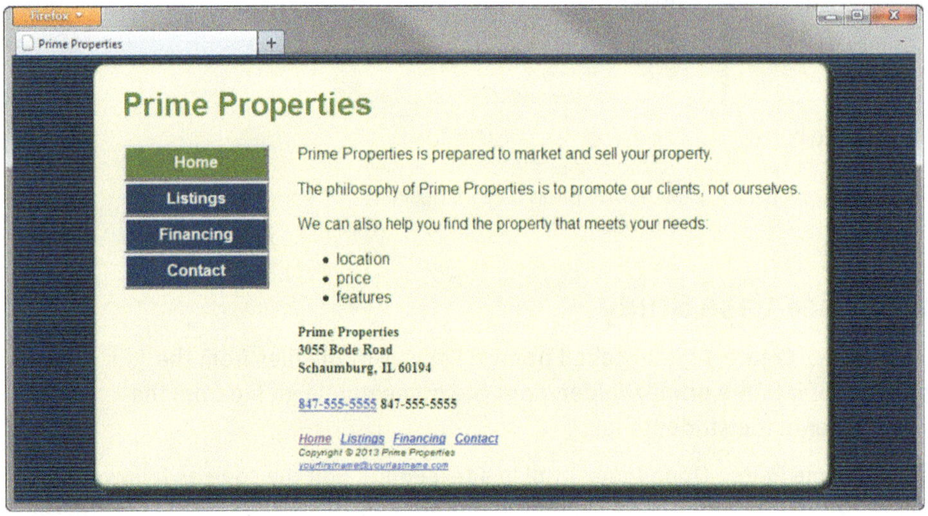

Figure 31 Temporary desktop browser display before new styles are configured

Task 3: Modify the Financing Page. Open financing.html in a text editor. Add the link element and viewport meta tag in a manner consistent with the home page. Reconfigure the header area and logo image in the same manner as the home page. Save and test your new financing.html page in a browser. Use the HTML validator to help you find syntax errors.

Task 4: Modify the Listings Page. Open listings.html in a text editor. Add the link element and viewport meta tag in a manner consistent with the home page. Reconfigure the header area and logo image in the same manner as the home page. Save and test your new listings.html page in a browser. Use the HTML validator to help you find syntax errors.

Task 5: Configure the Mobile CSS. Create the mobile style sheet based on the desktop style sheet. Open prime.css in a text editor. Save the file as primemobile.css. Edit the style rules as follows:

1. Modify the body element selector. Set margin and padding to `0`. There's no need to display the background image. Set the `background-image` property to the value `none`.
2. Modify the `wrapper` id selector. Set left margin to `0`, right margin to `0`, padding to `0`, width to `100%`, and minimum width to `0`.

3. Modify the `header` id selector. Recall that in Tasks 2, 3, and 4 you removed the logo image element from the web page background. Configure the small logo (primemobile.gif) as a background image with no repeats. Set the height to 70 pixels to correspond to the background image. Configure 0.4em bottom padding, no margin, and a 1 pixel `text-shadow` (use #000033 shadow color).
4. Configure an h1 element selector. Set left padding to 2em. The text "Prime Properties" will display in the header area on mobile devices. Set the `text-indent` property to 0.
5. Configure the `left` id selector. The mobile layout uses a single column. Set float to `none`, 100% width, 0 padding, and 0 margin.
6. Configure the anchor tags in the `left` id. Modify the style declaration for the `#left a` selector. Set padding to 0.3em. Set width to 92%.
7. Modify the `#left ul` selector. Set padding and margin to 0.
8. Modify the `right` id selector. Set padding to 0.5em, margin to 0, and font size to 90%.
9. Modify the `floatleft` class selector. Set the float property to `none`. Set right and bottom padding to 0.
10. Modify the h3 element selector. Set top padding to 0. Set margin to 0.
11. Modify the h2 element selector. Set margin to 0.
12. Modify the dd element selector. Set the `line-height` property to 100%.
13. Modify the `footer` id selector. Set top and bottom padding to 0.
14. Configure a new style rule to set a 0.3em margin for p, dt, dd, and ul elements in the content area (`right` id).

```
#right p, #right ul, #right dd, #right dt { margin: 0.3em; }
```

15. Modify the `nav` class (the repeated navigation in the footer section of the page). Use `display: none;` to prevent it from displaying.
16. Remember the telephone number hyperlink you created in Task 2? Configure the CSS for the phone number display as shown below:

```
#mobile { display: inline; }
#desktop { display: none; }
```

Save the primemobile.css file. Use the CSS validator to help you find syntax errors.

Task 6: Modify the Desktop CSS. Open prime.css in a text editor. Edit the style rules as follows:

1. Modify the `header` id selector. Set the text alignment to left. Recall that in Tasks 2, 3, and 4 you removed the logo image element from the web page background. Configure the desktop logo (primelogo.gif) as a background image that does not repeat. Set the height to 100 pixels, which corresponds to the height of the background image.
2. Configure an h1 element selector. Use the `text-indent` property to make this text available to screen readers but not display directly on the web page. The new style rule is

   h1 { text-indent: -99999px; }

3. Remember the telephone number hyperlink you created in Task 2? Configure the CSS for the phone number display as shown below:

```
#mobile { display: none; }
#desktop { display: inline; }
```

Save the prime.css file. Use the CSS validator to help you find syntax errors.

Display your pages in a desktop browser. The pages should look the same as they did before you started this case study. Next, test the mobile display. Either publish your pages to the Web and display with a mobile device/emulator OR temporarily modify the href value (change prime.css to primemobile.css) on the first link element. Display your page and reduce the width of the browser. Your mobile display should be similar to Figure 29 or 30. Select the hyperlinks to view the Listings and Financing pages. They should be similar to the home page. Prime Properties is mobile!

Web Project

In this case study, you configure the website to display in mobile devices using the single-column layout shown in Figure 14. You will create a new mobile style sheet and modify the web pages as indicated in Section 5.

Hands-On Practice Case Study

1. Create a new style sheet for mobile display.
2. Modify each web page to associate with the new style sheet for mobile display.
3. Display your pages in a desktop browser. The pages should look the same as they did before you started this case study. Next, display your pages in a mobile device or emulator. Your pages should be optimized for mobile display.

Answers

Checkpoint 1

1. Organizing a website into folders can help increase productivity by arranging the files into file type (such as images or media), file function (web page or script), and/or website section (products, services, and so on). Using folders and subfolders can be helpful when a project team is developing a large website.
2. The target attribute configures a hyperlink to open the file in a new browser window or tab.
3. Advantages of using CSS sprites on a website include reduced bandwidth (a condensed sprite image typically will have lower file size than multiple individual

images will have), reduced number of http requests by the browser (only one request must be made for the sprite image, instead of multiple requests for individual image files), and quick display of individual images in the sprite, which are configured to display in response to mouse movement.

Checkpoint 2

1. Web page areas can be configured specifically for hard copy. For example, navigation areas can be hidden, page breaks can be configured, and font typeface can configured in serif fonts. In addition, content useful for a person with a hard copy—such as a contact phone number or even a map—can be configured to display and print on the hard copy.
2. A single-column page layout with a small header, key navigation links, content, and page footer works well for mobile device display. Heading elements and lists are well suited for mobile web pages. Eliminate content that is not essential for mobile use. Avoid the use of tables and absolute positioning when configuring pages for mobile display.
3. False. Although well intended, `media="handheld"` is not a reliable way to target mobile devices. CSS media queries are used instead.

Review Questions

1. a
2. a
3. c
4. b
5. c
6. a
7. b
8. c
9. c
10. b
11. `media = "print"`
12. media queries
13. One Web
14. minimal
15. only

Credits

Tables

Chapter Objectives

In this chapter, you will learn how to . . .

- Create a table on a web page
- Apply attributes to format tables, table rows, and table cells
- Increase the accessibility of a table
- Style an HTML table with CSS

While back in the day tables were often used to format the layout of a web page, CSS is the page layout tool of choice for modern web developers. In this chapter, you'll become familiar with coding HTML tables to organize information on a web page.

1 Table Overview

VideoNote
Configure a Table

The purpose of a table is to organize information. In the past, before CSS was well supported by browsers, tables were also used to format web page layouts. An HTML table is composed of rows and columns, like a spreadsheet. Each individual table cell is at the intersection of a specific row and column.

Name	Birthday	Phone
Jack	5/13	857-555-5555
Sparky	11/28	303-555-5555

Figure 1 Table with three rows, three columns, and a border

- Each table begins with a `<table>` tag and ends with a `</table>` tag.
- Each table row begins with a `<tr>` tag and ends with a `</tr>` tag.
- Each cell (table data) begins with a `<td>` tag and ends with a `</td>` tag.
- Table cells can contain text, graphics, and other HTML elements.

Figure 1 shows a sample table with three rows, three columns, and a border. The sample HTML for this table is

```
<table border="1">
  <tr>
    <td>Name</td>
    <td>Birthday</td>
    <td>Phone</td>
  </tr>
  <tr>
    <td>Jack</td>
    <td>5/13</td>
    <td>857-555-5555</td>
  </tr>
  <tr>
    <td>Sparky</td>
    <td>11/28</td>
    <td>303-555-5555</td>
  </tr>
</table>
```

Notice how the table is coded row by row. Also, each row is coded cell by cell. This attention to detail is crucial for the successful use of tables. An example can be found in the student files (chapter8/table1.html).

Table Element

Table elements are block display elements that contain tabular information. The table begins with a **`<table>`** tag and ends with a **`</table>`** tag. See Table 1 for the common attributes of the table element.

Table 1 Commonly used attributes of the table element

Attribute	Value	Purpose
`align`	`left` (default), `right`, `center`	Horizontal alignment of the table (obsolete in HTML5)
`bgcolor`	Valid color value	Background color of the table (obsolete in HTML5)
`border`	0	Default; there is no visible border (obsolete in HTML5)
	1–100	Visible border with pixel width specified
`cellpadding`	Numeric value	Specifies the number of pixels of padding between the content of a table cell and its border (obsolete in HTML5)
`cellspacing`	Numeric value	Specifies the number of pixels of space between the borders of each cell in a table (obsolete in HTML5)
`summary`	Text description	Provides accessibility with a text description that gives an overview of and the context for the information in the table (at the time this was written, the summary attribute was obsolete in HTML5, but efforts were underway for reinstatement; check the text website for further information)
`title`	Text description	A brief text description that provides an overview of the table; may be displayed by some browsers as a tooltip
`width`	Numeric value or percentage	Specifies the width of the table (obsolete in HTML5)

Table Captions

The **caption element** is often used with a data table to describe its contents. The caption begins with a **`<caption>`** tag and ends with a `</caption>` tag. The text contained within the caption element displays on the web page above the table, although you'll see later in the chapter that you can configure the placement with CSS. The table shown in Figure 2 uses the caption element to set the table caption to "Bird Sightings". Notice that the caption element is coded on the line immediately after the opening `<table>` tag. An example can be found in the student files (chapter8/table2.html). The HTML for the table is

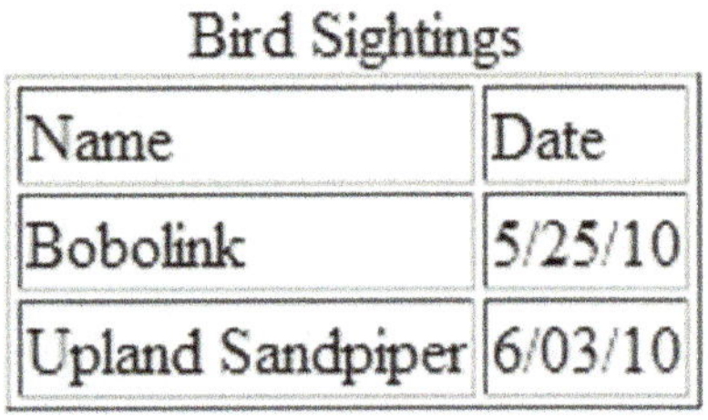

Bird Sightings

Name	Date
Bobolink	5/25/10
Upland Sandpiper	6/03/10

Figure 2 The caption for this table is "Bird Sightings"

```
<table border="1">
<caption>Bird Sightings</caption>
  <tr>
    <td>Name</td>
    <td>Date</td>
  </tr>
  <tr>
    <td>Bobolink</td>
    <td>5/25/10</td>
  </tr>
  <tr>
    <td>Upland Sandpiper</td>
    <td>6/03/10</td>
  </tr>
</table>
```

2 Table Rows, Cells, and Headers

Table Row Element

The **table row element** configures a row within a table on a web page. The table row begins with a <tr> tag and ends with a </tr> tag. See Table 2 for common attributes of the table row element.

Table 2 Commonly used attributes of the table row element

Attribute	Value	Purpose
align	left (default), right, center	Horizontal alignment of the table (obsolete in HTML5)
bgcolor	Valid color value	Background color of the table (obsolete in HTML5)

Table Data Element

The **table data element** configures a cell within a row in a table on a web page. The table cell begins with a <td> tag and ends with a </td> tag. See Table 3 for common attributes of the table data cell element.

Table 3 Commonly used attributes of the table data and table header cell elements

Attribute	Value	Purpose
align	left (default), right, center	Horizontal alignment of the table (obsolete in HTML5)
bgcolor	Valid color value	Background color of the table (obsolete in HTML5)
colspan	Numeric value	The number of columns spanned by a cell
headers	The id value(s) of a column or row header cell	Associates the table data cells with table header cells; may be accessed by screen readers
height	Numeric value or percentage	Height of the cell (obsolete in HTML5)
rowspan	Numeric value	The number of rows spanned by a cell
scope	row, col	The scope of the table header cell contents (row or column); may be accessed by screen readers
valign	top, middle (default), bottom	The vertical alignment of the contents of the cell (obsolete in HTML5)
width	Numeric value or percentage	Width of the cell (obsolete in HTML5)

Name	Birthday	Phone
Jack	5/13	857-555-5555
Sparky	11/28	303-555-5555

Figure 3 Using <th> tags to indicate column headings

Table Header Element

The **table header element** is similar to a table data element and configures a cell within a row in a table on a web page. Its purpose is to configure column and row headings. Text displayed within a table header element is centered and bold. The table header element begins with a **<th>** tag and ends with a **</th>** tag. See Table 3 for common attributes of the table data cell element. Figure 3 shows a table with column headings configured by <th> tags. The HTML for the table shown in Figure 3 is as follows (also see chapter8/table3.html in the student files). Notice that the first row uses <th> instead of <td> tags.

```
<table border="1">
  <tr>
    <th>Name</th>
    <th>Birthday</th>
    <th>Phone</th>
  </tr>
  <tr>
    <td>Jack</td>
    <td>5/13</td>
    <td>857-555-5555</td>
  </tr>
  <tr>
    <td>Sparky</td>
    <td>11/28</td>
    <td>303-555-5555</td>
  </tr>
</table>
```

Hands-On Practice 1

In this Hands-On Practice, you will create a web page similar to Figure 4 that describes two schools you have attended. Use the caption "School History Table." The table has three rows and three columns. The first row will have table header elements with the headings School Attended, Years, and Degree Awarded. You will complete the second and third rows with your own information within table data elements.

To get started, launch a text editor and open chapter2/template.html in the student files. Save the file as mytable.html. Modify the title element. Use table, table row, table header, table data, and caption elements to configure a table similar to Figure 4.

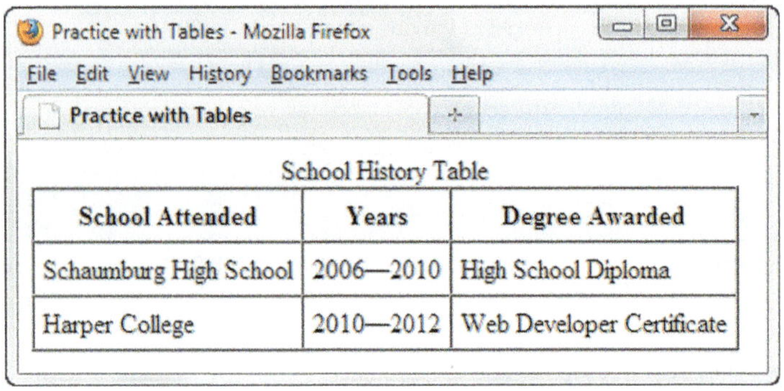

School Attended	Years	Degree Awarded
Schaumburg High School	2006—2010	High School Diploma
Harper College	2010—2012	Web Developer Certificate

Figure 4 School History Table

Hints:

- The table has three rows and three columns.
- To configure a border, use `border="1"` on the `<table>` tag.
- To eliminate space between the cell borders, use `cellspacing="0"` on the `<table>` tag.
- To configure padding within each cell, use `cellpadding="5"` on the `<table>` tag.
- Use the table header element for the cells in the first row.

A sample solution is found in the student files (chapter8/table4.html)[1]. Your HTML5 code will not pass W3C validation testing when using obsolete attributes such as `border`, `cellspacing`, and `cellpadding`. This chapter introduces these obsolete attributes because they are still valid in XHTML and are still used often on the Web. Don't worry, you'll get practice configuring a table with CSS properties later in the chapter.

3 Span Rows and Columns

You can alter the gridlike look of a table by applying the `colspan` and `rowspan` attributes to table data or table header elements. As you get into more complex table configurations like these, be sure to sketch the table on paper before you start typing the HTML.

<table>
<tr><td colspan="2">This spans two columns</td></tr>
<tr><td>Column 1</td><td>Column 2</td></tr>
</table>

Figure 5 Table with a row that spans two columns

The `colspan` Attribute

The `colspan` **attribute** specifies the number of columns that a cell will occupy. Figure 5 shows a table cell that spans two columns.

The HTML for the table is

```
<table border="1">
  <tr>
    <td colspan="2">This spans two columns</td>
  </tr>
  <tr>
    <td>Column 1</td>
    <td>Column 2</td>
  </tr>
</table>
```

<table>
<tr><td rowspan="2">This spans two rows</td><td>Row 1 Column 2</td></tr>
<tr><td>Row 2 Column 2</td></tr>
</table>

Figure 6 Table with a column that spans two rows

The `rowspan` Attribute

The **`rowspan` attribute** specifies the number of rows that a cell will occupy. An example of a table cell that spans two rows is shown in Figure 6.

The HTML for the table is

```
<table border="1">
  <tr>
    <td rowspan="2">This spans two rows</td>
    <td>Row 1 Column 2</td>
  </tr>
  <tr>
    <td>Row 2 Column 2</td>
  </tr>
</table>
```

An example of the tables in Figures 5 and 6 can be found in the student files (chapter8/table5.html).

---

[1]Website Case Study starter files are available for download from Pearson's CS Support website at http://cssupport.pearsoncmg.com.

Hands-On Practice 2

You will practice with the `rowspan` attribute in this Hands-On Practice. To create the web page shown in Figure 7, launch a text editor and open chapter2/template.html in the student files. Save the file as myrowspan.html. Modify the title element. Use table, table row, table head, and table data elements to configure the table.

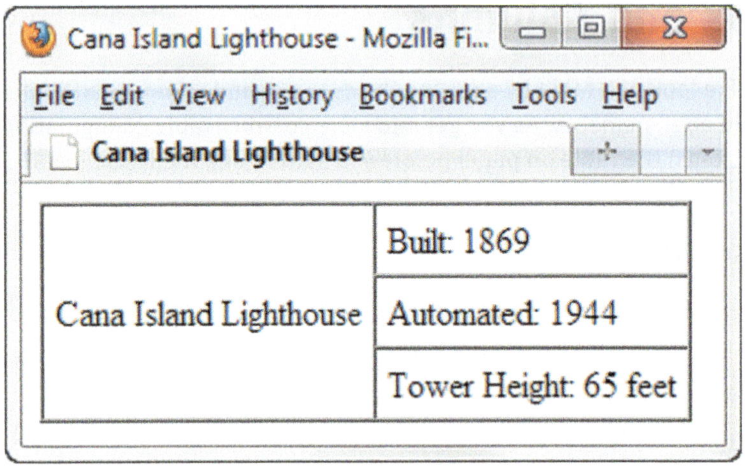

Figure 7 Practice with the `rowspan` attribute

1. Code the opening `<table>` tag. Configure a border with `border="1"`, eliminate space between the cell borders with `cellspacing="0"`, and configure padding within each cell with `cellpadding="5"`.
2. Begin the first row with a `<tr>` tag.
3. The table data cell with "Cana Island Lighthouse" spans three rows. Code a table data element. Use the `rowspan="3"` attribute.
4. Code a table data element that contains the text "Built: 1869".
5. End the first row with a `</tr>` tag.
6. Begin the second row with a `<tr>` tag. This row will only have one table data element because the cell in the first column is already reserved for "Cana Island Lighthouse".
7. Code a table data element that contains the text "Automated: 1944".
8. End the second row with a `</tr>` tag.
9. Begin the third row with a `<tr>` tag. This row will only have one table data element because the cell in the first column is already reserved for "Cana Island Lighthouse".
10. Code a table data element that contains the text "Tower Height: 65 feet".
11. End the third row with a `</tr>` tag.
12. Code the closing `</table>` tag.

Save the file and view it in a browser. A sample solution is found in the student files (chapter8/table6.html). The use of the `border`, `cellpadding`, and `cellspacing` attributes will cause your web page to fail HTML5 validation. However, these attributes are still valid in XHTML syntax. Notice how the "Cana Island Lighthouse" text is vertically aligned in the middle of the cell, which is the default vertical alignment. You can modify the vertical alignment using the `valign` attribute on the td element. While this example uses HTML attributes, the modern approach is to configure tables using CSS, which you'll explore later in this chapter.

4 Configure an Accessible Table

Focus on Accessibility

Tables can be useful to organize information on a web page, but what if you couldn't see the table and were relying on assistive technology like a screen reader to read the table to you? You'd hear the contents of the table just the way it is coded—row by row, cell by cell. This might be difficult to understand. This section discusses coding techniques to improve the accessibility of tables.

Bird Sightings

Name	Date
Bobolink	5/25/10
Upland Sandpiper	6/03/10

Figure 8 This simple data table uses <th> tags and the caption element to provide accessibility

For a simple informational data table like the one shown in Figure 8, the W3C Web Accessibility Initiative (WAI) Web Content Accessibility Guidelines 2.0 (WCAG 2.0) recommend the following:

- Use table header elements (<th> tags) to indicate column or row headings.
- Use the caption element to provide a text title or caption for the table.

An example web page is in the student files (chapter8/table7.html). The HTML is

```
<table border="1">
<caption>Bird Sightings</caption>
  <tr>
    <th>Name</th>
    <th>Date</th>
  </tr>
  <tr>
    <td>Bobolink</td>
    <td>5/25/10</td>
  </tr>
  <tr>
    <td>Upland Sandpiper</td>
    <td>6/03/10</td>
  </tr>
</table>
```

However, for more complex tables, the W3C recommends specifically associating the table data cell values with their corresponding headers. The technique that is recommended uses the id attribute (usually in a <th> tag) to identify a specific header cell and the **headers attribute** in a <td> tag. The code to configure the table in Figure 8 using headers and ids is as follows (also see chapter8/table8.html in the student files):

```
<table border="1">
<caption>Bird Sightings</caption>
  <tr>
    <th id="name">Name</th>
    <th id="date">Date</th>
  </tr>
  <tr>
    <td headers="name">Bobolink</td>
    <td headers="date">5/25/10</td>
  </tr>
```

```
  <tr>
    <td headers="name">Upland Sandpiper</td>
    <td headers="date">6/03/10</td>
  </tr>
</table>
```

Focus on Accessibility

FAQ What about the summary attribute?

At the time this was written, the **summary** attribute was deemed obsolete in HTML5, but efforts were underway for reinstatement. Check the text website for further information. The **summary** attribute was used for many years and is still valid in XHTML. The purpose of coding a **summary** attribute on a table element is to provide an overview of the purpose and organization of the table, setting the context for the information in the table. The information in the **summary** attribute is available to screen readers but does not display in the browser viewport. An example of using the **summary** attribute for the table shown in Figure 8 follows:

```
<table border="1" summary="A list of bird sightings with one bird
listed in each row. The first column contains the name of the bird.
The second column contains the date the bird was identified.">
```

New for the HTML5 specification, W3C suggests the following techniques to provide context for the information in a table: Configure descriptive text in the caption element, provide an explanatory paragraph directly on the web page, or simplify the table.

Focus on Accessibility

FAQ What about the scope attribute?

The **scope** attribute specifies the association of table cells and table row or column headers. It is used to indicate whether a table cell is a header for a column (**scope="col"**) or row (**scope="row"**). An example of the code for the table in Figure 8 that uses this attribute is as follows (also see chapter8/table9.html in the student files):

```
<table border="1">
<caption>Bird Sightings</caption>
   <tr>
      <th scope="col">Name</th>
      <th scope="col">Date</th>
   </tr>
   <tr>
      <td>Bobolink</td>
      <td>5/25/10</td>
   </tr>
   <tr>
      <td>Upland Sandpiper</td>
      <td>6/03/10</td>
   </tr>
</table>
```

As you reviewed the code sample in the previous page, you may have noticed that using the `scope` attribute to provide accessibility requires less coding than implementing the `headers` and `id` attributes. However, because of inconsistent screen reader support of the `scope` attribute, the WCAG 2.0 recommendations for coding techniques encourage the use of `headers` and `id` attributes rather than the `scope` attribute.

Checkpoint 1

1. What is the purpose of using a table on a web page?
2. What is the difference between the `cellpadding` and `cellspacing` table attributes?
3. Describe one coding technique that increases the accessibility of an HTML table.

5 Style a Table with CSS

Back in the day, it was common practice to configure the visual aesthetic of a table with HTML attributes. A more modern approach is to use CSS to style a table. In this section, you'll explore using CSS to style the border, padding, alignment, width, height, vertical alignment, and background of table elements. Table 4 lists corresponding CSS properties with the HTML attributes used to style tables.

Table 4 CSS properties used to style tables

HTML Attribute	CSS Property

`align`	To align a table, configure the `width` and `margin` properties for the table selector. For example, to center a table, use
	`table { width: 75%;`
	`margin: auto; }`
	To align items within table cells, use `text-align`

`width`	`width`
`height`	`height`
`cellpadding`	`padding`
`cellspacing`	`border-spacing`; a numeric value (px or em) or percentage. If you set a value to 0, omit the unit. One numeric value with unit (px or em) configures both horizontal and vertical spacing. Two numeric values with unit (px or em): The first value configures the horizontal spacing and the second value configures the vertical spacing. `border-collapse` configures the border area. The values are `separate` (default) and `collapse`. Use `border-collapse: collapse;` to remove extra space between table and table cell borders.
`bgcolor`	`background-color`
`valign`	`vertical-align` specifies the vertical placement of content. The values are numeric pixel or percentage, `baseline` (default), `sub` (subscript), `super` (superscript), `top`, `text-top`, `middle`, `bottom`, and `text-bottom`
`border`	`border`, `border-style`, `border-spacing`
none	`background-image`
none	`caption-side` specifies the placement of the caption. Values are `top` (default) and `bottom`

Hands-On Practice 3

In this Hands-On Practice, you will code CSS style rules to configure an informational table on a web page. Create a folder named ch8table. Copy the starter.html file from the chapter8 folder to your ch8table folder. We'll use embedded styles for ease of editing and testing your page. Open the starter.html file in a browser. The display should look similar to the one shown in Figure 9.

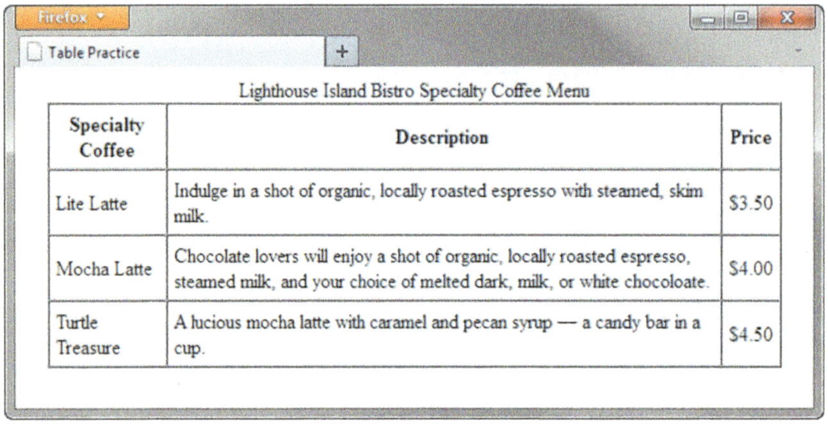

Lighthouse Island Bistro Specialty Coffee Menu

Specialty Coffee	Description	Price
Lite Latte	Indulge in a shot of organic, locally roasted espresso with steamed, skim milk.	$3.50
Mocha Latte	Chocolate lovers will enjoy a shot of organic, locally roasted espresso, steamed milk, and your choice of melted dark, milk, or white chocoloate.	$4.00
Turtle Treasure	A lucious mocha latte with caramel and pecan syrup — a candy bar in a cup.	$4.50

Figure 9 This table is configured with HTML

Launch a text editor and open starter.html from your ch8table folder.

1. Review the web page code and notice the attributes on the `<table>` tag that configure the border, width, alignment, cell padding, and cell spacing of the table. Delete these attributes from the `<table>` tag. You will code embedded CSS style rules to replace their functions.

2. Configure the table element selector. Locate the embedded styles in the head section of the web page. Add a style rule for the table element selector in this area that configures the table to be centered, have a border, and have a width of 600px.

```
table { margin: auto;
        border: 1px solid #5c743d;
        width: 600px; }
```

   Save the file as menu.html. Open your page in a browser. Notice that there is a border surrounding the entire table but not surrounding each table cell.

3. Configure the td and th element selectors. Add a style rule that configures a border and padding. Configure these selectors to use Arial or the default sans-serif font typeface.

```
td, th { border: 1px solid #5c743d;
         padding: 5px;
         font-family: Arial, sans-serif; }
```

   Save the file and open your page in a browser. Each table cell should now be outlined with a border and should display text in a sans-serif font.

4. Notice the empty space between the borders of the table cells. The `border-spacing` **property** can be used to eliminate this space. Add a `border-spacing: 0;` declaration to the table element selector. Save the file and open your page in a browser.

5. Configure the caption to be displayed with Verdana or the default sans-serif font typeface, bold font weight, 1.2em font size, and 5 pixels of bottom padding. Configure a style rule as follows:

```
caption { font-family: Verdana, sans-serif;
          font-weight: bold;
          font-size: 1.2em;
          padding-bottom: 5px; }
```

6. Let's experiment and configure background colors for the rows instead of cell borders. Modify the style rule for the td and th element selectors and remove the border declaration. The new style rule for the cells is

```
td, th { padding: 5px;
         font-family: Arial, sans-serif; }
```

7. Create a new class called `altrow` that sets a background color.

```
.altrow { background-color: #eaeaea; }
```

8. Modify the `<tr>` tags in the HTML. Assign the second and fourth `<tr>` tags to the `altrow` class. Save the file and open your page in a browser. The table area should look similar to the one shown in Figure 10.

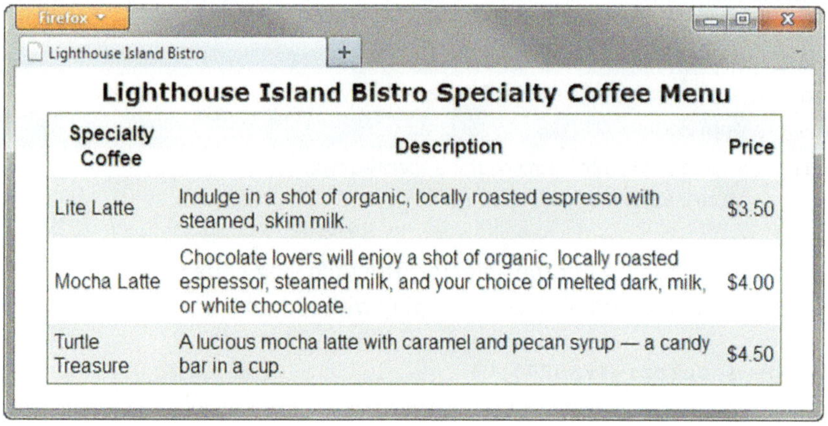

Specialty Coffee	Description	Price
Lite Latte	Indulge in a shot of organic, locally roasted espresso with steamed, skim milk.	$3.50
Mocha Latte	Chocolate lovers will enjoy a shot of organic, locally roasted espressor, steamed milk, and your choice of melted dark, milk, or white chocoloate.	$4.00
Turtle Treasure	A lucious mocha latte with caramel and pecan syrup — a candy bar in a cup.	$4.50

Figure 10 Rows are configured with alternating background colors

Notice how the background color of the alternate rows adds subtle interest to the web page. Compare your work with the sample in the student files (chapter8/menu.html). In this Hands-On Practice, you configured the display of an HTML table using CSS. You'll see this coding technique used increasingly in the future.

FAQ **Is there a way to create a table-like page layout with CSS?**

Yes, if you'd like to explore using CSS to style table-like layouts on web pages, check out the CSS `display` property. The CSS `display` property configures whether and how an element is displayed. You've already worked with `display: none`, `display: block`, and `display: inline`. Internet Explorer 8 was the last major browser to add support for the `display: table` property values. Rachel Andrew's article, "Everything You Know About CSS Is Wrong" (http://www.digital-web.com/articles/everything_you_know_about_CSS_Is_wrong), encourages developers to embrace the `display: table` coding methods. Be aware that this technique is still quite limited. For example, there is no built-in mechanism to emulate the `rowspan` or `colspan` attribute in HTML tables. However, this is in the works with the CSS3 draft recommendation at http://www.w3.org/Style/CSS/current-work, which includes new CSS specifications for working with multicolumn layouts and grid positioning.

6 CSS3 Structural Pseudo-Classes

In the previous section, you configured CSS and applied a class to every other table row to configure alternating background colors, often referred to as "zebra striping." You may have found this to be a bit inconvenient and wondered if there was a more efficient method. Well, there is! CSS3 **structural pseudo-class selectors** allow you to select and apply classes to elements based on their position in the structure of the document, such as every other row. CSS3 pseudo-classes are supported by current versions of Firefox, Opera, Chrome, Safari, and Internet Explorer 9. Earlier versions of Internet Explorer do not support CSS3 pseudo-classes, so consider using this coding technique only for enhancements to a web page. Table 5 lists common CSS3 structural pseudo-class selectors and their purpose.

Table 5 Common CSS3 structural pseudo-classes

Pseudo-Class	Purpose
`:first-of-type`	Applies to the first element of the specified type
`:first-child`	Applies to the first child of an element (CSS2 selector)
`:last-of-type`	Applies to the last element of the specified type
`:last-child`	Applies to the last child of an element
`:nth-of-type(n)`	Applies to the "nth" element of the specified type Values: a number, `odd`, or `even`

To apply a pseudo-class, write it after the selector. The following code sample will configure the first item in an unordered list to display with red text.

```
li:first-of-type { color: #FF0000; }
```

Hands-On Practice 4

In this Hands-On Practice, you will rework the table you configured in Hands-On Practice 3 to use CSS3 structural pseudo-class selectors to configure color.

1. Launch a text editor and open menu.html in your ch8table folder (it can also be found as chapter8/menu.html in the student files). Save the file as menu2.html.

2. View the source code and notice that the second and fourth tr elements are assigned to the `altrow` class. You won't need this class assignment when using CSS3 structural pseudo-class selectors. Delete `class="altrow"` from the tr elements.

3. Examine the embedded CSS and locate the `altrow` class. Change the selector to use a structural pseudo-class that will apply the style to the even-numbered table rows. Replace `.altrow` with `tr:nth-of-type (even)` as shown in the following CSS declaration:

```
tr:nth-of-type(even) { background-color: #eaeaea; }
```

4. Save the file and open your page in a browser. The table area should look similar to the one shown in Figure 10 if you are using a modern browser that supports CSS3 structural pseudo-classes.

5. Let's configure the first row to have a dark-gray background (#666) and light-gray text (#eaeaea) with the `:first-of-type` structural pseudo-class. Add the following to the embedded CSS:

```
tr:first-of-type { background-color: #666;
                   color: #eaeaea; }
```

6. Save the file and open your page in a browser. The table area should look similar to the one shown in Figure 11 if you are using a modern browser that supports CSS3 structural pseudo-classes. A sample solution is available in the student files (chapter8/menucss.html).

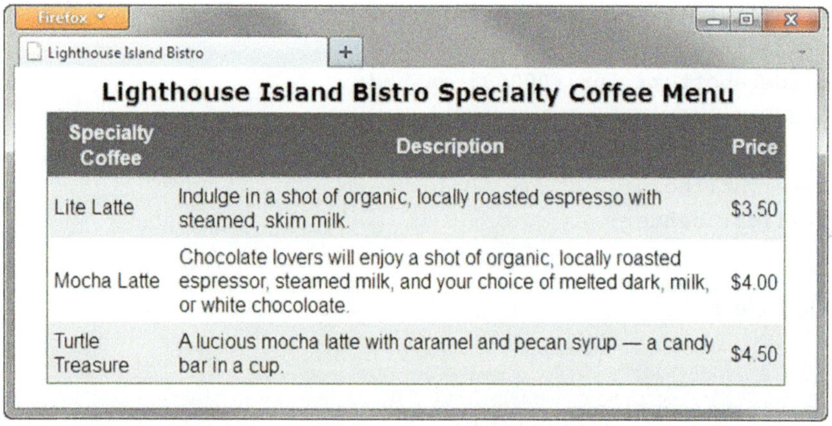

Figure 11 CSS3 pseudo-class selectors style the table rows

CSS structural pseudo-classes are convenient to use, but be aware that Internet Explorer 8 and earlier versions do not support this technology. Although browser support will increase in the future, today it's best to apply these pseudo-classes with progressive enhancement in mind.

7 Configure Table Sections

There are a lot of configuration options for coding tables. Table rows can be put together into three types of groups: table head with `<thead>`, table body with `<tbody>`, and table footer with `<tfoot>`.

These groups can be useful when you need to configure the areas in the table in different ways, using either attributes or CSS. The `<tbody>` tag is required if you configure a `<thead>` or `<tfoot>` area, although you can omit either the table head or table footer if you like. When you use table row groups, the `<thead>` and `<tfoot>` sections must be coded *before* the `<tbody>` section to pass W3C XHTML validation. The code sample in this section uses HTML5 syntax with the `<tfoot>` coded after the `<tbody>`, which is more intuitive.

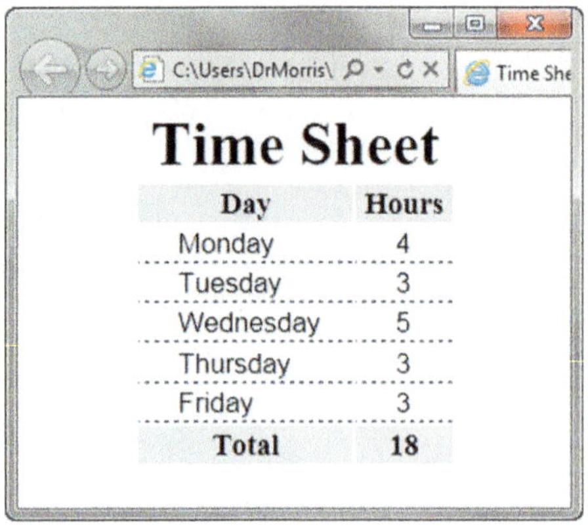

Figure 12 CSS configures the thead, tbody, and tfoot element selectors

The following code sample (see chapter8/tfoot.html in the student files) configures the table shown in Figure 12 and demonstrates the use of CSS to configure a table head, table body, and table footer with different styles.

The CSS styles a centered 200-pixel-wide table with a caption that is rendered in large, bold font; a table head section with a light-gray (#eaeaea) background color; a table body section styled with slightly smaller text (.90em) using Arial or sans-serif font; table body td element selectors set to display with some left padding and a dashed bottom border; and a table footer section that has centered, bold text and a light-gray background color (#eaeaea). The CSS code is

```
table { width: 200px;
        margin: auto; }
caption { font-size: 2em;
          font-weight: bold; }
thead { background-color: #eaeaea; }
tbody { font-family: Arial, sans-serif;
        font-size: .90em; }
tbody td { border-bottom: 1px #000033 dashed;
           padding-left: 25px; }
tfoot { background-color: #eaeaea;
        font-weight: bold;
        text-align: center; }
```

The HTML for the table is

```
<table>
<caption>Time Sheet</caption>
   <thead>
      <tr>
         <th id="day">Day</th>
         <th id="hours">Hours</th>
      </tr>
   </thead>
   <tbody>
      <tr>
         <td headers="day">Monday</td>
         <td headers="hours">4</td>
      </tr>
      <tr>
         <td headers="day">Tuesday</td>
         <td headers="hours">3</td>
      </tr>
```

```
        <tr>
            <td headers="day">Wednesday</td>
            <td headers="hours">5</td>
        </tr>
        <tr>
            <td headers="day">Thursday</td>
            <td headers="hours">3</td>
        </tr>
        <tr>
            <td headers="day">Friday</td>
            <td headers="hours">3</td>
        </tr>
    </tbody>
    <tfoot>
        <tr>
            <td headers="day">Total</td>
            <td headers="hours">18</td>
        </tr>
    </tfoot>
</table>
```

This example demonstrates the power of CSS in styling documents. The `<td>` tags within each table row group element selector (thead, tbody, and tfoot) inherited the font styles configured for their parent group element selector. Notice how a contextual selector configures the padding and border only for `<td>` tags that are contained within (actually, "children of") the `<tbody>` element. Sample code is located in the student files (chapter8/tfoot.html). Take a few moments to explore the web page code and open the page in a browser.

Checkpoint 2

1. Describe a reason to configure a table with CSS properties instead of HTML attributes.
2. List three elements that are used to group table rows.

Chapter Summary

This chapter introduces both the HTML techniques used to code tables to organize information and the CSS properties that configure the display of tables on web pages. Visit the text website at http://www.webdevfoundations.net for examples, the links listed in this chapter, and updated information.

Key Terms

`<caption>`
`<table>`
`<tbody>`
`<td>`
`<tfoot>`
`<th>`
`<thead>`
`<tr>`
`:first-child`
`:first-of-type`
`:last-child`
`:last-of-type`
`:nth of type`
align attribute
border attribute
border-collapse property
border-spacing property
caption-side property
cell
cellpadding attribute
cellspacing attribute
colspan attribute
headers attribute
rowspan attribute
scope attribute
summary attribute
title attribute
vertical-align property
valign attribute

Review Questions

Multiple Choice

1. Which HTML attribute specifies the distance between the edges of each cell?
   a. cellpad
   b. cellpadding
   c. cellspacing
   d. cellborder

2. Which HTML attribute specifies the distance between the cell text and the cell border?
   a. cellpad
   b. cellpadding
   c. cellspacing
   d. cellborder

3. Which HTML tag pair is used to group rows in the footer of a table?
   a. <footer> </footer>
   b. <tr> </tr>
   c. <tfoot> </tfoot>
   d. <td> </td>

4. Which HTML element uses a border attribute to display a table with a border?
   a. <td>
   b. <tr>
   c. <table>
   d. <tableborder>

5. Which HTML tag pair is used to specify table headings?
   a. <td> </td>
   b. <th> </th>
   c. <head> </head>
   d. <tr> </tr>

6. Which HTML attribute associates a table data cell with a table header cell?
   a. head
   b. headers
   c. align
   d. th

7. Which HTML tag pair is used to begin and end a table row?
   a. <td> </td>
   b. <tbody> </tbody>
   c. <table> </table>
   d. <tr> </tr>

8. Which of the following is the intended use of tables on web pages?
   a. configuring the layout of an entire page
   b. organizing information
   c. forming hyperlinks
   d. configuring a résumé

9. Which CSS property specifies the background color of a table?
   a. `background`
   b. `bgcolor`
   c. `background-color`
   d. `table-color`
10. Which CSS pseudo-class applies to the first element of a specified type?
    a. `:first-of-type`
    b. `:first-type`
    c. `:first-child`
    d. `:first`

Fill in the Blank

11. The CSS ____________________ property can be used to configure the color and width of a table border.
12. The ____________________ attribute specifies the vertical alignment of the contents of a cell in a table.
13. Use the _____________ attribute to configure a table cell to occupy more than one row in the table.
14. ____________________ is an attribute of the table element that provides accessibility.
15. Use the ___________________ element to provide a brief description of a table that displays on the web page.

Apply Your Knowledge

1. **Predict the Result.** Draw and write a brief description of the web page that will be created with the following HTML code:

```
<!DOCTYPE html>
<html lang="en">
<head>
<title>Predict the Result</title>
<meta charset="utf-8">
</head>
<body>
<table>
   <tr>
      <th>Year</th>
      <th>School</th>
      <th>Major</th>
   </tr>
   <tr>
      <td>2006-2010</td>
      <td>Schaumburg High School</td>
      <td>College Prep</td>
   </tr>
   <tr>
      <td>2010-2012</td>
      <td>Harper College</td>
      <td>Web Development Associates Degree</td>
   </tr>
</table>
</body>
</html>
```

2. **Fill in the Missing Code.** This web page should have a table with a background color of #cccccc and a border. Some CSS properties and values, indicated by "_", are missing. Fill in the missing code.

```
<!DOCTYPE html>
<html lang="en">
<head>
<title>CircleSoft Web Design</title>
<meta charset="utf-8">
<style>
table { "_":"_";
        "_":"_"; }
</style>
</head>
<body>
<h1>CircleSoft Web Design</h1>
<table>
<caption>Contact Information</caption>
   <tr>
      <th>Name</th>
      <th>Phone</th>
   </tr>
   <tr>
      <td>Mike Circle</td>
      <td>920-555-5555</td>
   </tr>
</table>
</body>
</html>
```

3. **Find the Error.** Why doesn't the table information display in the order it was coded?

```
<!DOCTYPE html>
<html lang="en">
<head>
<title>CircleSoft Web Design</title>
<meta charset="utf-8">
</head>
<body>
<h1>CircleSoft Web Design</h1>
<table>
<caption>Contact Information</caption>
<tr>
   <th>Name</th>
   <th>Phone</th>
</tr>
<tr>
   <tr>Mike Circle</td>
   <td>920-555-5555</td>
</tr>
</table>
</body>
</html>
```

Hands-On Exercises

1. Write the HTML for a two-column table that contains the names of your friends and their birthdays. The first row of the table should span two columns and contain the following heading: Birthday List. Include at least two people in your table.
2. Write the HTML for a three-column table to describe the courses you are taking this semester. The columns should contain the course number, course name, and instructor name. The first row of the table should use `th` tags and contain descriptive headings for the columns. Use the table row grouping tags `<thead>` and `<tbody>` in your table.
3. Write the HTML for a table with three rows, two columns, and no border. The cell in the first column of each row will contain one of the following terms: HTML5, XML, and XHTML. The corresponding cell in the second column of each row will contain a definition of the term. Configure alternating rows to use the background color #CCCCCC.
4. Use CSS to configure a table that has a border around both the entire table and the table cells. Write the HTML to create a table with three rows and two columns. The cell in the first column of each row will contain one of the following terms: HTML, XML, and XHTML. The corresponding cell in the second column of each row will contain a definition of the term.
5. Modify the table you created in Hands-On Exercise 1 to be centered on the page, use a background color of #CCCC99, and display text in Arial or the browser default sans-serif font. Configure this table using CSS instead of obsolete HTML attributes. Place an e-mail link to yourself on the web page. Save the file as mytable.html.
6. Create a web page about your favorite sports team with a two-column table that lists the positions and starting players. Use embedded CSS to style the table border, background color, and center the table on the web page. Place an e-mail link to yourself on the web page. Save the file as sport8.html.
7. Create a web page about your favorite movie that uses a two-column table containing details about the movie. Use CSS to style the table border and background color. Include the following in the table:
   - Title of the movie
   - Director or producer
   - Leading actor
   - Leading actress
   - Rating (G, PG, PG-13, R, NC-17, NR)
   - A brief description of the movie
   - An absolute link to a review about the movie

   Place an e-mail link to yourself on the web page. Save the page as movie8.html.
8. Create a web page about your favorite music CD that uses a four-column table. The column headings should be as follows:
   - **Group:** Place the name of the group and the names of its principal members in this column.
   - **Tracks:** List the title of each music track or song.
   - **Year:** List the year the CD was recorded.
   - **Links:** Place at least two absolute links to sites about the group in this column.

   Include an e-mail link to yourself on the web page. Save the page as band8.html.

9. Create a web page about your favorite recipe. Organize the ingredients and directions in a single table. Use two columns for the ingredients. Use a row that spans two columns to contain the instructions for creating your culinary delight. Place an e-mail link to yourself on the web page. Save the page as recipe8.html.

Web Research

Search the Web and find a web page configured with one or more HTML tables. Print the browser view of the page. Print out the source code of the web page. On the printout, highlight or circle the tags related to tables. On a separate sheet of paper, create some HTML notes by listing the tags and attributes related to tables found on your sample page, along with a brief description of their purpose. Hand in the browser view of the page, source code printout, and your HTML notes page to your instructor.

Focus on Web Design

Good artists view and analyze many paintings. Good writers read and evaluate many books. Similarly, good web designers view and scrutinize many web pages. Surf the Web and find two web pages, one that is appealing to you and one that is unappealing to you. Print out each page. Create a web page that answers the following questions for each of your examples:

a. What is the URL of the website?

b. Does this page use tables? If so, for what purpose (page layout, organization of information, or another reason)?

c. Does this page use CSS? If so, for what purpose (page layout, text and color configuration, or another reason)?

d. Is this page appealing or unappealing? List three reasons for your answer.

e. If this page is unappealing, what would you do to improve it?

WEB SITE CASE STUDY

Using Tables

This chapter incorporates an HTML table in four websites.

JavaJam Coffee House

Figure 25 in the chapter "HTML Basics" shows a site map for JavaJam. Use the JavaJam website in the chapter entitled "Page Layout" as a starting point. You will modify the

Menu page (menu.html) to display information in an HTML table. You will use CSS to style the table. You have three tasks in this case study:

1. Create a new folder for this JavaJam case study.
2. Modify the style sheet (javajam.css) to configure style rules for the new table.
3. Modify the Menu page to use a table to display information as shown in Figure 13.

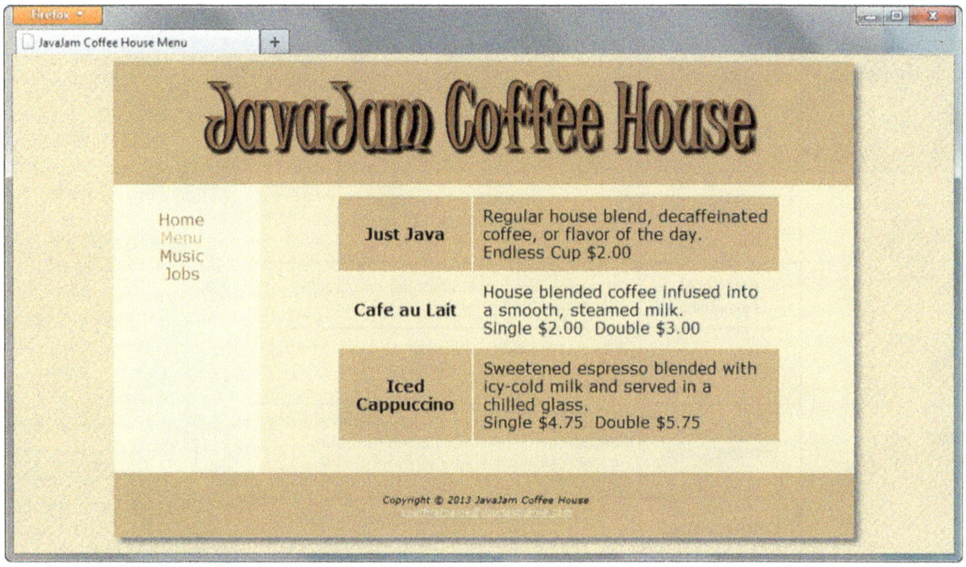

Figure 13 Menu page with a table

Hands-On Practice Case Study

Task 1: Create a Folder. Create a folder called javajam8. Copy all the files from the Chapter 6 javajam6 folder into the javajam8 folder.

Task 2: Configure the CSS. Modify the external style sheet (javajam.css). Open javajam.css in a text editor. Review Figure 13 and note the menu descriptions, which are coded in an HTML table. Add style rules to the javajam.css external style sheet to configure a table that is centered, has td and th selectors with 10 pixels of padding, and displays a background color of #ccaa66 in alternate rows (use a class or the `:nth-of-type` pseudo-class to configure odd table rows). Save the javajam.css file.

Task 3: Modify the Menu Page. Open menu.html in a text editor. The menu descriptions are configured with a description list. Replace the description list with a table that has three rows and two columns. Use th and td elements where appropriate. Save your page and test it in a browser. If the page does not display as you intended, review your work, validate the CSS, validate the HTML, modify as needed, and test again.

Fish Creek Animal Hospital

Figure 29 in the chapter "HTML Basics" shows a site map for Fish Creek. Use the JavaJam website in the chapter entitled "Page Layout" as a starting point.
You will modify the Services page (services.html) to display

information in an HTML table. You will use CSS to style the table. You have three tasks in this case study:

1. Create a new folder for this Fish Creek case study.
2. Modify the style sheet (fishcreek.css) to configure style rules for the new table.
3. Modify the Services page to use a table to display information as shown in Figure 14.

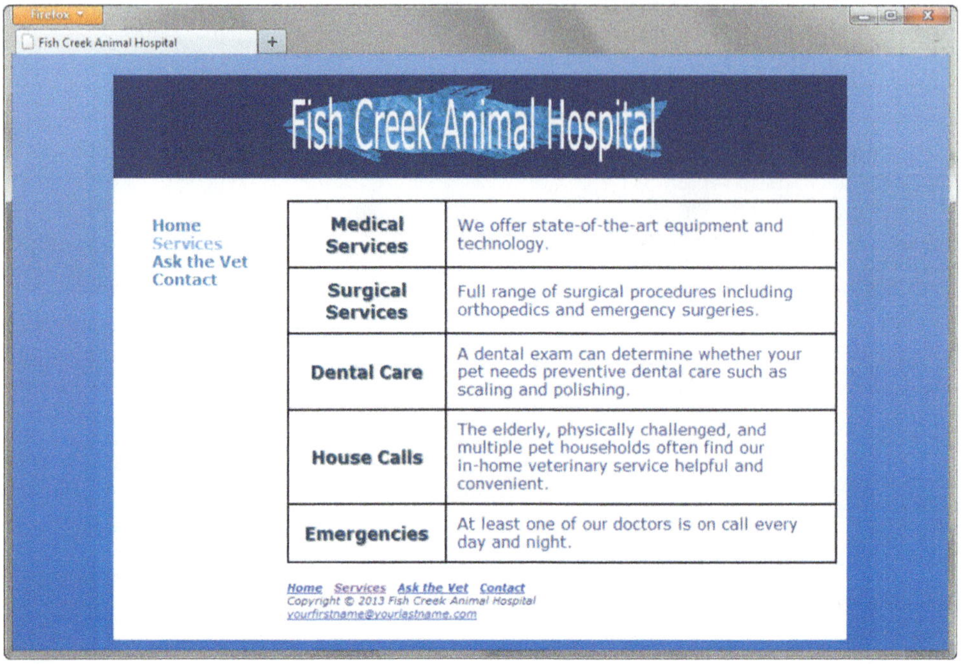

Figure 14 Services page with a table

Hands-On Practice Case Study

Task 1: Create a Folder. Create a folder called fishcreek8. Copy all of the files from the Chapter 6 fishcreek6 folder into the fishcreek8 folder.

Task 2: Configure the CSS. Modify the external style sheet (fishcreek.css). Open fishcreek.css in a text editor. Review Figure 14 and note the services descriptions, which are coded in an HTML table. Add style rules to the fishcreek.css external style sheet as indicated:

1. Configure a table that has a solid, dark-blue, 2 pixel border.
2. Configure the borders in the table to collapse.
3. Configure td and th element selectors with 10 pixels of padding and a solid, dark-blue, 1 pixel border.

Save the fishcreek.css file.

Task 3: Modify the Services Page. Open services.html in a text editor. The services descriptions are configured with an unordered list. Replace the unordered list with a table that has five rows and two columns. Use th and td elements where appropriate. *Hint*: Assign the th element to the category class. Save your page and test it in a browser. If the page does not display as you intended, review your work, validate the CSS, validate the HTML, modify as needed, and test again.

Pacific Trails Resort

Figure 33 in the chapter "HTML Basics" shows a site map for Pacific Trails. Use the Pacific Trails Resort website in the chapter entitled "Page Layout" as a starting point. You will modify the Yurts page (yurts.html) to display additional information in an HTML table. You will use CSS to style the table. You have three tasks in this case study:

1. Create a new folder for this Pacific Trails case study.
2. Modify the style sheet (pacific.css) to configure style rules for the new table.
3. Modify the Yurts page to use a table to display information as shown in Figure 15.

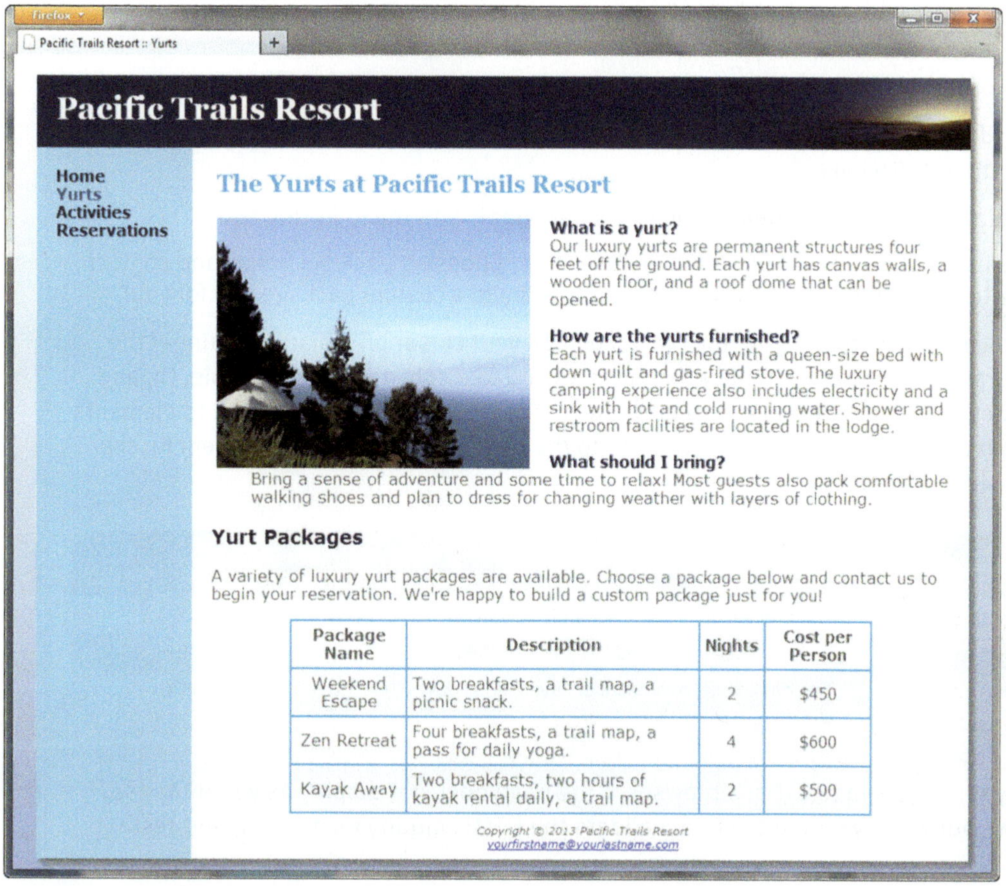

Figure 15 Yurts page with a table

Hands-On Practice Case Study

Task 1: Create a Folder. Create a folder called pacific8. Copy all the files from the Chapter 6 pacific6 folder into the pacific8 folder.

Task 2: Configure the CSS. Modify the external style sheet (pacific.css). Open pacific.css in a text editor. Add styles to configure the table on the Yurts page as shown in Figure 15.

1. Configure the table. Code a new style rule for the table element selector that configures a centered table with a 1 pixel solid-blue border (#3399cc), 600 pixel width, and no cell spacing (use `border-spacing: 0;`).

2. Configure the table cells. Code a new style rule for the td and th element selectors that configure 5 pixels of padding and a 1 pixel solid-blue border (#3399cc).
3. Center the td content. Code a new style rule for the td element selector that centers text (use `text-align: center;`).
4. Configure the `.text` class. Notice that the content in the table data cells that contain the text description is not centered. Code a new style rule for a class named `text` that will override the td style rule and left-align the text (use `text-align: left;`).
5. Configure alternate-row background color. The table looks more appealing if the rows have alternate background colors, but it is still readable without them. Apply the `:nth-of-type` CSS3 pseudo-class to configure the odd table rows with a light-blue background color (#F5FAFC).
6. Save the pacific.css file.

Task 3: Modify the Yurts Page. Open yurts.html in a text editor.

1. Add a blank line above the footer div. Configure an h3 element with the following text: "Yurt Packages".
2. Below the new h3 element, configure a paragraph with the following text:

   A variety of luxury yurt packages are available. Choose a package below and contact us to begin your reservation. We're happy to build a custom package just for you!
3. You are ready to configure the table. Position your cursor on a blank line under the paragraph and code a table with four rows and four columns. Use the table, th, and td elements. Use the summary attribute on the table element. Assign the td elements that contain the detailed descriptions to the class named `text`. The content for the table is as follows.

Package Name	Description	Nights	Cost per Person
Weekend Escape	Two breakfasts, a trail map, a picnic snack	2	$450
Zen Retreat	Four breakfasts, a trail map, a pass for daily yoga	4	$600
Kayak Away	Two breakfasts, two hours of kayak rental daily, a trail map	2	$500

Save your page and test it in a browser. If the page does not display as you intended, review your work, validate the CSS, validate the HTML, modify as needed, and test again.

Prime Properties

Figure 37 in the chapter "HTML Basics" shows a site map for Prime Properties. Use the Prime Properties website in the chapter entitled "Page Layout" as a starting point. You will modify the Listings page (listings.html) to display the information in an HTML table. You will use CSS to style the table. You have three tasks in this case study:

1. Create a new folder for this Prime Properties case study.
2. Modify the style sheet (prime.css) to configure style rules for the new table.
3. Modify the Listings page to use a table to display information as shown in Figure 16.

Figure 16 Listings page with tables

Hands-On Practice Case Study

Task 1: Create a Folder. Create a folder called prime8. Copy all the files from the Chapter 6 prime6 folder into the prime8 folder.

Task 2: Configure the CSS. Modify the external style sheet (prime.css). Open prime.css in a text editor. Review Figure 16 and note the property listing information, which is coded in two HTML tables. Add style rules to the prime.css external style sheet to configure the following:

1. A table with a background color (#ffffff), 80% width, no border, and a 10 pixel bottom margin
2. A th element selector with left-aligned text in a green color (#006600)
3. A td element selector that is aligned vertically to the top and has 10 pixels of padding
4. No top margin for the paragraphs and h3 elements in the table

Save the prime.css file.

Task 3: Modify the Listings Page. Open listings.html in a text editor. The listings information currently uses the <h3>, image, paragraph, and unordered lists elements. You will reconfigure this area with two tables—one for each real estate listing. Each table will have two rows. Refer to Figure 16. The first row in each table consists of one table cell which spans two columns that contain the real estate listing name. The second row in each table consists of two table cells. The first table cell in this row contains the image (remove the `floatleft` class from the image element). The second table cell contains the paragraph and unordered list.

Save your page and test it in a browser. If the page does not display as you intended, review your work, validate the CSS, validate the HTML, modify as needed, and test again.

Web Project

See the Web Project case study in the chapters entitled "Web Design" and "Page Layout" for an introduction to the web project. You will modify the design of one of the pages to display information in an HTML table. Use CSS to style the table.

Hands-On Practice Case Study

1. Choose one of your project web pages to modify. Sketch a design of the table you plan to create. Decide on borders, background color, padding, alignment, and so on.
2. Modify your project's external CSS file (project.css) to configure the table (and table cells) as needed.
3. Update your chosen web page and add the HTML code for a table.

Save and test the page. Modify both the web page and the project.css file as needed. Test and modify until you have achieved the look you want.

Answers

Checkpoint 1

1. Tables are often used to organize tabular information on a web page.
2. The cellspacing attribute configures the amount of empty space between the cells in a table. The cellpadding attribute configures the amount of empty space between the information contained within the cells and the edges of the cells.
3. Among the various coding techniques that improve the accessibility of a table are the summary attribute, the title attribute, and configuring headers for columns or rows.

Checkpoint 2

1. Using CSS properties instead of HTML attributes to configure table characteristics provides for flexibility and easier maintenance.
2. The thead, tbody, and tfoot elements are used to group table rows.

Review Questions

1. c
2. b
3. c
4. c
5. b
6. b
7. d
8. b
9. c
10. a
11. border
12. valign
13. rowspan
14. summary or title
15. caption

Credits

All photographs except those noted below © Terry Ann Morris

"Checkpoint" icon (green check mark), "Web Site Case Study" icon (blue "WWW"), "FAQ" icon (orange caption bubble), "Focus on Accessibility" icon (orange key) © Fotolia LLC

"Hands-On Practice" icon (green hand); empty green, yellow, purple, red, and blue icons © Piotr M./Fotolia LLC

Index

Page references followed by "f" indicate illustrated figures or photographs; followed by "t" indicates a table.